THE PRACTICE OF HARMONY

sixth edition

Peter Spencer

The Florida State University

Barbara A. Bennett

University of California, Riverside

PEARSON

Boston Columbus Indianapolis New York San Francisco Upper Saddle River
Amsterdam Cape Town Dubai London Madrid Milan Munich Paris Montreal Toronto
Delhi Mexico City São Paulo Sydney Hong Kong Seoul Singapore Taipei Tokyo

Editorial Director: Craig Campanella
Editor in Chief: Sarah Touborg
Executive Editor: Richard Carlin
Editorial Assistant: Lily Norton
Vice President Director of Marketing: Brandy Dawson
Executive Marketing Manager: Kate Stewart Mitchell
Managing Editor: Melissa Feimer
Project Manager: Marlene Gassler
Senior Manufacturing Manager: Mary Fischer
Senior Operations Specialist: Brian Mackey
Creative Director, Cover: Jayne Conte
Cover Designer: Bruce Kenselaar
Cover Photo Credit: Misha/Fotolia
Senior Media Editor: David Alick
Media Project Manager: Rich Barnes
Full-Service Project Management: Lynn Steines, S4Carlisle Publishing Services
Composition: S4Carlisle Publishing Services
Printer/Binder: RR Donnelly Menasha
Cover Printer: Lehigh-Phoenix Color/Hagerstown

Library of Congress Cataloging-in-Publication Data

Spencer, Peter
The practice of harmony / Peter Spencer.—6th ed.
p. cm.
Includes index.
ISBN-13: 978-0-205-71719-4
ISBN-10: 0-205-71719-5
1. Harmony—Textbooks. I. Title.
MT50.S746 2011
781.2'5—dc23

2011025852

10 9 8 7 6 5 4 3 2 1

ISBN 10: 0-205-71719-5
ISBN 13: 978-0-205-71719-4
Exam Copy ISBN 10: 0-205-21442-8
Exam Copy ISBN 13: 978-0-205-21442-6

Contents

Preface

Almost all music majors in colleges and universities in the United States are required to study music theory. A large portion of music theory involves the study of tertian harmony, that is, the general harmonic practice of composers from about 1700 to 1900. A thorough grasp of the basic principles of this practice is a prerequisite to the full appreciation and comprehension of the works of every composer from Bach to Brahms. One should not forget, however, that over a hundred years have elapsed since Brahms's death, and in that time a number of harmonic practices have grown that demand attention, albeit at an elementary level. The object of the sixth edition of *The Practice of Harmony* is, therefore, to give the music student, regardless of his or her major, a thorough understanding of the basic materials of harmony.

The book is divided into four parts:

Part One: Foundations—Designed to ensure that the student has a solid grasp of fundamentals before advancing to subject matter in which these fundamentals are used as the basis for further development. These early chapters establish the pedagogical strategy that is employed throughout most of the remainder of the book. The materials are presented in an additive manner, so that the student uses what was learned in one chapter to comprehend the materials in the next. Such an approach allows coverage of not only the rudiments of music theory, but also the principles behind the rudiments. Because the authors are convinced that understanding is most effectively reached by doing, each chapter contains a large number of exercises, most of which have time goals designed to force the student to operate quickly—indeed automatically.

Upon successfully completing this portion of the book, the student will be in a position to make automatic responses to questions related to reading in G, F, and C clefs; major and minor scales; key signatures and scale degrees; and all intervals, triads, and principles of rhythmic notation.

Parts Two and Three: Harmony in Common Practice—Designed to develop a complete understanding of the principles of tertian harmony as they pertain to common practice. Parts Two and Three, "The Diatonic Vocabulary" and "The Chromatic Vocabulary," respectively, continue to stress learning by doing. After each new concept has been introduced, several pages of carefully graduated exercises follow to ensure that the student completely understands that concept before approaching a new one. This method favors writing over analysis, for understanding involves more than the ability merely to analyze; it also involves a working knowledge of the problems that are inevitably encountered when musical pitches are committed to paper. One cannot begin to reach a true understanding of a Beethoven sonata, for instance, unless one has wrestled, even at a very low level, with the same kind of harmonic problems that confronted Beethoven himself. Analysis can be illuminating only to the student who understands some of the reasons for the notes in the first place. Not that analysis has been ignored; in addition

*Upon completion of each group of exercises, the preceding text will be torn out and, along with the exercises, inserted in a loose-leaf binder. The student can insert additional staff paper as needed.

to examples for analysis in the text, more elaborate *exercises* for analysis are included. New to the sixth edition is an appendix with a study guide for analysis, two musical excerpts with a process to guide the student through an analysis, and a list by topic of pieces for analysis.

Part Four: Post-Common Practice Harmony—Designed to introduce the student to some of the more important harmonic procedures that have either evolved from or developed as a reaction to common practice. In keeping with the philosophy embraced in the previous parts, the materials in Part Four are presented concisely and reinforced by a wide variety of exercises. The absence of a continuing "common practice" in relation to several of these materials, however, precludes the possibility for the same kind of step-by-step development of concepts that students encounter in the earlier parts of the text. Nonetheless, in the spirit of the rest of the book, the emphasis in Part Four is also on the exposition of theoretical procedures rather than on individual composers' interpretations of them. The pursuit of *stylistic* considerations is beyond the scope or intention of *The Practice of Harmony,* for such considerations fall more naturally into the purview of advanced theoretical studies.

In summation, *The Practice of Harmony* is designed for students of basic theory. The authors have given considerable thought to the kind of people for whom this book would be valuable, and consequently has endeavored to present the material in an entirely systematic manner, simply and logically, so that the subject matter is not only comprehensible to the student, but also easily taught by the instructor. The sixth edition features additional exercises, both preliminary and advanced; an answer appendix of selected exercises; as well as a number of improvements to the musical examples.

PETER SPENCER
BARBARA A. BENNETT

PART ONE

FOUNDATIONS

1

*Clefs and Basic Pitch Notation**

Four clefs are in common use:

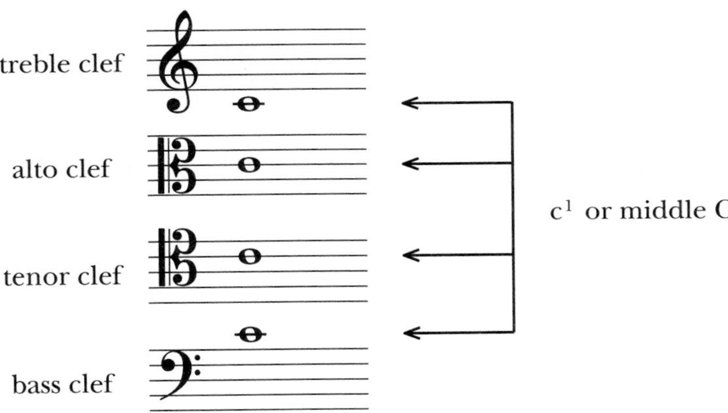

Note:

a. The treble clef is called a *G clef* because the symbol is a corruption of the letter G, the "center" of which encircles g^1, the second line of the staff.

b. The alto and tenor clefs are called *C clefs* because the symbol (the same for each) is a corruption of the letter C, the center of which encircles c^1, the third line of the staff for the alto clef and the fourth line for the tenor clef.

c. The bass clef is called an *F clef* because the symbol is a corruption of the letter F, the "center" of which encircles f, the fourth line of the staff.

*Because Chapter 6, *The Notation of Rhythm*, is not dependent upon the contents of the first five chapters, this chapter may be studied concurrently with Chapters 1 through 5.

d. The term *pitch class* is used to describe a class of pitches with the same letter name. Thus, all C's (C, c, c^1, etc.) are members of the same pitch class. In addition, all pitches and their *enharmonic equivalents* belong to the same pitch class (for example, F♯ and G♭, or E♯ and F).

Because there are only seven letter names for pitches (A B C D E F G), but at least seven audible octave transpositions of any given pitch, each pitch has its own special designation.

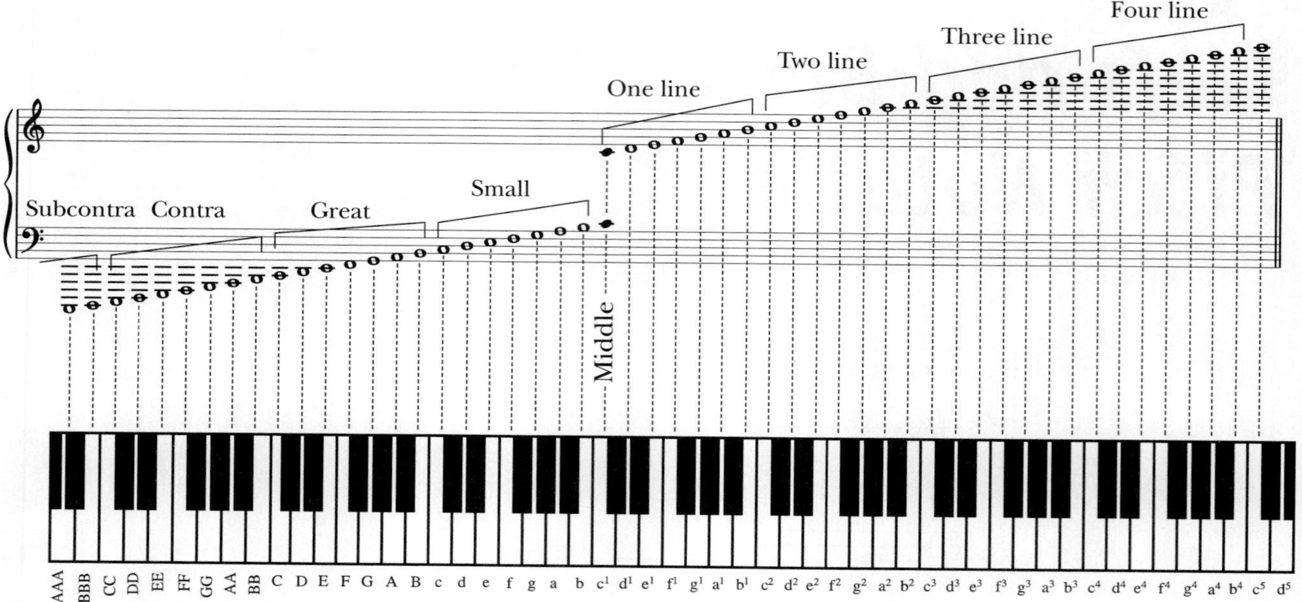

Raymond Elliott, FUNDAMENTALS OF MUSIC, 3rd ed., © 1971, p. 15. Reprinted by permission of Prentice Hall, Inc., Upper Saddle River, NJ.

Note:

a. The shortest movement from one pitch to another, called a half step or semitone, sometimes involves a change in letter name and sometimes does not.

b. When a change of name is not involved, the pitch is raised or lowered a half step by the use of either a sharp (♯) or a flat (♭). The pitch may also be changed by two half steps without altering the letter name by the use of a double sharp (𝄪) or a double flat (𝄫).

c. E to F and B to C are the only unaltered pitches that are one half step apart. C to D, D to E, F to G, G to A, and A to B are two half steps apart; this space or interval is called a whole step or a whole tone.

In a more recent system for pitch designation, introduced by the International Acoustic Society, the lowest C on the piano is C1. Under this designation, middle C is C4, and the piano's highest C is C8. This system, though still not embraced by the majority of writers of music texts, is universally used in electronic and computer-generated music.

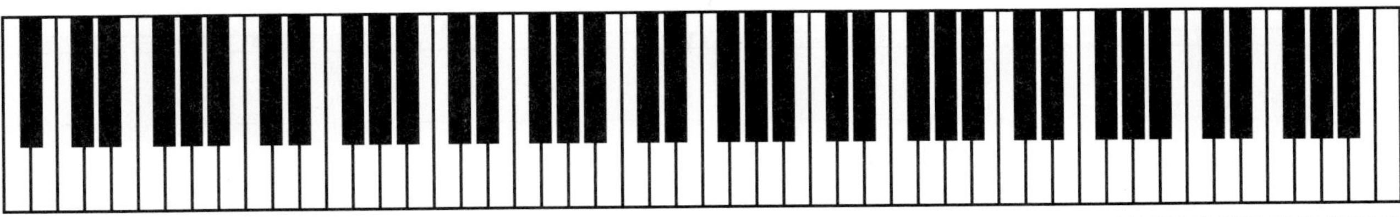

SUGGESTIONS AND STRATEGIES

Most students are more familiar with the G and F clefs than with the C clefs. You can, however, use the G and F clefs as a reference for the alto clef in the following manner:

Imagine middle C belonging to both the treble and bass clefs. The alto clef may then be considered to link the two clefs together, so that middle C becomes a part of both of them. If you think of the clef in this way, you will quickly learn to read the lines and spaces.

EXERCISES

A. Write the letter name for each note in the manner indicated. Time goal—45 seconds per line (middle C = c^1).

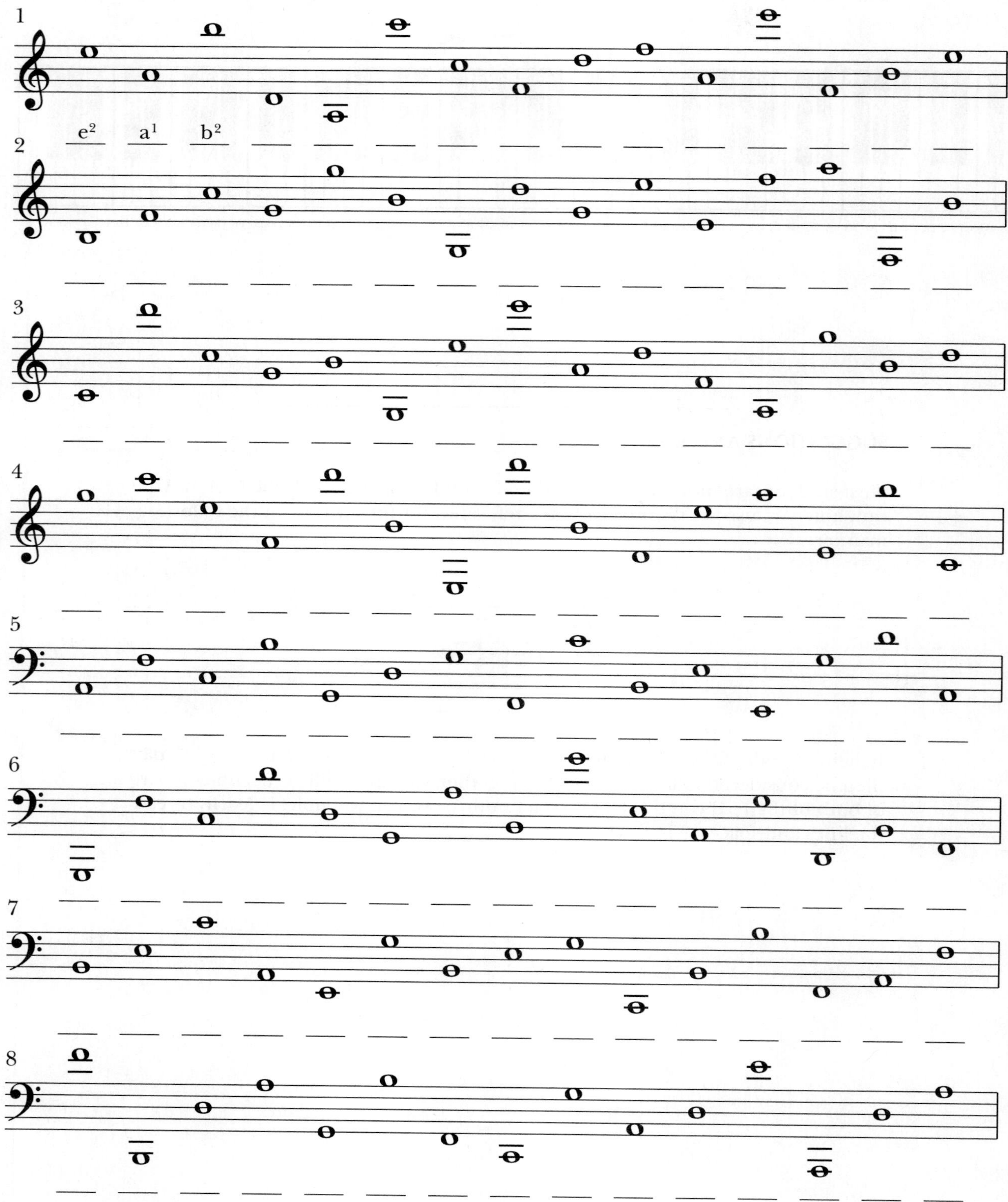

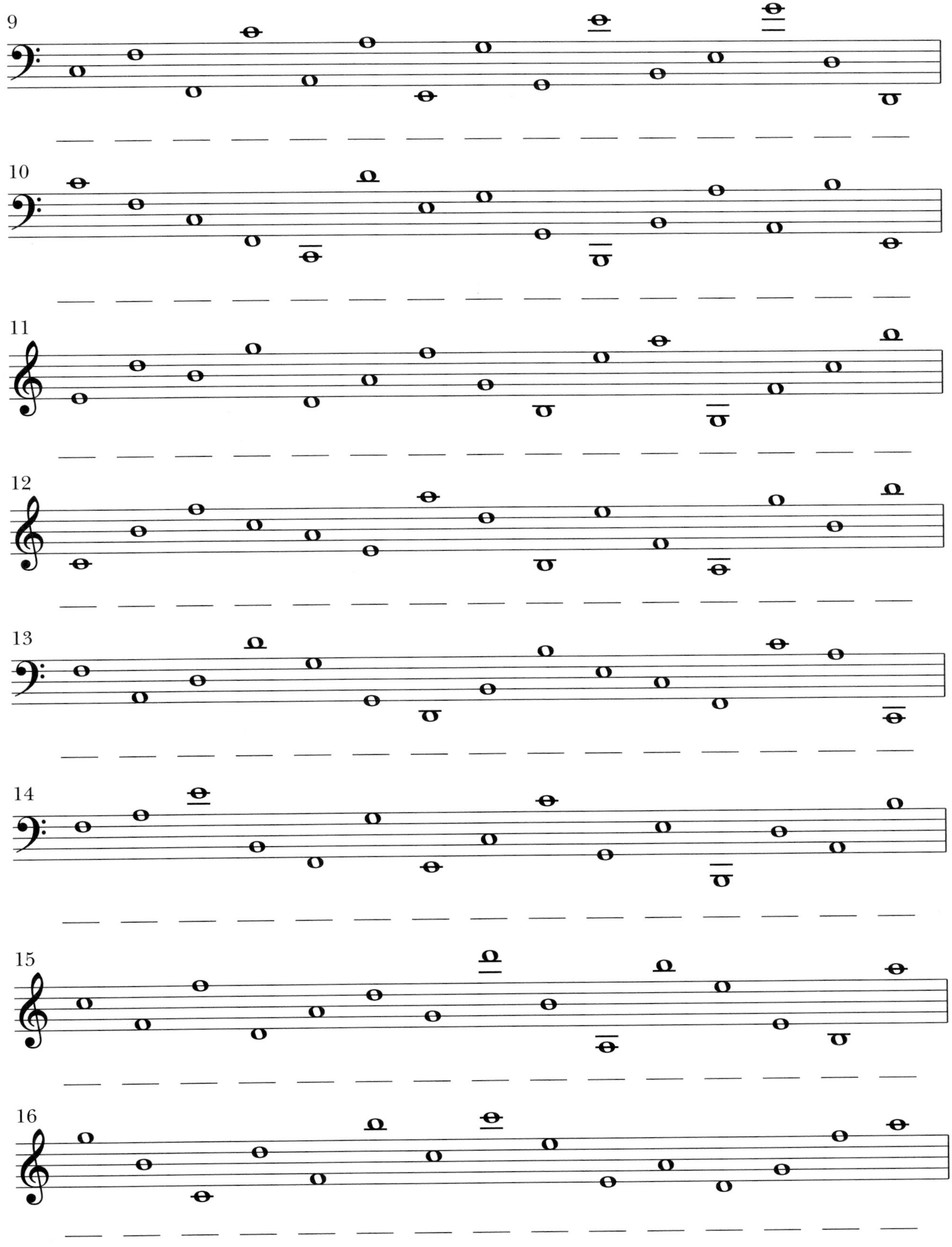
9
10
11
12
13
14
15
16

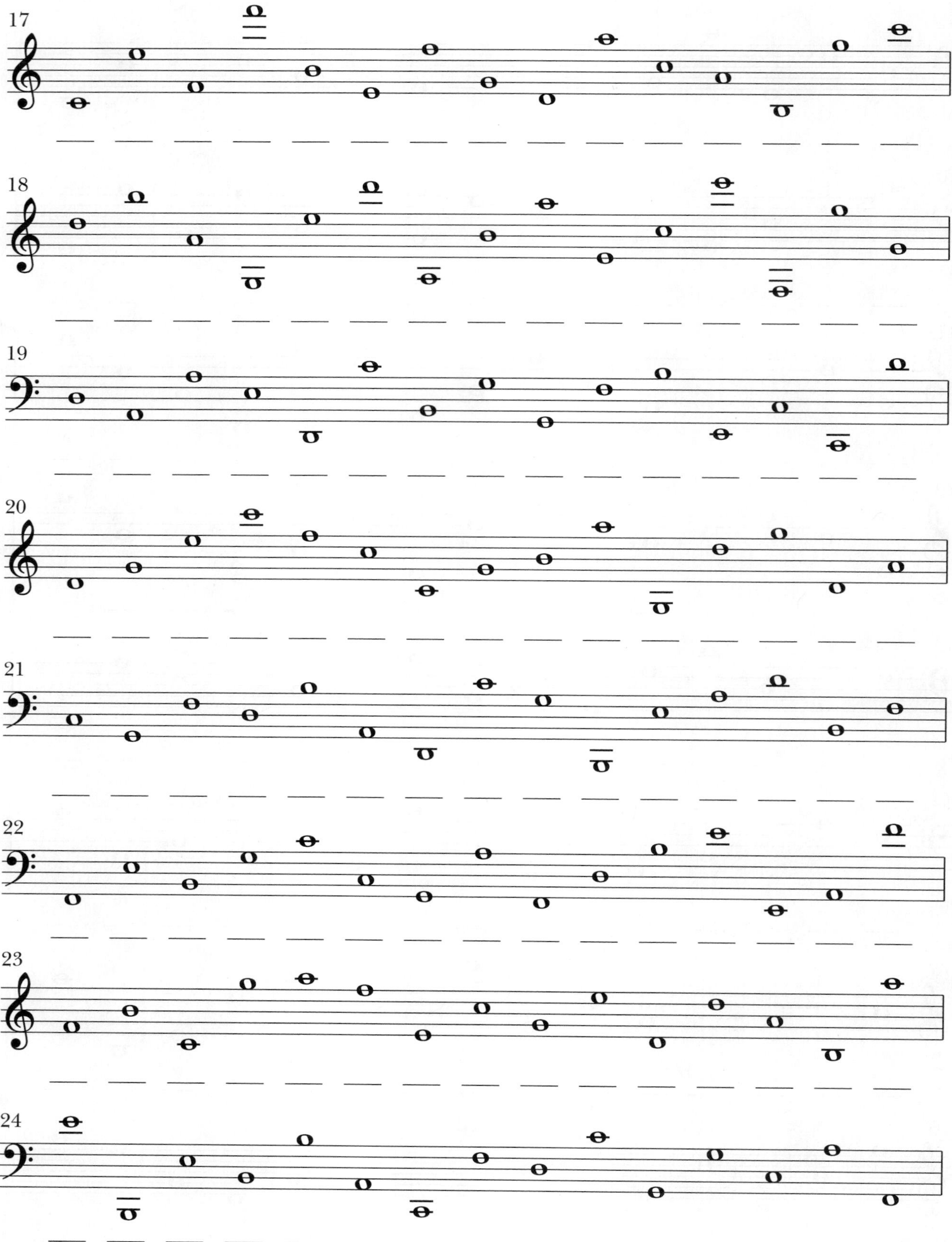
17
18
19
20
21
22
23
24

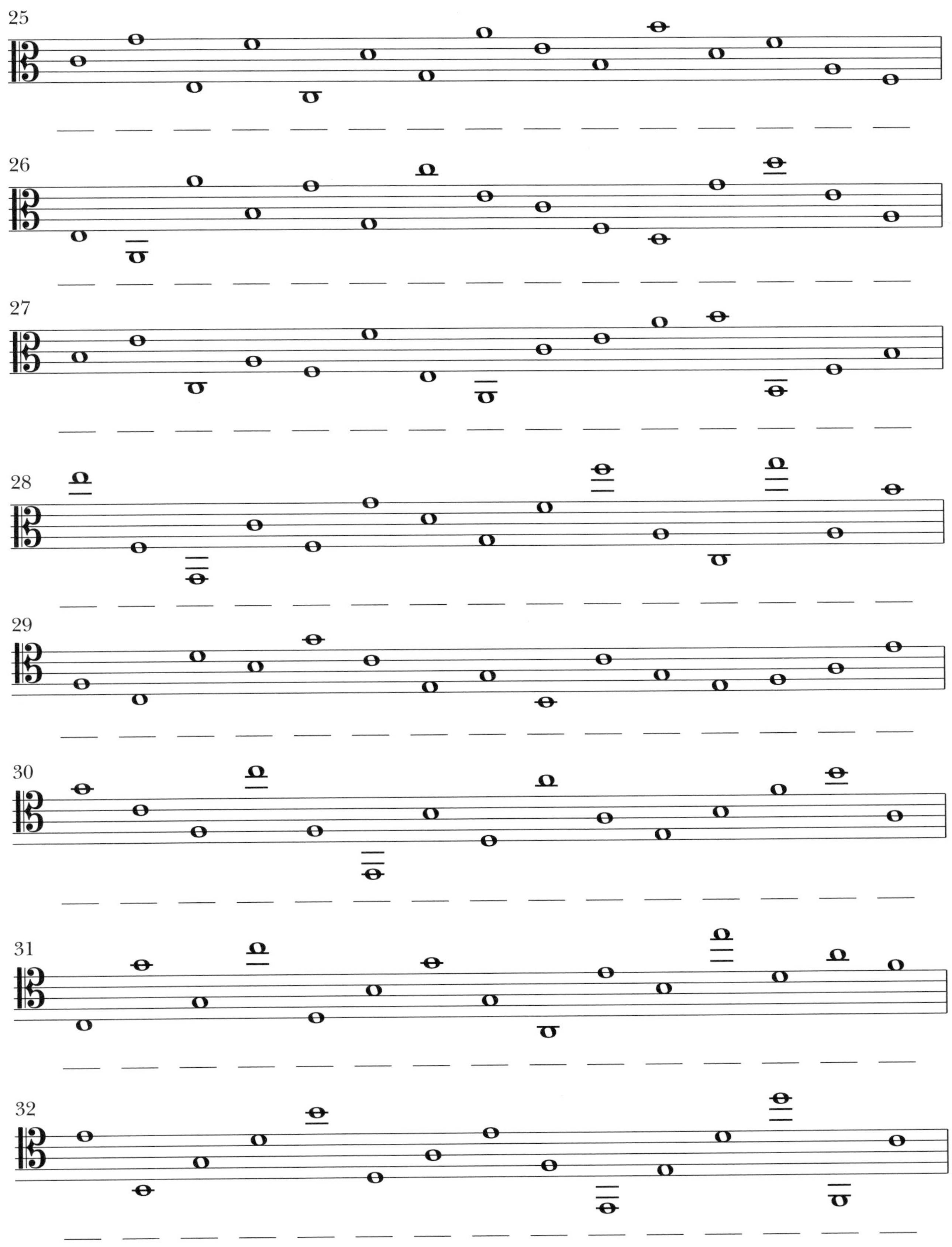
25
26
27
28
29
30
31
32

B. Notate the specifed pitches. Time goal—45 seconds per line (middle C = c^1).

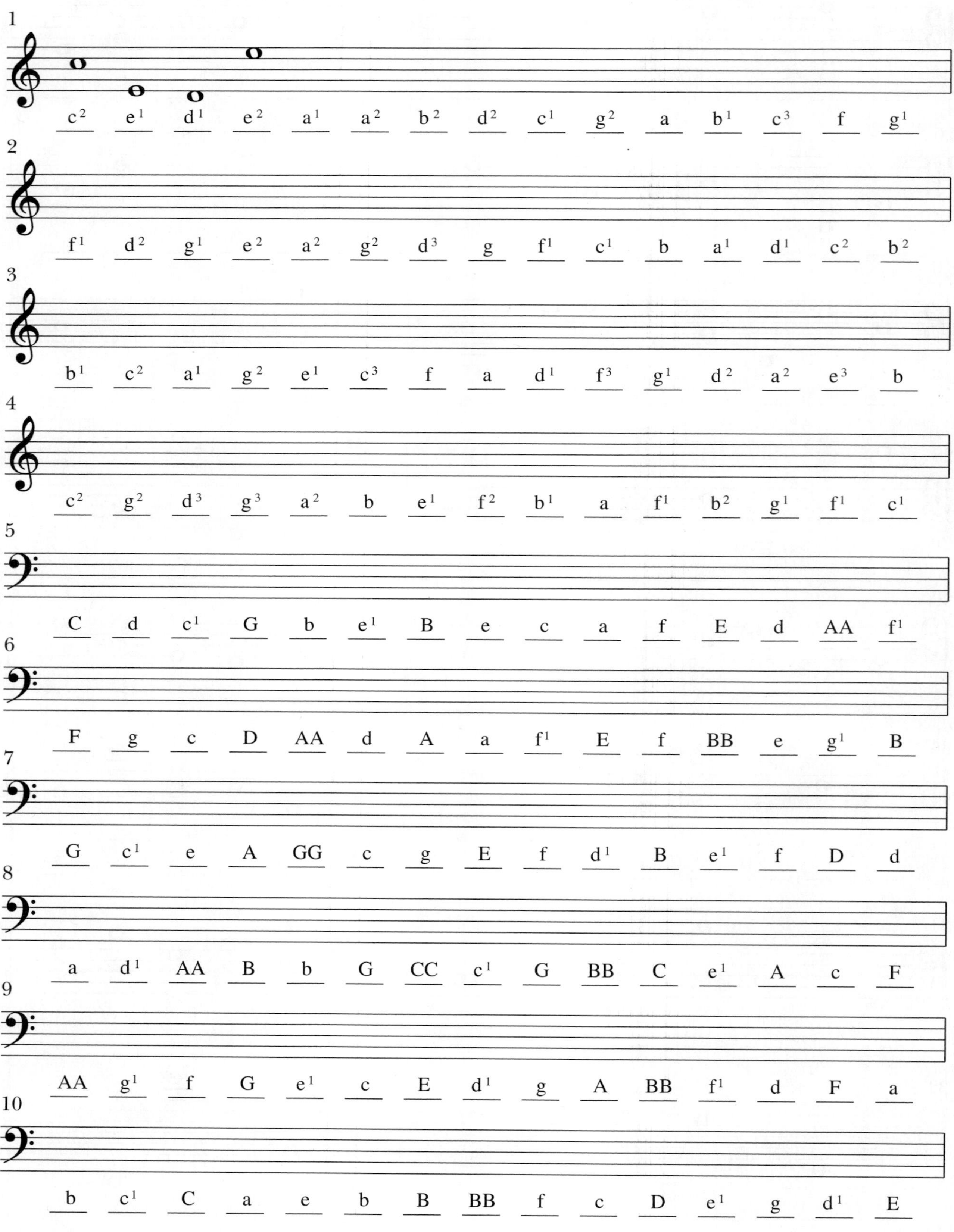

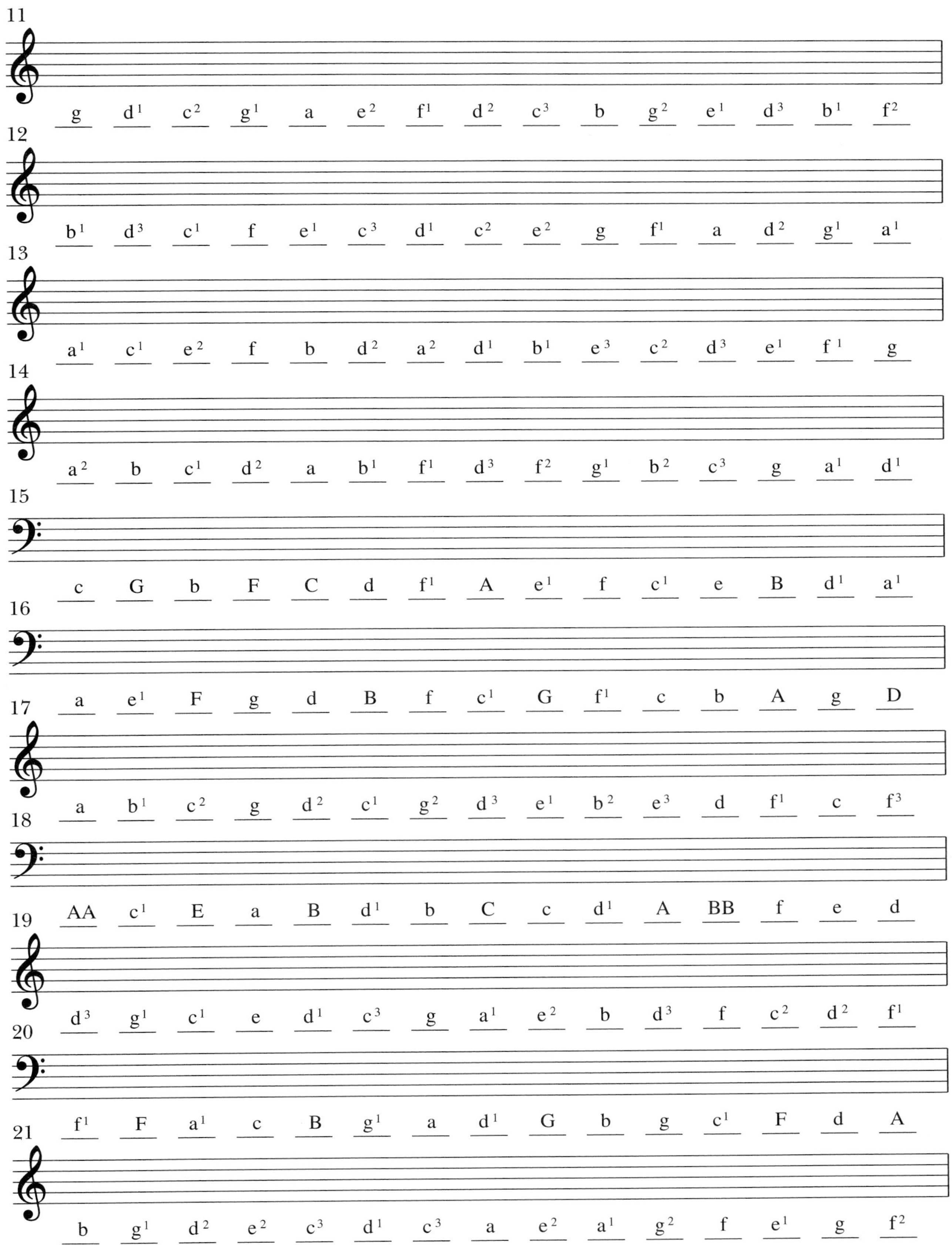
11
g d^1 c^2 g^1 a e^2 f^1 d^2 c^3 b g^2 e^1 d^3 b^1 f^2
12
b^1 d^3 c^1 f e^1 c^3 d^1 c^2 e^2 g f^1 a d^2 g^1 a^1
13
a^1 c^1 e^2 f b d^2 a^2 d^1 b^1 e^3 c^2 d^3 e^1 f^1 g
14
a^2 b c^1 d^2 a b^1 f^1 d^3 f^2 g^1 b^2 c^3 g a^1 d^1
15
c G b F C d f^1 A e^1 f c^1 e B d^1 a^1
16
a e^1 F g d B f c^1 G f^1 c b A g D
17
a b^1 c^2 g d^2 c^1 g^2 d^3 e^1 b^2 e^3 d f^1 c f^3
18
AA c^1 E a B d^1 b C c d^1 A BB f e d
19
d^3 g^1 c^1 e d^1 c^3 g a^1 e^2 b d^3 f c^2 d^2 f^1
20
f^1 F a^1 c B g^1 a d^1 G b g c^1 F d A
21
b g^1 d^2 e^2 c^3 d^1 c^3 a e^2 a^1 g^2 f e^1 g f^2

22

e C c^1 AA G f e^1 D g F d^1 g BB E f^1

23

g b^1 d^2 c^1 d^1 a c^2 d^1 e^1 b e^2 e c^3 d^1 f^1

24

c^1 B d f^1 e b c d^1 f C E BB g e^1 A

25

g a c^2 f g^1 B d b^1 e^1 b a^1 e c^1 d^2 c

26

d^1 f B e^1 a b^1 c^1 e g b a^1 g^1 A e^1 f^1

27

g a^1 g^1 d c^1 f B d^2 e e^1 f^1 c a d^1 b

28

f g^1 g d^1 b A d b^1 c a c^2 f^1 a^1 e^1 c^1

29

F a^1 d^1 c B g^1 c^2 c^1 g A e^1 f d e f^1

30

e^1 d f^1 G b^1 d^1 c g^1 c^2 a^1 A a c^1 f F

31

F a e^1 b G G f^1 e c^1 A c^2 d^1 B c b^1

32

a^1 f d^1 g f^1 A c^1 B c^1 c^2 b g^1 a e^1 b^1

C. Notate the specified pitches. Time goal—45 seconds per line (middle C = C4).

1
C4 E4 D4 E5 A4 A5 B5 D5 B3 G5 A3 B4 C6 F3 G4

2
F4 D5 G4 E5 A5 G5 D6 G3 E4 C4 B3 A4 B4 C5 A3

3
B4 C5 A4 G5 E4 C6 F3 G4 D4 F6 F4 G5 D6 E6 B3

4
C5 G5 D6 G6 A5 B3 E4 F5 B4 A3 F4 B5 G3 C6 C4

5
C2 D3 C4 G2 B3 E4 B2 E3 C3 A3 F3 C2 D3 A1 F4

6
F2 G3 C3 D2 A1 D3 F2 A3 F4 E2 C1 B1 E3 G4 F3

7
G2 C4 E3 A2 G1 C3 G3 E4 F3 D4 E2 F4 F2 D2 B1

8
A3 D4 A1 B2 B3 C2 F2 A2 B1 G2 D3 F3 F4 D2 C1

9
A1 G4 F3 G2 E4 C3 E2 D4 G3 A2 B1 F4 D3 F2 A3

10
B3 C4 C2 A3 E3 A1 B2 B1 F3 C3 D2 E4 G3 D4 E2

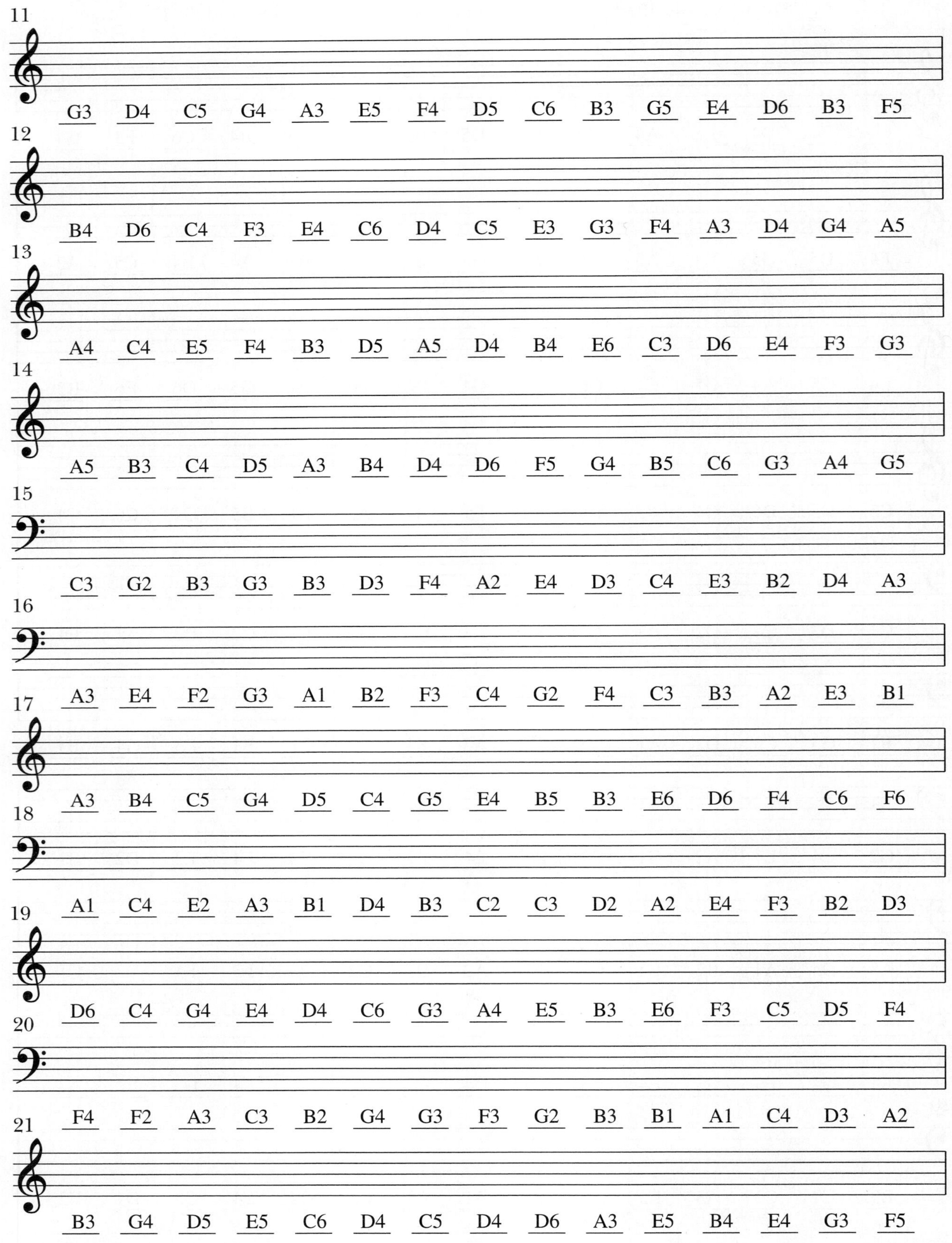
11
G3 D4 C5 G4 A3 E5 F4 D5 C6 B3 G5 E4 D6 B3 F5
12
B4 D6 C4 F3 E4 C6 D4 C5 E3 G3 F4 A3 D4 G4 A5
13
A4 C4 E5 F4 B3 D5 A5 D4 B4 E6 C3 D6 E4 F3 G3
14
A5 B3 C4 D5 A3 B4 D4 D6 F5 G4 B5 C6 G3 A4 G5
15
C3 G2 B3 G3 B3 D3 F4 A2 E4 D3 C4 E3 B2 D4 A3
16
A3 E4 F2 G3 A1 B2 F3 C4 G2 F4 C3 B3 A2 E3 B1
17
A3 B4 C5 G4 D5 C4 G5 E4 B5 B3 E6 D6 F4 C6 F6
18
A1 C4 E2 A3 B1 D4 B3 C2 C3 D2 A2 E4 F3 B2 D3
19
D6 C4 G4 E4 D4 C6 G3 A4 E5 B3 E6 F3 C5 D5 F4
20
F4 F2 A3 C3 B2 G4 G3 F3 G2 B3 B1 A1 C4 D3 A2
21
B3 G4 D5 E5 C6 D4 C5 D4 D6 A3 E5 B4 E4 G3 F5

22

E3 C2 C4 A1 G2 F3 E4 D2 G3 F2 C3 G2 B1 E2 D4

23

G3 B4 D5 C4 D4 A3 C5 D6 E4 A4 D5 E5 C6 B3 F4

24

C4 B2 D3 F4 E3 B3 C3 D4 F3 C2 E2 B1 G3 E4 D2

25

G3 A3 C5 F3 G4 B2 D3 B4 E4 B3 A4 B3 E5 D5 C3

26

D4 F3 B2 E4 A3 B4 C4 E3 B3 F4 A2 G4 C3 A4 D3

27

G3 A4 G4 D3 C4 F3 B2 D5 E3 C5 F4 C3 A3 D4 D5

28

F3 A3 G4 D4 B3 A4 D3 B4 C3 E3 F4 C5 B4 E4 C4

29

F4 A4 C3 D3 B3 G3 A2 B2 E4 G4 D4 C5 F3 A3 E3

30

E4 D3 F4 G2 B3 D4 D3 G4 C5 A4 C3 A3 C4 A3 F2

31

F2 A3 E4 B3 G2 D3 F4 E3 C4 A2 C5 D4 F3 C3 B4

32

A4 F3 D5 G3 F4 A2 C4 B2 C3 C5 B3 G4 B1 B2 D4

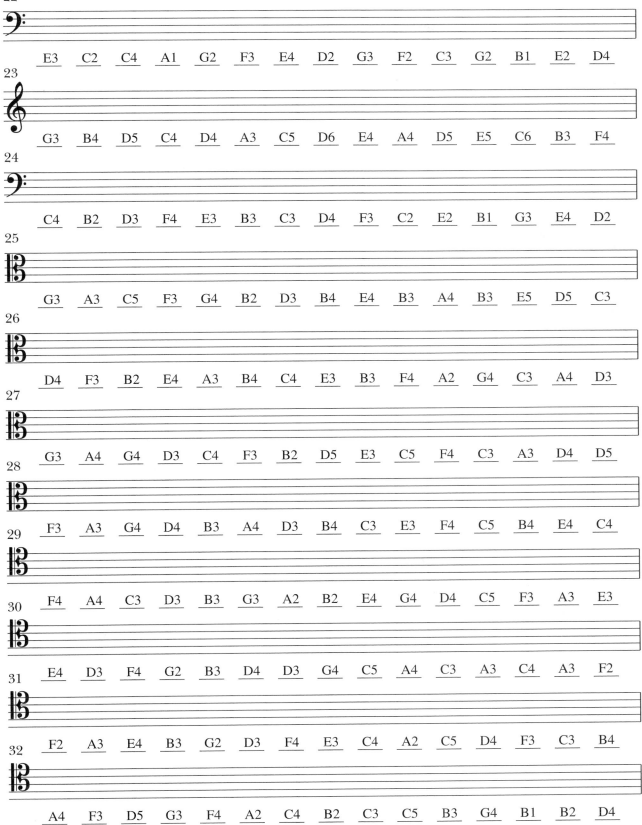

2 Scales

Strictly speaking, a scale is an ascending, ordered arrangement of pitches. In the tertian harmonic system, which is basic in the study of music theory, two scale types occur: the *major scale* and the *minor scale*. The minor scale has three variants: the *natural minor*, the *melodic minor*, and the *harmonic minor*.

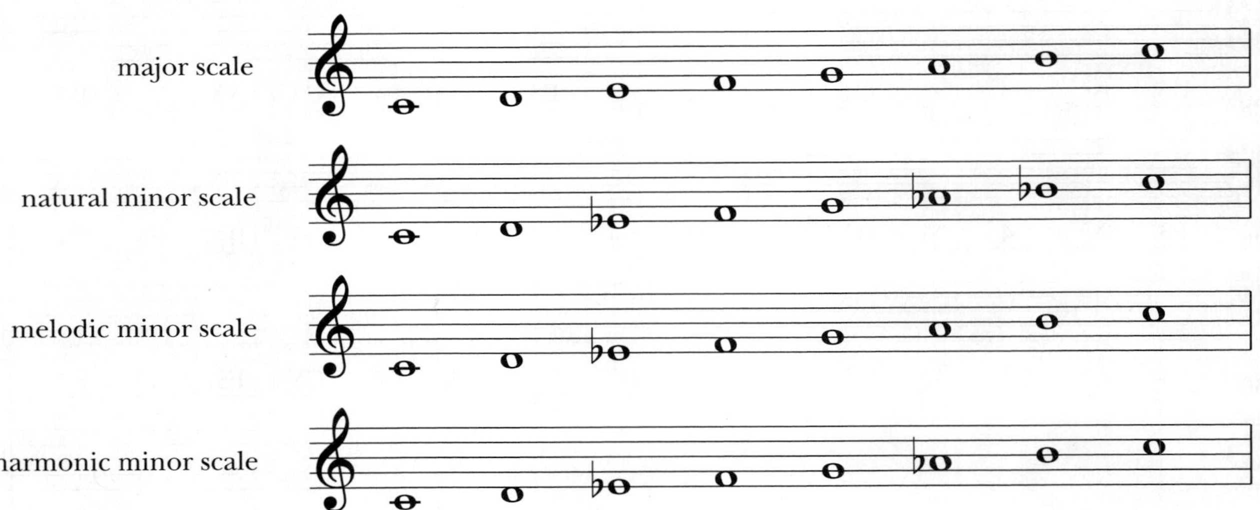

Note:

a. Each scale consists of eight pitches, the first and last being an octave apart.

b. Because any one of the scales may be built upon any given pitch, each scale has its own characteristic organization. In each case, this organization is most clearly seen when one examines not the pitches themselves, but the intervals between the pitches.

c. In all the scales, the interval between adjacent pitches is called a second. It is a *major second* if the interval between the pitches is two half steps and a *minor second* if the interval is one half step. (In the harmonic minor scale, there is one interval of three half steps. This interval is called an *augmented second.*)

THE MAJOR SCALE

The major scale may be viewed as consisting of two tetrachords (four-note groups) separated by two half steps. Each tetrachord contains five half steps.

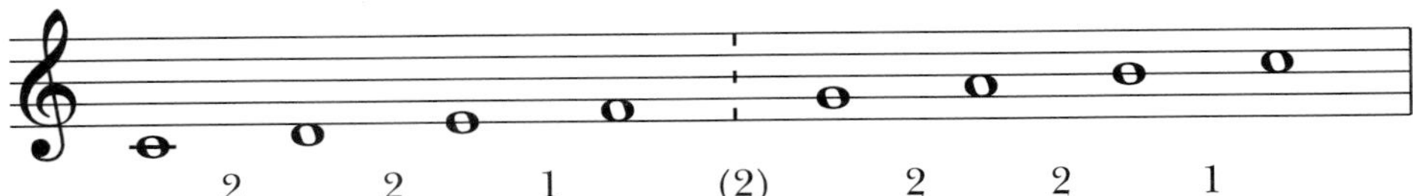

Note:
Each tetrachord has the same intervallic properties—two half steps, followed by two half steps, followed by one half step. Thus, the major scale may be expressed as

2-2-1-(2)-2-2-1

THE MINOR SCALE

The minor scale may also be viewed as consisting of two tetrachords separated by two half steps. The upper tetrachord, however, differs for each variant. Like the major scale, each tetrachord contains five half steps.

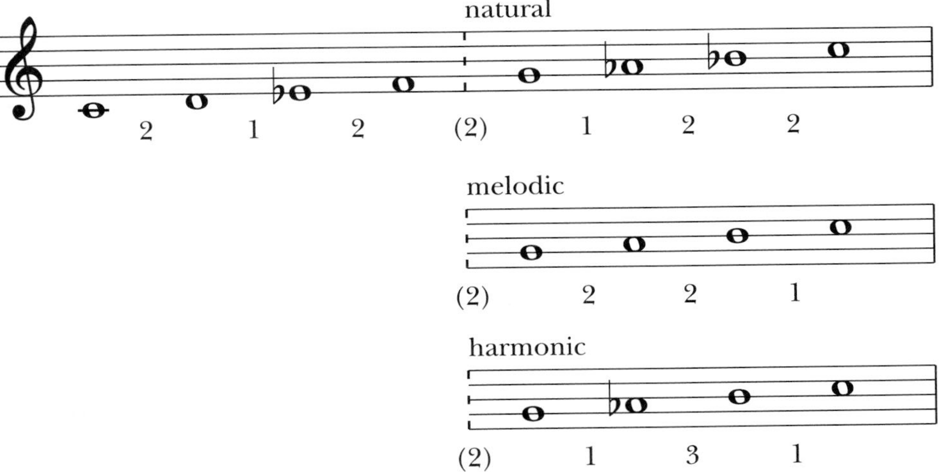

Note:

a. All three variants have the same lower tetrachord:

2-1-2

b. The upper tetrachord of the *natural* minor scale is the retrograde of the major tetrachord (i.e., the major tetrachord written backward). The scale, therefore, may be expressed as

2-1-2-(2)-1-2-2

c. The upper tetrachord of the *melodic* minor scale is the same as that of the major tetrachord. The scale, therefore, may be expressed as

2-1-2-(2)-2-2-1

d. The upper tetrachord of the *harmonic* minor scale is palindromic (i.e., it reads the same forward and backward). The scale, therefore, may be expressed as

2-1-2-(2)-1-3-1

NAMING SCALES

A scale is named by identifying its lowest note and by describing its type, that is, major or variety of minor. Thus the following scale

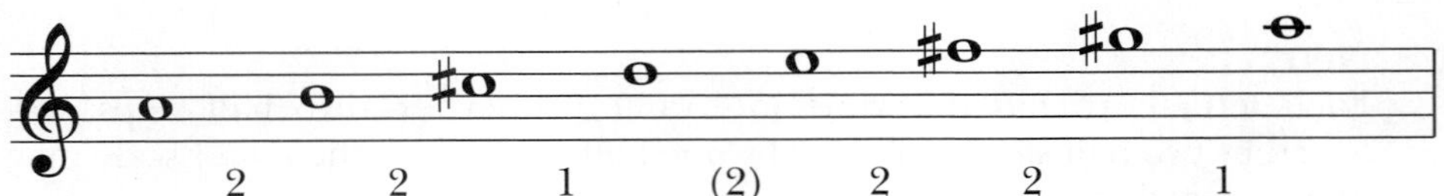

is A major and

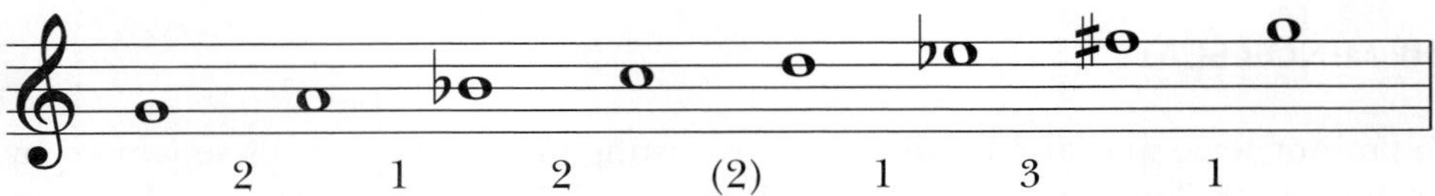

is g harmonic minor.

The major scale, by convention, is assigned an uppercase letter (e.g., A), and the minor a lowercase letter (e.g., g).

SCALES IN DESCENT

In this chapter each scale has been presented as an ascending series of pitches. In addition, a scale may be written as a descending series without altering its intervallic organization, except in the case of the melodic minor.

The descending melodic minor scale has exactly the same intervallic organization as the ascending (and descending) *natural minor.*

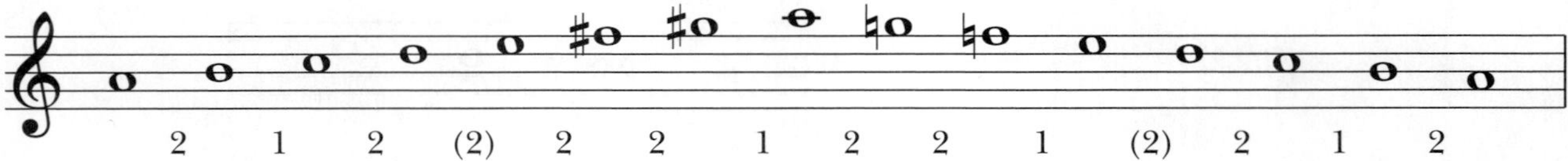

a melodic minor (ascending and descending)

THE SYNTHETIC MINOR SCALE

No effort has been made in this part of the text to explain when and why the various forms of the minor scale are used. In Chapter 10, the text shows that the minor scale may, for practical purposes, be considered a synthesis of all three forms, containing ten pitches:

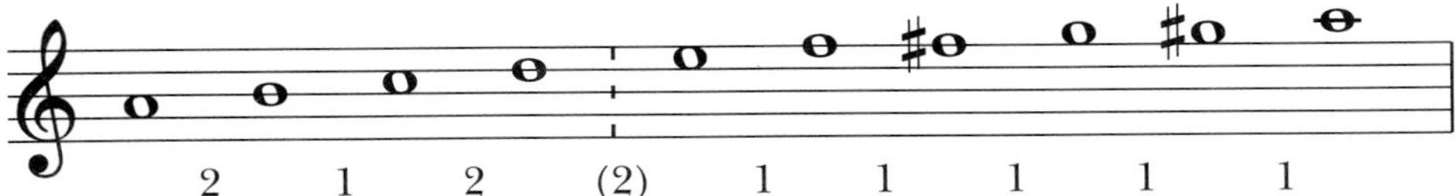

Note:

a. The upper part of the scale, now a hexachord (six-note group), has an intervallic organization entirely of half steps.

b. Considerations of voice leading and melodic activity will determine which pitches from the hexachord are appropriately employed in a given musical situation. These issues are discussed in Part Two.

MODES

The study of the scalar structure of modes is not a necessary foundation for the majority of the chapters in this book; however, the fact that modes may be derived from the major scale makes an introductory study of them possible at this point. The reader may wish to refer, therefore, to the beginning of Chapter 28, in which the derivation of the seven modes from the major scale is shown, followed by each mode's essential characteristics.

SUGGESTIONS AND STRATEGIES

When identifying scales (Exercise A), remember that the interval between pairs of pitches without accidentals in front of them is always two half steps, unless the pitches are E to F and B to C, in which case the interval is one half step. If you fill in these intervals first, you will soon notice patterns that help you to identify scale-types.

Experiment with pairs of pitches that have one or two accidentals associated with them. Are there observations to be made that are similar to the ones above?

In the second group of exercises, your first step should be to write the correct intervallic organization for the given scale, and then make the adjustments when you rewrite it.

Remember:

1. that the first and last pitches do not require any alteration;
2. that all alterations involve adding, changing, or removing accidentals; the note-heads remain unaltered.

The last group of exercises (Exercise C) involves writing specified scales from a given note. Follow these procedures:

a) write the scale with note-heads only, so that the first and last note are an octave apart (do not remove the accidental from the first note);
b) write the intervallic organization for the given scale-type;
c) place accidentals in front of the note-heads as necessary.

EXERCISES

A. Identify each scale by analyzing its tetrachord structure. Time goal—30 seconds per scale.

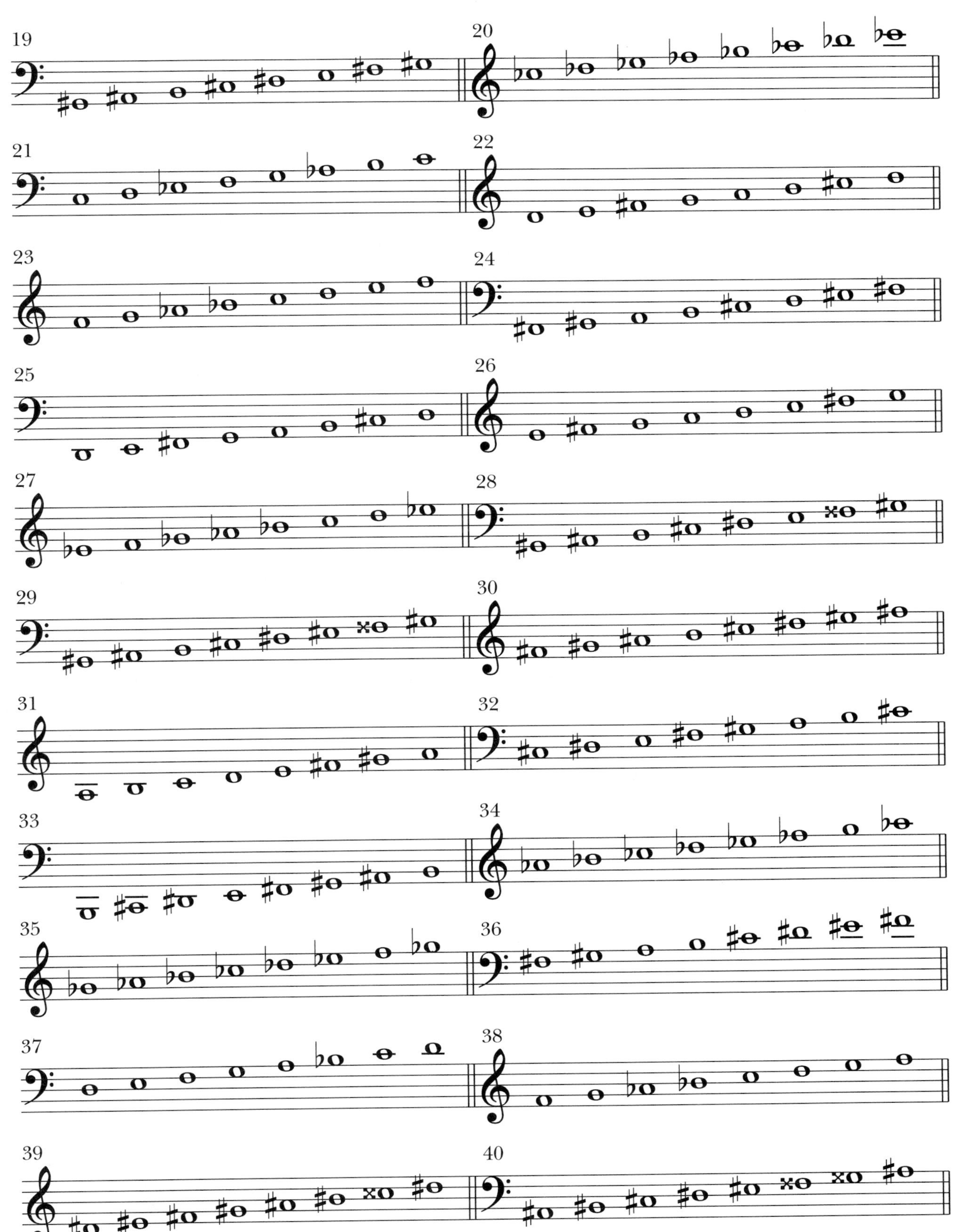
19
20
21
22
23
24
25
26
27
28
29
30
31
32
33
34
35
36
37
38
39
40

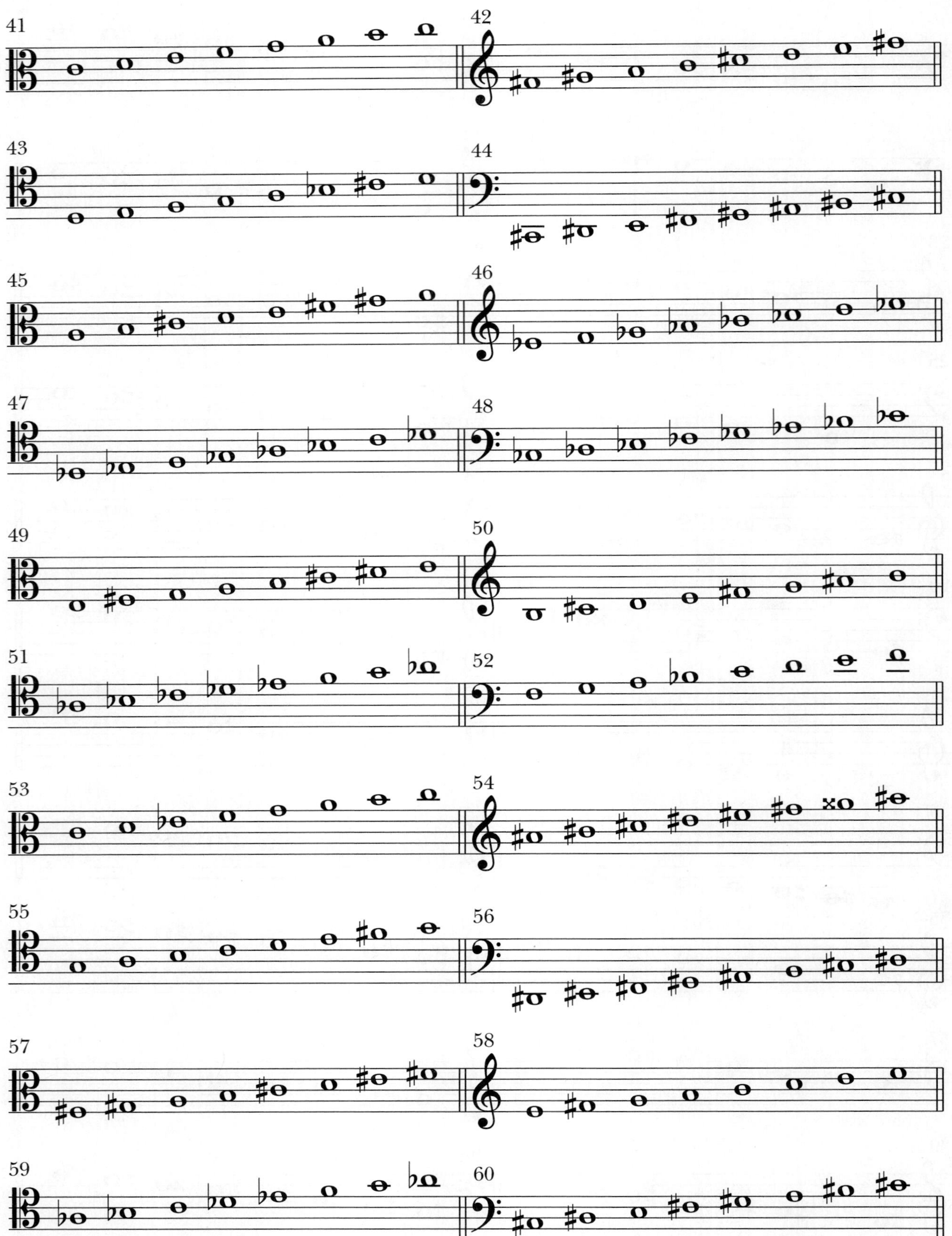
41
42
43
44
45
46
47
48
49
50
51
52
53
54
55
56
57
58
59
60

B. Identify the error(s) in each scale and write the scale correctly. Time goal—45 seconds per scale.

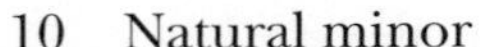

10 Natural minor

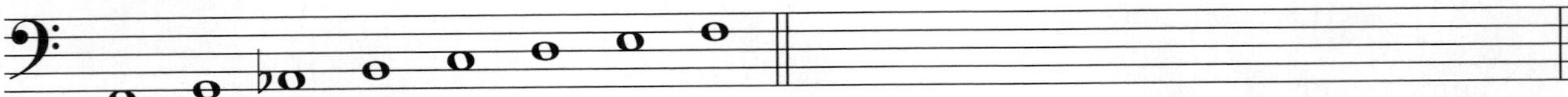

11 Major

12 Harmonic minor

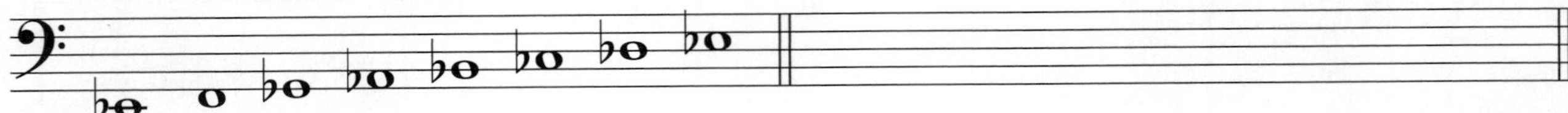

13 Natural minor

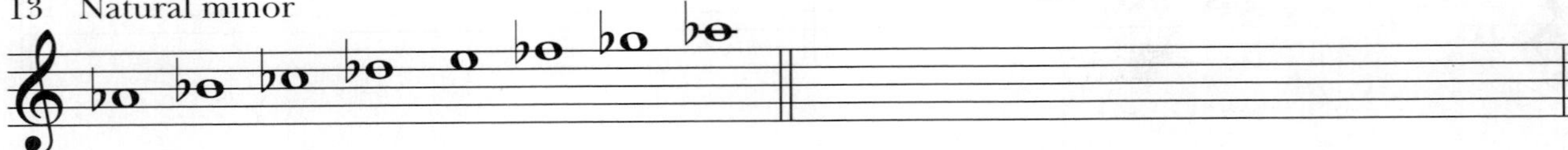

14 Harmonic minor

15 Natural minor

16 Harmonic minor

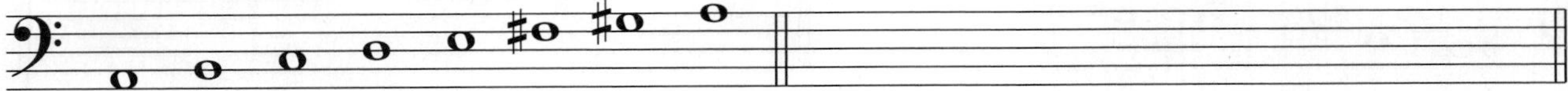

17 Melodic minor

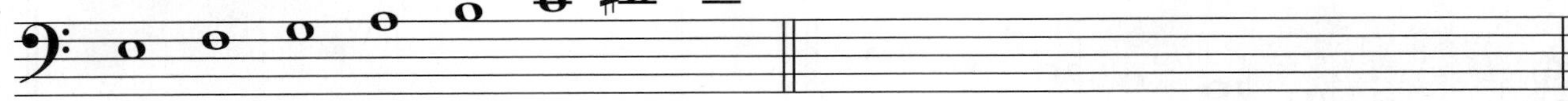

18 Harmonic minor

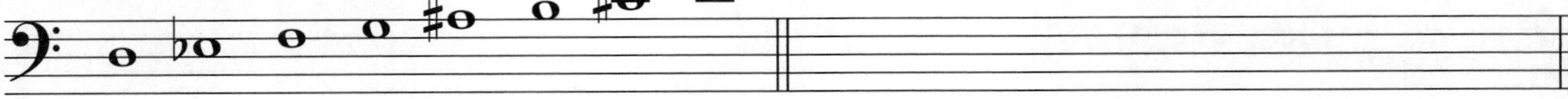

19 Melodic minor

20 Major
21 Harmonic minor
22 Major
23 Natural minor
24 Melodic minor
25 Natural minor
26 Harmonic minor
27 Major
28 Melodic minor
29 Natural minor

30 Harmonic minor
31 Melodic minor
32 Melodic minor
33 Major
34 Harmonic minor
35 Harmonic minor
36 Melodic minor
37 Major
38 Natural minor
39 Melodic minor
40 Natural minor

C. Write the specified scales. Time goal—20 seconds per scale.

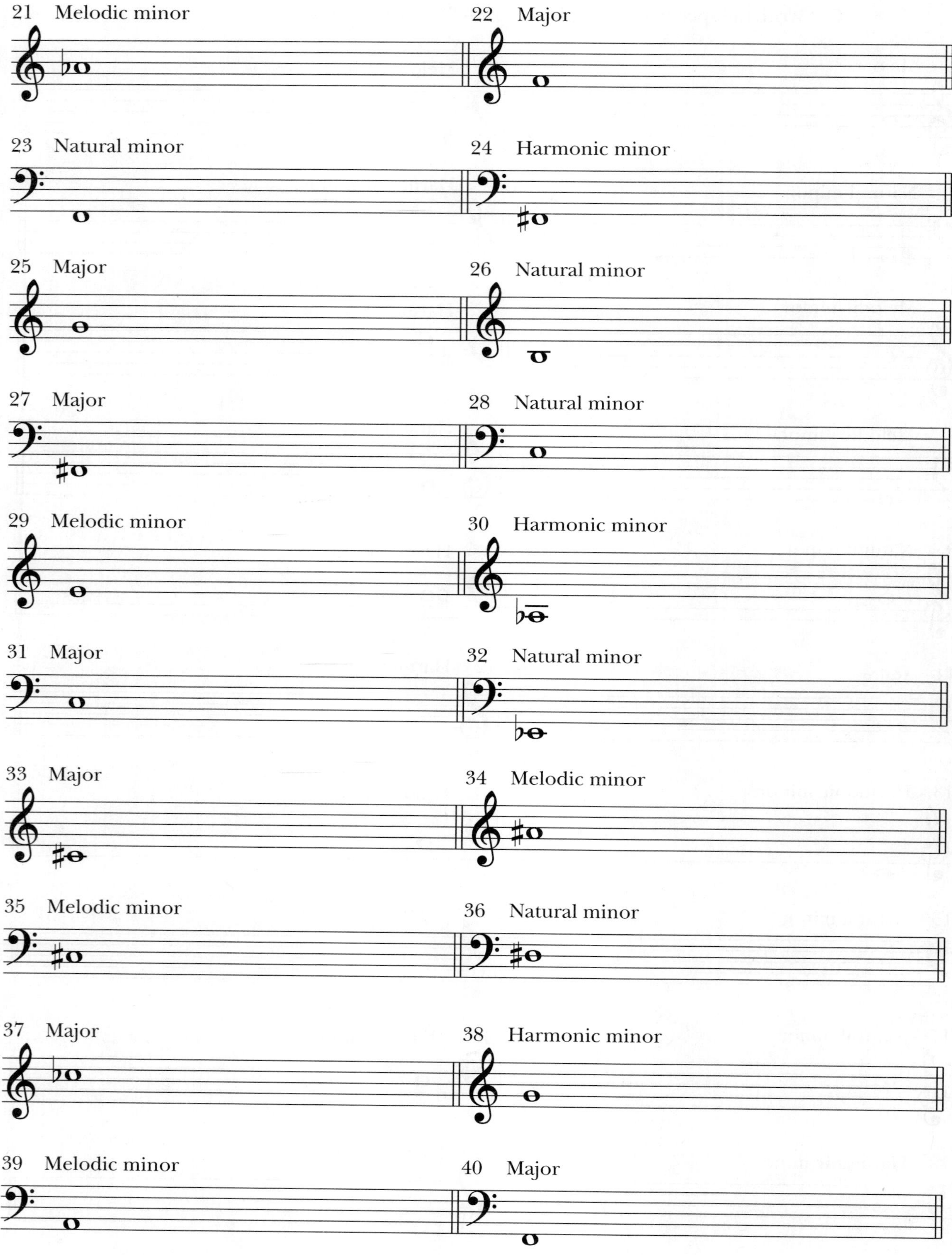
21 Melodic minor
22 Major
23 Natural minor
24 Harmonic minor
25 Major
26 Natural minor
27 Major
28 Natural minor
29 Melodic minor
30 Harmonic minor
31 Major
32 Natural minor
33 Major
34 Melodic minor
35 Melodic minor
36 Natural minor
37 Major
38 Harmonic minor
39 Melodic minor
40 Major

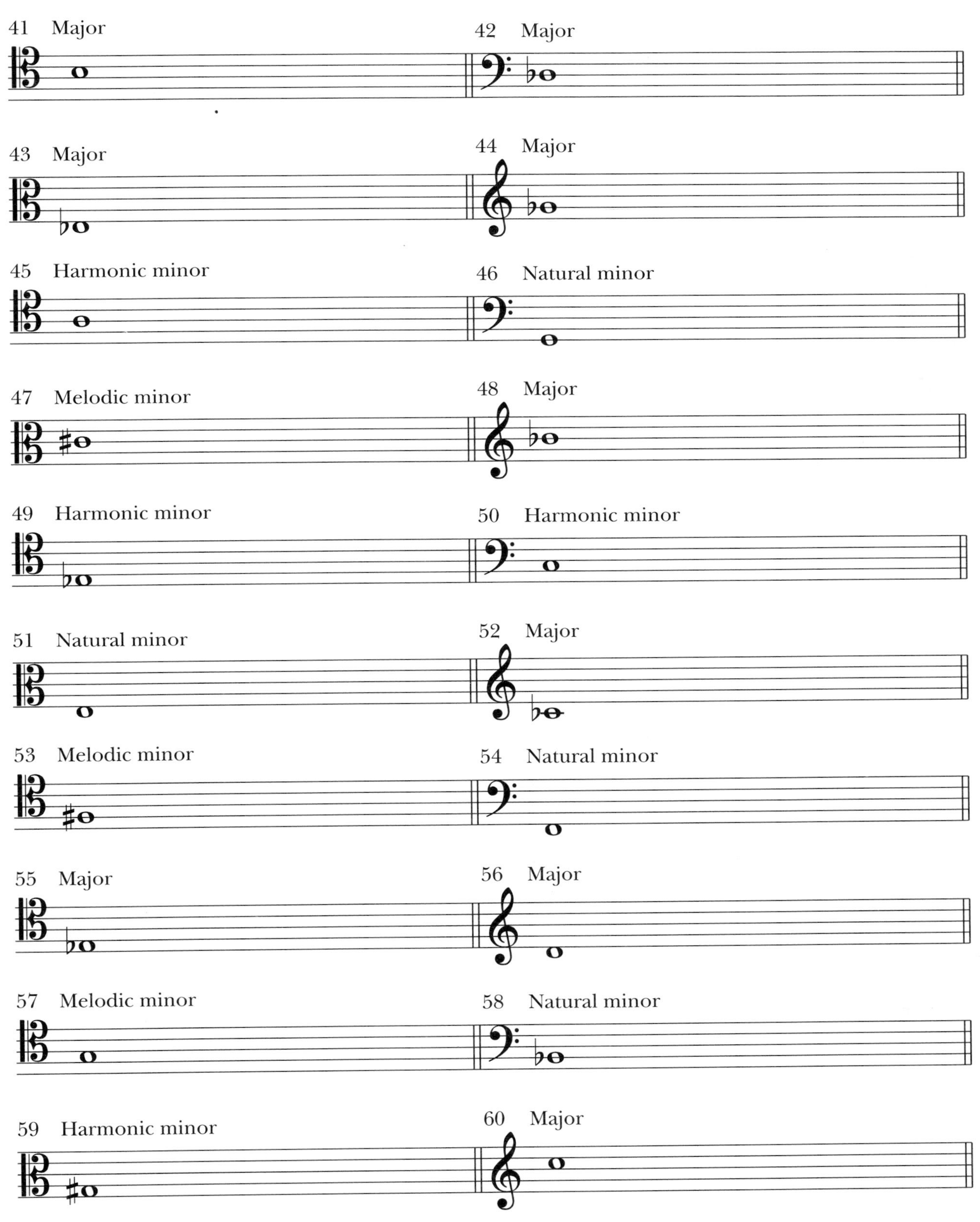
41 Major
42 Major
43 Major
44 Major
45 Harmonic minor
46 Natural minor
47 Melodic minor
48 Major
49 Harmonic minor
50 Harmonic minor
51 Natural minor
52 Major
53 Melodic minor
54 Natural minor
55 Major
56 Major
57 Melodic minor
58 Natural minor
59 Harmonic minor
60 Major

3
Key Signatures and Scale Degrees

A *key signature,* which appears to the right of the clef sign as an arrangement of sharps or flats, gives two essential pieces of information to the musician.

1. It tells the performer which pitches are to be raised by a sharp, or lowered by a flat.
2. It indicates (by implication) that there is a central pitch around which the other pitches are organized. This pitch is the lowest member of the scale (the scale may be major or minor), is called the *tonic,* and is the pitch after which the key is named. For example, if the tonic is A, the key is either A major or a minor, depending on the number of accidentals.

Key signatures are all derived from the major scale in a completely logical manner. Let us examine key signatures made up of sharps first.

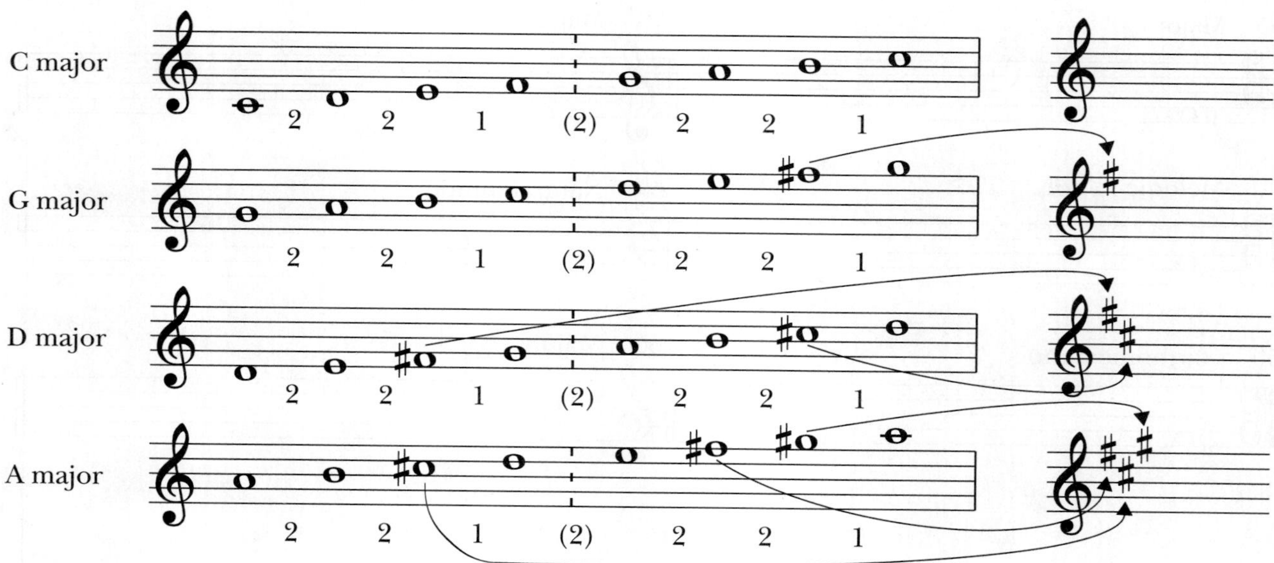

Note:

a. Each scale begins with the second tetrachord of the previous scale.

b. In each case a new accidental is introduced to the scale as a result of having to sharp the third pitch of the second tetrachord.

c. The key signatures show an "accumulation" of accidentals, F♯ always appearing first, C♯ second, and so on.

The remainder of the major scales with sharps and their derived key signatures are

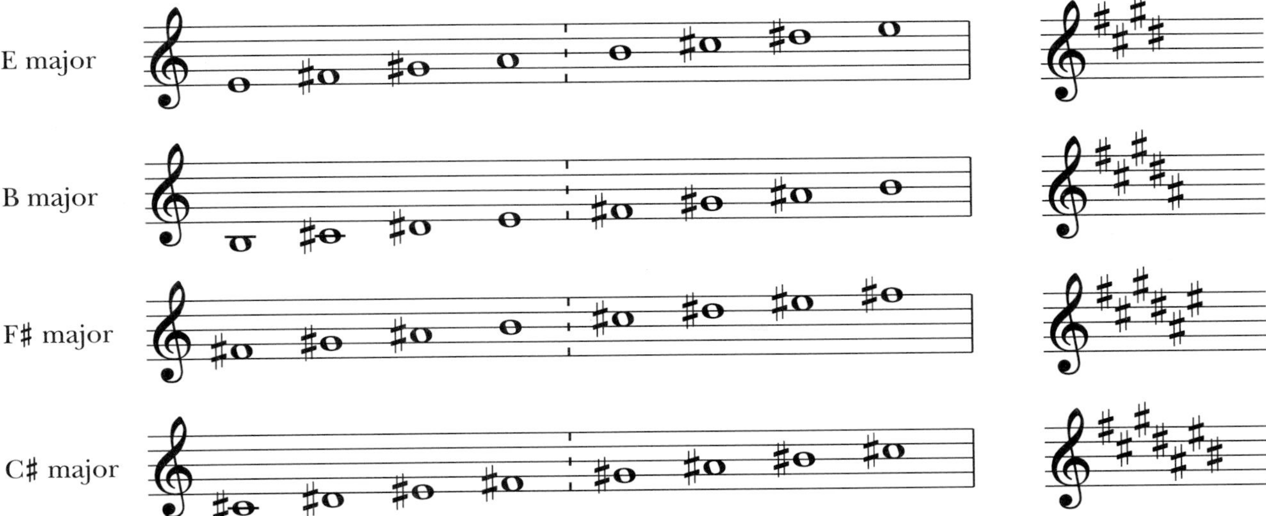

The key signatures with flats are derived from the major scale in a manner similar to the derivation of key signatures with sharps.

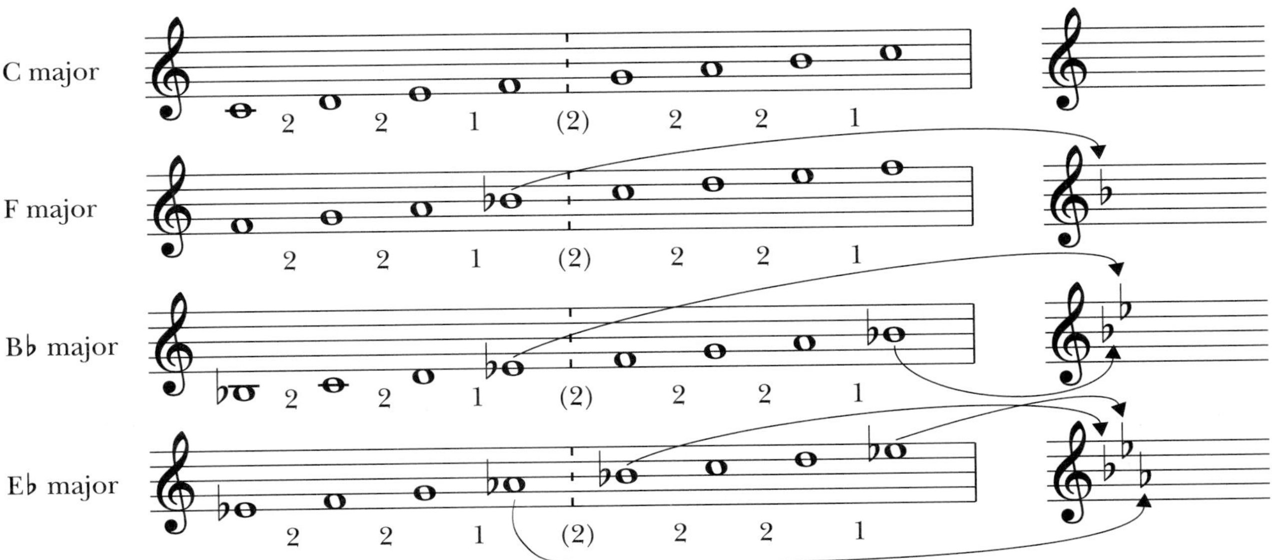

Note:

a. Each scale ends with the first tetrachord of the previous scale, and the last pitch of that tetrachord gives the new tonic.

b. In each case a new accidental is introduced to the scale as a result of having to flat the fourth pitch of the first tetrachord.

c. As with the sharps, the flat key signatures show an accumulation of accidentals, B♭ always appearing first, E♭ second, and so on.

The remainder of the major scales with flats and their derived key signatures are

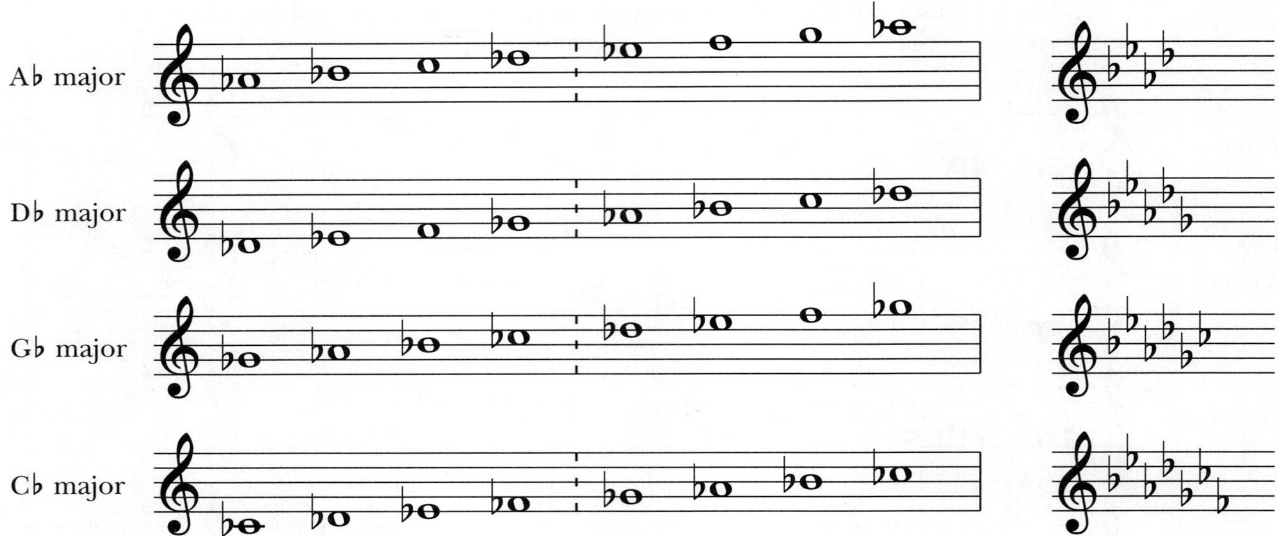

The writing of a key signature renders it unnecessary to put an accidental beside each altered pitch in the scale. Thus, with a key signature, the A♭ major scale appears as

Each major key has a companion minor key with the same signature. The companion key is known as the *relative minor.* The tonic of the relative minor is the *sixth* pitch of the major key's scale. Therefore, if the major key is A, the major scale in that key is

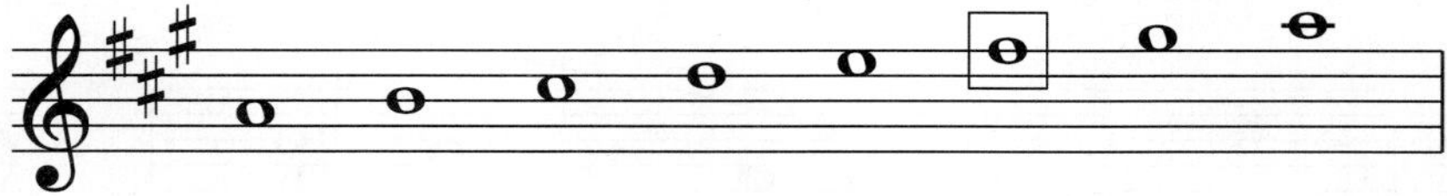

The sixth pitch (or scale step, or degree) is F♯, and so the relative minor key of A major is f♯ minor. The key signatures

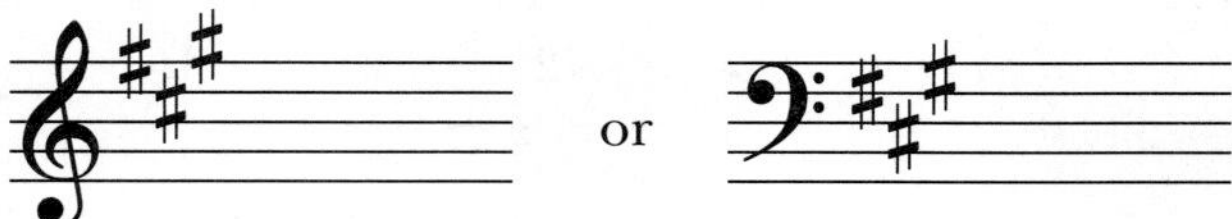

indicate a tonic of A or F♯. Examination of the organization of the music quickly reveals which one of the two is the tonic.

The key signatures for the major scales and their relative minors are shown below:

For each tonic there are, of course, three minor scales; however, the key signature is not affected by this variation. If the natural minor scale is being used the accidentals in the key signature ensure the correct formation of the scale. In the case of the harmonic minor, the seventh degree of the scale has to be raised a half step by an accidental placed beside it; and both the sixth and seventh degrees have to be raised similarly if the melodic minor is being used.

Key: g minor

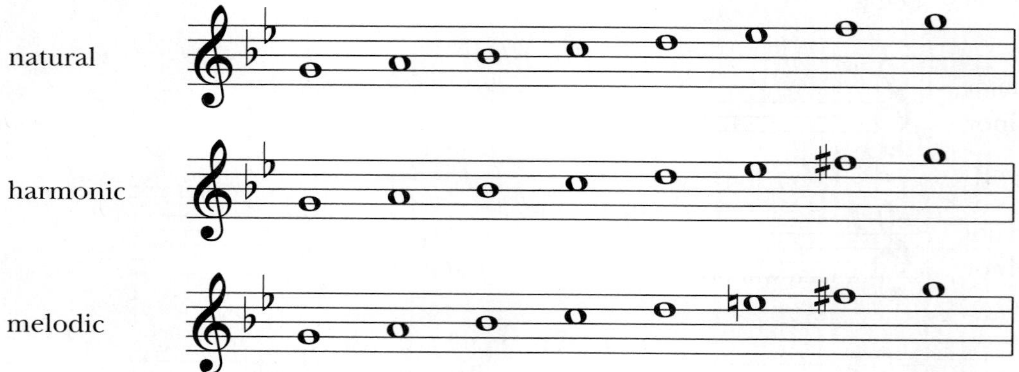

Each scale degree, irrespective of key, has both a name and a number (written in Roman) by which to identify it. (Roman numerals are sometimes written in lowercase letters; see Chapter 5).

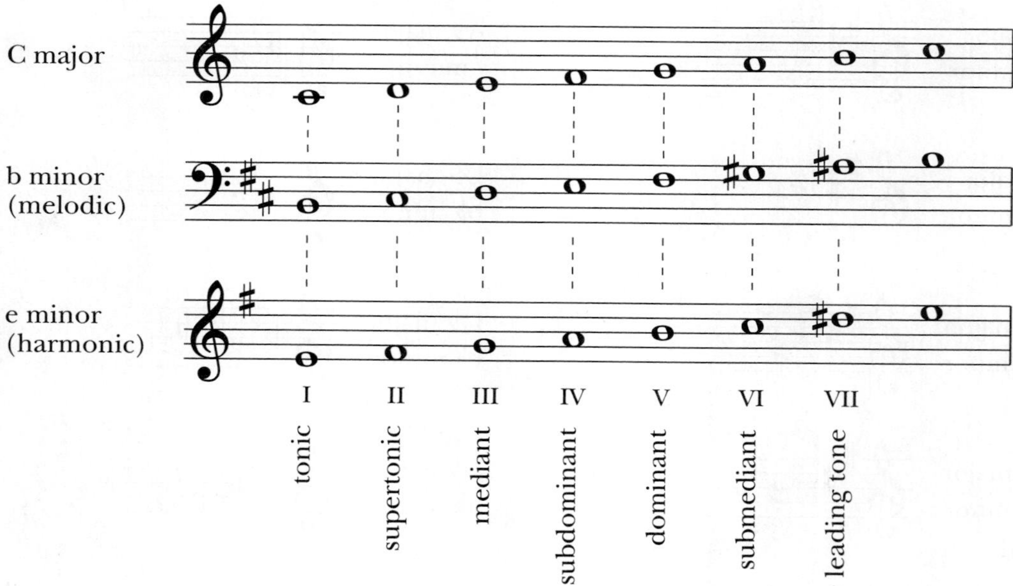

The natural minor has no leading tone because the leading tone must *always* be a half step below the tonic. The seventh scale degree in the natural minor is called the *subtonic.*

SUGGESTIONS AND STRATEGIES

Although it is important to understand how key signatures are derived, it is equally important to be able to notate them without having to think about the process. Thus, you should practice doing so in each clef until you can commit them to paper almost automatically.

There are various memory devices (*mnemonics*) to help you in this regard. One of the simplest is to invent a seven-word sentence, in which the first letter of each word represents each of the sharps and the order in which they occur. One sentence, in fact, will do for both sharps and flats. For the ordering of the latter, simply read the sentence backward.

Make up some imaginative sentences. They should begin with the letters:

F – C – G – D – A – E – B

Study the following example for proper placement of sharps and flats in all four clefs

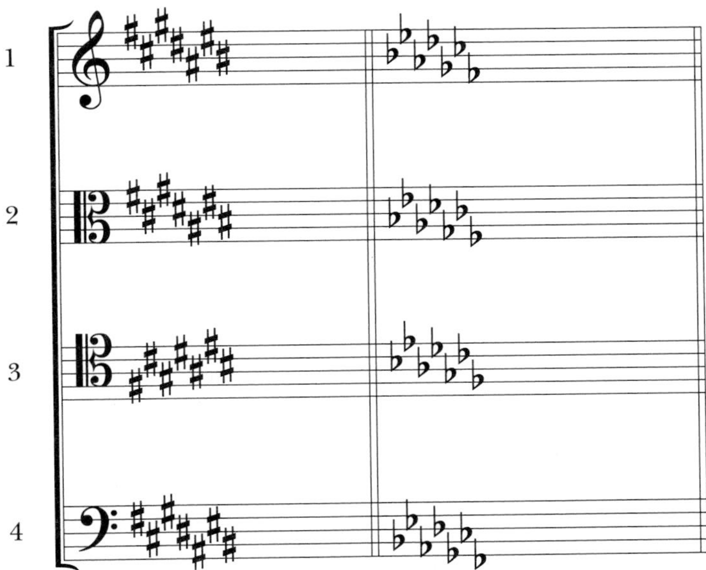

EXERCISES

A. Identify the *major* key signatures. Time goal—20 seconds per line.

B. Identify the *minor* key signatures. Time goal—20 seconds per line.

C. Supply the specified *major* key signatures. Time goal—60 seconds per line.

D. Supply the specified *minor* key signatures. Time goal—60 seconds per line.

E. Using accidentals where necessary, write the specified scales without key signatures. Then write the key signature, as shown. Time goal—30 seconds per scale.

10 a natural minor

11 f harmonic minor

12 b♭ melodic minor

13 C♭ major

14 g harmonic minor

15 a harmonic minor

16 e melodic minor

17 e♭ melodic minor

18 B major

19 c♯ harmonic minor

20 d♯ melodic minor

21 g natural minor

22 a♯ harmonic minor

23 D♭ major

24 a melodic minor

25 F♯ major

26 e♭ natural minor

27 d harmonic minor

28 c melodic minor

29 b♭ harmonic minor

30 f♯ natural minor

31 a♯ melodic minor

32 b harmonic minor

33 C♯ major

34 c♯ melodic minor

35 d natural minor

36 G♭ major

37 f♯ melodic minor

38 f natural minor

39 c melodic minor

40 b melodic minor

F. Write the signatures of the given keys and the pitch(es) for the specified scale degrees. Lowercase letters indicate minor keys. Time goal—40 seconds per line.

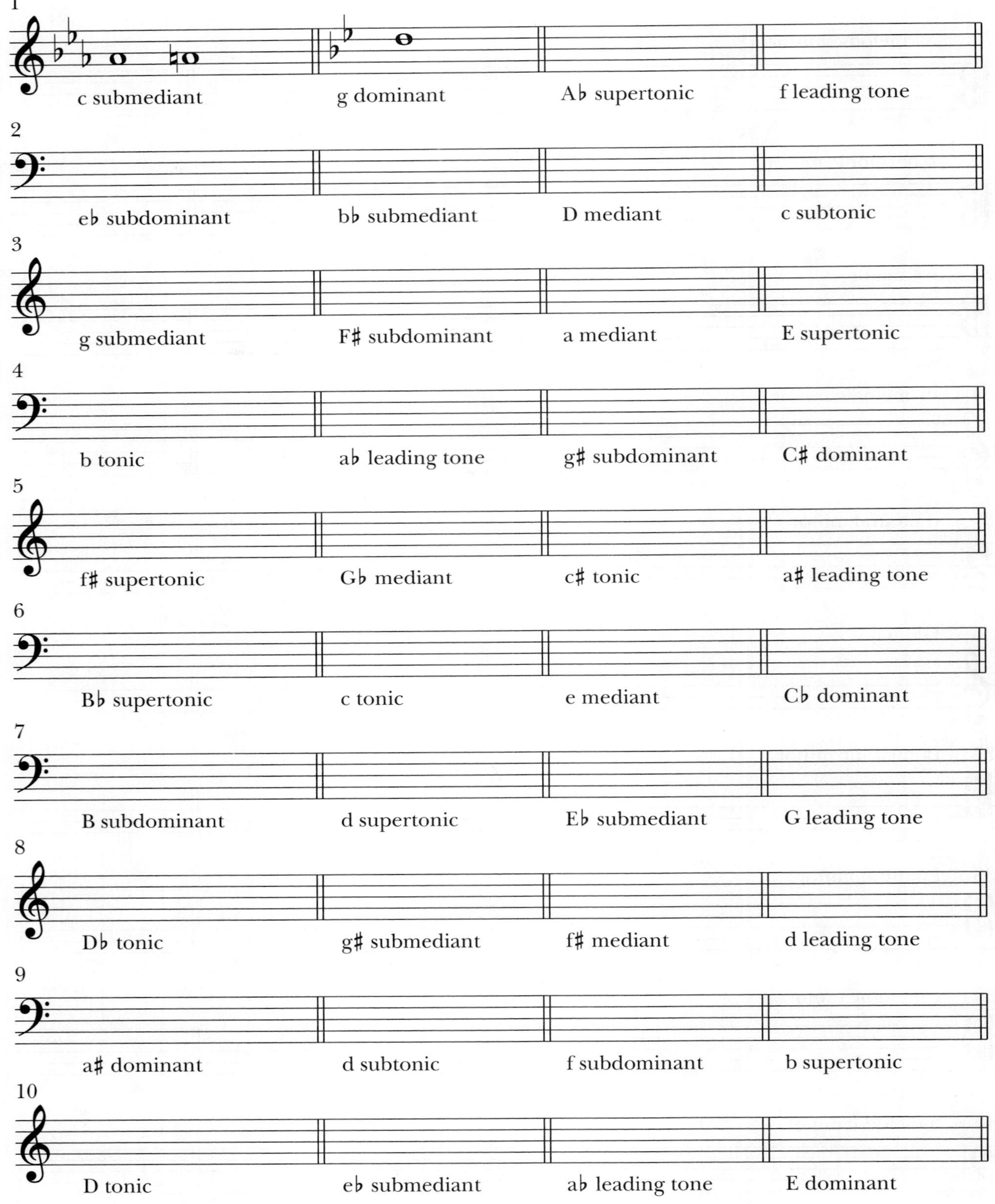

G. Using accidentals where necessary, write the specified scales around the given scale degrees without key signatures. Then write the key signature, as shown. Time goal—30 seconds per scale.

10 Major
leading tone
11 Major
mediant
12 Harmonic minor
submediant
13 Melodic minor
submediant
14 Natural minor
tonic
15 Harmonic minor
supertonic
16 Harmonic minor
leading tone
17 Melodic minor
dominant
18 Major
subdominant
19 Major
tonic

20 Natural minor
submediant
21 Melodic minor
submediant
22 Major
dominant
23 Natural minor
subdominant
24 Major
mediant
25 Natural minor
supertonic
26 Melodic minor
submediant
27 Natural minor
dominant
28 Melodic minor
leading tone
29 Melodic minor
leading tone

30 Major
mediant
31 Melodic minor
mediant
32 Major
tonic
33 Melodic minor
dominant
34 Harmonic minor
mediant
35 Melodic minor
submediant
36 Harmonic minor
leading tone
37 Major
mediant
38 Natural minor
subdominant
39 Melodic minor
supertonic
40 Major
tonic

4 Intervals

The spatial relationship between two pitches is called an interval. In Chapter 2, to enable the notation of scales, the interval of the second was introduced. To notate an interval with accuracy one needs to know the following:

1. The precise names of the intervals.
2. The correct spelling of the intervals.
3. The number of half steps the intervals contain.

The major scale provides an excellent starting point for a formal study of intervals.

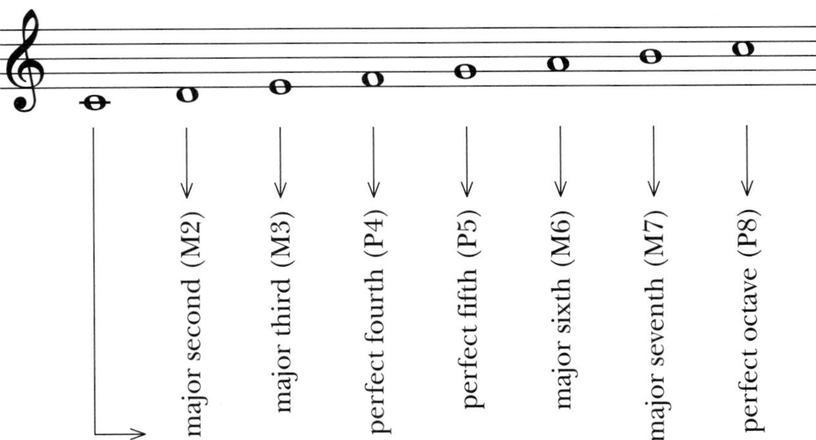

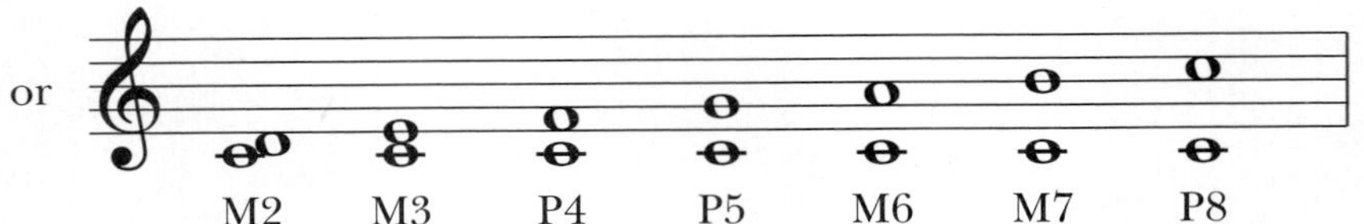

Note:

a. Each interval has a qualitative and a quantitative component in the description of its name. Take, for example, the major sixth. *Major* describes quality (type); *sixth* describes quantity (numerical value).

b. The quantity of each interval (e.g., third, sixth, etc.) coincides precisely with the number of note names as well as the number of lines and spaces on the staff it contains. For example, the perfect fifth, C up to G, is called a fifth because there are five note names in the interval—C D E F G. It is important to understand that the interval C up to G is *always* a fifth in quantity even if an accidental is placed beside either or both of the notes, thus altering its quality.

c. Each interval with a precise name (M2, P4, M7, etc.) spans a characteristic number of half steps. The major scale above shows that

M2 spans two half steps
M3 spans four half steps
P4 spans five half steps
P5 spans seven half steps
M6 spans nine half steps
M7 spans eleven half steps
P8 spans twelve half steps

An understanding of these three points is most valuable, since it enables one to write or identify all of the intervals above without reference to the major scale.

THE QUALITY OF INTERVALS

The major scale contains all the perfect and major intervals within the span of an octave. The qualities, *but not the quantities,* of these intervals may be altered by the appropriate placing of accidentals in the following manner.

1. A *perfect* or *major* interval may be made larger by a half step. This interval is then said to be *augmented.*

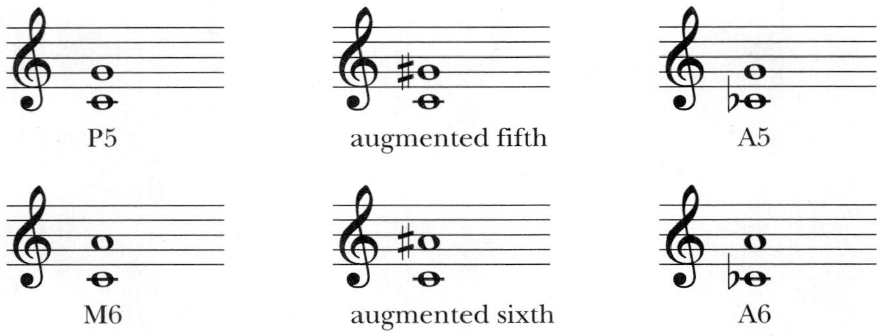

2. A *perfect* interval may be made smaller by a half step. This interval is then said to be *diminished.*

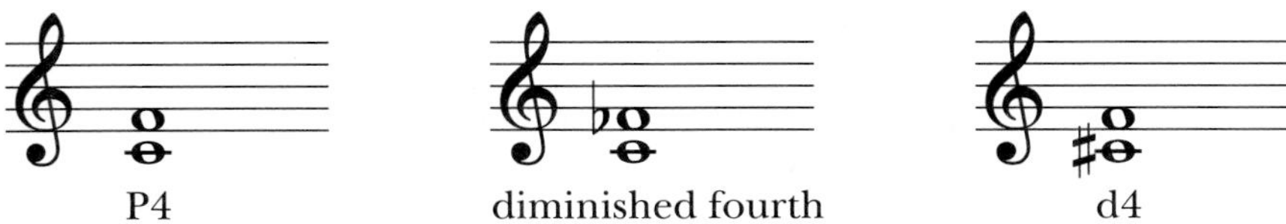

P4 diminished fourth d4

3. A *major* interval may be made smaller by a half step. This interval is then said to be *minor.*

M3 minor third m3

4. A *minor* interval may be made smaller by a half step. This interval is then said to be *diminished.*

m7 diminished seventh d7

Note:

- **a.** The quality of a perfect interval (unisons, 4, 5, 8) can never be altered to produce a major or minor interval. Nor can a major or minor interval (2, 3, 6, 7) be so altered to produce a perfect one.
- **b.** Perfect unisons, fourths, fifths, and octaves are traditionally called *perfect consonances.*
- **c.** Major and minor thirds and sixths are called *imperfect consonances.*
- **d.** Major and minor seconds and sevenths, and all augmented and diminished intervals, are called *dissonances.*
- **e.** The augmented fourth and diminished fifth, both intervals with the same number of half steps (six), are sometimes referred to as *tritones,* because six half steps equal three (tri-) whole steps (tones).
- **f.** The standard abbreviations for interval quality are:

  P for Perfect
  M for Major
  m for minor
  A or $^{+}$ for Augmented
  d or $^{\circ}$ for diminished

The following chart is an easy way to figure out the number of half steps in any simple interval starting with a perfect unison, which consists of zero half steps, and ending with a perfect octave, which comprises twelve half steps. The first column indicates the quality of the interval. Going across the table are the number of half steps, from unison (zero half steps) to octave (twelve half steps).

The first row in this table represents the minor quality. A minor second will have one half step; a minor third contains three half steps; a minor sixth, eight half steps; and a minor seventh, ten half steps.

The second row is the major quality. Notice that the number of half steps in the major quality is always one more half step than the minor quality. For example: The minor second has one half step separating the two pitches, whereas the major second has two half steps. A minor third is separated by three half steps whereas a major third has four half steps.

The third row is perfect. A perfect unison contains no half steps; a perfect fourth has five half steps; a perfect fifth seven half steps; and a perfect octave twelve half steps.

The fourth row is the tritone. Tritones consist of six half steps. Depending on its harmonic function, the tritone will be spelled either as an augmented fourth or a diminished fifth.

Any interval—save the unison, which may not be diminished—may be augmented or diminished. Augmented intervals go to the next number up, while diminished intervals go to the next number down. For example, a major third is made up of four half steps, while the augmented third consists of five half steps. Note, however, that the perfect fourth also comprises five half steps. Therefore, an augmented third and a perfect fourth will sound alike but be spelled differently. For example, C to E-sharp is identified as an augmented third, while C to F is identified as a perfect fourth.

				QUANTITY					
Quality	**Unison**	**Second**	**Third**	**Fourth**	**Tritone**	**Fifth**	**Sixth**	**Seventh**	**Octave**
Minor		1	3				8	10	
Major		2	4				9	11	
Perfect	0			5		7			12
Aug4 / Dim5					6				

Another method for determining quality is based on referencing all the white-note intervals (no sharps or flats). Understanding the makeup of the piano keyboard is crucial to working with this method. The piano keyboard consists of seven white notes and five black notes, a total of twelve half steps. The black notes are grouped in a recurring pattern of two and three. The distance between each black note and the adjacent white note, up or down, is one half step. There are two places on the keyboard where adjacent white notes have no black note in between, the spaces created to form the black note pattern. These white-note half steps are located between B and C, and between E and F, and are identified as minor seconds—the distance of one half step. All other adjacent white notes are major seconds—the distance of two half steps. There are two white-note minor seconds and five white-note major seconds.

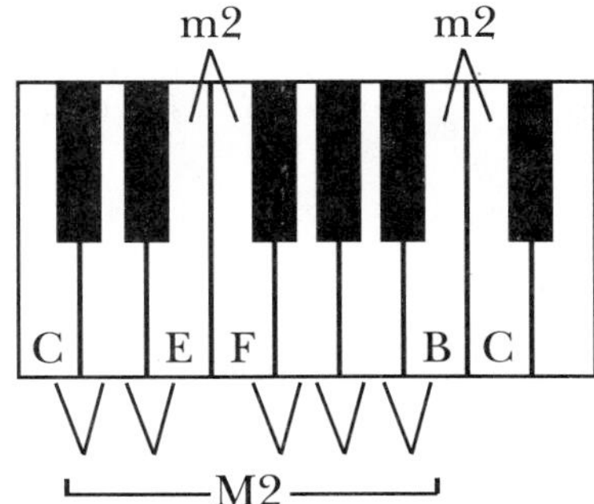

Keeping in mind where the white-note minor seconds are, the quality of white-note thirds can be determined by observing if the white-note half step is contained within the third or not. If the half step is within, the third is minor (smaller); if the half step is outside the third, the third is major (larger). There are three white-note major thirds and four minor thirds.

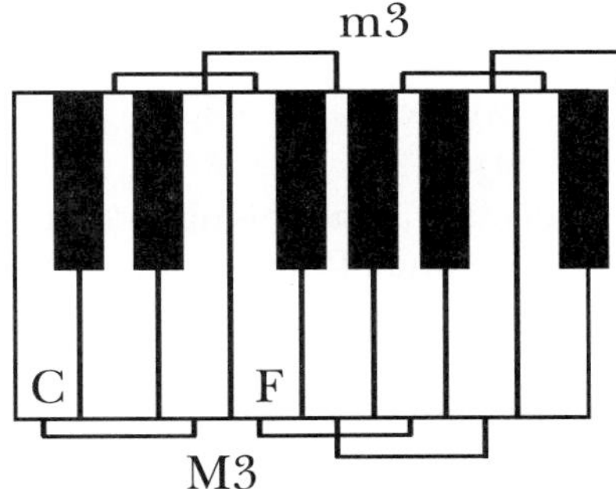

With the exception of the intervals using B and F, all white-note fourths and fifths are perfect. The fourth from F to B contains no white-note half steps, it is larger than every other white-note fourth, and therefore, the fourth from F to B is augmented. The fifth from B to F contains both white-note half steps, making that fifth diminished.

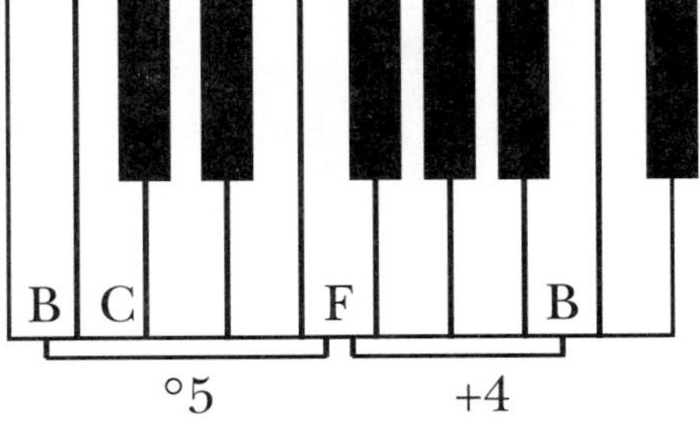

Intervals of the sixth and seventh are minor if both white-note half steps are within, and major if only one white-note half step is within. There are three white-note minor sixths and four major sixths. There are two white-note major sevenths and five minor sevenths.

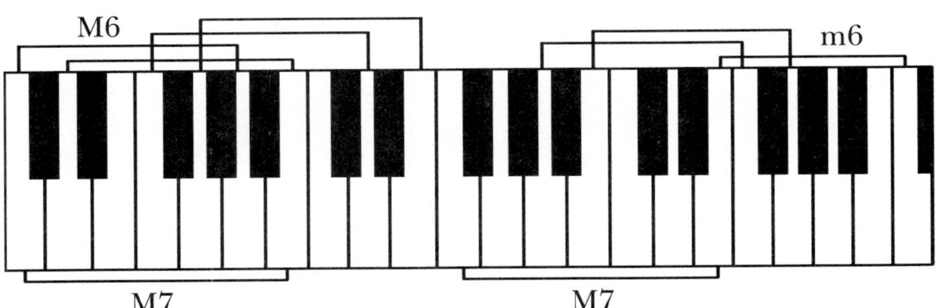

Once the identification of all the white-note intervals has been thoroughly absorbed, adding sharps and/or flats to one or both notes to increase or decrease the quality should be relatively easy.

THE INVERSION OF INTERVALS

An interval is inverted either by raising its lower pitch an octave or by lowering its upper pitch an octave.

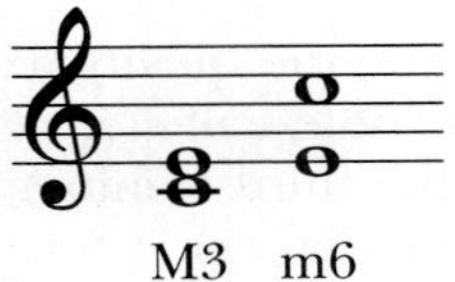

M3 m6

P5 P4

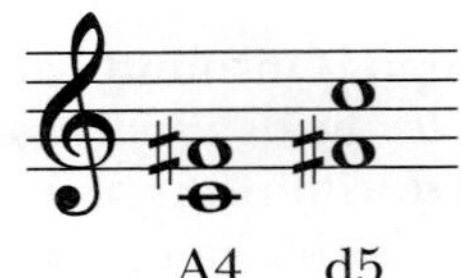

A4 d5

Note:

a. An interval and its inversion always span an octave. Such intervals are said to be *complementary.*

b. The sum of the intervals' quantity is always nine. (It is not eight, as one might suppose, because one of the pitch names is counted twice.)

c. With the exception of the perfect interval, the quality of an interval changes when it is inverted.

A major interval becomes minor.
A minor interval becomes major.
An augmented interval becomes diminished.
A diminished interval becomes augmented.

d. The sum of the half steps in complementary intervals is always twelve. For example, a major sixth (nine half steps) added to its inversion, a minor third (three half steps), produces a perfect octave (twelve half steps).

Or:

M6 + m3 = P8
9 + 3 = 12

COMPOUND INTERVALS

All intervals greater than an octave are said to be *compound.* For example:

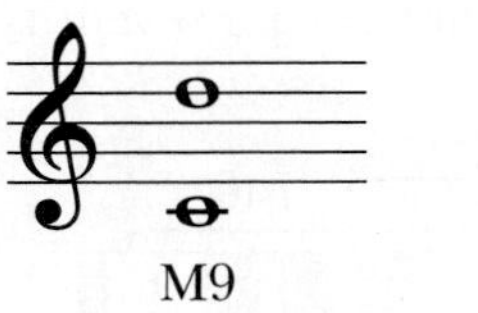

M9

P11

A12

m13

If one raises the lower pitch an octave in each interval above, the results are as follows:

M2

P4

A5

m6

Thus,

M9 = M2 + 7
P11 = P4 + 7
A12 = A5 + 7
m13 = m6 + 7

A compound interval, therefore, between one and two octaves in span is created by expanding the simple interval by an octave. The quality of the compound interval is the same as that of the simple one. Its quantity is determined by adding seven to the quantity of the simple interval.

SUGGESTIONS AND STRATEGIES

Identifying and writing intervals accurately is most easily done if you know all the white-note intervals. The examples that follow show you how to apply this principle.

Identifying an Ascending or Descending Interval

or

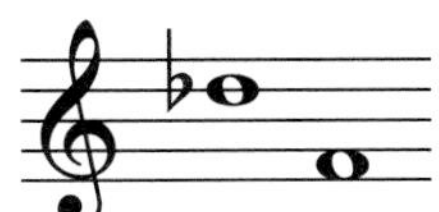

If one note has an accidental, begin with the white-note analysis, then determine what adding the accidental does to the space between the notes—increases or decreases it.

1. Find the quantity of the interval by counting the number of letter names involved.	FGABCD = a sixth
2. The sixth from F to D contains only one white-note second.	F to D = M6
3. The given note is D♭.	The flat makes the interval a half step smaller, so it is a minor sixth (m6)

If both notes have the same accidental, the interval can be analyzed as if the notes are white.

or

1. Find the quantity of the interval by counting the number of letter names involved.	ABCDE = a fifth
2. Without altering the note-names, lower *both* pitches by a half step.	We now have A and E
3. White-note fifths, except B to F, are perfect.	The interval is a perfect fifth (P5).

If both notes have different accidentals, again begin with the white-note analysis, then determine what each accidental does to the space between the notes.

or

1. Find the quantity of the interval by counting the number of letter names involved.	FGA = a third
2. F to A does not contain any white-note seconds.	F to A = M3
3. The given note is F♯.	The sharp makes the interval a half step smaller—a minor third
4. The given note is A♭.	The flat makes the interval a half step smaller—a diminished third (d3)

PRELIMINARY EXERCISES

A. The following are quantity only exercises; thus, there is no need for clefs.

Identify the quantity of the following intervals.

Write the indicated interval above the given note.

Write the indicated interval below the given note.

7 8 4 2 5 6 4 7 6 3

B. The following are white-note only exercises: quantity and quality.

Identify the following intervals.

Write the indicated interval above the given note.

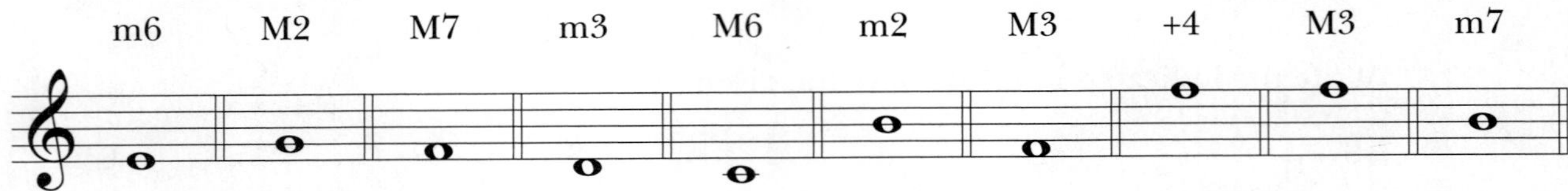

Write the indicated interval below the given note.

M6 °5 M7 P8 P4 M2 P5 m6 m2 m7

EXERCISES

A. Identify the intervals. Time goal—20 seconds per line.

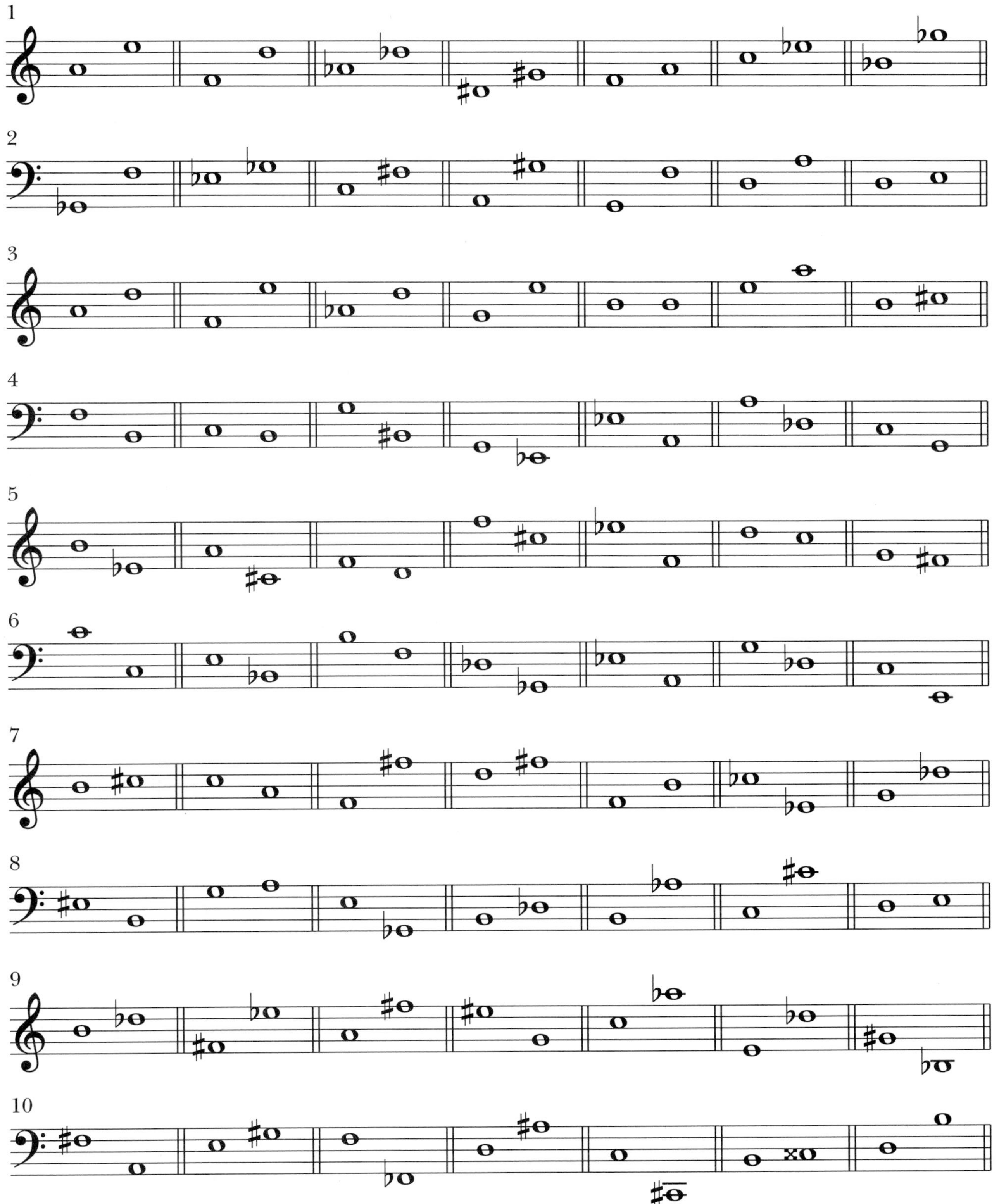

11
12
13
14
15
16
17
18
19
20

B. Most of the following intervals are spelled incorrectly. Rewrite the wrong intervals correctly without changing the first of the two pitches. Time goal—20 seconds per line.

10
M2
M7
°4
11
M6
°3
°6
12
+3
+1
+2
13
P4
M3
+6
14
M7
M7
°7
15
°5
M6
M3
16
+2
°4
m6
17
°7
+3
P5
18
P5
M2
P8
19
°8
°4
°7
20
°3
+6
+3

C. Write the specified intervals above or below the given pitches as indicated. Time goal—30 seconds per line.

11
P8↑ P4↑ m6↓ m7↑ °5↑ M2↓
12
M3↓ °4↓ +3↑ +2↓ +8↑ P1
13
M6↑ M7↓ +1↓ °3↓ °6↑ °5↑
14
+3↑ m6↓ P8↓ m2↓ M7↑ P5↓
15
P8↑ +1↓ °6↓ M3↓ m2↑ °8↓
16
M2↑ m6↑ P5↓ +8↑ °4↑ m3↓
17
P1 °8↑ M6↓ +5↓ °3↓ +2↑
18
+4↑ °7↓ °5↓ M3↑ m7↑ °4↓
19
m3↑ m7↑ °4↓ P4↓ +8↓ °7↓
20
°8↓ +5↓ °7↑ +6↓ m2↑ +1↓

21
+1 ↑ P4 ↑ m6 ↓ °3 ↓ +6 ↓ m3 ↑
22
+3 ↑ M2 ↓ °8 ↑ +4 ↑ °7 ↓ +2 ↓
23
P5 ↓ M3 ↑ M6 ↓ +2 ↑ m2 ↓ +5 ↓
24
°8 ↑ +3 ↓ m7 ↑ P1 °6 ↓ °5 ↓
25
M6 ↓ +4 ↑ °5 ↑ m6 ↓ P4 ↓ m3 ↑
26
M7 ↑ °6 ↑ M2 ↓ m7 ↓ +8 ↓ m2 ↑
27
+2 ↑ °5 ↓ P1 M3 ↓ +5 ↑ °4 ↑
28
P5 ↑ °3 ↑ M2 ↓ °7 ↓ °6 ↑ m2 ↓
29
P8 ↑ M6 ↓ +6 ↑ M7 ↓ m6 ↑ °3 ↓
30
+8 ↑ °7 ↑ P1 °4 ↓ P5 ↓ +1 ↓

D. Write and identify the inversions of the given intervals. Time goal—60 seconds per line.

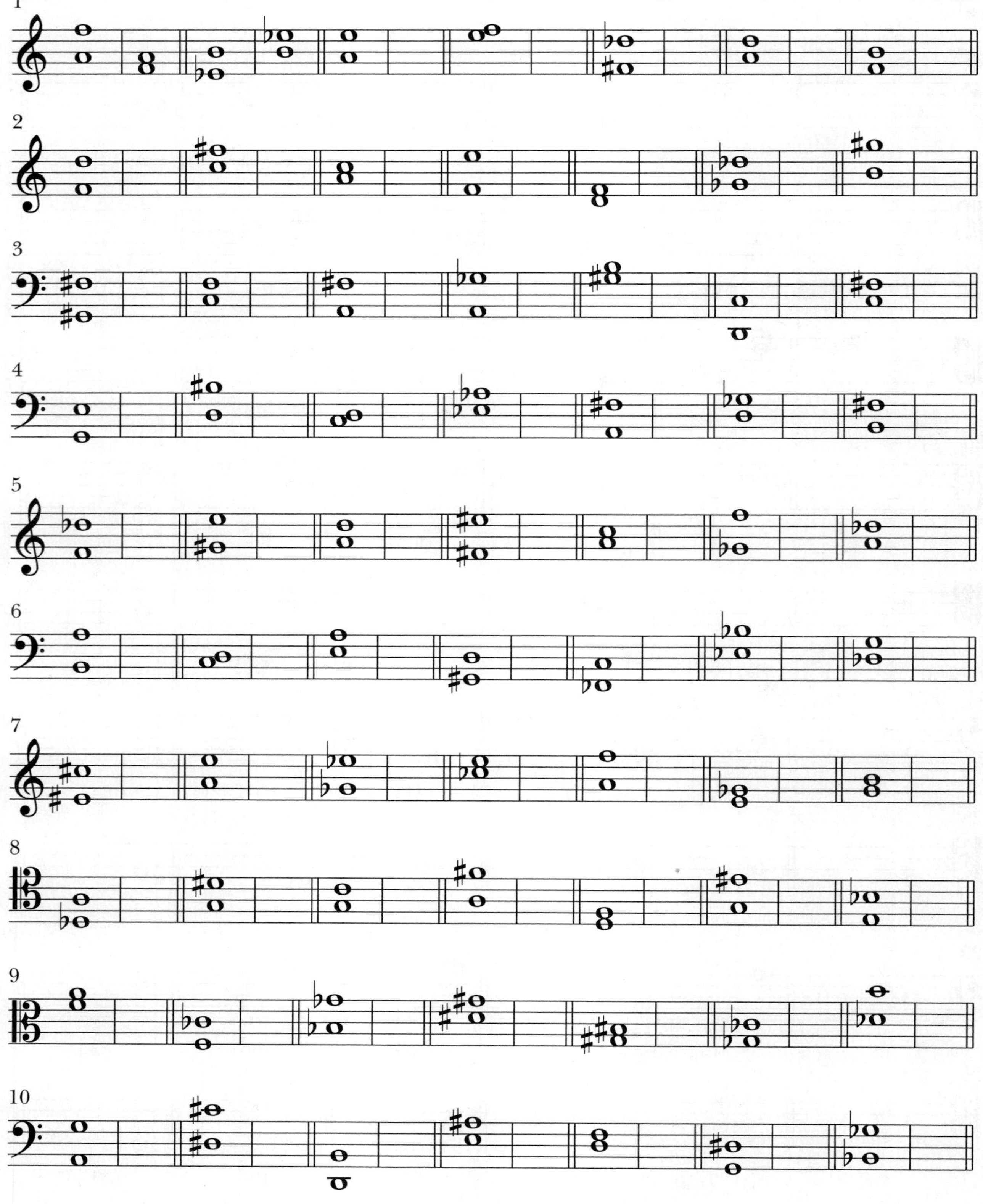

E. Rewrite the given intervals as compound intervals. In each case identify the compound interval. Time goal—75 seconds per line.

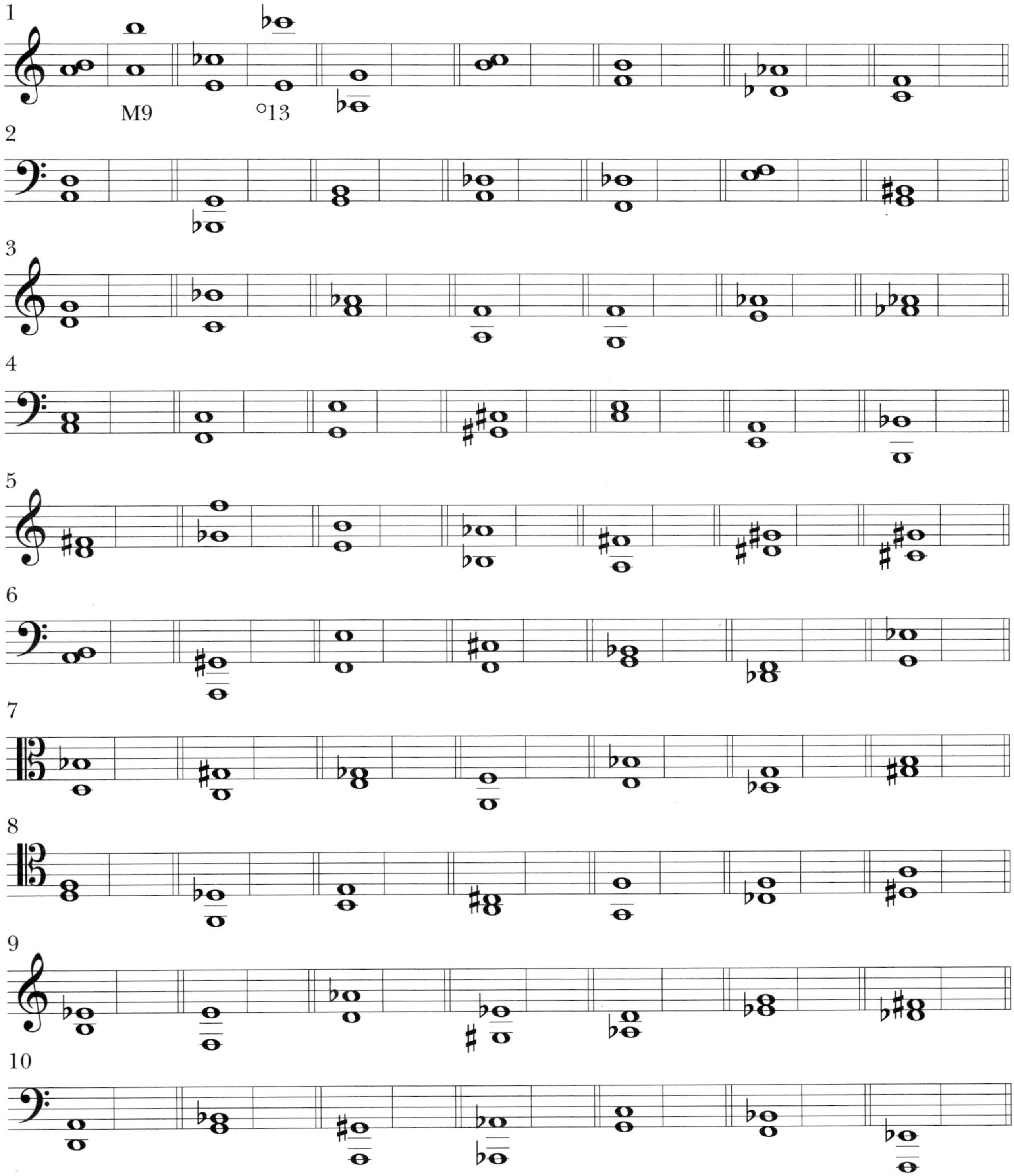

5
Triads

A triad is a three-note chord. In traditional harmony, a triad is a three-note chord built in intervals of thirds. As seen in the previous chapter, for two pitches to be separated by a third, the pitches must be either on adjacent lines or in adjacent spaces. There is no other way of spelling the interval correctly. The three letters that form a triad are always the same, regardless of the addition of flats and sharps. For instance, the triad with the root letter of A is always spelled A-C-E. In addition, triads are always spelled from the root up. The following shows which letters go together to form a triad: A-b-C-d-E-f-G-a-B-c-D-e-F-g-A. Any three consecutive uppercase letters, or any three consecutive lowercase letters, form the letter grouping for a triad.

TYPES OF TRIADS

Triads contain two kinds of thirds: the major third (four half steps) and the minor third (three half steps). These thirds in combination make possible the formation of four triad types.

1. The *major triad:* constructed by writing a major third and a minor third upon it.

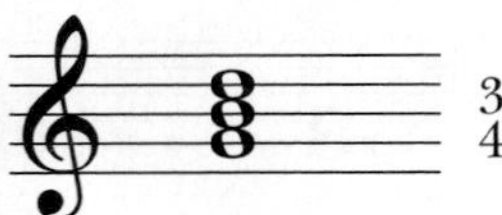

2. The *minor triad:* constructed by writing a minor third and a major third upon it.

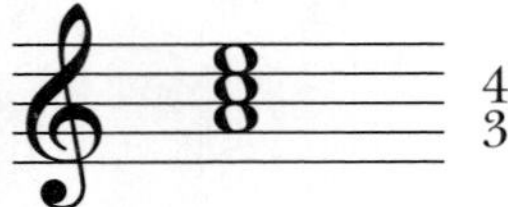

3. The *augmented triad:* constructed by writing one major third upon another.

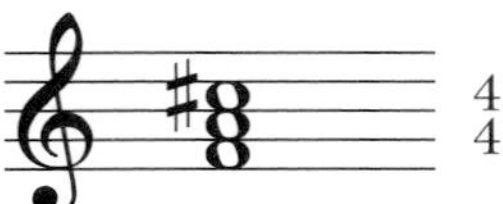

4. The *diminished triad:* constructed by writing one minor third upon another.

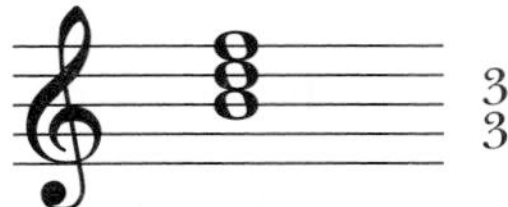

Note:

a. The lowest note of the triad is called the *root.*

b. The middle note is called the *third,* because it is an interval of a third above the root.

c. The highest note is called the *fifth,* because it is an interval of a fifth above the root.

d. In the major and minor triads, the fifth is *perfect.*

e. In the augmented triad, the fifth is *augmented.*

f. In the diminished triad, the fifth is *diminished.*

TRIADS IN MAJOR AND MINOR KEYS

Triads are named after the scale degree upon which they are built. Thus, the triad built on the first scale degree is called the tonic triad, on the second scale degree the supertonic, and so on. In the key of C major and its relative minor, a minor, the triads on all the scale degrees are as follows:

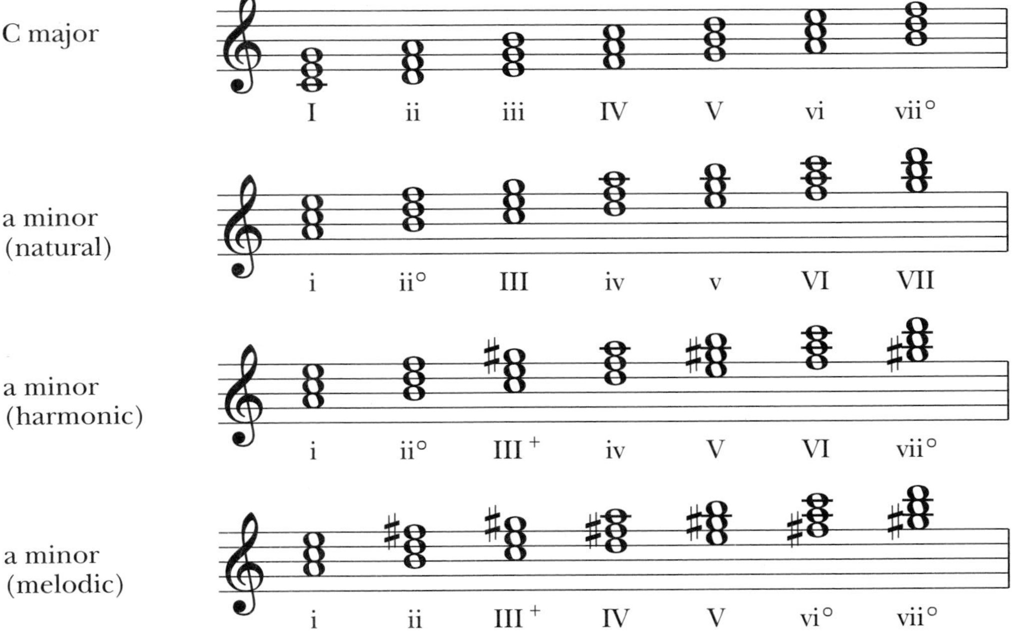

Note:
Capital Roman numerals are used for major triads (I), small Roman numerals for minor triads (ii), capital Roman numerals followed by plus signs for augmented triads (III^{+}), and small Roman numerals followed by circles for diminished triads (vii°).

It is important to appreciate that the qualities of the triads in the major and minor keys are governed by the intervallic organizations of the major and minor scales. In all major keys, therefore, the tonic triad will be major, the supertonic will be minor, and so on. The chart below shows the distribution of the four types of triads in the major and minor keys.

	MAJOR	**MINOR**		
		Natural	**Harmonic**	**Melodic**
Major Triads	I, IV, V	III, VI, VII	V, VI	IV, V
Minor Triads	ii, iii, vi	i, iv, v	i, iv	i, ii
Augmented Triads			III^{+}	III^{+}
Diminished Triads	vii°	ii°	ii°, vii°	vi°, vii°

The following is a chart of triad construction by scale degrees. Observe that, with the exception of the tonic triad, all the other triads contain either scale degree six or scale degree seven. Triads that contain scale degrees six or seven in minor keys will therefore have two quality possibilities—quality according to the key signature, and quality with a raised 6 or raised 7. Remember to read from the root up.

Chord Member	**Scale Degree**						
Fifth	5	6	7	1	2	3	4
Third	3	4	5	6	7	1	2
Root	1	2	3	4	5	6	7
Minor Keys	**Chord Quality**						
Key signature quality	i	ii°	III	iv	v	VI	VII
Raised 6 or 7 quality	i	ii	III^{+}	IV	V	vi°	vii°
Major Keys	**Chord Quality**						
Major key quality	I	ii	iii	IV	V	vi	vii°

SUGGESTIONS AND STRATEGIES

A useful starting point in quickly identifying the quality of a triad is to know the quality of all the white-note triads (triads in C major). Follow with analyzing the effect of adding sharps or flats to the root, third, or fifth.

With the exception of triads built on B-flat and B-natural, the following obervations may be useful in helping you to identify triads quickly (Exercise A).

If the root and the fifth of a triad have no accidentals, or the same accidental, the triad is major or minor. Determine the triad's quality by identifying the quality of the third.

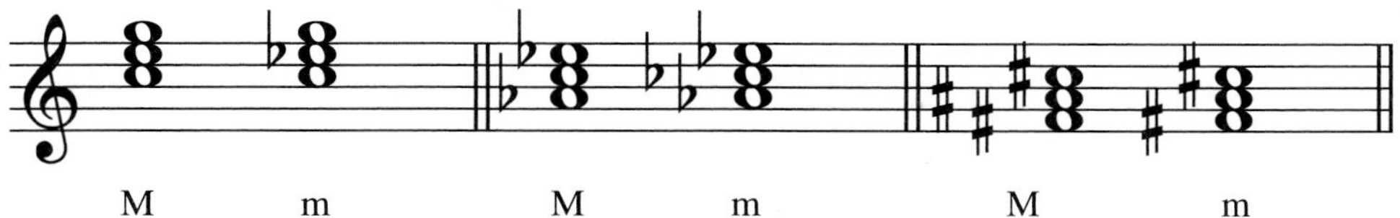

If the root of a triad is natural and the fifth is sharp, or if the root is flat and the fifth is natural, or if the root is sharp and the fifth is double-sharp, the triad is augmented.

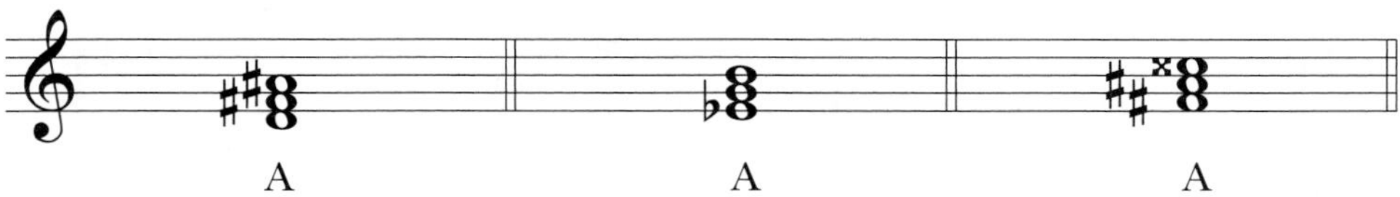

If the root of a triad is natural and the fifth is flat, or if the root is sharp and the fifth is natural, or if the root is flat and the fifth is double-flat, the triad is diminished.

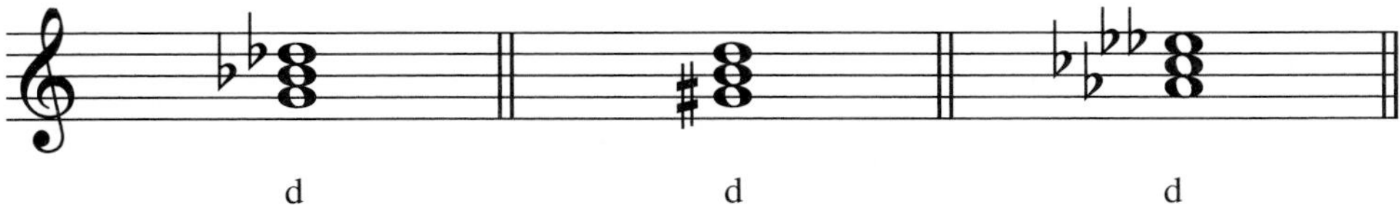

The same observations may be used to check your construction of triads for accuracy (Exercise B). For example, if you think you have written a major triad, but the root and fifth do not match with respect to accidentals, you know you have made a mistake (again, with the exception of triads built on B♭ and B♮). Similar checks may be made for augmented and diminished triads.

Finally, try to figure out why the observations made in the previous examples do not apply to triads whose roots are B♭ or B♮. If you succeed, you will have arrived at some useful conclusions about the organization of steps and half steps in the diatonic scale.

EXERCISES

A. Identify the quality of each triad. Time goal—45 seconds per line.

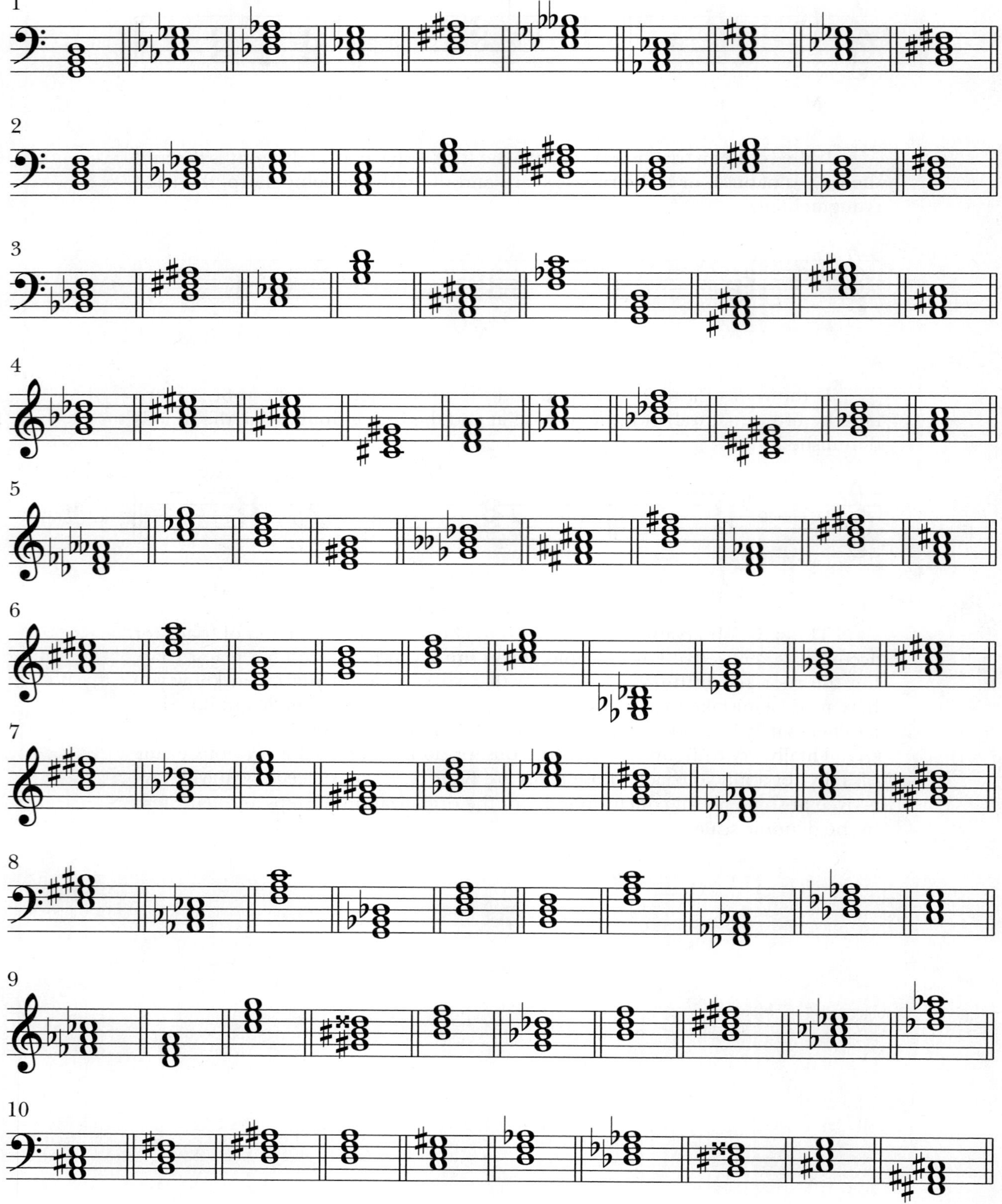

11
12
13
14
15
16
17
18
19
20

B. Using the given note as either the root (r), third (3), or fifth (5), write the specified triad. Time goal—75 seconds per line.

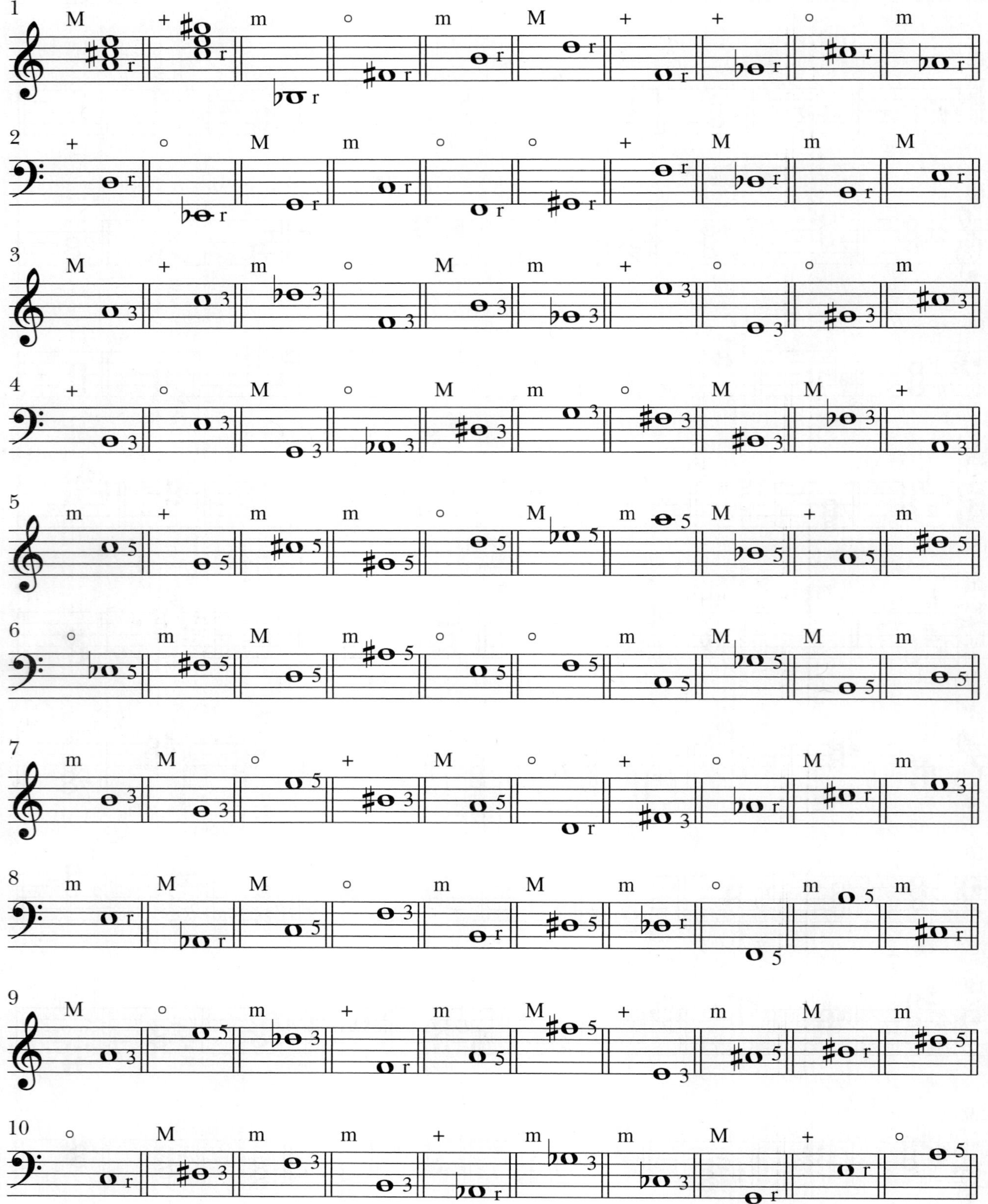

11 + M m + ○ M + ○ M +
12 m ○ + M + + M m + m
13 M ○ m M ○ + M ○ + +
14 + M + M m ○ M + m +
15 M m ○ m + ○ M ○ m M
16 m + M + M + m ○ m M
17 M m m + m ○ M m ○ m
18 + m ○ m + m M ○ + +
19 + M + ○ + m M M + ○
20 m M ○ m M m m + ○ M

C. Supply the signature of the given key, and write the triad on the specified scale degree. Time goal—60 seconds per line.

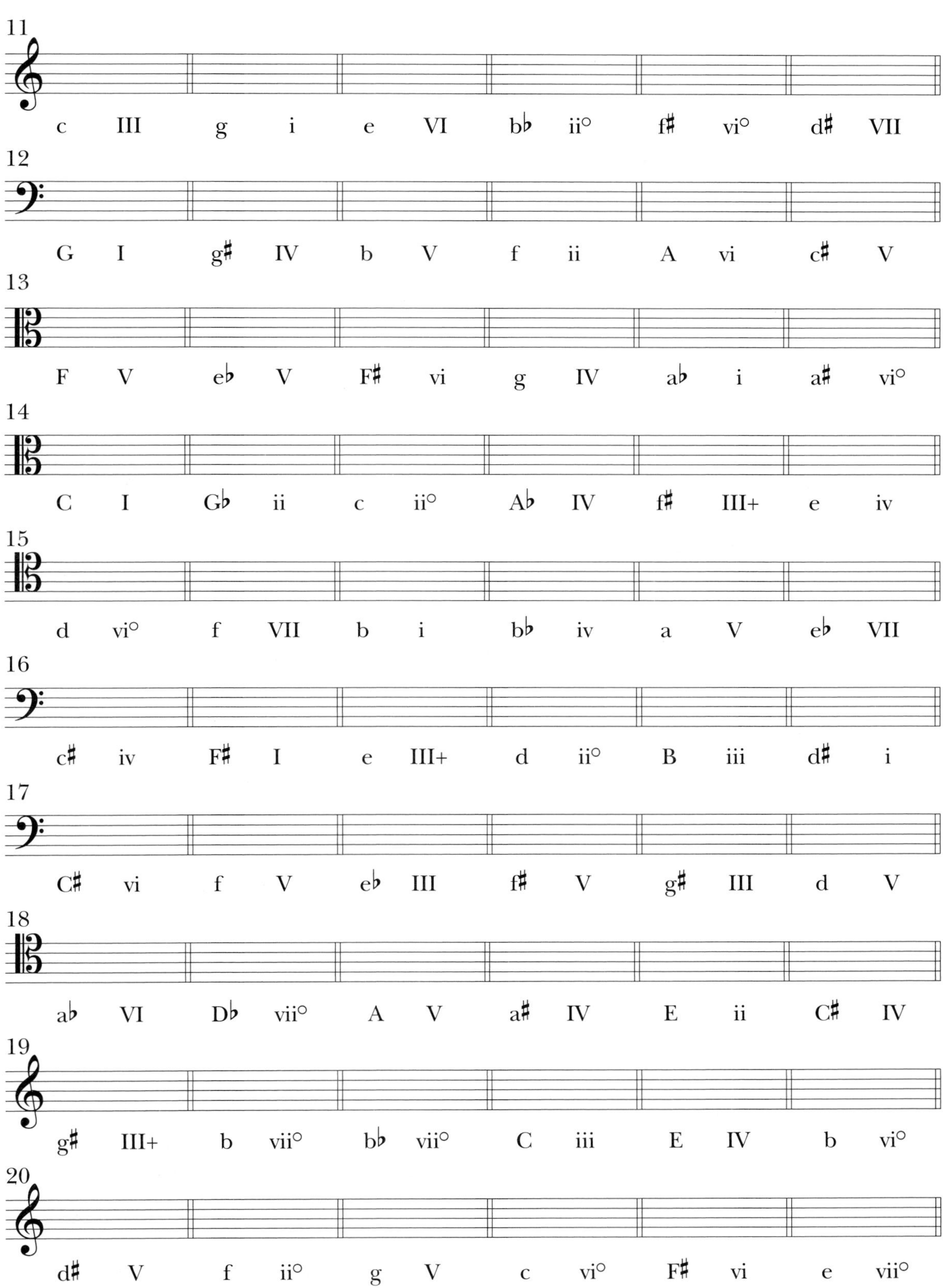
11
c III g i e VI b♭ ii° f♯ vi° d♯ VII
12
G I g♯ IV b V f ii A vi c♯ V
13
F V e♭ V F♯ vi g IV a♭ i a♯ vi°
14
C I G♭ ii c ii° A♭ IV f♯ III+ e iv
15
d vi° f VII b i b♭ iv a V e♭ VII
16
c♯ iv F♯ I e III+ d ii° B iii d♯ i
17
C♯ vi f V e♭ III f♯ V g♯ III d V
18
a♭ VI D♭ vii° A V a♯ IV E ii C♯ IV
19
g♯ III+ b vii° b♭ vii° C iii E IV b vi°
20
d♯ V f ii° g V c vi° F♯ vi e vii°

D. Write the specified key signature, the triad, and the triad's quality in the manner indicated. Time goal—100 seconds per line.

11 Subdominant
c♯ mel. min.
F maj.
d har. min.
f♯ mel. min.
G♭ maj.
a nat. min.
12 Leading tone
f har. min.
e har. min.
a♯ mel. min.
B♭ maj.
g mel. min.
e♭ har. min.
13 Mediant
f nat. min.
a♭ mel. min.
c nat. min.
b mel. min.
c♯ nat. min.
d♯ nat. min.
14 Tonic
E maj.
c har. min.
A maj.
f♯ nat. min.
a♯ nat. min.
b♭ har. min.
15 Subdominant
G maj.
b har. min.
d mel. min.
e♭ nat. min.
c♯ nat. min.
f har. min.
16 Supertonic
e nat. min
a har. min.
C♯ maj.
g mel. min.
a♯ har. min.
g♯ har. min.
17 Submediant
e♭ nat. min.
d♯ mel. min.
c mel. min.
f♯ har. min.
b♭ nat. min.
B maj.
18 Dominant
b nat. min.
a mel. min.
A♭ maj.
f mel. min.
a♭ nat. min.
e mel. min.
19 Submediant
c♯ har. min.
D♭ maj.
d♯ har. min.
c♯ mel. min.
e♭ mel. min.
d nat. min.
20 Leading tone
a♭ har. min.
F maj.
D maj.
g♯ mel. min.
b♭ mel. min.
C♯ maj.

6
The Notation of Rhythm

Rhythm is the duration of the sounds (notes) and silences (rests) in music.

NOTE VALUES

The note with the longest duration is the breve. The duration of each note in the table below is half that of the note immediately above it.

SYMBOL	NAME	EQUIVALENT REST
	breve (rarely used)	
	whole note	
	half note	
	quarter note	
	eighth note	
	sixteenth note	
	thirty-second note	
	sixty-fourth note	

A rest is used to account for the time during which a note is not sounding.

A note's duration may be increased by one half by placing a dot after the note, thus:

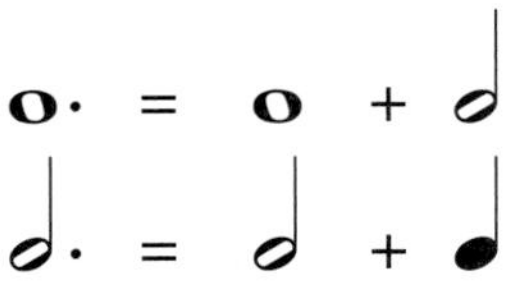

𝅝. = 𝅝 + 𝅗𝅥

𝅗𝅥. = 𝅗𝅥 + ♩

A second dot increases the duration by half the value of the first dot.

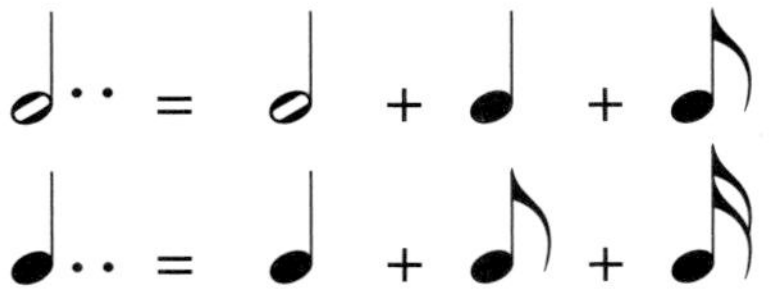

𝅗𝅥.. = 𝅗𝅥 + ♩ + ♪

♩.. = ♩ + ♪ + 𝅘𝅥𝅯

Because dots cannot always produce the desired duration, notes may be tied together:

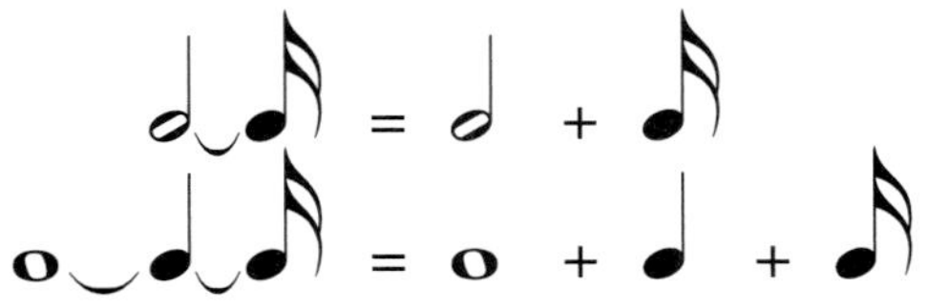

𝅗𝅥‿𝅘𝅥𝅯 = 𝅗𝅥 + 𝅘𝅥𝅯

𝅝‿♩‿𝅘𝅥𝅯 = 𝅝 + ♩ + 𝅘𝅥𝅯

METER SIGNATURES

A meter (or time) signature (e.g., $\frac{3}{4}$, $\frac{6}{8}$, $\frac{4}{4}$,) gives the performer two pieces of information:

1. The lower number tells which note value is used as the basic unit of organization within the measure.
2. The upper number tells how many notes of a given value are in the measure.

For example, $\frac{3}{4}$ informs that the measure is organized in quarter notes and that there are three quarter notes in the measure.

Determining the number of beats in a measure requires additional understanding of the type of meter being used.

There are two types of meter—*simple* and *compound.* In simple meter the note value that represents the beat may be divided into durations that are related to the beat by multiples of two. For example:

beat = ♩
simple division = ♪ ♪ or ♪ 𝅘𝅥𝅯 𝅘𝅥𝅯

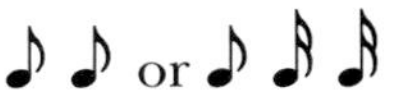

In compound meter the note value that represents the beat may be divided into durations that are related to the beat by multiples of three. For example:

beat = ♩.
compound division = ♪ ♪ ♪

Notice that the beat value in compound meter is a dotted note and that the lower number in the time signature represents the division of the beat value, whereas the beat value in simple meter is the lower number in the time signature.

The vast majority of music of the seventeenth, eighteenth, and nineteenth centuries is constructed in measures that have either two (duple), three (triple), or four (quadruple) beats to the measure. The chart below shows the most commonly found meter signatures.

	SIMPLE		COMPOUND	
	METER SIG.	DURATION OF BEAT	METER SIG.	DURATION OF BEAT
DUPLE	2/2 (¢)	𝅗𝅥	6/4	𝅗𝅥.
	2/4	♩	6/8	♩.
	2/8	♪	6/16	♪.
TRIPLE	3/2	𝅗𝅥	9/4	𝅗𝅥.
	3/4	♩	9/8	♩.
	3/8	♪	9/16	♪.
QUADRUPLE	4/2	𝅗𝅥	12/4	𝅗𝅥.
	4/4 (C)	♩	12/8	♩.
	4/8	♪	12/16	♪.

PRINCIPLES OF NOTATION

The procedure for the notation of rhythm in music is very difficult to codify because a given rule frequently has exceptions. One reason for these frequent exceptions is that a common practice has evolved that is not necessarily the outcome of a strict logic; another, that visual considerations overcome, in some cases, procedures that may be theoretically more correct.

What follows, therefore, is an explanation of a number of principles that constitute the basis for the notation of rhythm. One should remember that, generally speaking, music is notated in such a way that the organization of the beat and its subdivisions is clear to the performer.

Flags and Beams

All pitches of a duration less than a quarter note are made up of note heads (•), stems (|), and flags (𝅮). The stem is attached to the right of the note head and points up if the note head is placed below the middle line of the staff, and to the left, pointing down, if the note head is on or above the middle line. The flag is always placed on the right of the end of the stem.

In instrumental music (and in some editions of vocal music), flags are replaced by beams. For example:

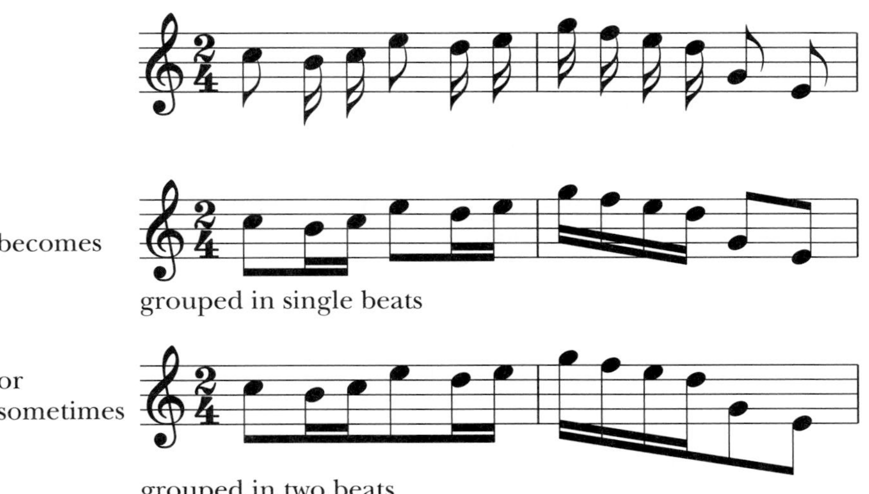

Notice that when groups of notes are embraced by a single beam, the stems always go in the same direction, the direction being determined by the placement of the note heads.

A beam is used for the duration of a fraction of a beat only if the remainder of the beat is occupied by a rest.

If a beam crosses a beat, either it must span the measure completely or it must span a whole number of beats completely. For example:

is undesirable because the beaming in the first measure obscures the fact that e is the first note of the second beat. The correct notation is:

is unsatisfactory for two reasons:

1. The first eighth note should be beamed to the sixteenth notes.
2. Beats two and three should not be beamed together without beaming the whole measure together.

Of the three possible solutions that follow, the first is the most common and the last the least common.

Referring to the beat value as the grouping value might aid in proper grouping of notes. Study the following example, carefully making note of the groupings in $\frac{3}{4}$ versus the groupings in $\frac{6}{8}$. Each meter has the equivalence of six eighth-notes.

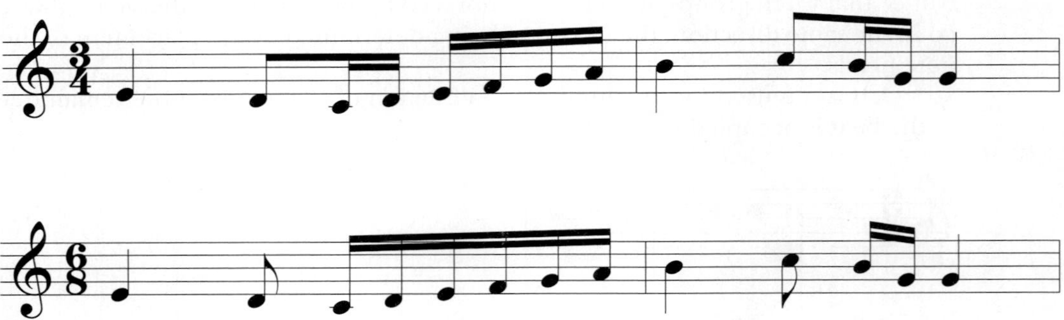

Since triple-meter measures cannot be divided in half without breaking into the beat, the first and second, or second and third, beats are occasionally beamed together.

Dots and Ties

Dots and ties are used to extend the duration of given note values. Dotted notes may be used anywhere within a measure provided that the beat is not obscured. For example:

is acceptable because the performer has no difficulty in understanding the temporal organization, but

is unacceptable because the performer would have difficulty in seeing where the second and third beats fall. Rhythmic dots always go after the note head. If the note is in a space, the dot goes in the same space. If the note is on a line, the dot goes in the space above.

Ties are used within a measure when the use of dots would create confusion. The example directly above, for instance, can be rewritten with ties so that the beats may be clearly seen.

Ties are also used to extend a note value across a bar line.

Notice that the tie symbol (‿) always connects *note heads* and curves in the opposite direction to the stems.

Borrowed Divisions

Simple meter is used when the beat is divided into multiples of two. It is possible, however, to insert compound divisions of the beat into music written in simple meter, and simple divisions into music written in compound meter. For example:

In the example above, three eighth notes occupy the duration of two in the third beat. This is a *borrowed division.*

Notice that the three eighth notes are connected by a single beam and that a small "3" is written below the beam for the sake of clarification. This group of three is called a *triplet.*

Study the borrowed divisions in the following examples.

Augmentation and Diminution

The duration of a pitch is augmented by doubling its value and diminished by halving its value.

Thus, a piece of music in $\frac{2}{4}$ may be rewritten in $\frac{4}{4}$ by doubling the value of each of the original notes and rests. For example:

Rests

In any measure each beat, or part of each beat, must be accounted for by a note or a rest. The principles for writing rests, therefore, are very similar to those for writing notes, with some exceptions.

1. Rests may not be tied.
2. It is not the common practice to follow a rest with a dot. For example, 𝄽 𝄾 is preferable to 𝄽.
3. A whole rest is used to indicate an empty measure, *regardless of the meter.*
4. Rests may be included in beamed groups.

SUGGESTIONS AND STRATEGIES

In the set of rhythmic equations (Exercise A), the following is worth observing:

Because there are 4 ♩ in a 𝅝

There are also 4 ♩. in a 𝅝.

The number of notes equal to a whole note is the number of the type of note in the equation (4 quarter notes = a whole note; 16 sixteenth notes = a whole note; and so on).

When correcting the errors in Exercise C, be consistent in notating the stems, beams, and flags. In a single exercise, either notate them above or below the note heads.

In Exercise D, in spite of the errors in notation, the number of beats in each measure is correct.

When writing notes with stems (but not necessarily beams) on the middle line of the staff, remember that the stem is *always* notated below the note head.

You will find that Exercise E is done most easily if you begin by adding the bar lines before correcting the errors in notation.

For exercises C, D, and E, do not change the order of the rhythms or the actual duration of the rhythm. The given rhythmic notation may need to be changed in order to show proper beat groupings. For instance, a quarter note value that does not begin a beat may need to be written as two eighth notes tied together, but not beamed together (part of two different beats), or two quarter notes tied together may need to be written as a half note.

EXERCISES

A. Write the numerical solution for each rhythmic equation. Time goal—90 seconds per column.

1 2 3 4

6

8

8

B. Rewrite the given melodies in the specified meters, using rhythmic augmentation or diminution.

6
7
8
9
10

C. Rewrite the given rhythms using correct beaming procedures.

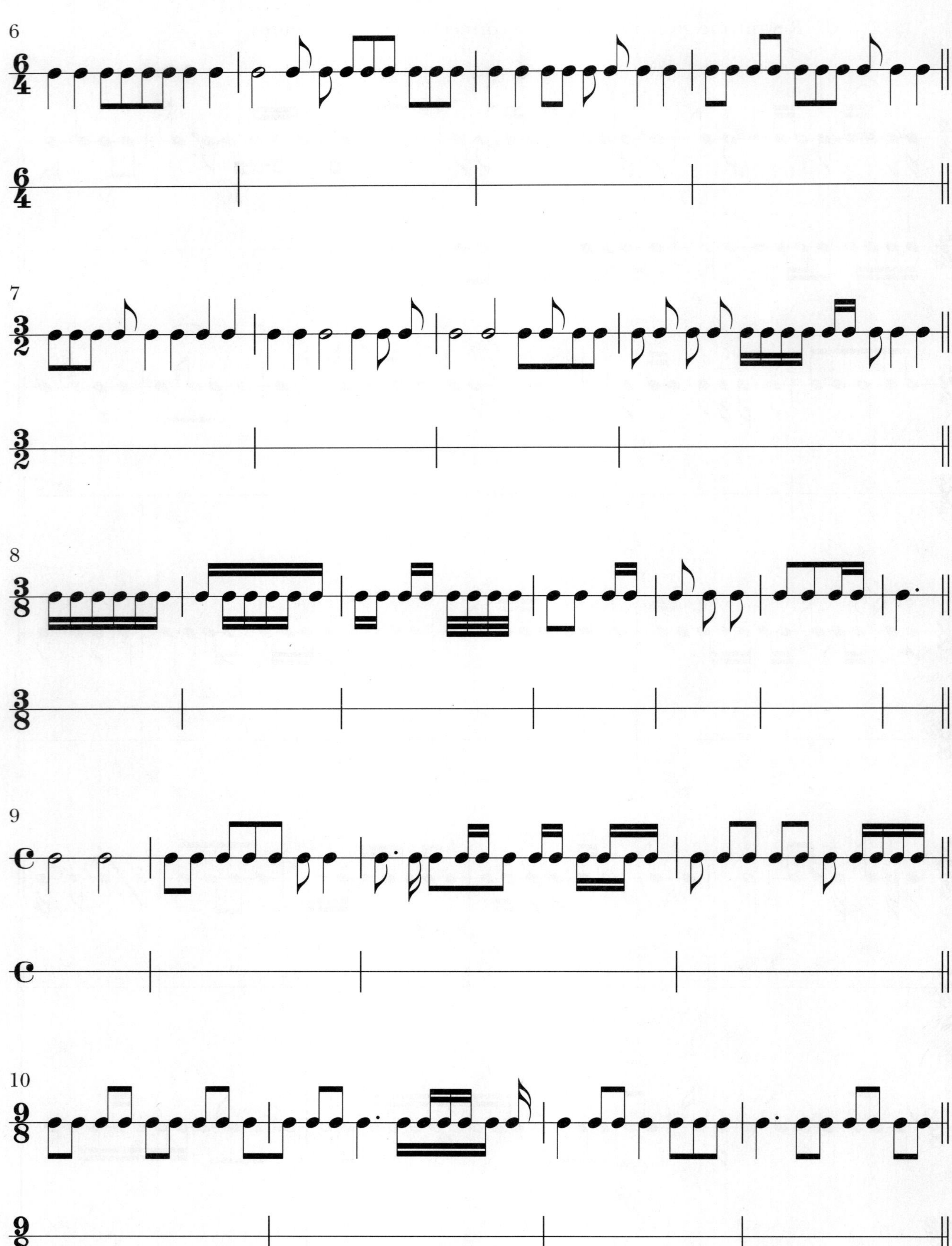
6
7
8
9
10

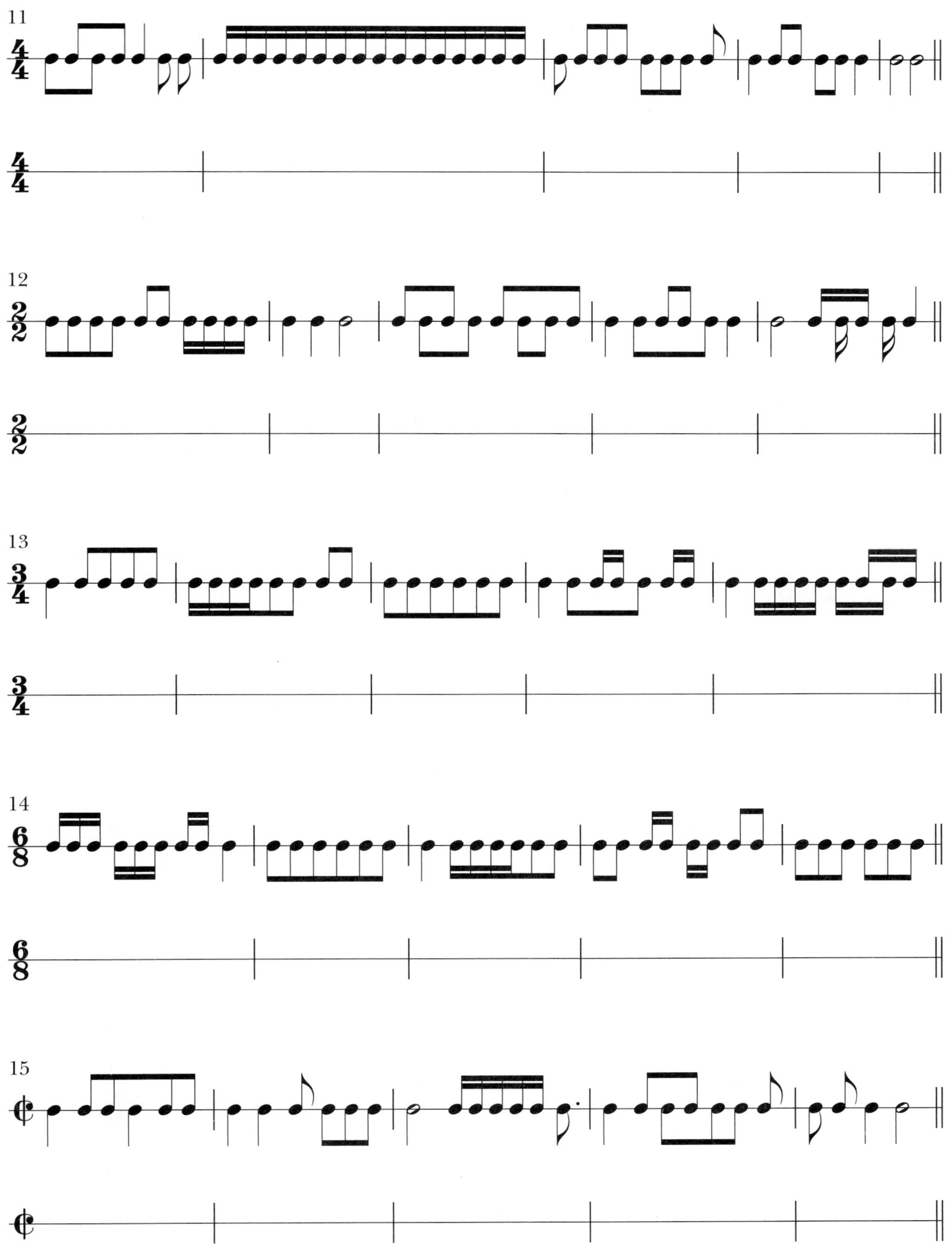
11
12
13
14
15

D. Correct the errors of notation in the following melodies.

6
7
8
9
10

11
12
13
14
15

E. Rewrite the following melodies with bar lines, and correct errors of notation.

6
7
8
9
10

11
12
13
14
15

16
17
18
19
20

21
22
23
24
25

26
3
27
28
29
30

PART TWO

HARMONY IN COMMON PRACTICE

The Diatonic Vocabulary

7

Four-Part Vocal Writing

Although composers write harmonic music for voice or instruments, or both, in a wide variety of parts, students customarily begin the study of harmony by writing for voices in four parts. There are three good reasons for this approach. First, by writing for voices rather than for instruments, the student learns to be sensitive to linear problems that arise in individual parts, for singers cannot depress a key or cover a hole to make their pitch; they must create their own. Second, the four voices—soprano, alto, tenor, and bass (SATB)—embrace a three-octave range over which the ear has relatively little difficulty in distinguishing between one pitch and another. Third, the majority of chords in common usage have either three or four different pitches.

The ranges of the four voices are:

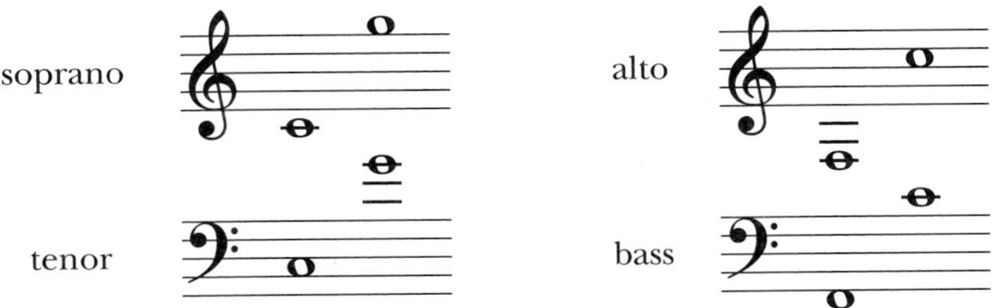

Notice that the soprano and alto ranges are duplicated an octave lower by the tenor and bass.

Because triads have only three different pitches, in a four-part setting one of those pitches has to be doubled. The problem of doubling is one that has plagued writers of music theory books for the better part of a century. Rules for the doubling of certain members of the triad vary from book to book, and some are so complex that the student is literally terrified to commit a pitch to paper.

For over three centuries composers have treated the problem of doubling with such considerable freedom that a series of elaborate rules is at best unrealistic, at worst stultifying. The guidelines below will help the student develop an approach to doubling that is not only simple and practical, but also as representative of composers' practices as any other approach.

1. In major and minor triads, in root position and first inversion, the most commonly doubled pitch is the root.
2. If the root is not doubled, the third or the fifth of the triad is doubled, producing an alternate doubling. When using an alternate doubling, double scale degrees 1, 2, 4, or 5. The purpose for using alternate doublings is to produce desirable voice leading.
3. Pitches that have strong resolution tendencies are not doubled, for example, the leading tone. Such pitches are called *sensitive* pitches. In general, altered pitches are not doubled.

Triads may be written in *close* or *open structure.* In close structure in four parts, the soprano, alto, and tenor voices are placed as close together as the chord tones will allow.

Note:

a. The stems are written above the note head for the soprano and tenor and below the note head for the alto and bass.
b. There is no restriction upon the distance between the tenor and bass.
c. The triads are said to be in *root position* because the roots are in the bass.
d. The fourth example is the dominant triad in a minor key, thus requiring an accidental.

In open structure, the soprano, alto, and tenor voices are not placed as close together as possible.

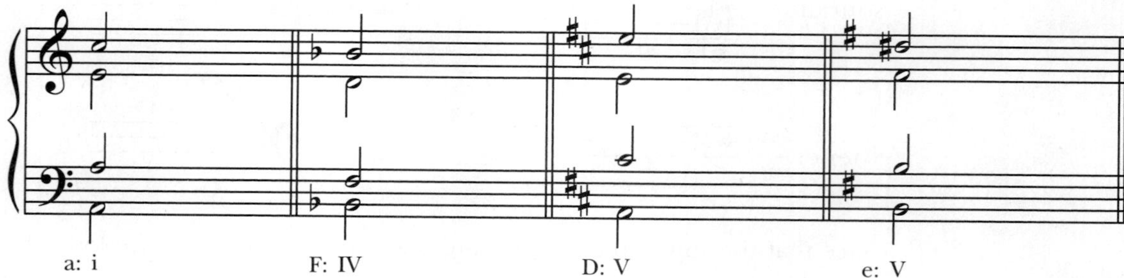

Note:

a. There is a space of an octave between the soprano and alto in the third example. Except for the tenor and bass, adjacent voices should not exceed this interval.
b. In the same example, the fifth is doubled (scale degree 2) producing an alternate doubling. Although this is not incorrect, it is not the most common doubling.
c. The fourth example is the dominant triad in a minor key, thus requiring an accidental.

EXERCISES

A. The key, triad, soprano part, and structure (close or open) are given. Add alto, tenor, and bass parts, and then rewrite each chord in the structure that differs from the one given, being careful to pay attention to voice ranges. All triads are in root position.

B. All of the chords below are tonic (I or i), dominant (V), or subdominant (IV or iv) triads. For each one identify the key, triad, and structure (open or close).

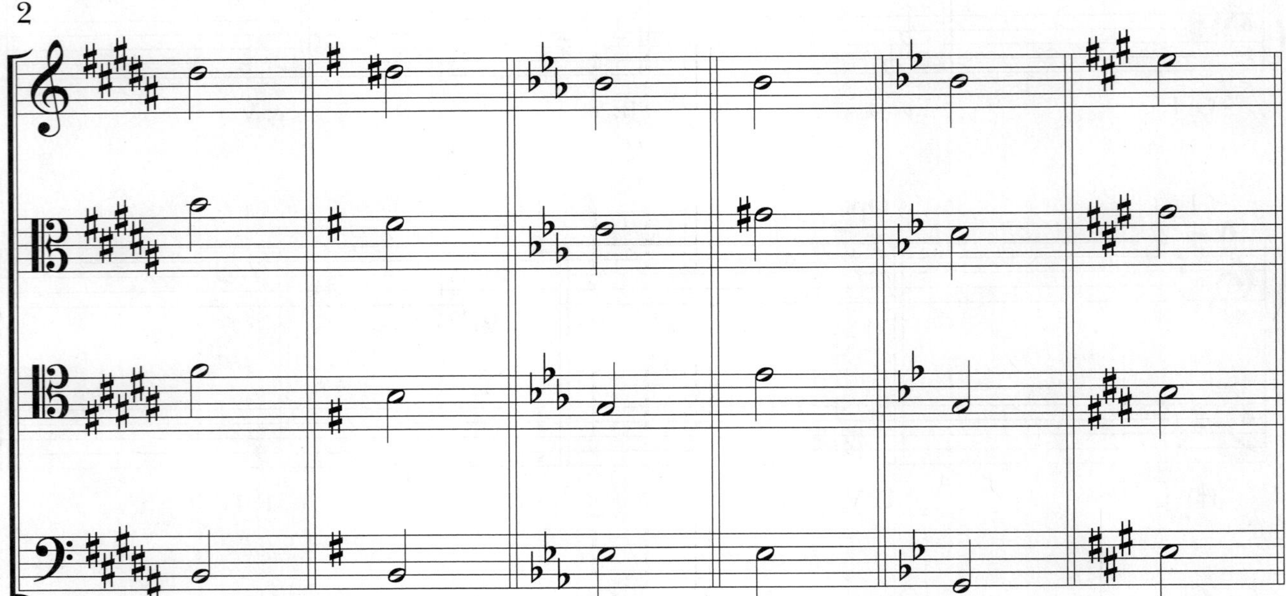

8
Primary Triads in Root Position

The tonic, subdominant, and dominant triads are called the *primary triads.* In the major keys, the primary triads are all major (I, IV, V), whereas in the minor keys, only the dominant triad is major (i, iv, V).

> ***Note:***
> There is the possibility of IV and v in minor keys, but the more commonly used qualities for the subdominant and dominant triads are iv and V.

CADENCES

The word *cadence* is derived from the Latin verb *cadere,* which means "to fall." Cadences in music are analogous to those punctuation marks in English that subdivide sentences into phrases and clauses. Thus, cadences occur at points of relative repose. A complete musical sentence is referred to as a *period,* and each major subdivision as a *phrase.*

1. The *authentic cadence* is the cadence that most decisively terminates the last phrase of a period. It is represented by the harmonic progression V–I.
2. The *plagal cadence,* IV–I, is also used at the end of a period but more rarely than the authentic cadence because it is harmonically less decisive. It is sometimes described as the "amen cadence" due to its use at the end of hymns.
3. The *half cadence,* analogous to a comma, occurs in the middle of a musical period and typically terminates an internal phrase. This cadence is represented by several harmonic progressions such as I–V, IV–V, ii–V, and vi–V. The essence of the half cadence is arrival at the *dominant.*
4. The *deceptive cadence* is most commonly represented by the progression V–vi, although V may be followed by other chords. Since this cadence involves the movement to a chord that is not a primary triad, it will be discussed later.

A cadence does not occur every time one of the progressions described above is encountered. For a listener to perceive a cadence, the music must create a feeling of repose. Such a feeling is frequently achieved by a coincidental relaxation of harmonic, melodic, and rhythmic motion.

ROOTS A FOURTH AND FIFTH APART

Three procedures are common to all of the following progressions:

1. The root is doubled in both chords.
2. Two pitches in each progression move in parallel stepwise motion.
3. There is one common tone (a pitch common to both chords), and it remains in the same voice.

Note:

a. In the V–I and V–i progressions, the *leading tone* moves up to the *tonic.* This movement is its natural tendency.

b. Each progression is provided with a harmonic analysis that includes the key of the excerpt and the scale degree and quality of each triad. Students are encouraged to use this standard format to check the accuracy of their answers to the exercises.

If, in the soprano voice in a V–I progression, the fifth of the dominant triad moves to the root of the tonic triad, and the leading tone has resolved to the tonic note, the tonic triad will be incomplete, having three roots and a third. This voicing is acceptable.

Additionally, if the leading tone is in the alto or tenor voice and a third below the adjacent upper voice, it may resolve downwards, allowing a complete tonic triad.

ROOTS A SECOND APART

Two procedures are common to the following progressions:

1. The root is doubled in both chords.
2. The top three voices move in contrary motion to the bass.

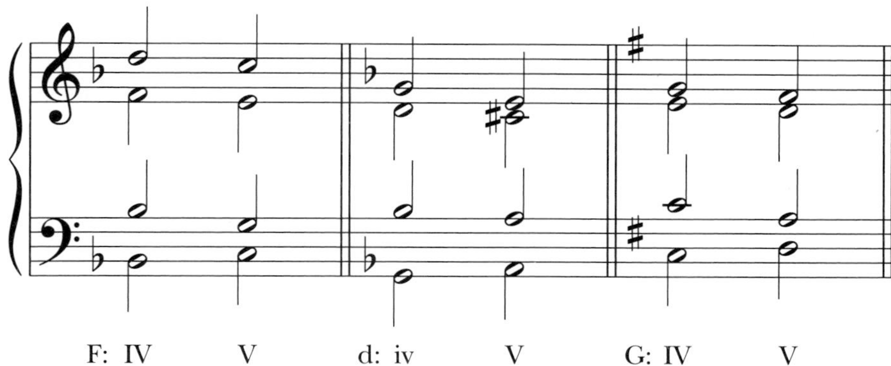

RESTRICTIONS IN VOICE LEADING

The contents of Part Two of this book represent a synthesis of harmonic techniques commonly practiced by composers over a period of about three hundred years, from 1600 through 1900. Composers throughout this period were usually careful, particularly in choral writing, to avoid the following movements of the voices between adjacent chords:

1. Parallel or consecutive movement by leap or step between any two voices in octaves.

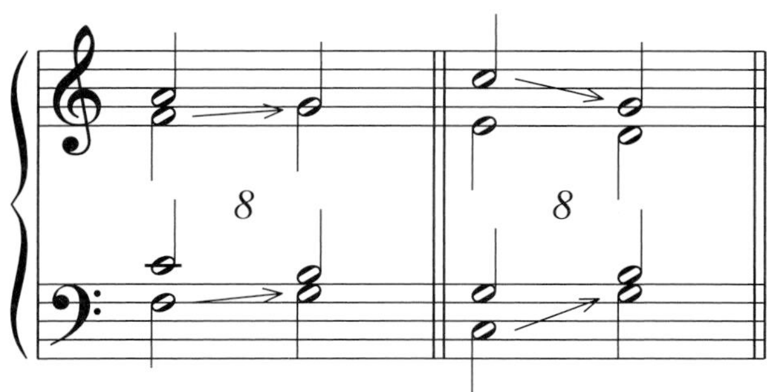

Note:

a. In the first example, *parallel octaves* are caused by the stepwise motion of the alto and bass voices.

b. In the second example, *consecutive octaves* are caused by the soprano and bass voices, which leap in opposite directions from c^2 to g^1 and c to g, respectively.

2. Parallel or consecutive movement between any two voices in perfect fifths.

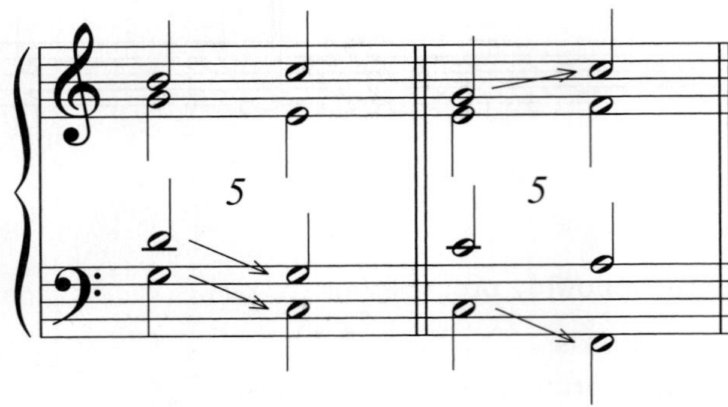

Note:

a. In the first example, *parallel fifths* are caused by tenor and bass voices, which, after a leap in the same direction, remain a perfect fifth apart.

b. In the second example, *consecutive fifths* are caused by the soprano and bass voices, which, after a leap in opposite directions, remain a (compound) perfect fifth apart.

3. Hidden octaves or fifths—the leap in the same direction by outer voices to a perfect octave or fifth.

Note:

a. In both examples, *hidden octaves* and *fifths* are caused by the soprano and bass voices, which leap to (compound) perfect octaves and fifths.

b. The condition for hidden octaves or fifths exists only if both outer voices leap to a (compound) octave or fifth.

4. The overlapping or crossing of voices.

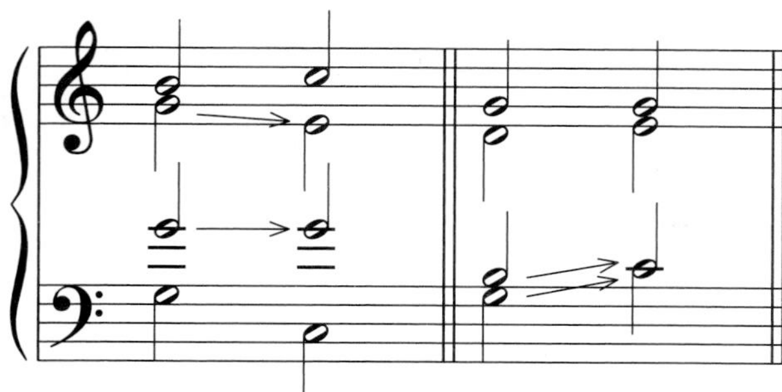

Note:

a. In the first example, the alto and tenor voices quite properly double g^1. The motion of the alto to e^1 while the tenor sustains the higher g^1 causes the overlapping (or crossing) of voices.

b. In the second example, the tenor and bass voices move in the same direction to middle C. The bass, however, "passes through" the tenor's b to arrive at middle C and in doing so causes the overlapping of voices.

As a general principle, motion in the inner parts should be as smooth as possible—for example, repeated notes, stepwise motion, leaps less than a sixth. Large leaps and diminished and augmented intervals should be treated with great care, because they are difficult to sing. In fact, good harmony is very often the result of combining good harmonic motion with good linear movement of the individual voices.

PRIMARY TRIADS IN COMBINATION

Study the following examples. They show how primary triads in root position are typically used in a simple four-voice texture.

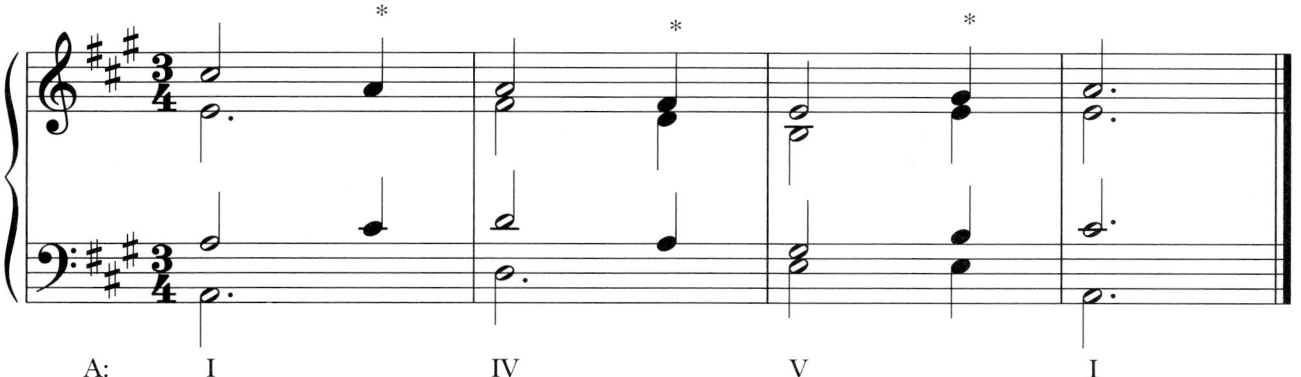

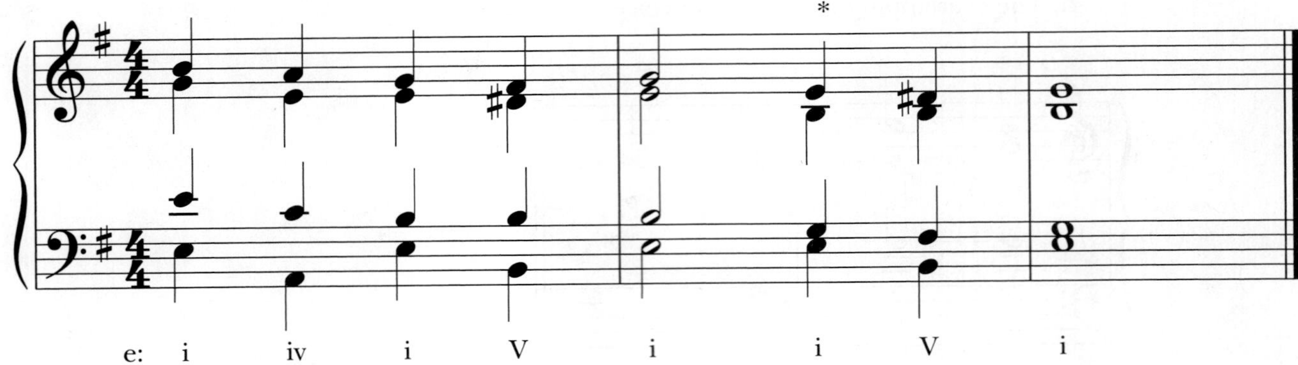

Note:

a. In both examples, the principle of *revoicing* over a stationary bass note (see asterisks) is exemplified. Two or three of the upper voices move in such a way that the doubling is not altered.

b. The subdominant triad follows the tonic in both examples. Rarely does the subdominant follow the dominant triad.

c. The final chord of the cadence falls on a strong beat.

d. Each of the examples terminates with a *perfect authentic cadence.* For an authentic cadence to be classified as perfect, the penultimate chord must be a dominant in root position and the final chord must be a tonic in root position with the tonic note in the soprano voice. All other dominant-to-tonic cadences are called *imperfect authentic cadences.*

e. In the second example, the movement from the first triad to the second triad (i–iv) has all voices moving to different pitches, not retaining the common tone. This is acceptable voice leading, since no restrictions have been disregarded, and is the first example of alternative voice leading.

THE FUNCTION OF PRIMARY TRIADS

The main function of the primary triads is to establish the key of a piece of music. The composer realizes this goal by judiciously using the tonic, dominant, and subdominant triads at the beginning of a composition and by exploiting one of the four cadence types at the end of phrases. Music in which these two conditions are not realized is typically nebulous from a tonal standpoint.

SUGGESTIONS AND STRATEGIES

For Parts Two and Three of the text, you should get into the habit of preparing for part writing, and checking the exercises by following procedures that are applicable from one chapter to the next. Let's look at some examples of the formats for this chapter.

1. Bass Given—Exercises A, B, D, E, and H.

Preparation

Enter the key

Remember that for a given key signature, the key can be major or minor. The clearest indication is given by the bass, particularly at the cadence.

Make a complete Roman numeral analysis

Remember to use uppercase Roman numerals for major triads, and lowercase for minor.

Part Writing

Choose a structure for the first chord—open or close

Observe conventional doubling and spacing procedures

Follow conventional voice leading procedures with regard to root movement

Resolve sensitive pitches correctly—leading tone (additional sensitive pitches will be added in later chapters)

Checking

Wrong notes including the omission of necessary accidentals

Parallel octaves and fifths

Improperly resolved leading tones

Awkward melodic intervals—augmented and diminished intervals

2. Bass Not Given—Exercises C and F.

Preparation

Enter the key

Notate the Bass Line

Examine the soprano line to see what chords are suggested, and begin by notating the first note, and then the cadence (authentic, half, or plagal). You may need to assign one or more soprano notes to the same harmony (stationary bass note). The remainder of the bass line will now be easy to complete. (Remember that you have only the roots of the tonic, subdominant, and dominant triads at your disposal.) Avoid choosing harmonies that would create parallel fifths or octaves between the soprano and bass voices.

Make a complete Roman numeral analysis

Part Writing and Checking

Proceed as described above.

Chapter 8 exercises A through F can all be accomplished by following the root movement procedures described on pages 106–107. Exercise H requires flexibility in following procedures, such as not holding a common tone, moving all voices in the same direction, or the use of incomplete triads, but may still be accomplished with smooth voice leading.

EXERCISES

A. Add parts for alto and tenor. (The student should begin by making a Roman numeral analysis of each progression.)

B. Add parts for soprano, alto, and tenor.

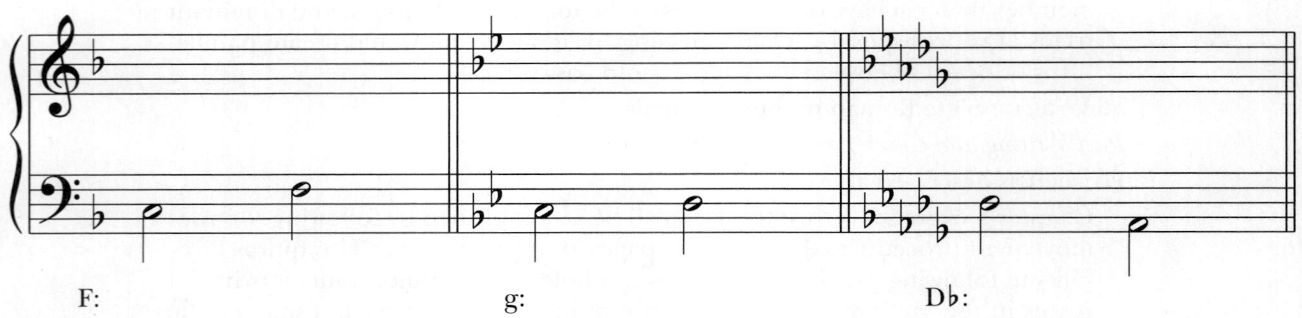

C. Add parts for alto, tenor, and bass.

D. Add parts for alto and tenor. (The student is advised to determine the key in each case before proceeding.)

E. Add parts for soprano, alto, and tenor.

F. Add parts for alto, tenor, and bass.

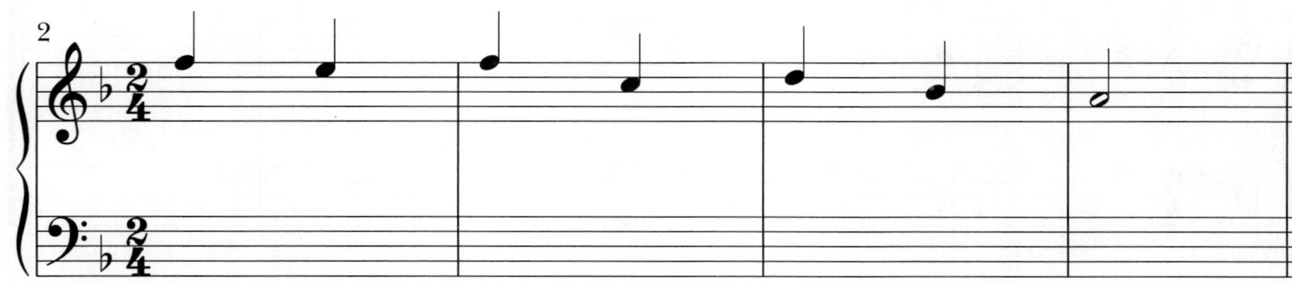

G. Identify the key and provide a harmonic analysis of the following phrases (see **Note:** b on page 106). Draw dotted lines between the common tones and arrows between the notes that move in observation of voice leading procedures.

1

2

H. Add parts for alto and tenor.

THE DOMINANT SEVENTH

Seventh chords will be covered in detail in Chapter 15; however, because the relationship between the dominant and the tonic is crucial to understanding tonality, a brief description, along with SATB examples, is warranted here. Music literature consisting purely of primary harmonies frequently employs dominant sevenths.

A triad is a three-note chord with each of the notes separated by an interval of a third; hence, the triad chord comprises a root, third, and fifth. Triads may be built on any degree of the scale.

Seventh chords are classified as extended harmonies of a triad. A seventh chord is based on a triad plus the addition of an interval of a third above the fifth (i.e., root, third, fifth, and seventh). The harmony can be "extended" beyond the seventh chord by adding more intervals of a third, thereby creating possibilities such as ninth, eleventh, and thirteenth chords. All of the intervallic numbers (e.g., third, fifth, seventh) represent their relationship to the root; thus, a seventh chord is a triad with the addition of a seventh above the root.

Although seventh chords may be built on virtually any degree of a scale, the seventh chords occur most frequently and most prominently as dominant sevenths (V7). Thus, the dominant seventh chord is a dominant triad (built on the fifth degree of a scale) with an added seventh above the root. As with all seventh chords, the dominant seventh chord would comprise a root and intervals of a third, fifth, and seventh above the root.

In both major and minor keys, the dominant seventh should always be represented as a major-minor seventh chord; that is, a major triad with a minor seventh. In major keys, the dominant seventh occurs naturally. In minor keys, however, the dominant triad is naturally minor. To convert a minor dominant triad into a major dominant triad, an accidental (sharp or natural sign) is applied to the third above the dominant root to raise it by a half step. This, in effect, produces a leading tone to the tonic and creates a major dominant triad. To complete the dominant seventh in a minor key, add a minor seventh above the root of the dominant triad.

Study the following examples, observing the bass movement (scale degree 5 to scale degree 1), construction of the V7, and the resolution of the notes of the V7.

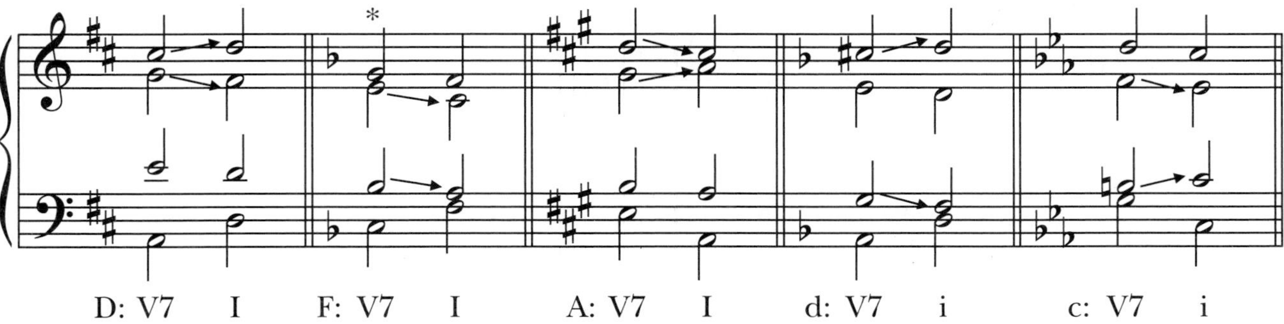

* Alternate resolution of leading tone.

Note:

a. In minor keys, the V7 requires an accidental (the leading tone of the key)
b. The seventh of the V7 resolves down by step
c. The leading tone resolves up by step
d. The I (i) chord is incomplete, consisting of three roots and a third (see Chapter 15, page 181, for more explanation)

9 Primary Triads in First Inversion

A triad is said to be inverted when a pitch other than its root (the pitch on which the triad is constructed) is in the bass voice.

When the *third* is in the bass the triad is in *first inversion.*

When the *fifth* is in the bass the triad is in *second inversion.*

Note:

Triads in second inversion are introduced in Chapter 10.

CHORD SYMBOLIZATION: FIGURED BASS

Figured bass is a musical shorthand that originated in the sixteenth century. To save time, a composer, instead of writing a complete score, would provide a keyboard player in an ensemble with a bass line underneath which various Arabic numerals were written. The numeral (or numerals) under each bass note indicated to the performer which intervals above the bass were to be played. Usually, the numeral was expressed as a simple interval, although the performer was at liberty to perform that interval in any octave he wished.

Examine the following example:

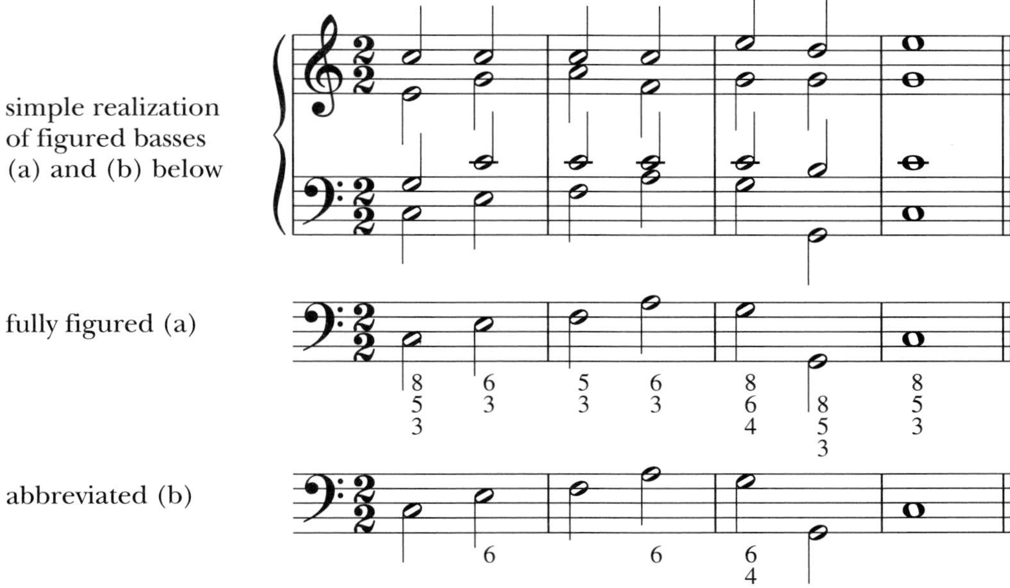

The figures under bass line (a) show all of the intervals that appear in the realization. But in practice this would be an extremely cumbersome form of shorthand. Thus, (b) is written, from which the performer may deduce that

1. The absence of any figures indicates a triad in root position.
2. 6 indicates a chord in first inversion. This chord is commonly referred to as a 6 chord.
3. $^6_4$ indicates a chord in second inversion. This chord is commonly referred to as a $^6_4$ chord.

Each interval is considered to be diatonic unless altered by placing an accidental in front of the figure. Occasionally, a figure has a diagonal line through it, which indicates that the interval is raised by a half step. An isolated accidental indicates that the third above the bass is raised or lowered.

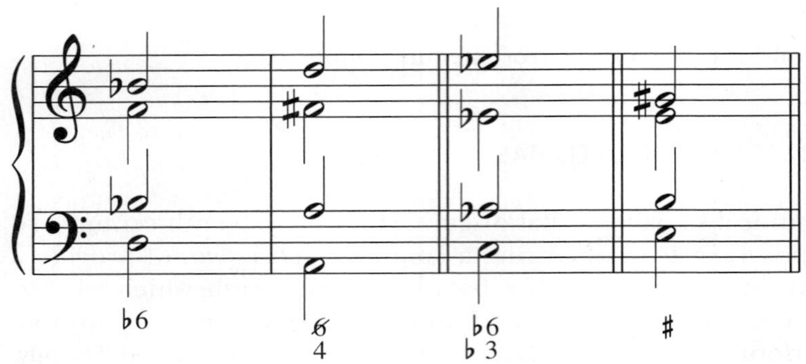

PRIMARY TRIADS IN FIRST INVERSION

Primary triads in first inversion follow the same basic principles regarding doubling and voice leading as primary triads in root position. However, a strict adherence to voice leading procedures is not possible with the use of inversions since the bass voice is now a note that in root position would be in an upper voice.

Study the following examples, making note of movement to and from first inversion triads:

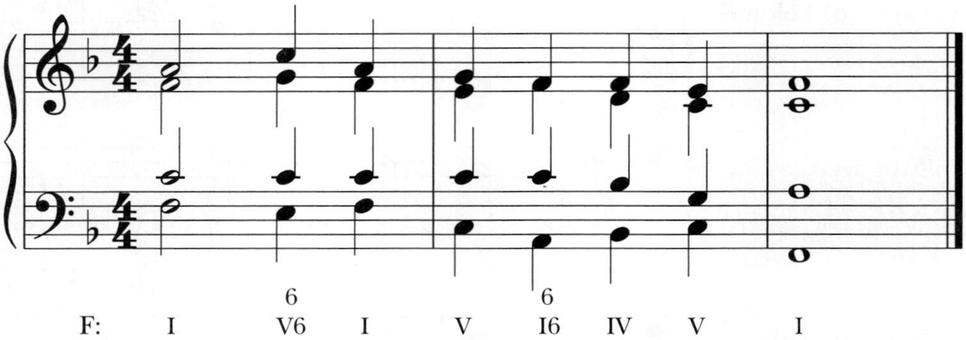

6 6
F: I V6 I V I6 IV V I

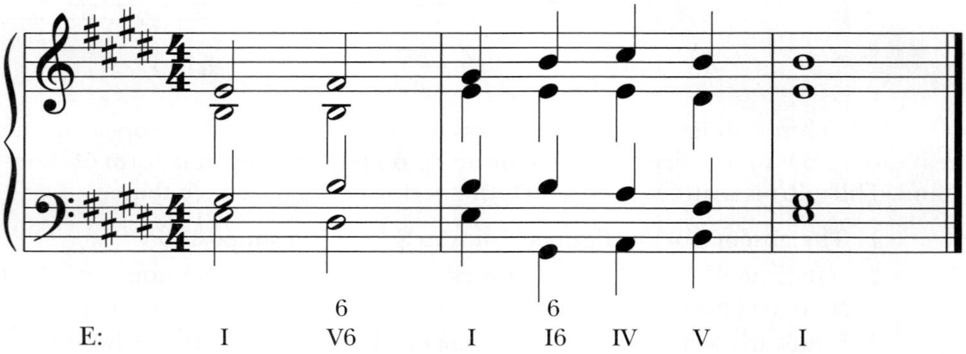

6 6
E: I V6 I I6 IV V I

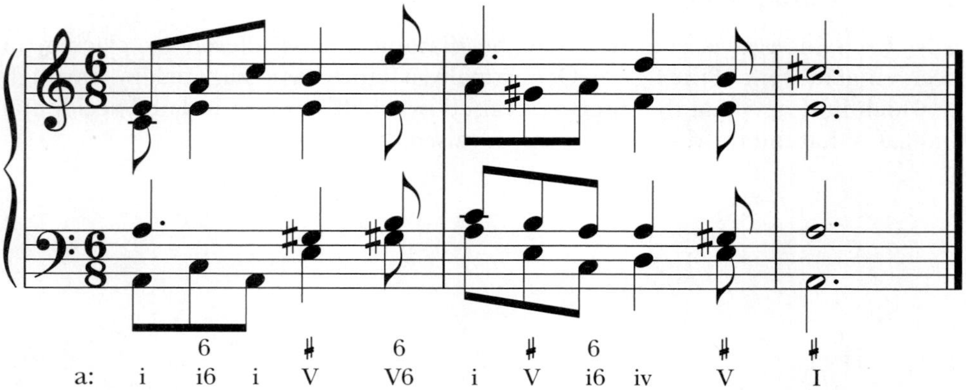

6 ♯ 6 ♯ 6 ♯ ♯
a: i i6 i V V6 i V i6 iv V I

Note:

a. The introduction of the primary triad in first inversion allows bass notes to be written on the third, sixth, and seventh scale degrees, in addition to the first, fourth, and fifth. Thus, a bass line that is more melodic than was previously possible can be created.

b. The figured bass and the harmonic analysis indicate when a triad is inverted.

c. At least one of the upper voices tends to move in contrary motion to the bass.

d. Observe the alternate doubling for the I6 chord in Example two.

e. Example three ends with a *picardy third,* a major tonic in a minor key.

The exercises that follow are associated with triads in root position and first inversion. The discussion of triads in second inversion begins on page 128.

SUGGESTIONS AND STRATEGIES

The procedures for doing the exercises in which the bass is given (A through D) are essentially the same as those suggested for Chapter 8. Exercises E and F, however, require some different decisions.

1. **Soprano Given**—Exercise E

   In the last chapter, the bass line could be constructed from only three scale degrees—tonic, subdominant, dominant. The inclusion of the first inversion of the primary triads allows an additional three—mediant (I6), submediant (IV6), and leading tone (V6). How do we manage these new resources?

   In the *Preparation* phase, follow the procedures described on page 111 in the last chapter. Then increase the melodic interest of the bass line by the appropriate use of first inversion. Smooth voice leading should still be applied to the alto and tenor voices, using alternate doubling, incomplete triads, or all voices moving, when appropriate.

2. **Roman Numeral Analysis Given**—Exercise F

   Preparation

   Notate the bass line, being careful to observe the chords that are in first inversion.

   Part Writing and Checking

   Proceed as described on page 111 of Chapter 8.

   Additional Part Writing Considerations

   The use of alternate doublings and changing notes rather than holding common tones may become more frequent. Be aware that bass lines with a significant upward motion will require careful placement of the tenor to avoid cross voicing. Soprano lines with large leaps will require careful placement of the alto to avoid cross voicing. Voice leading does not need to be carried across a rest.

EXERCISES

A. Add parts for alto and tenor.

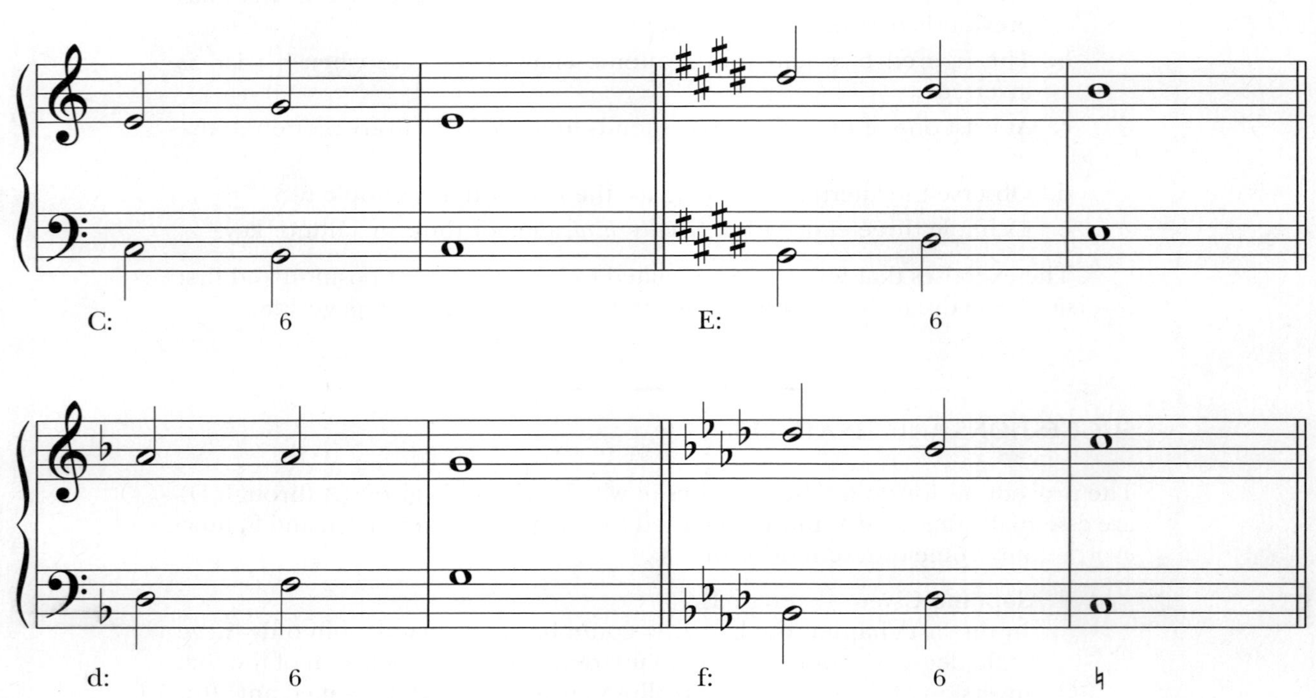

B. Add parts for soprano, alto, and tenor.

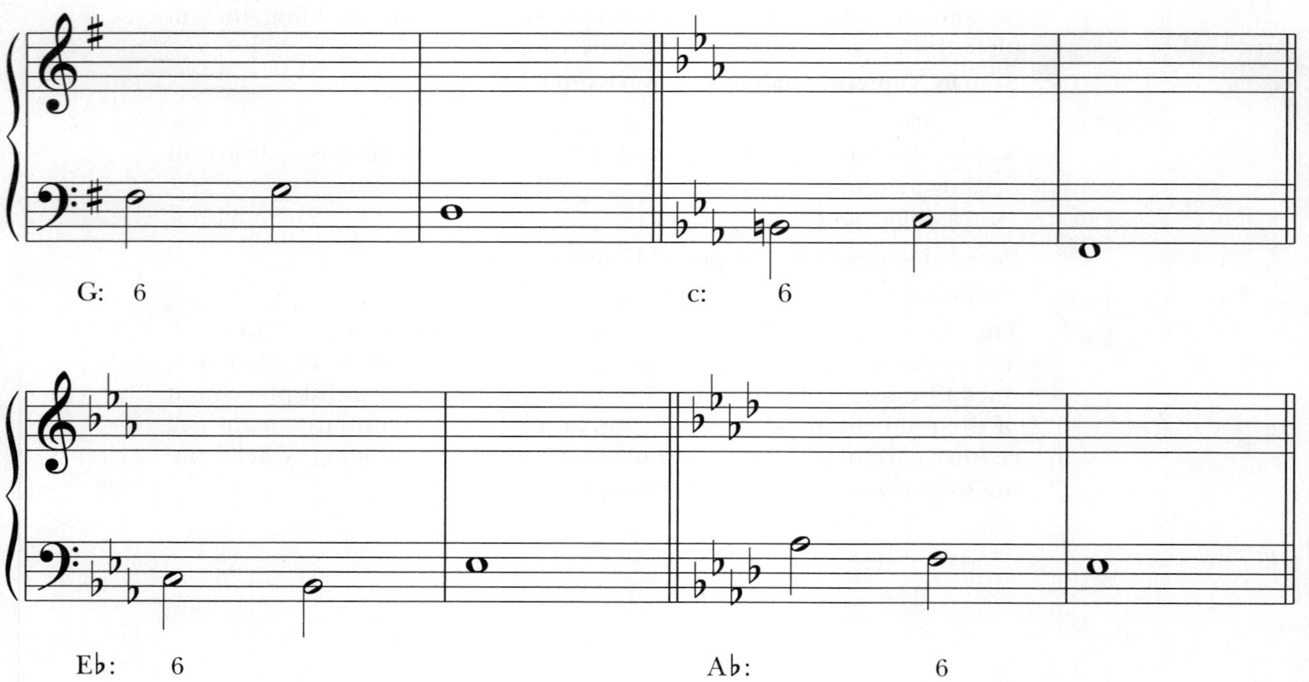

C. Add parts for alto and tenor.

D. Add parts for soprano, alto, and tenor.

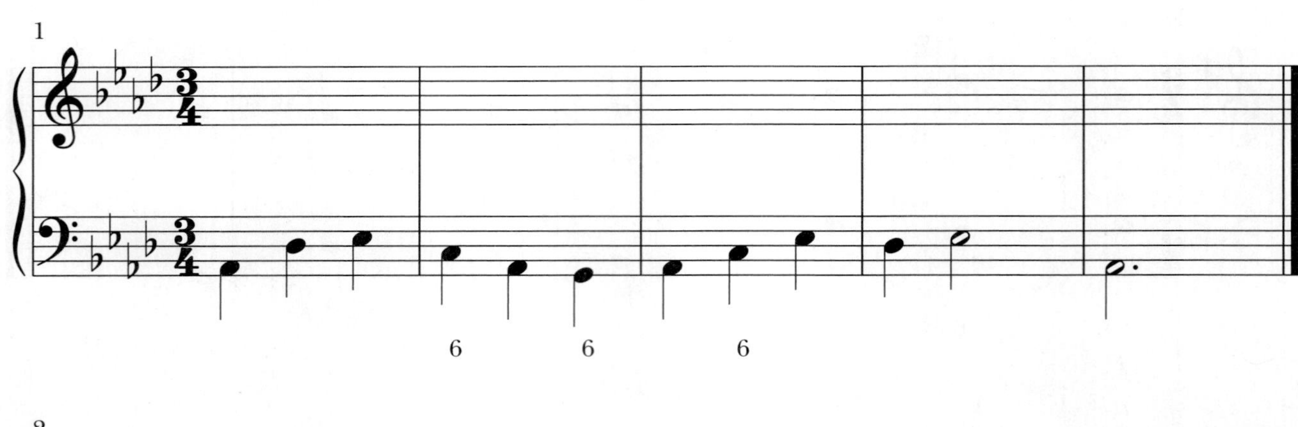

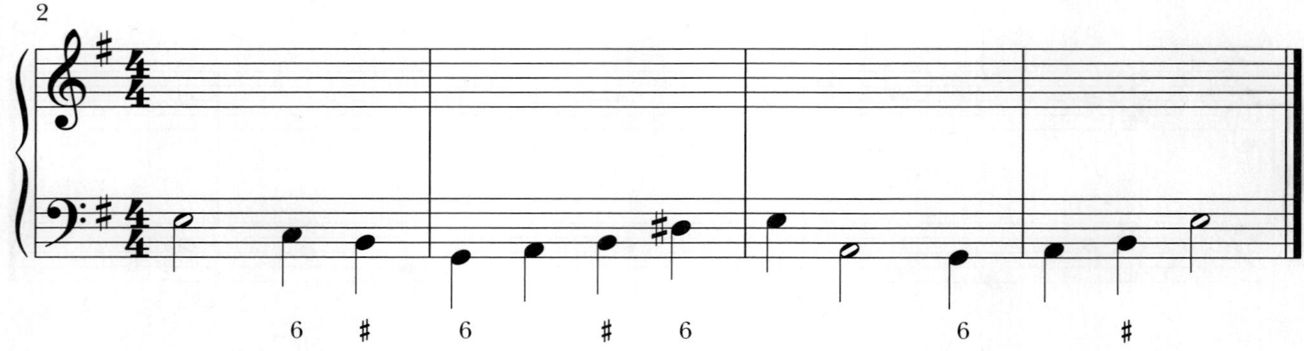

E. Add parts for alto, tenor, and bass, using suitable first inversions.

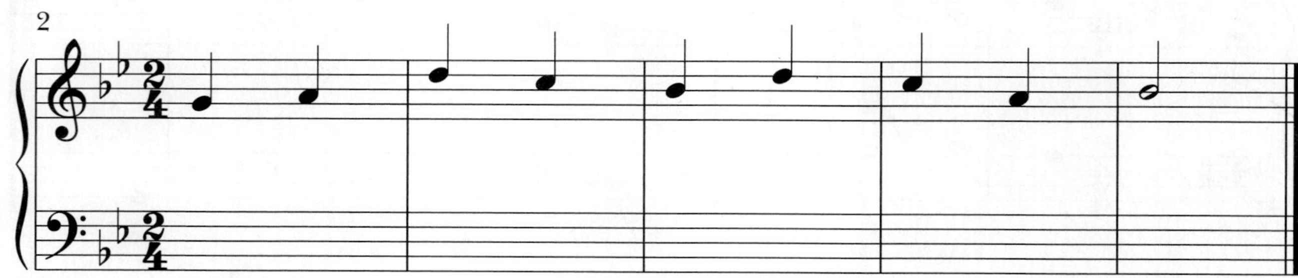

F. Using the given progressions, invent four-measure phrases for soprano, alto, tenor, and bass. The harmonic rhythm is given (see model).

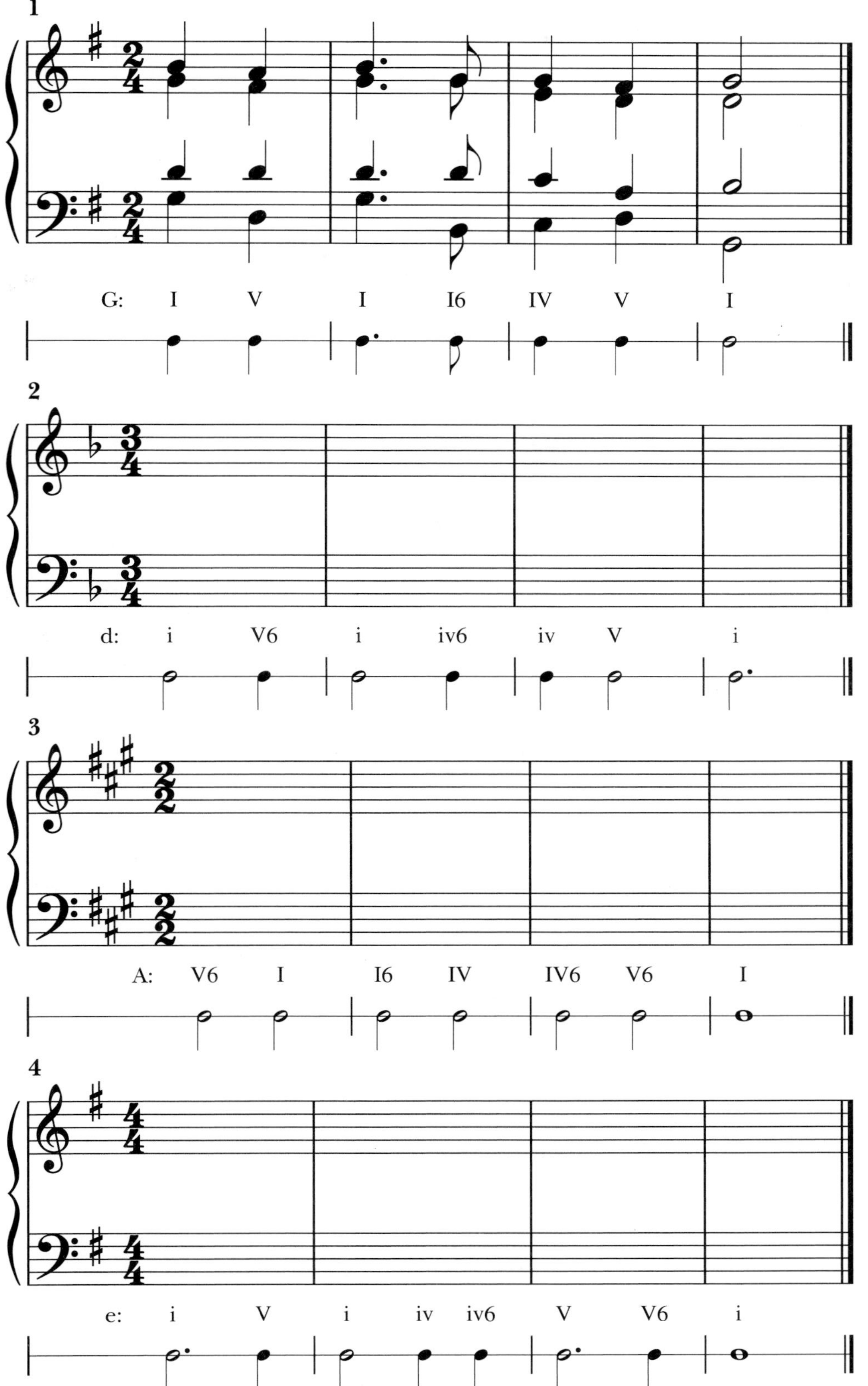

G. Make a harmonic analysis of the following phrases. Indicate first inversions with the appropriate symbol.

H. Add parts for alto and tenor.

10
Primary Triads in Second Inversion

Primary triads in second inversion are used far less frequently than primary triads in root position and first inversion, because in second inversion the interval of a fourth occurs between the bass and an upper voice. This interval, although melodically consonant, is considered to be dissonant as a vertical structure, and thus, complete freedom in the use of the chord is prohibited.

There are three common uses of the $^6_4$ chord:

1. The Cadential $^6_4$ Chord
2. The Passing $^6_4$ Chord
3. The Auxiliary $^6_4$ Chord

There is also an "arpeggiated" $^6_4$ chord, which occurs primarily in instrumental music as a result of an arpeggiated bass line. This chord lies outside the scope of this text.

THE CADENTIAL $^6_4$ CHORD

As the title suggests, the cadential $^6_4$ chord occurs at cadence points. Study the following examples:

D: I V I IV I IV I$^{6}_{4}$ V I

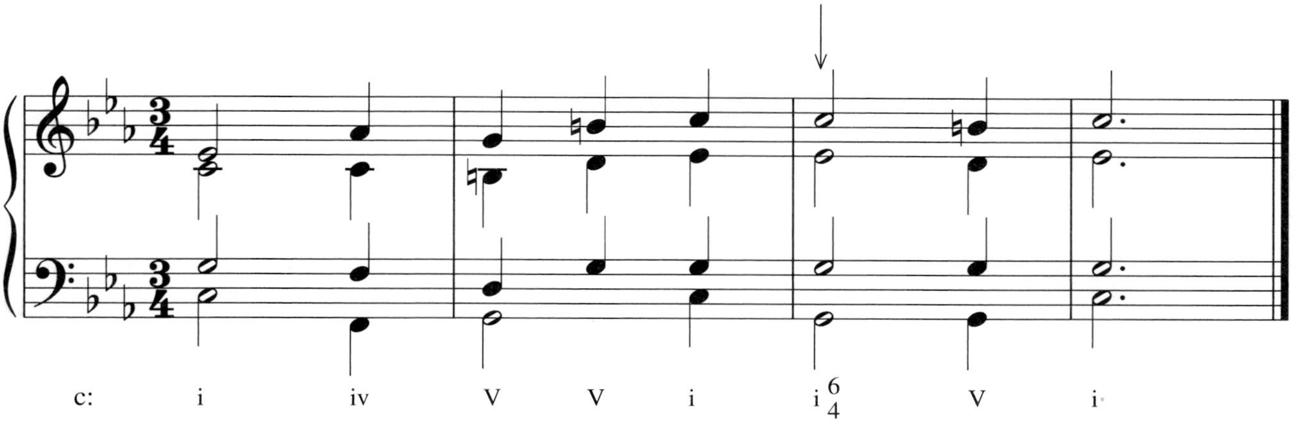

c: i iv V V i i$^{6}_{4}$ V i

Note:

a. The bass is doubled.
b. The chord occurs in a metrically strong position.
c. The chord's root and third resolve down by step.

THE PASSING $^{6}_{4}$ CHORD

The passing $^{6}_{4}$ chord is used when the bass line moves stepwise. It most commonly separates a triad in root position from its first inversion, as the example shows:

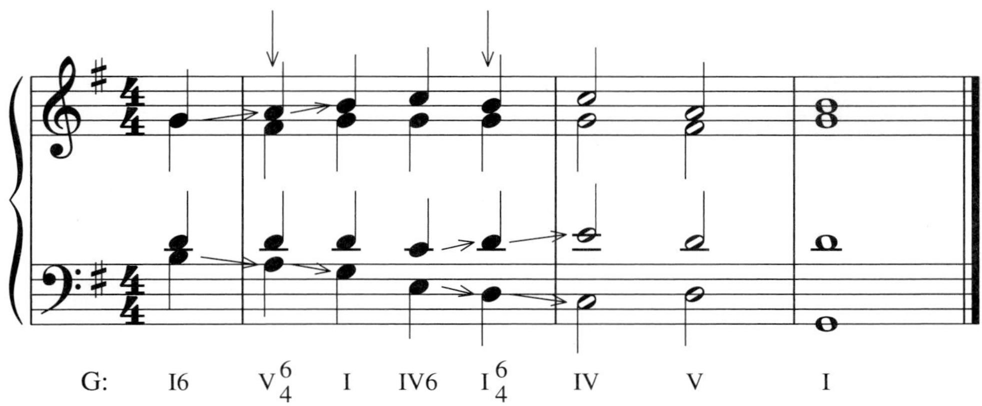

Note:

a. The bass is doubled.

b. The chord occurs both accented and unaccented, although the latter is more common.

c. One of the upper voices proceeds in contrary motion to the bass.

THE AUXILIARY $^6_4$ CHORD

The auxiliary $^6_4$ chord is purely decorative and occurs when the bass is stationary, thus:

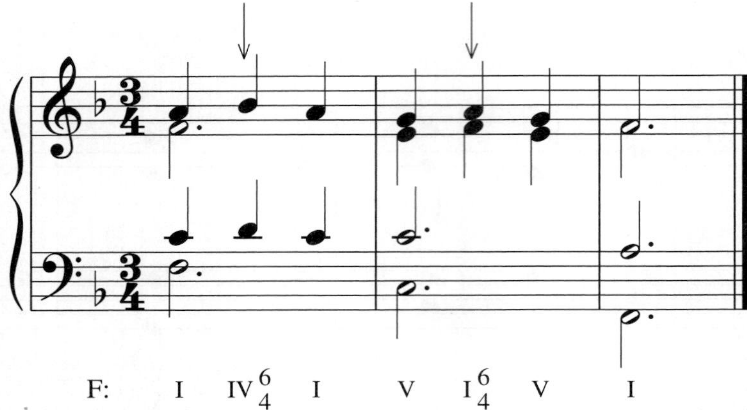

Note:

a. The bass is doubled.

b. The chord is unaccented.

c. The bass note remains stationary during the approach to, and departure from, the chord. Two upper voices move by step away and then back.

SUGGESTIONS AND STRATEGIES

When you work on the exercises in which the figured bass is given, get into the habit of identifying the six-four chords by type. For example, in addition to adding Roman numerals to the figures, you may choose to write the following symbols below the chords:

C = Cadential $^6_4$
P = Passing $^6_4$
A = Auxiliary $^6_4$

Following this procedure will help you to remember that these sonorities are used only under specific circumstances.

....

Exercise E is arguably the most difficult of the exercises in this section, because the addition of $^6_4$ chords greatly increases the number of possible bass lines. The musical examples below may give you some ideas that will help you to include $^6_4$ chords in the musical phrases. Arabic numerals indicate the scale degrees used in the soprano voice.

1. Cadence patterns in the soprano that accommodate the cadential six-four:

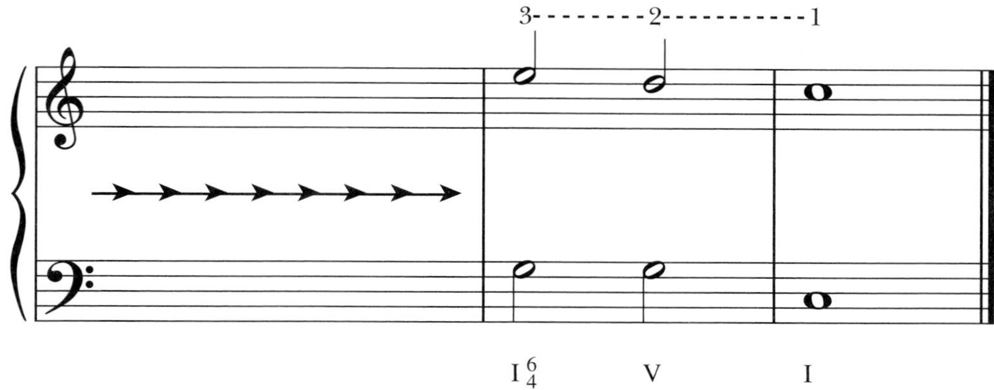

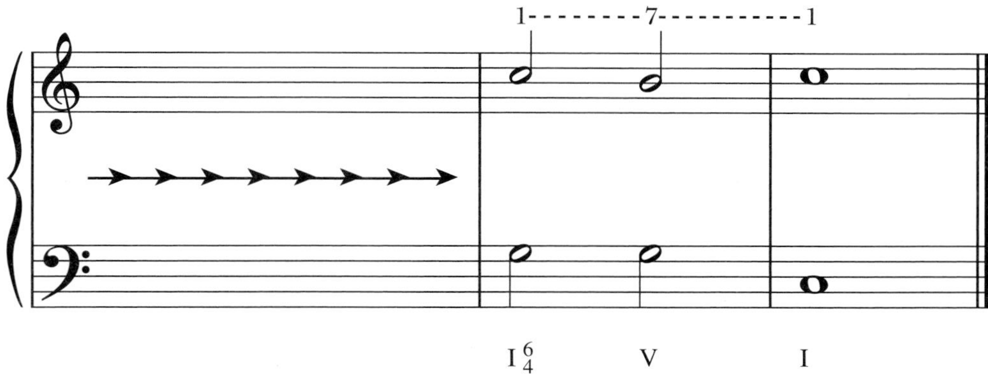

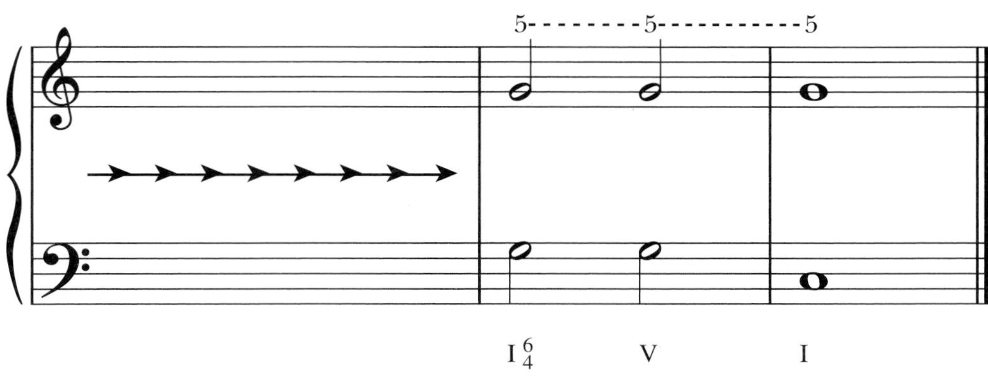

2. Stepwise patterns in the soprano that accommodate the passing six-four:

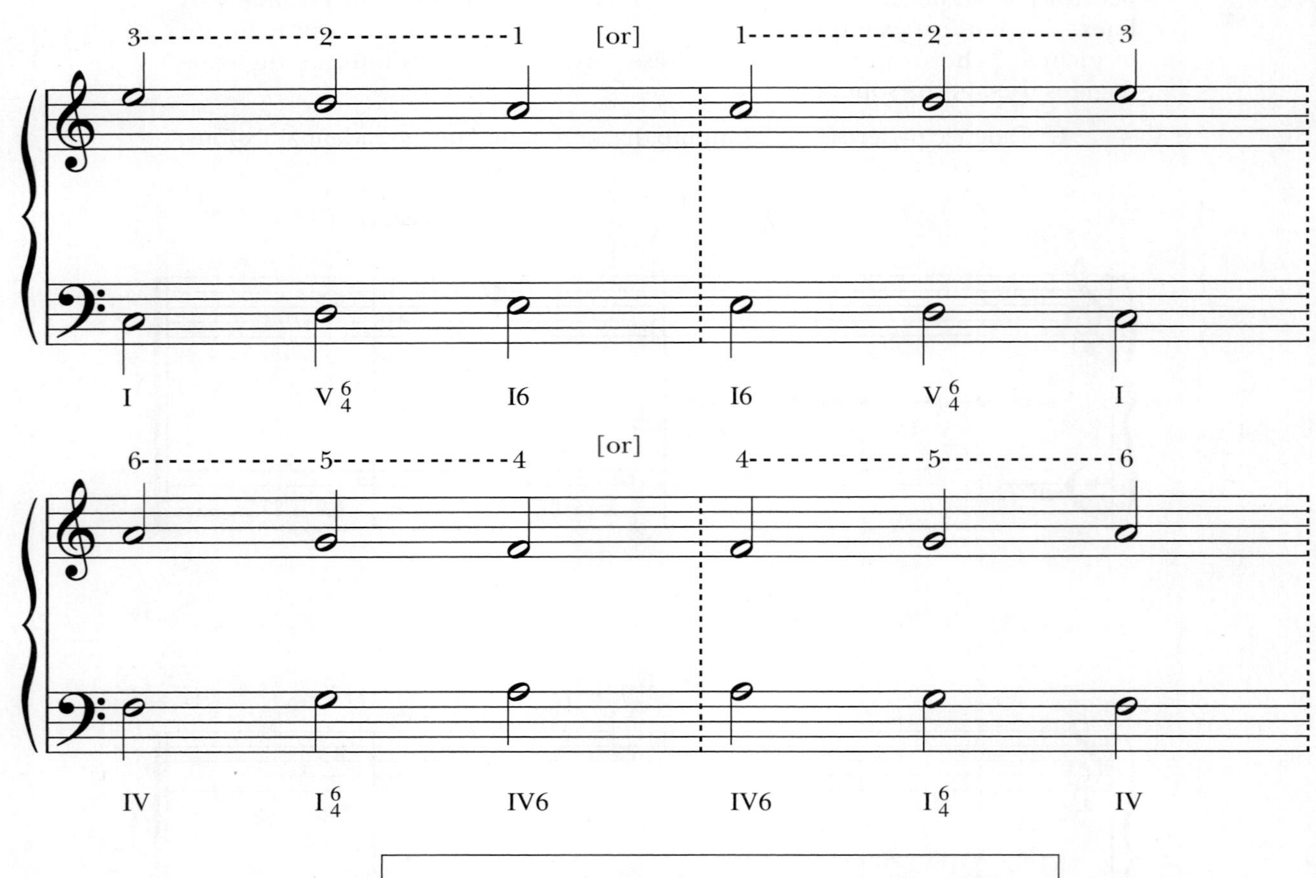

Remember that, in the $\frac{6}{4}$ chord, the **bass** is doubled.

EXERCISES

A. Add parts for alto and tenor.

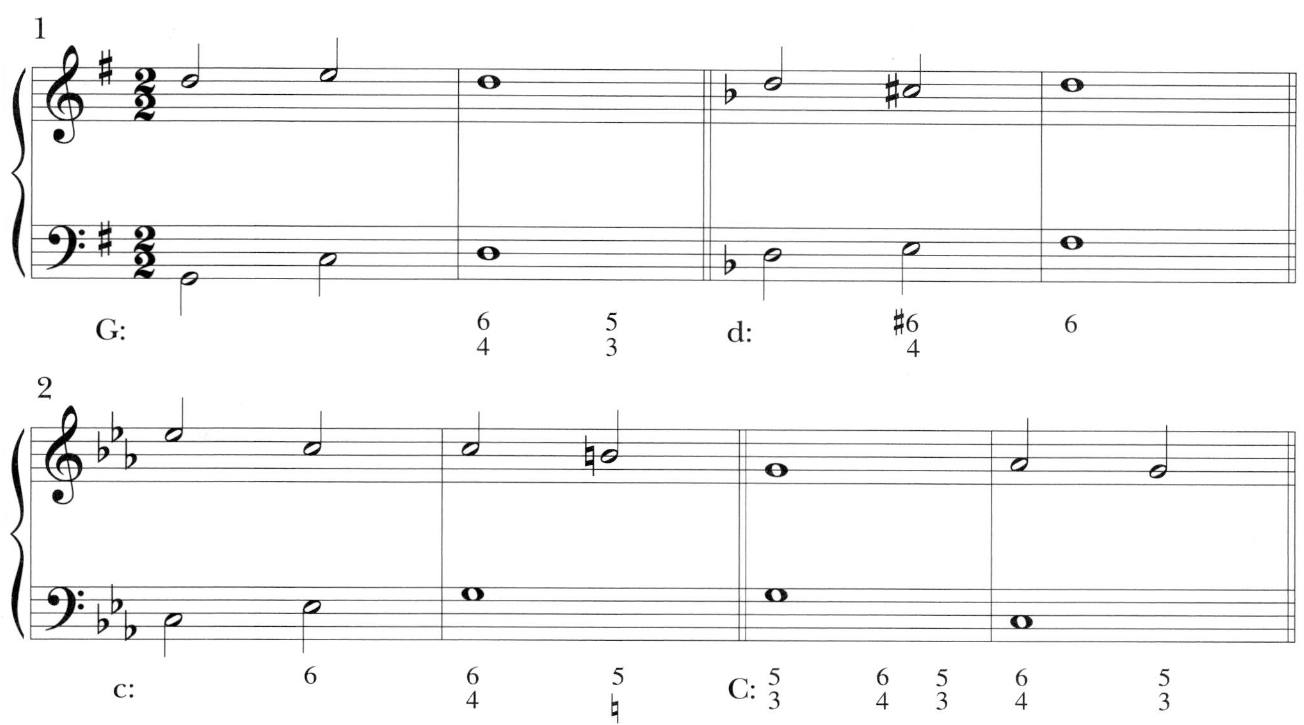

B. Add parts for soprano, alto, and tenor.

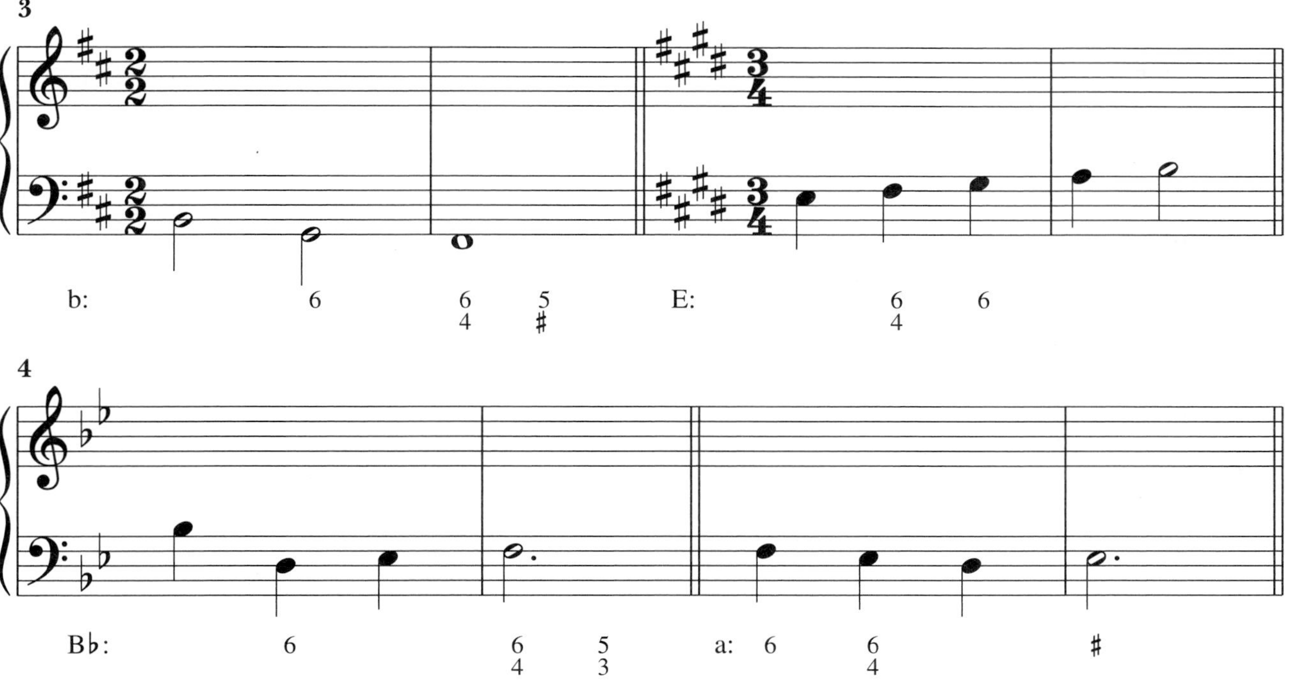

Note:
When the figured bass symbols indicate the use of a cadential $^6_4$ chord, the figures $^5_3$ (or $^5_♮$ or $^5_♯$) follow them. These figures are included to show the linear motion of two of the upper parts.

C. Add parts for alto and tenor.

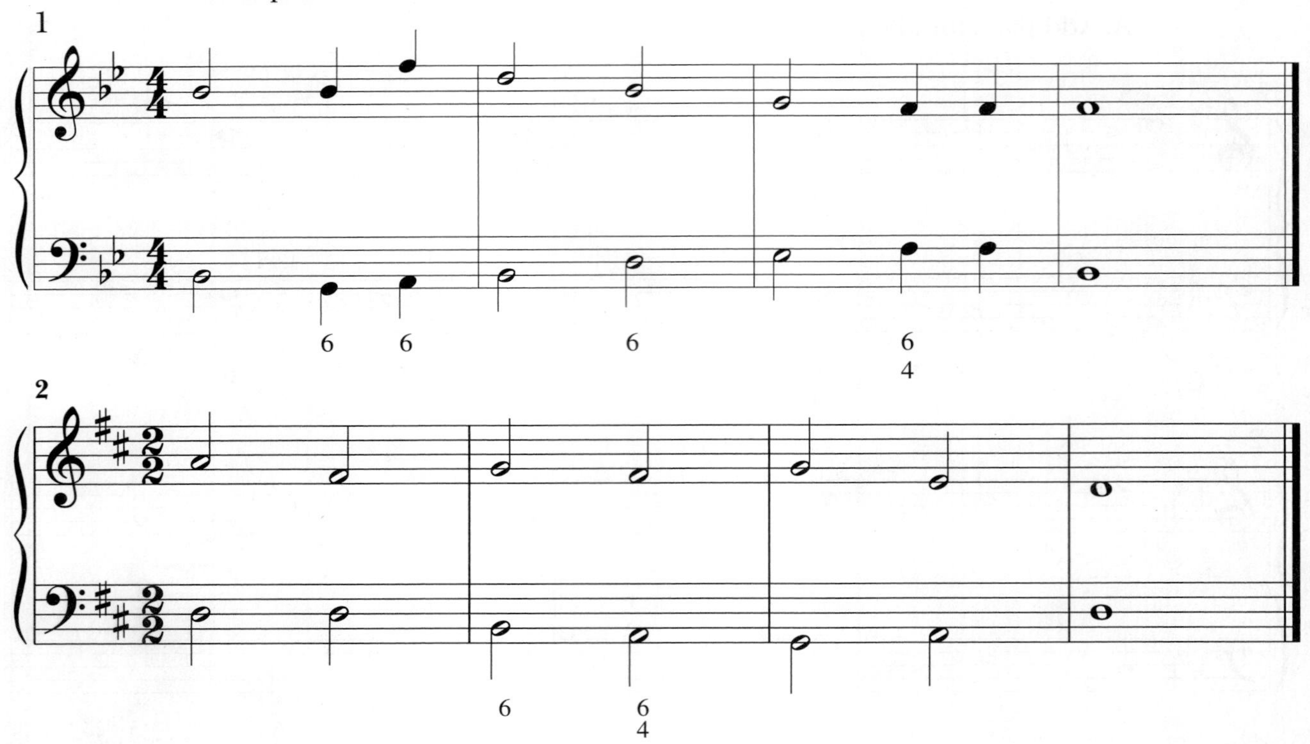

D. Add parts for soprano, alto, and tenor.

E. Add parts for alto, tenor, and bass. (Use first and second inversions.)

1

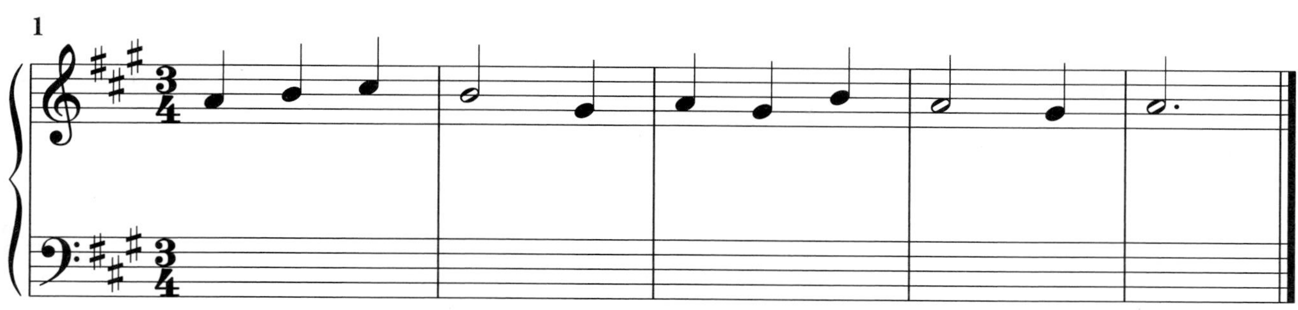

2

3

4

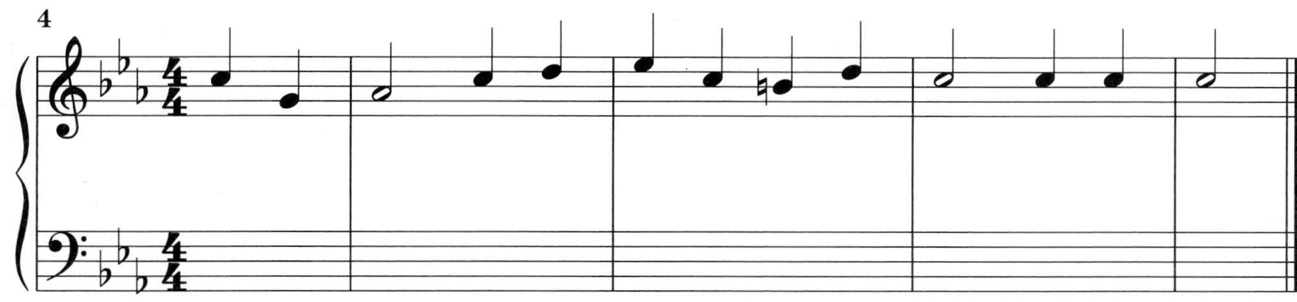

F. Using the given progressions, invent four-measure phrases for soprano, alto, tenor, and bass. The harmonic rhythm is given.

G. Make a harmonic analysis of the following phrases. Indicate all inversions with the appropriate symbols. Identify each six-four chord as to type (P = passing, C = cadential, A = auxiliary).

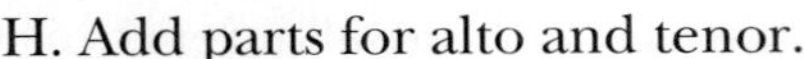

H. Add parts for alto and tenor.

1

2

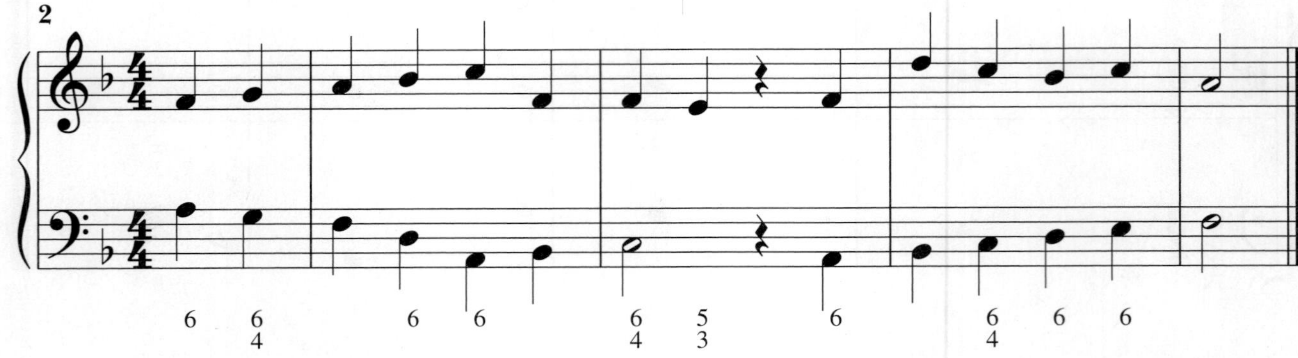

I. Add parts for soprano, alto, and tenor.

1

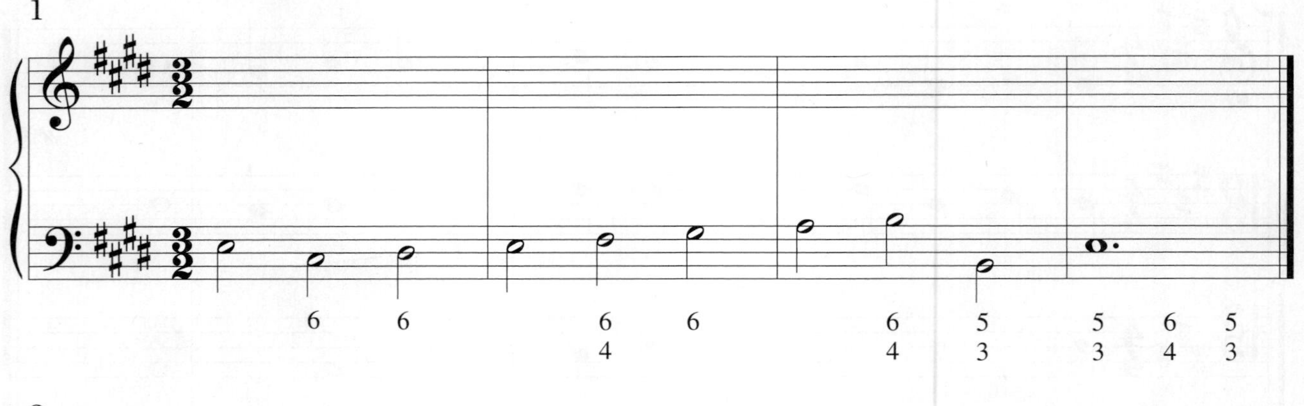

2

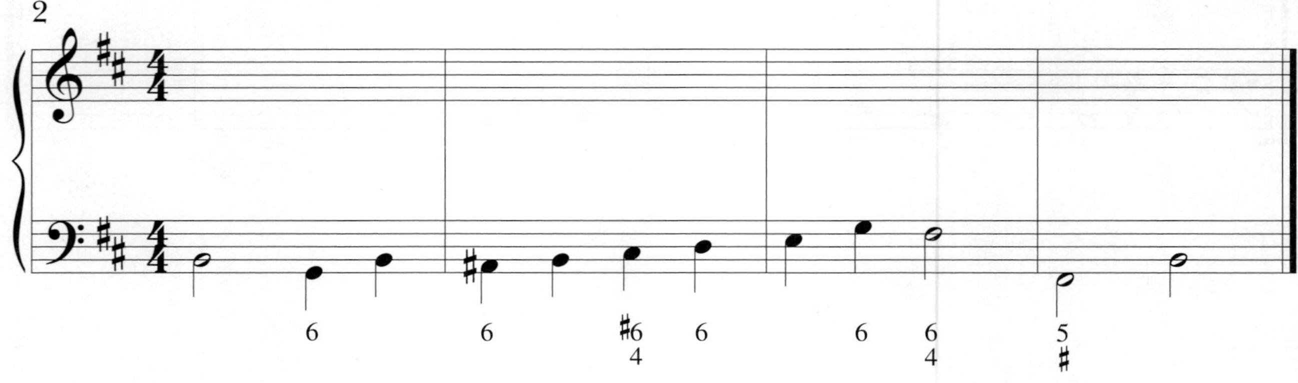

11
Secondary Triads

The *supertonic, mediant, submediant, subtonic,* and *leading tone triads* are the secondary triads.

Unlike the primary triads, which are either major or minor, the secondary triads include major, minor, augmented, and diminished triads, depending on the scale degree and scale type. Refer to page 67 for a listing of triad qualities in major and minor keys.

The following table shows the usage and principal doublings of the secondary triads.

	TRIAD	USAGE			DOUBLING
		Root Pos.	First Inv.	Second Inv.	
Major Keys	ii	yes	yes	no	root
	iii	yes	yes	no	root
	vi	yes	yes	no	root
	vii°	no	yes	no	third
Minor Keys	ii	no	rare	no	third
	III	yes	yes	no	root
	VI	yes	yes	no	root
	VII	yes	yes	no	root
	ii°	no	yes	no	third
	vi°	no	yes	no	third
	vii°	no	yes	no	third
	III+	no	yes	no	third

Note:

a. Secondary triads are not used in second inversion.

b. In minor keys the minor form of the supertonic triad is not used in root position, and is rarely used in first inversion.

c. Where the root is the principally doubled pitch (i.e., in major and minor triads), doubling procedures are the same as those for the primary triads.

d. The diminished and augmented triads are used in first inversion only.

e. Neither the root nor the fifth is doubled in the diminished or the augmented triad. In both cases the interval between the two pitches is unstable (dissonant), and thus the pitches are sensitive. In particular, the fifth of each triad has a strong tendency toward resolution—*downward* in the diminished triad, and *upward* in the augmented triad.

The addition of the secondary triads to the primary triads gives the student the potential to use a different chord on every scale degree. To do so indiscriminately, however, would certainly produce unsatisfactory music, and yet it is often difficult to exercise discrimination when such a wide variety of resources exists. The following observations will help the student in this respect.

CHORD RELATIONSHIPS

Harmonic movement may be considered strong, neutral, or weak, depending upon (1) *root* movement and (2) *bass* movement. For a given harmonic progression, movements in root position (assuming diminished and augmented triads are not employed) tend to be stronger than those that involve inversions. Since, however, inversions create melodic interest in the bass, a successful harmonization is the result of a proper balance between root and bass movement.

1. The strongest harmonic movement occurs when roots are separated by ascending fourths or descending fifths. Particularly strong is a progression that makes use of consecutive chords in any part of the following chord sequence: I–IV–VII–III–VI–II–V–I.

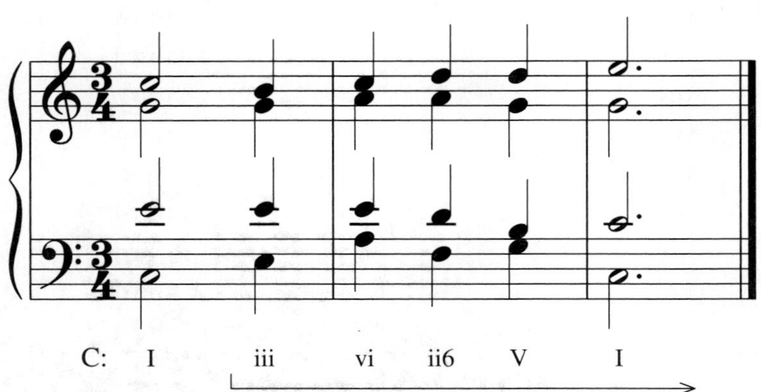

Movement in the opposite direction, descending fourths or ascending fifths, also produces strong harmonic motion but tends to lead away from, rather than toward, cadence points. The term *retrogression* is often applied to this kind of motion. A sequence of retrogressive harmonies is commonly followed by movement in ascending fourths to terminate a phrase or period.

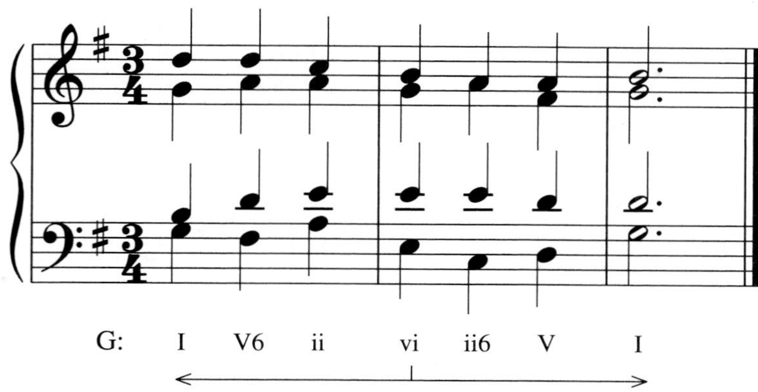

2. Chords a third apart progress weakly in a harmonic sense because there are always two common tones which may be held in the same voices or moved. They may be used effectively, however, in maintaining a smooth motion in preparation for a cadence.

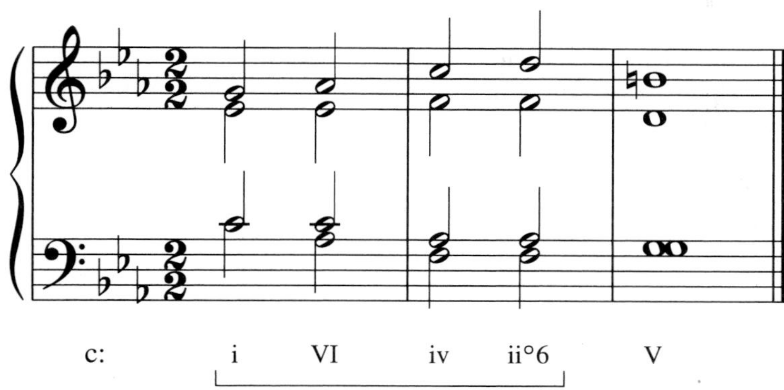

Harmonic strength (or lack thereof) differs little between chords in ascending or descending thirds.

3. Chords a second apart lack the harmonic drive of those a fourth or fifth apart, but because no common tones exist, they give a greater impression of harmonic motion than do those a third apart.

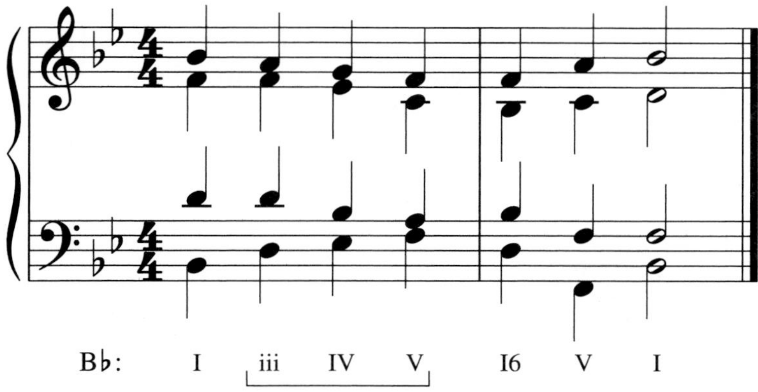

Harmonic movement in ascending seconds is generally considered to be stronger than that in descending seconds.

4. The deceptive cadence, V–vi or V–VI (when the dominant is followed by the submediant in a cadential situation), is said to be deceptive because the ear, which expects a tonic chord after the dominant, is deceived by the submediant chord. This cadence is used to prolong musical activity, since the composer must reach a cadence terminating with the tonic to conclude the phrase satisfactorily.

5. The leading tone triad, followed by the tonic triad, vii°6 –i, is said to have a "dominant function," and so the progression below may be considered a weak form of an authentic cadence. Observe the use of an alternate doubling in the iv chord.

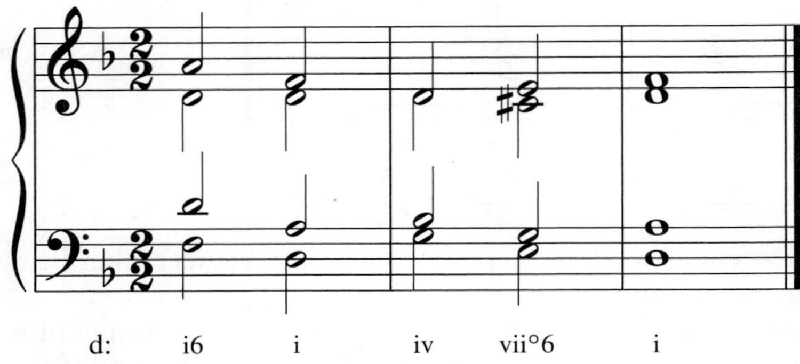

THE SIXTH AND SEVENTH SCALE DEGREES IN MINOR KEYS

In Chapter 2, the concept of a minor scale consisting of a minor tetrachord and a chromatic hexachord was introduced. Certain problems in part writing are more easily solved by using this scale as a point of reference than by trying to determine which of the three forms of the traditional minor scale to employ. The fact is that under a wide variety of circumstances, a harmonization will contain elements of more than one of the forms of the minor scale—in other words, it will be based upon the synthetic minor scale.

Generally speaking, when the lower note of either of the chromatic scale degrees (sixth and seventh) is employed, if the voice which contains that note moves by step, it will do so *downward*. Conversely, when the higher note is employed, stepwise motion will be *upward*.

Study the following examples carefully:

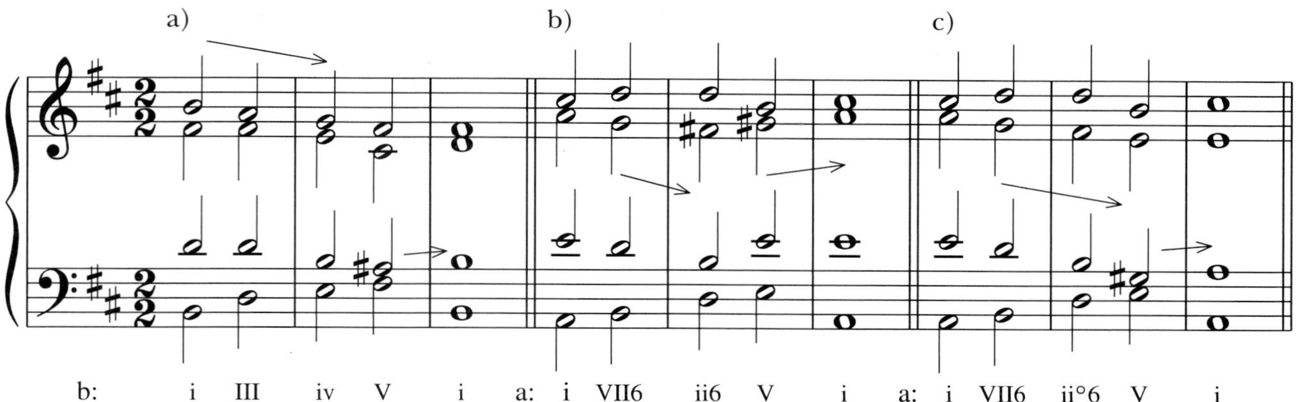

Note:

Harmonically, c) differs from b) only in the substitution of ii°6 for ii6. As a result of the altered pitch, however, the subsequent voice-leading in the middle voices is quite different.

SUGGESTIONS AND STRATEGIES

For Exercises A through E, follow these procedures:

Preparation

Enter the Key

Except for Exercise E, make a Roman numeral analysis, and pay careful attention to the qualities of the triads. Remember that you may now encounter diminished and augmented triads in addition to major and minor.

Part Writing

As well as paying attention to structure, doubling, and spacing, remember the following:

Six-four chords—double the *bass* (the fifth of the chord)

Diminished and augmented triads (in first inversion)—double the *bass* (the third of the chord)

Dominant and leading tone triads—resolve the *leading tone* properly (in minor keys, the seventh note of the scale has to have an accidental to make it a leading tone)

Checking

In addition to looking for bad parallel motion, wrong notes, awkward melodic intervals, and so on, look for six-four chords [is the bass doubled?], diminished triads in first inversion [is the bass doubled?], and leading tones in dominant and leading tone triads [do they resolve to the tonic?]

Progressive and Retrogressive Harmonic Motion

The following circle shows how the diatonic triads are related to each other through the interval of the fifth—the perfect fifth except for IV to vii°.

Counterclockwise motion around the circle produces *progressive* harmonic activity, while *clockwise* motion produces *retrogressive* harmonic activity.

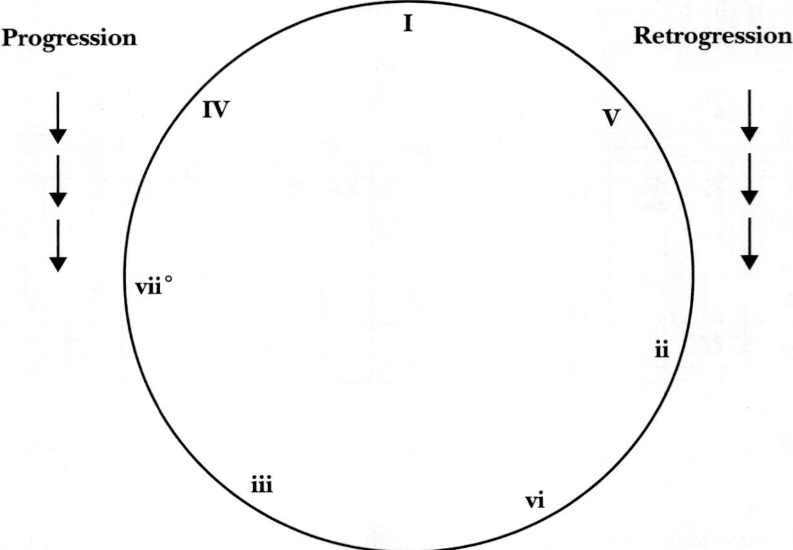

After completing each of your exercises, check the relationships between chords that are a fifth apart. Musical phrases that feature predominantly progressive harmonic motion tend to be perceived as driving toward the cadence more powerfully than those that do not feature such motion.

What follows is a summary of root movement progressions and voice leading procedures for four-voice SATB (Roman numerals, all uppercase, will be used for ease of presentation; this does not indicate quality).

1. Root movement of a fourth or a fifth: I–IV–VII–III–VI–II–V–I
   a. Hold the common tone in the same upper voice
   b. Move the other two upper voices by step in the same direction
2. Root movement of a second: I–II–III–IV–V–VI–VII–I
   a. The bass steps up or down; move the upper three voices in contrary motion to the bass, to the closest note of the second chord
   b. V moving to VI often requires an alternate doubling for the VI (doubling scale degree 1), resulting from the leading tone moving up to the tonic
3. Root movement of a third: I–VI–IV–II–VII–V–III–I
   a. Hold the two common tones in the same upper voices
   b. Move the other upper voice by step

Function Substitutions

With the addition of secondary triads to the chord vocabulary, and using root movement progressions 1 and 2 found above, tonic, dominant, and predominant function may be illustrated.

TONIC (after V)	DOMINANT (before I)	PREDOMINANT (before V)
I (i)	V	IV (iv)
vi (VI)	vii°	ii (ii°)

The mediant triad (iii, III) possesses characteristics of both tonic and dominant chords. This triad is not prevalent in music literature, although by no means is it to be avoided. The root movement of thirds progression places the mediant triad between the dominant and the tonic. Thus, as the mediant triad follows the dominant, it could function as a tonic substitution. As the mediant precedes the tonic, it could function as a dominant. Typically, the minor and the major versions of the mediant triad function to extend the tonic, whereas the augmented version of the mediant functions as a dominant.

PRELIMINARY EXERCISE

Add parts for alto and tenor.

A. Root movement of a fourth or fifth

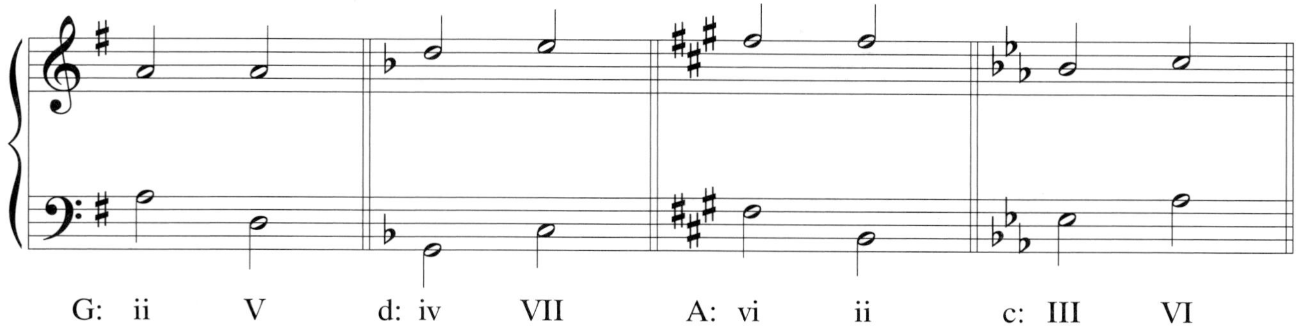

B. Root movement of a second

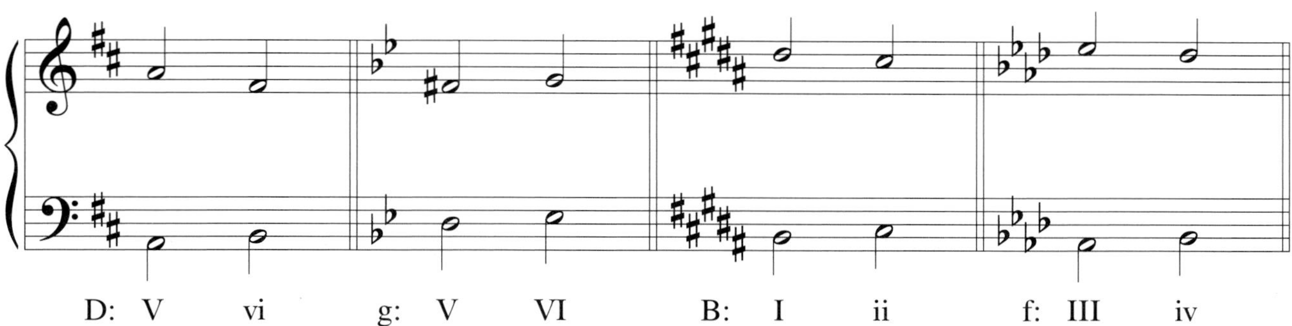

C. Root movement of a third

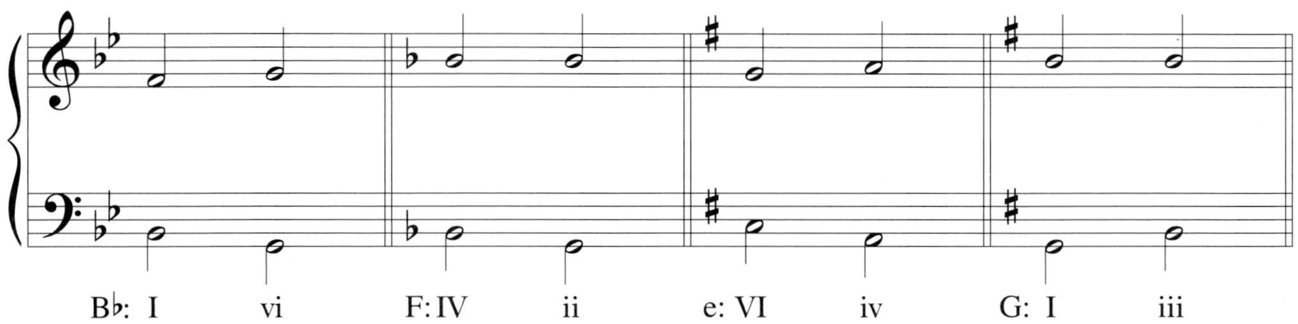

D. Use of first inversion

EXERCISES

A. Add parts for alto and tenor.

B. Add parts for soprano, alto, and tenor.

C. Add parts for alto and tenor.

D. Add parts for soprano, alto, and tenor.

E. Using the given progressions, invent four-measure phrases for soprano, alto, tenor, and bass. The harmonic rhythm is given.

F. Make a complete harmonic analysis of the following phrases.

1

2

12
The Harmonization of Melodies I

In the last chapter it was emphasized that the introduction of secondary triads created the potential for a wide variety of harmonic progressions; as a result, musical problems may be encountered. These problems are brought into particularly sharp focus when students are confronted with a melody to harmonize; they face what seems to be a bewildering array of possibilities, and, consequently, they have difficulty in deciding where to begin.

Using the melody below as a model, the author describes a method that can be effectively applied to the harmonization of melodies in general. Students should follow the steps carefully and should routinely put the steps into practice when they begin their own harmonizations.

1. Determination of key.

   The possibilities are F major and d minor. The key is F major for at least two reasons:

   a. The melody begins and ends on f (although this fact does not automatically preclude d minor).

b. C♮ the dominant in F, appears frequently. If the melody were in d, one would expect c♯ (the leading tone), rather than C♮ (the subtonic), to predominate.

2. Analysis of phrase structure, leading to identification of cadences. Cadences, which are points of relative repose, serve to terminate phrases (see Chapter 8). Clearly, the melody comes to rest in two places—on the dotted half note c^2 in measure 4, and on the final f^1. The arrival at c^2 strongly suggests a half cadence (conclusion on V); and one would expect an authentic cadence (V–I) to conclude on the final tonic note.

This melody, in fact, exhibits two very common characteristics with respect to phrase structure:

a. Each phrase is four measures long.

b. The first phrase (antecedent) ends with a half cadence; the second phrase (consequent) ends with an authentic cadence.

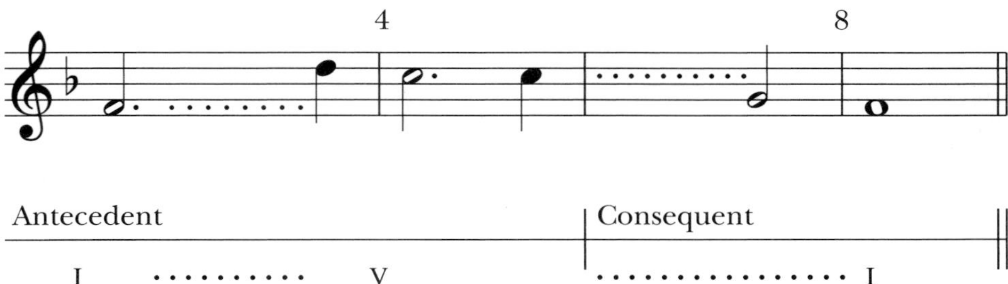

Keep a mental picture of this diagram: it will be encountered frequently.

3. Working backward from cadences, assignation of chords whose relationships represent strong harmonic motion (descending fifths, ascending seconds)—this phase ends when such motion is no longer possible.

Since the harmonic goal for each phrase is now known, it makes sense to try to reach the final cadence as clearly as possible.

Phrase One: Strong half cadences: a) ii–V b) IV–V] both fit the melody

a. To continue to achieve strong harmonic motion, ii should be preceded by vi (descending fifths) or by I (ascending seconds). The E♮ does not belong to either harmony:

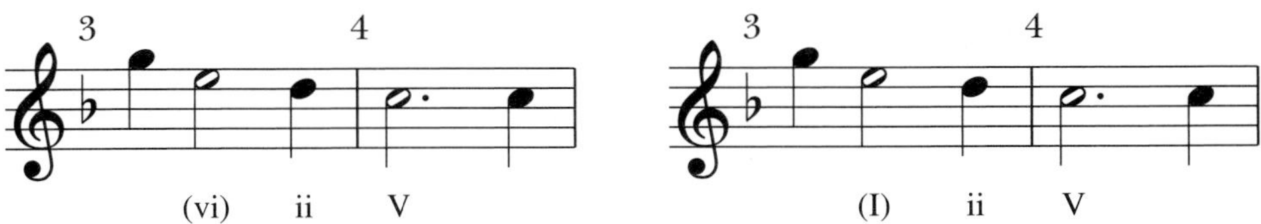

b. To continue to achieve strong harmonic motion, IV should be preceded by I (descending fifths), or by iii (ascending seconds). The latter fits the melody. In fact, ascending seconds may be projected back to c^2 in the second measure before the pattern breaks down. Thus, the solution to the end of phrase one is:

Phrase Two: Strong authentic cadence: V–I

To continue to achieve strong harmonic motion, V should be preceded by ii (descending fifths), or by IV (ascending seconds). In this case, descending fifths may be effectively projected back to the beginning of the seventh measure (note that long notes may have multiple harmonies), and thus, the solution is:

4. Assignation of chords from the beginning of phrases to link with chords already assigned—strength of harmonic movement is less critical in this phase than establishment of tonality.

   The harmonic goals for the phrases cannot be effectively realized unless the tonality (key) is clear in the first place. Thus, the harmonization of the remaining pitches in the melody should reinforce the key, in this case F major. Primary triads serve this purpose very well:

Note:

a. In the beginning of each phrase, the rate of change of harmony is relatively slow compared with that in the end of each phrase. The rhythmic configuration that emerges from these changes of harmony is called the *harmonic rhythm.* Frequently, harmonic rhythm is faster at the end of phrases than at the beginning.

b. In measure 6, the first and second notes have been assigned a subdominant and tonic triad, respectively; the third and fourth have been assigned a mediant and leading tone triad. This harmonization has been chosen to exploit the melodic pattern wherein the second pair of notes represents a transposition, by a step down, of the first pair. The repetition of a pattern at a different pitch level creates what is known as a *sequence*. Attention has been drawn to this melodic sequence by the harmonic sequence that accompanies it.

5. Construction of bass line with concentration on melodic interest, accomplished by appropriate use of inversions.

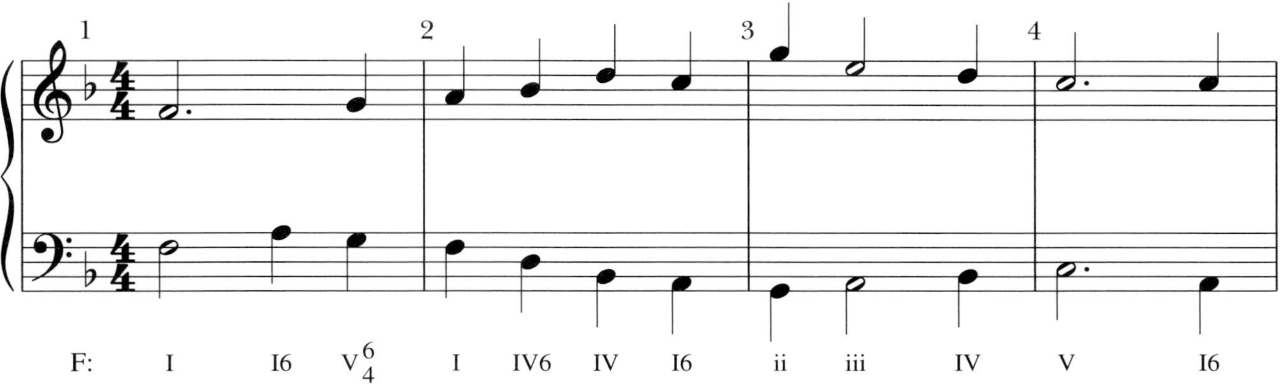

Several different bass lines could obviously be written. The previously established progressions to the cadences suggested largely conjunct (by step) motion in the first phrase and rather more disjunct (by leap) motion in the second. *Contrary motion* between the two voices is used throughout. Although such motion is not always manageable, it is desirable because it gives the outer voices melodic independence and usually facilitates the part writing in the inner voices. When you begin a phrase with a long melodic note (measure one), you can use the same harmony in both root position and first inversion under that note, to give the phrase forward movement.

6. Addition of inner voices to complete harmonization.

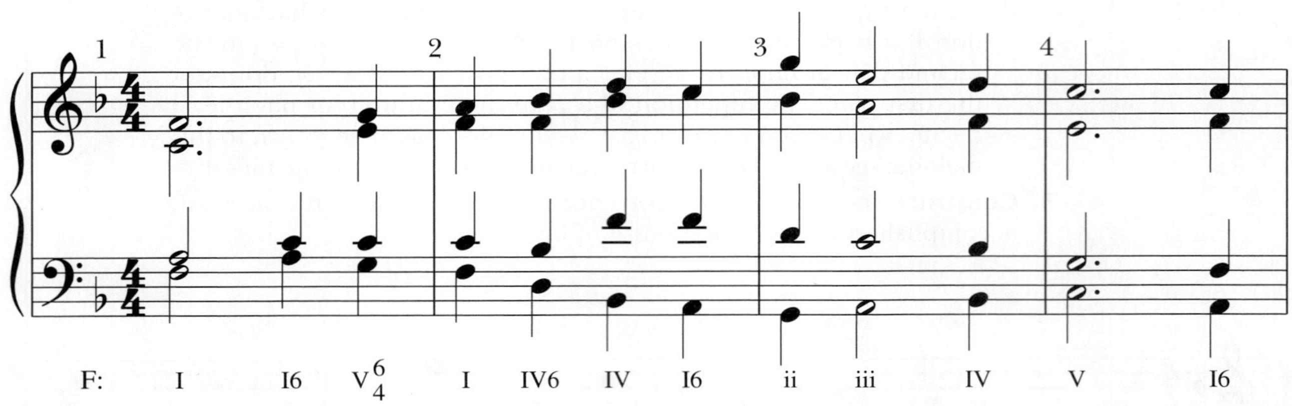

Note:

In the complete harmonization, an effort has been made to give the inner voices, as well as the outer, an interesting melodic line. Although it is not always possible to achieve such a line (e.g., the alto voice in the second phrase), linear considerations should not be ignored. The combination of a logical harmonic progression and fluid linear activity typically leads to an effective musical setting.

SUGGESTIONS AND STRATEGIES

For both Exercise A and Exercise B, look for melodic patterns that suggest the use of six-four chords, particularly the cadential six-four. Each melody note should be harmonized (Chapter 16 addresses the use of nonchord tones in a melody).

The two-phrase melodies to harmonize in Exercise B follow the antecedent-consequent phrase structure described earlier in this chapter. The combination of two phrases related to one another in this manner is called a *period*—provided that:

1. There is an authentic cadence at the end of the second phrase.
2. The cadence at the end of the first phrase is less conclusive than that at the end of the second phrase.
3. There is a logical relationship between the contents of the two phrases. This relationship is typically established through the use of similar melodic, harmonic, and rhythmic elements.

The melodic similarities between the phrases in 1 and 2 are very clear, and they exist in 3, but not quite so obviously.

In the *Preparation* phase, therefore, determine what the cadences are, and what other similarities exist. Remember that you can save yourself time and energy by harmonizing identical melodic material in the two phrases in the same way. By doing so you will also help to unify the phrases, and strengthen the periodic structure.

EXERCISES

A. Harmonize the following one-phrase melodies.

B. Harmonize the following two-phrase melodies.

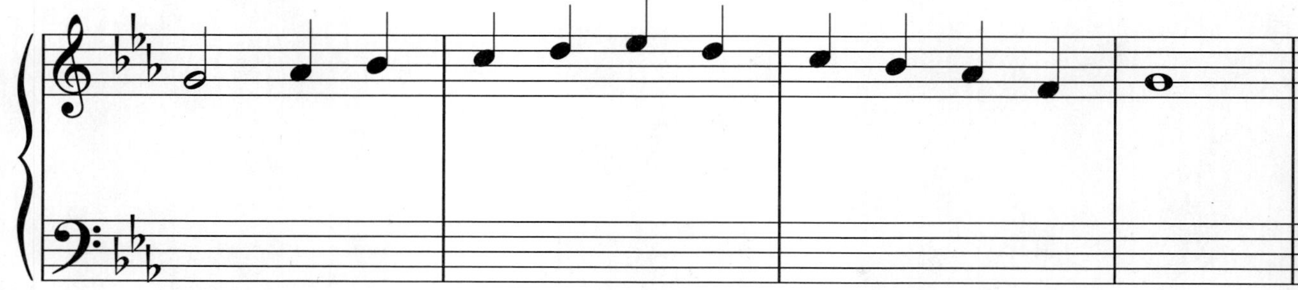

2
3

13
Nonchord Tones I

Passing Tones, Neighboring Tones, Changing Tones, Appoggiaturas, Escape Tones, Anticipations

A nonchord tone is a tone that does not belong to the prevailing harmony. It may be diatonic (belonging to the key) or chromatic (not belonging to the key). Nonchord tones are also called nonharmonic or embellishment tones.

THE PASSING TONE

The passing tone (P or PT) is a nonchord tone that is approached by step and resolved by step in the same direction. A *step* is typically an augmented unison, or a major or minor second.

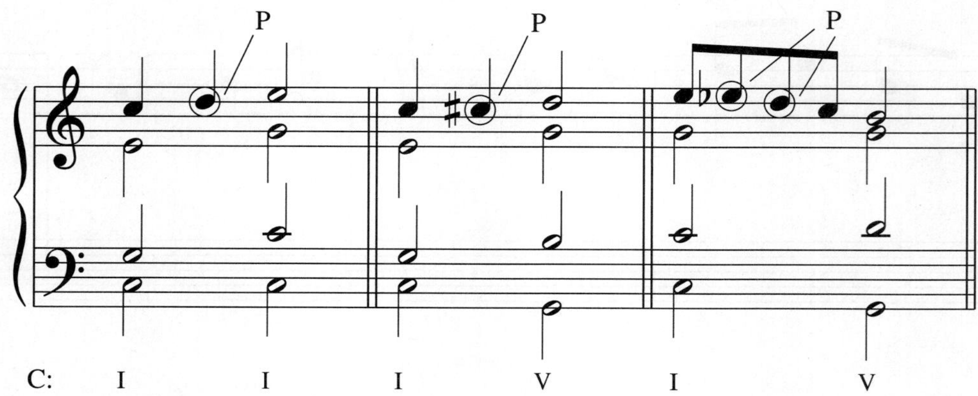

Note:

a. The C♯ and the E♭ are *chromatic* passing tones because they are not diatonic notes in the key of C.

b. The last example contains two adjacent passing tones. Such a procedure is common.

THE NEIGHBORING TONE

The neighboring tone (N or NT) is a nonchord tone that is approached by step and resolved by step in the opposite direction.

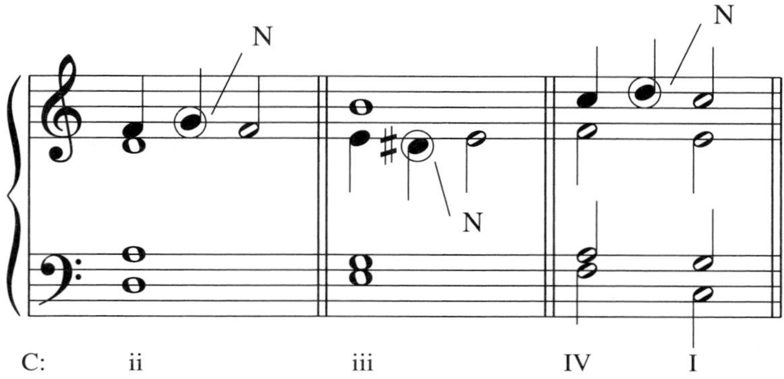

Note:

a. Upper neighboring tones are shown in the first and third examples; a lower neighboring tone is shown in the second.

b. The D♯ represents a chromatic neighboring tone.

Passing tones and neighboring tones are usually unaccented, but they do not have to be. They occur in all voices.

The following examples show them both unaccented and accented.

F: I V vi N ii ii6 V N P N P
N N P I6 ii6 I 6 4 N V I P
F: I V vi N ii ii6 V N P P N P
P N P I6 ii6 P I 6 4 V I P

CHANGING TONES

Changing tones (CT) are nonchord tones that occur in pairs and separate a chord tone from its repetition. The first is approached by step; the second is approached by leap and resolved by step. In each movement there is a change in direction.

Changing tones may be accented or unaccented and occur in all voices. They are more frequently used, however, in instrumental than vocal music.

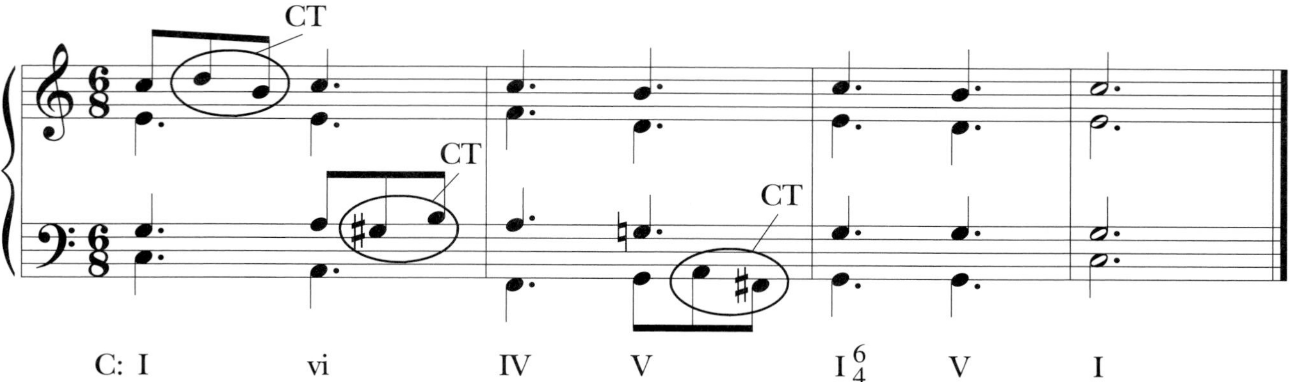

Note:

a. The first changing tone may be above or below the chord tone that precedes it.

b. A changing tone may be a diatonic or chromatic pitch.

c. A pair of changing tones may be regarded as the combination of an upper and lower neighboring tone.

THE APPOGGIATURA

The appoggiatura (Ap) is a nonchord tone that is approached by leap and resolved by step, usually in the opposite direction. It is typically accented and most frequently occurs in the soprano (or top) voice.

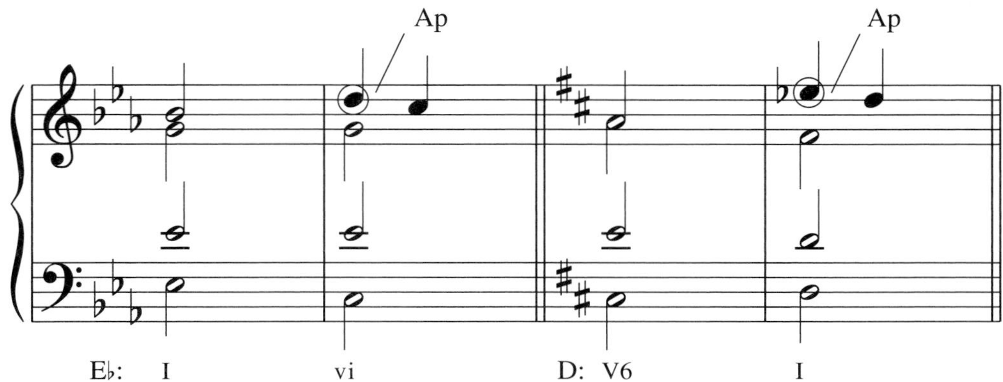

Note:

As the second example shows, the appoggiatura may be a chromatic pitch.

THE ESCAPE TONE

The escape tone (ET) is a nonchord tone that is approached by step and resolved by leap, usually in the opposite direction. It is typically unaccented and most frequently occurs in the soprano (or top) voice.

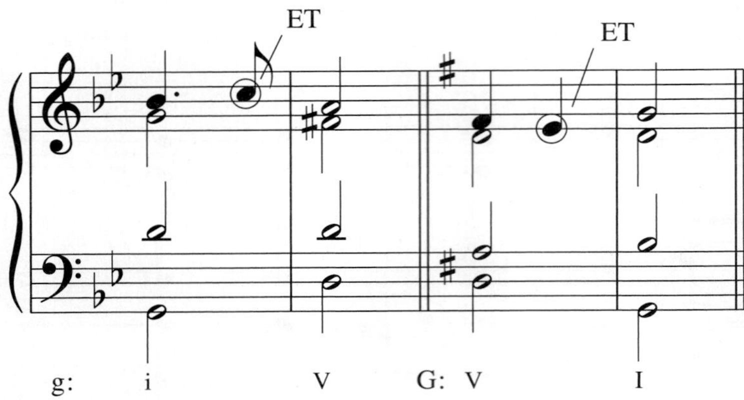

Note:
As the first example shows, the escape tone may be of shorter duration than the pitch that precedes it.

THE ANTICIPATION

The anticipation (An) is a nonchord tone that is approached by step or leap, and it becomes a chord tone with a subsequent change in harmony. It is unaccented and usually occurs in the soprano (or top) voice.

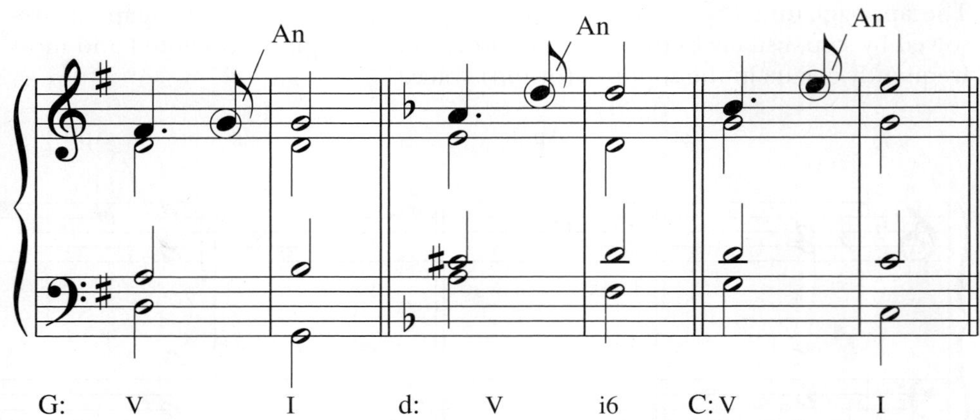

Note:
The anticipation is generally of shorter duration than the chord tone that precedes it.

SUGGESTIONS AND STRATEGIES

In Exercises A through E, you will use nonchord tones to embellish or smoothen one or more of the four parts.

You must be careful, however, when you add these tones to a harmonic setting devoid of them that you do not create part writing errors.

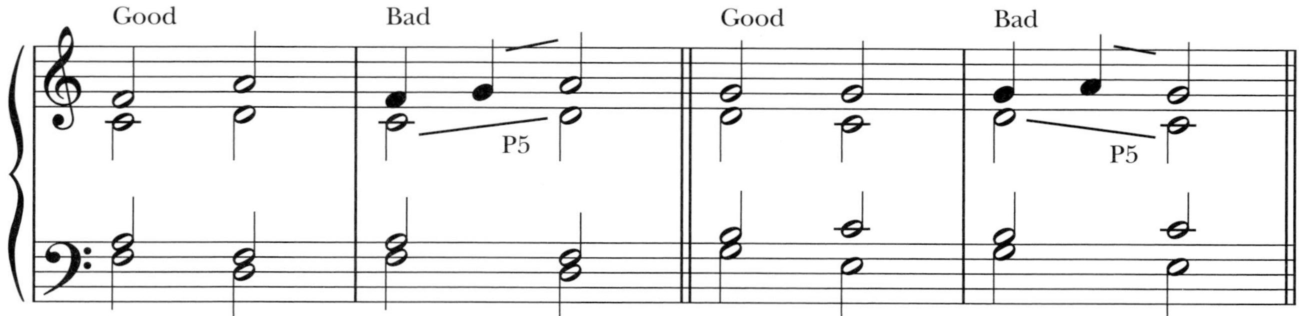

The addition of the passing tone and neighboring tone to the original progressions creates *parallel fifths*.

Conversely, if an error in part writing exists before the introduction of a nonchord tone, the addition of the nonchord tone does not negate the error.

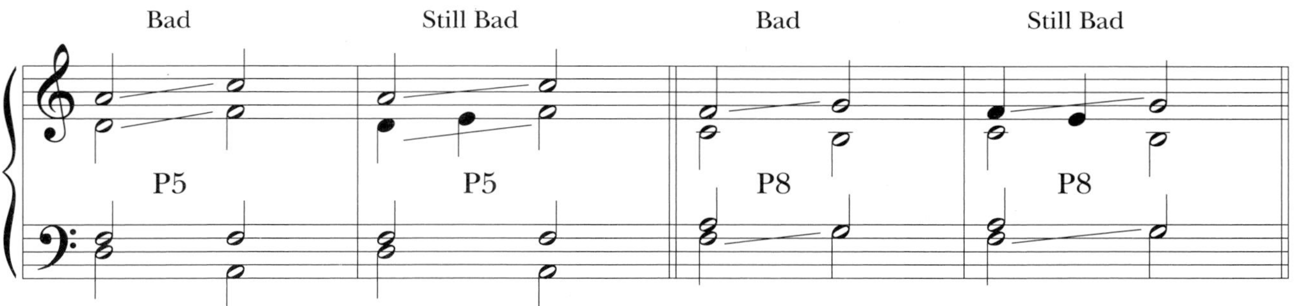

These two progressions contain parallel fifths and parallel octaves, respectively. The addition of the passing tone and escape tone does not rectify the errors.

EXERCISES

A. Elaborate the following harmonizations by the addition of passing tones and neighboring tones. Label each one.

B. Add parts for alto and tenor, introducing passing tones and neighboring tones where appropriate.

C. Add parts for soprano, alto, and tenor.

D. Harmonize the following melodies, introducing passing tones and neighboring tones where appropriate.

1

2

3

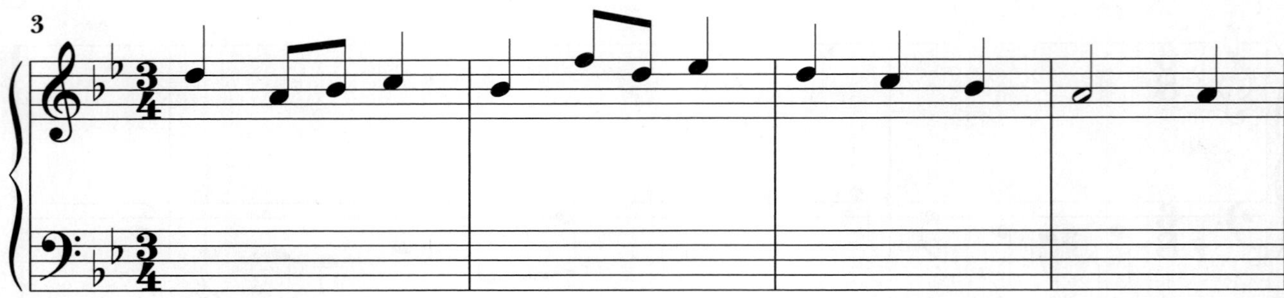

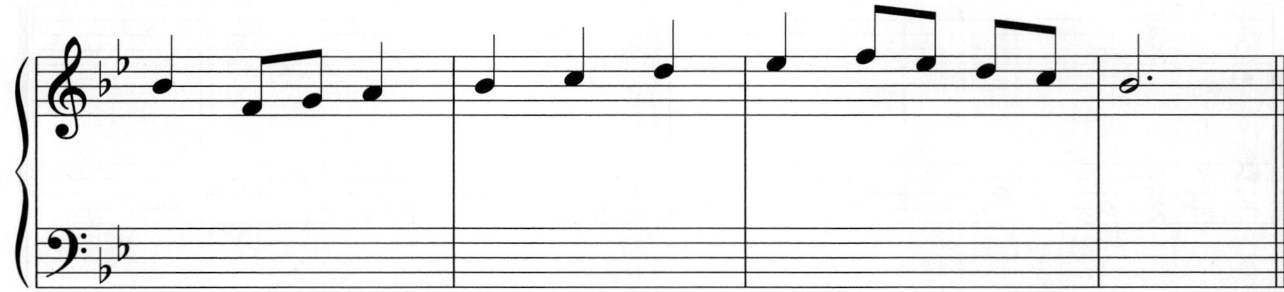

E. Add parts for alto and tenor. In the space provided, write an elaborated version introducing changing tones, appogiaturas, escape tones, and anticipations.

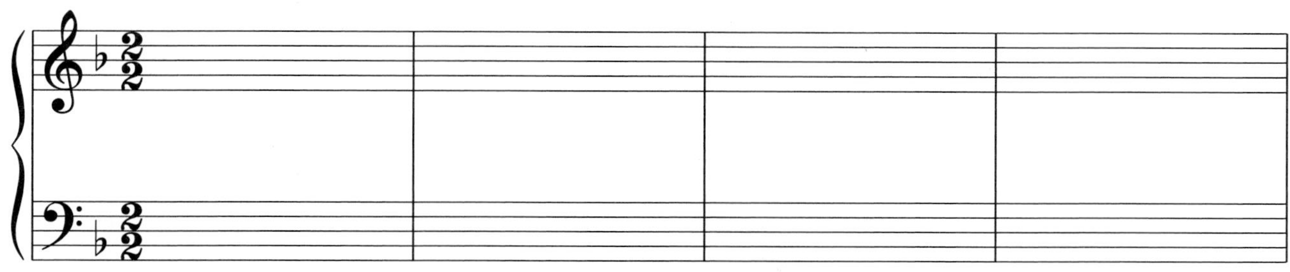

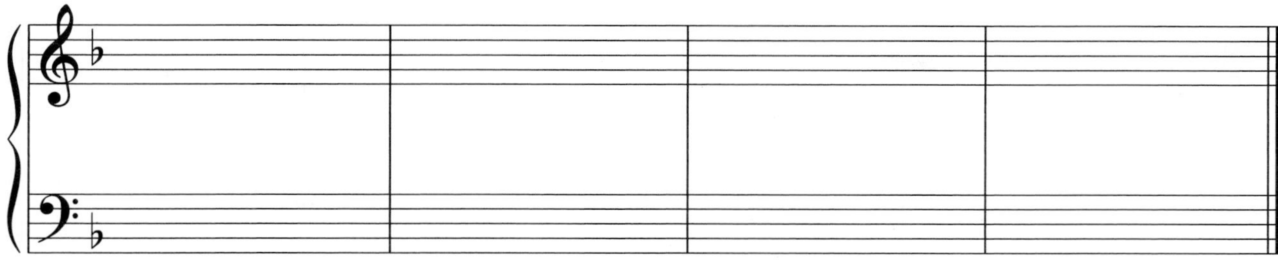

2

F. Make a complete harmonic analysis of the following phrases. Circle and label all nonchord tones.

3

4

14
Nonchord Tones II

Suspensions and Pedal Points

SUSPENSIONS

The suspension is a nonchord tone that is the result of retaining a tone from a previous harmony and that resolves downward by step. It is accented.

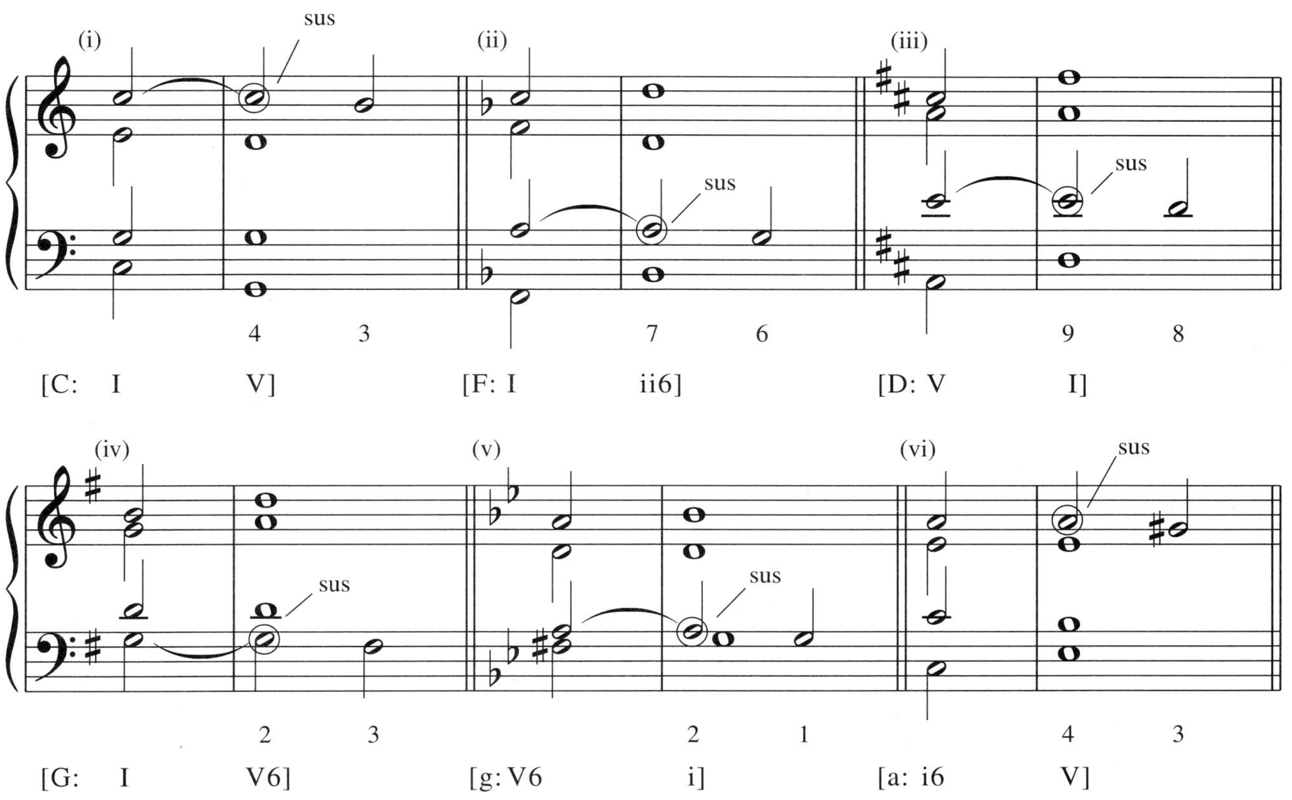

Note:

a. The change in harmony may or may not involve motion in the bass.

b. A suspension may occur in any voice. If it occurs in the bass, however, it is described by the interval that forms a dissonance with it, as shown in (iv).

c. Except in the cases of the 9–8 and 2–1 suspension, the pitch of resolution is not doubled.

d. The suspended pitch may be tied to the previous one or may be sounded again. If sounded again, it is known as an *articulated* suspension.

e. The suspension is in a stronger position metrically than its resolution.

A suspension may be written to resolve upwards by step. Suspensions of this kind are usually called *retardations.*

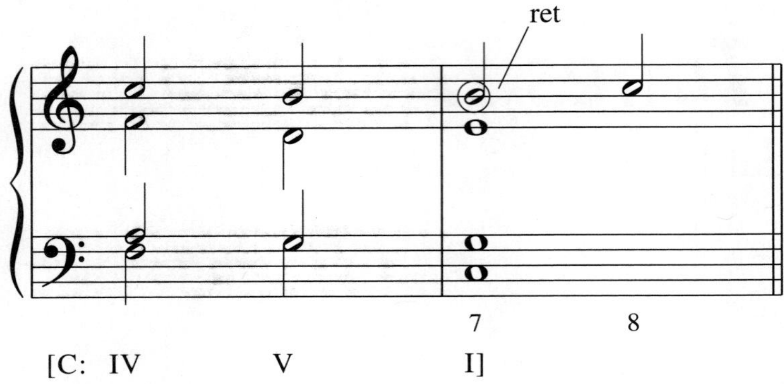

When working with suspensions, the student should get used to thinking in terms of three events: preparation (consonance)–suspension (dissonance)–resolution (consonance).

Usually, only two harmonies are involved; the suspension delays the completion of the second one. It is possible (though rare), for the resolution to coincide with a change of harmony, thus:

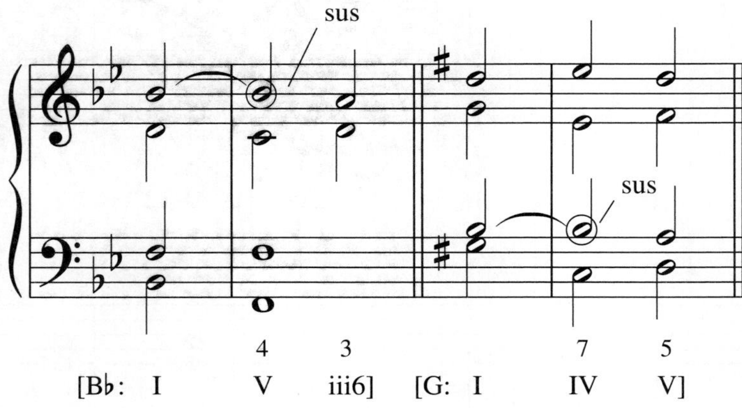

Note:

a. The change in harmony may or may not involve motion in the bass.

b. In the second example, the figured bass symbols (7–5) suggest a leap in the suspension's resolution. The unusual figures are produced by the ascending bass line; the suspended b resolves normally.

PEDAL POINT

A pedal point, or pedal, is a sustained pitch, usually in the bass, above which is juxtaposed a series of changing harmonies. Pedal points are named after the scale degrees upon which they are built, for example, "tonic pedal," "supertonic pedal," and so forth. In practice, however, they tend to occur most frequently on the tonic or dominant.

The Tonic Pedal

The tonic pedal is often used at the end of a piece of music to prolong the tonic harmony.

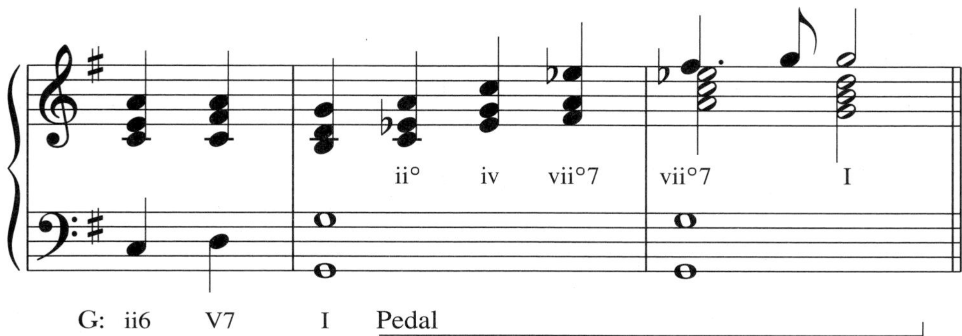

The Dominant Pedal

The main function of the dominant pedal is to create tension and thus to prepare the listener for the subsequent musical event, which is usually the resolution to the tonic.

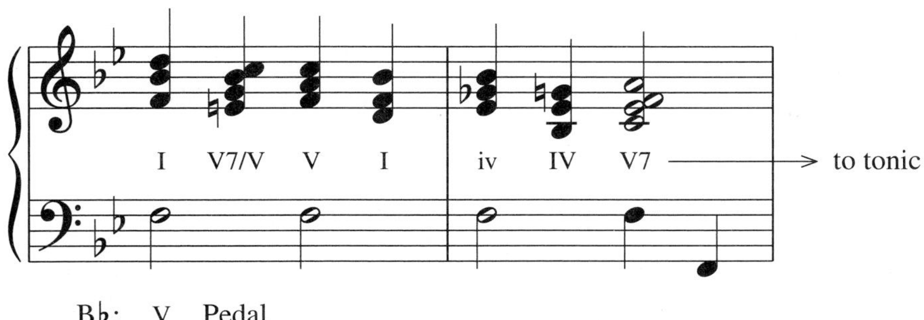

Note:
In the examples above, the pedals interact both consonantly and dissonantly with the chords above them. This interaction is the essence of the writing of pedal points, and their effectiveness is dependent upon the skill with which the composer controls the harmonic activity in the upper voices.

EXERCISES

A. Add to the given voice a second one so that the indicated suspensions are created. (Observe that the first interval in each example is consonant as a result of writing the suspension correctly.)

1

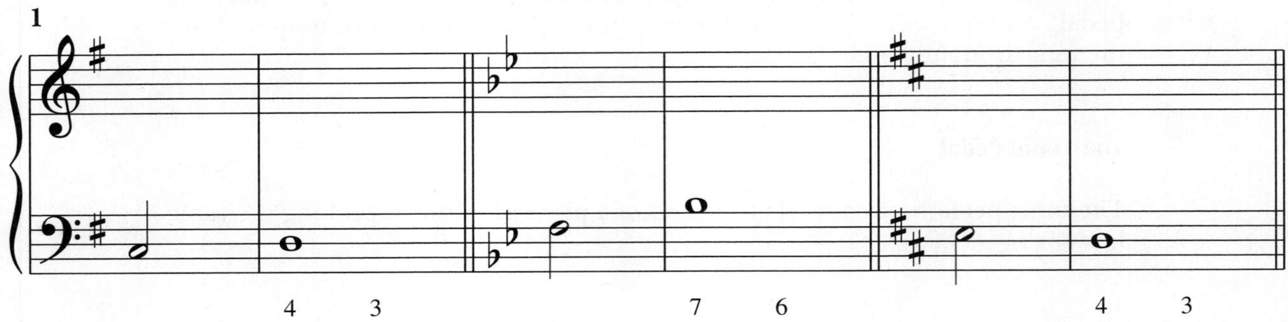

2

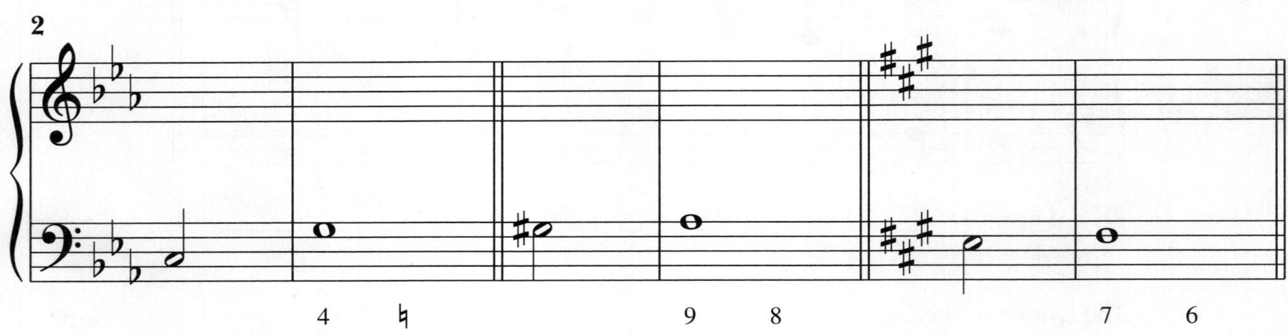

3

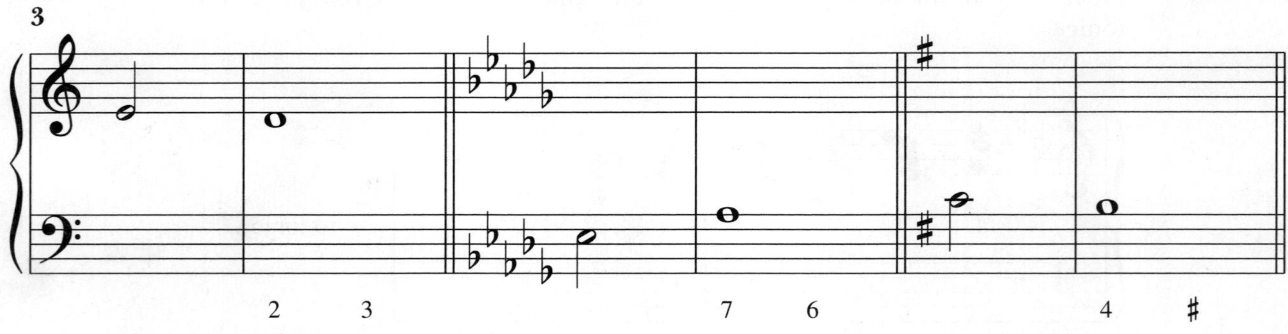

4

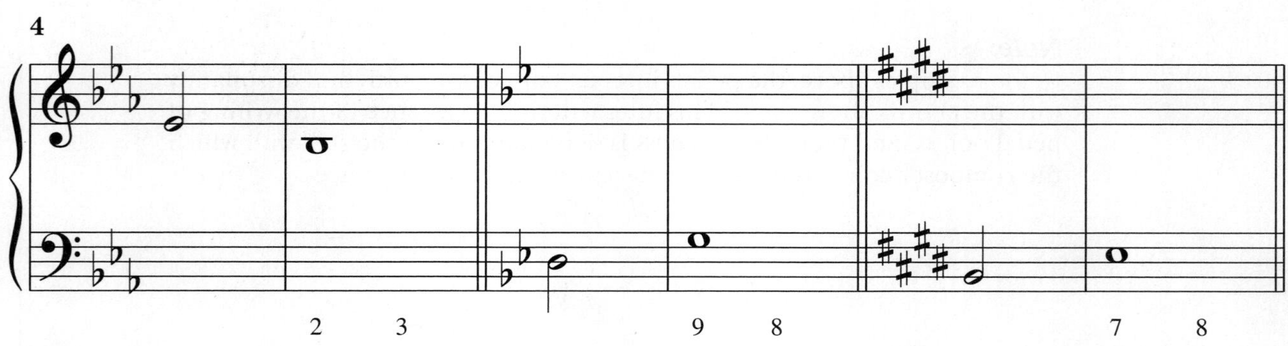

B. Add parts for alto and tenor.

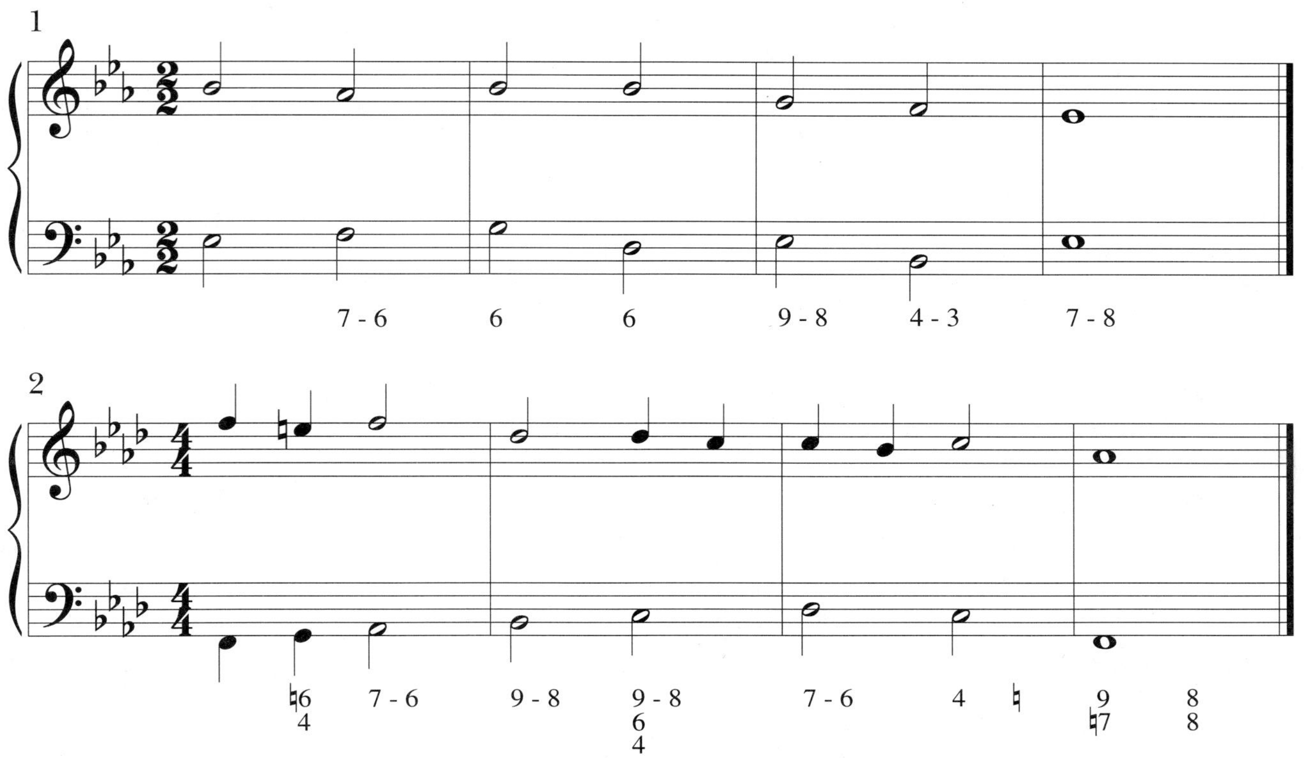

C. Add parts for soprano, alto, and tenor.

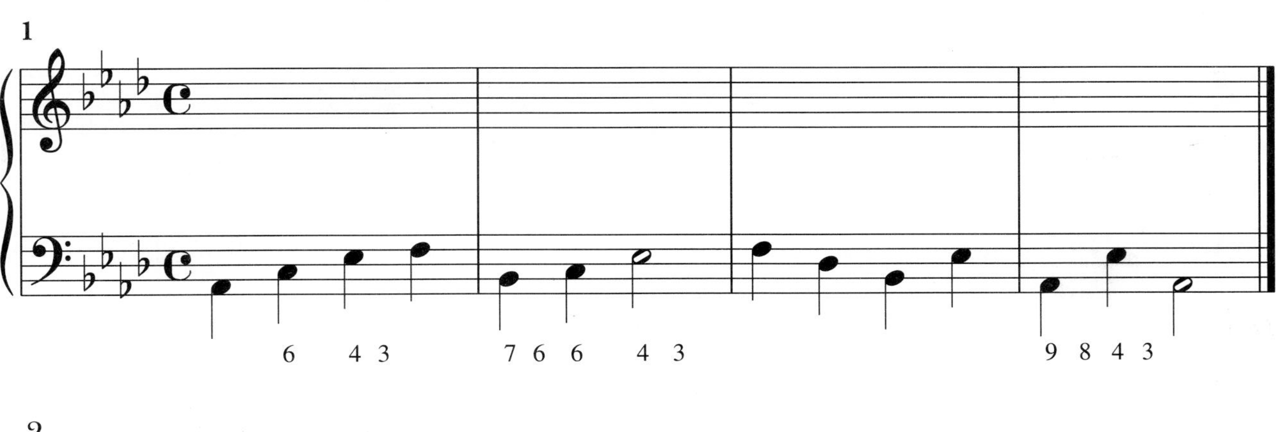

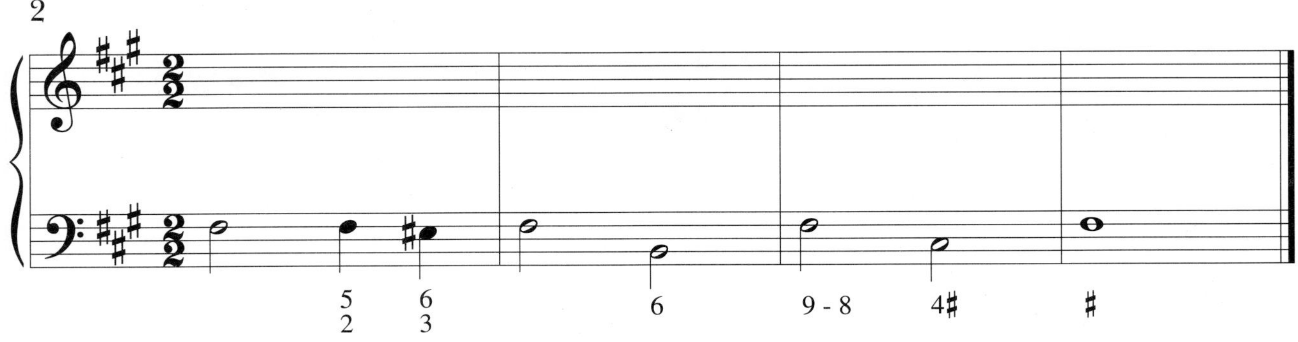

D. Add parts for alto, tenor, and bass. All tied notes should be treated as suspensions.

1

2

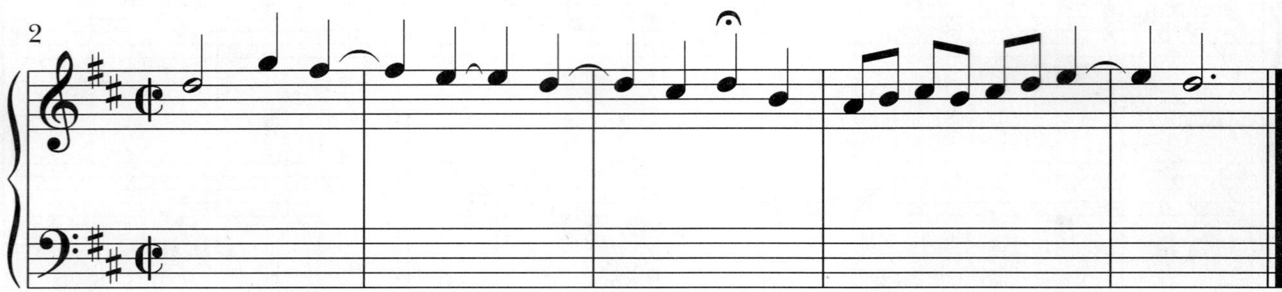

E. Add parts for alto, tenor, and bass. Use pedal points where appropriate.

1

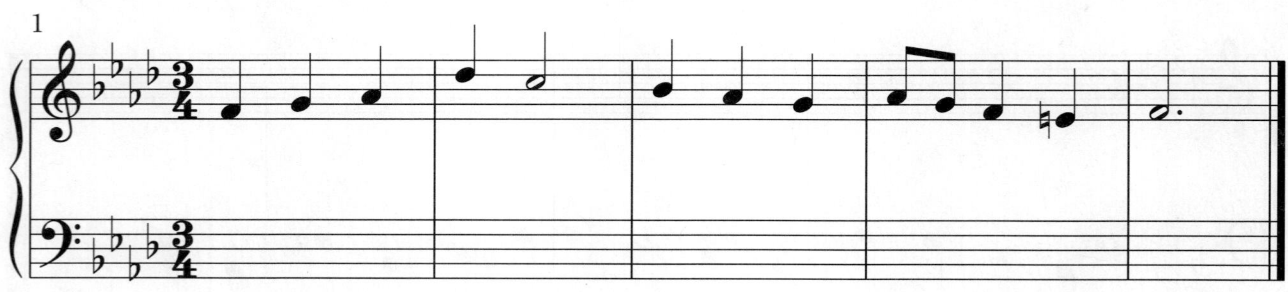

2

F. Make a complete harmonic analysis of the following phrases. Circle and label all nonchord tones.

15
Diatonic Seventh Chords

A seventh chord is constructed by adding to a triad a pitch that is a seventh above its root.

The result is a sonority (chord) with four pitches stacked in thirds. The quality of the seventh varies with the scale degree upon which it is built, as follows:

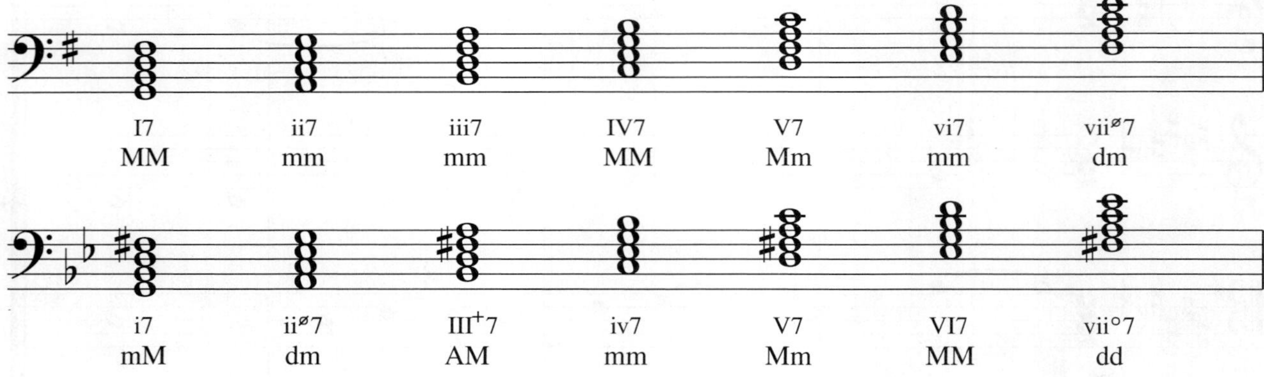

The diagram shows the seventh chords in the major and harmonic minor scales. Notice that under the Roman numerals, the qualities of the seventh chords are described. The first symbol shows the quality of the triad, and the second symbol shows the quality of the interval of the seventh. Although the augmented-major and minor-major seventh chords occur in the minor key, they are not often used.

FIGURED BASS SYMBOLS FOR SEVENTH CHORDS

The example below shows a seventh chord in root position and in its three inversions. For each one, the complete figured bass is given, and the most commonly used abbreviation.

7 5 3	6 5 3	6 4 3	6 4 2
7	6 5	4 3	4 2

Seventh chords in root position and in inversion are described by their figured bass symbols. For example, a seventh chord in first inversion is called a "six-five chord."

THE SEVENTH CHORD IN FOUR-PART WRITING

The seventh in the seventh chord is nearly always treated in one of two ways:

1. It resolves *downward* by step. This is its most natural resolution and the one most frequently encountered.
2. It remains as a common tone. Such a resolution is referred to as *passive.*

Study the following examples carefully:

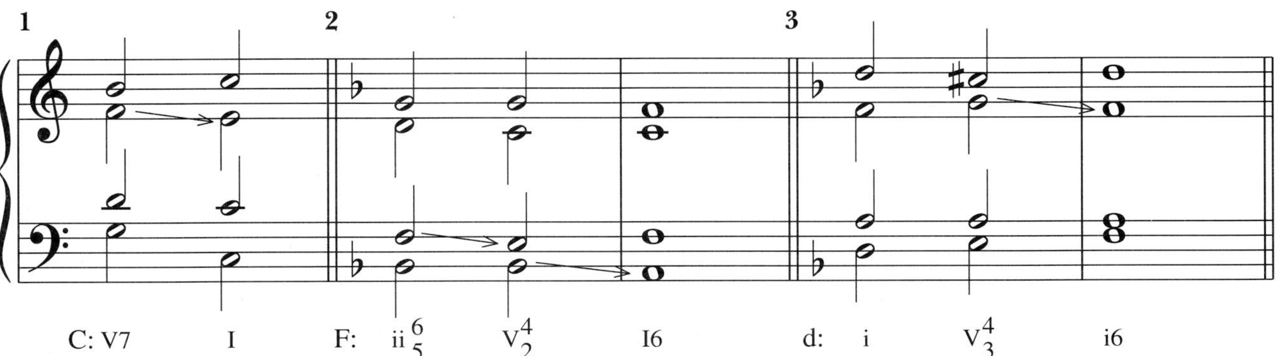

Note:

a. The seventh is never doubled; it is a sensitive pitch.

b. Occasionally the fifth is omitted from the seventh chord, as in 4. By doing so, parallel fifths are prevented. When the fifth is omitted, the root is doubled.

c. In some examples (see 2, 4, and 7), the seventh is "prepared" and treated in a manner similar to a suspension. This is a common procedure in part writing the chord.

d. The seventh chord usually resolves by a root movement of a descending fifth. With the exception of vii°7–i, this is the chord's most natural resolution, and the one most frequently encountered.

e. The seventh chord is used freely in all inversions.

THE FUNCTION OF DIATONIC SEVENTH CHORDS

Because seventh chords are dissonant sonorities, they should be used sparingly. They have two important functions:

1. To add intensity to harmonic motion, particularly at cadence points.
2. To create harmonic color.

With reference to the first function, the dominant seventh (V7) and the supertonic seventh (ii7) are more widely used than other seventh chords. With reference to the second function, care must be taken that when seventh chords are used for harmonic color, they are used systematically. The presence of a seventh chord in a passage otherwise devoid of them is likely to be unsatisfactory.

SUGGESTIONS AND STRATEGIES

When the dominant seventh in root position resolves by descending fifth to the tonic triad in root position, be very careful to avoid parallel (or consecutive) fifths.

The first example below shows the error, and the second and third examples show how that error may be corrected.

To avoid the incorrect part writing, the fifth has to be omitted in one of the two chords. This procedure is perfectly acceptable.

....

In the tonic seventh chord, I7, the seventh is the leading tone. It does not, however, function as such in this context. The correct resolution is to resolve the seventh downward by step.

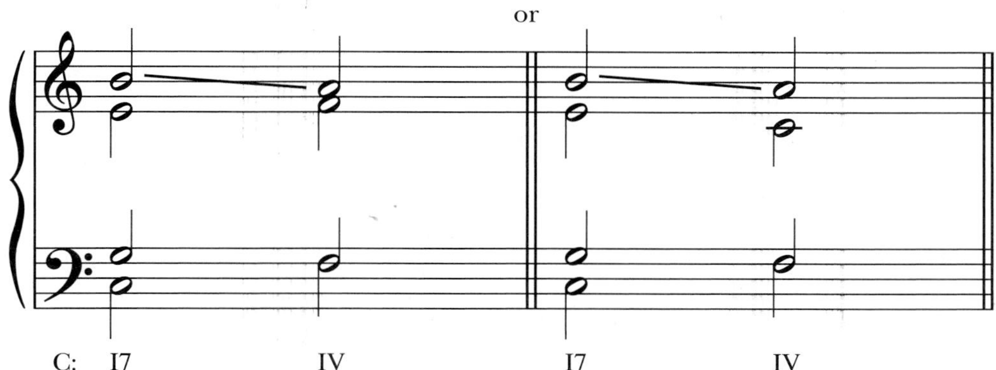

When harmonizing the melodies in Exercise E, you may find it easier to begin by following the previously described procedures, and creating a version that contains no sevenths. Then modify the melodies by the appropriate addition of sevenths, making certain, of course, that the sevenths are resolved properly.

EXERCISES

A. Write, in four voices, the following seventh chords.

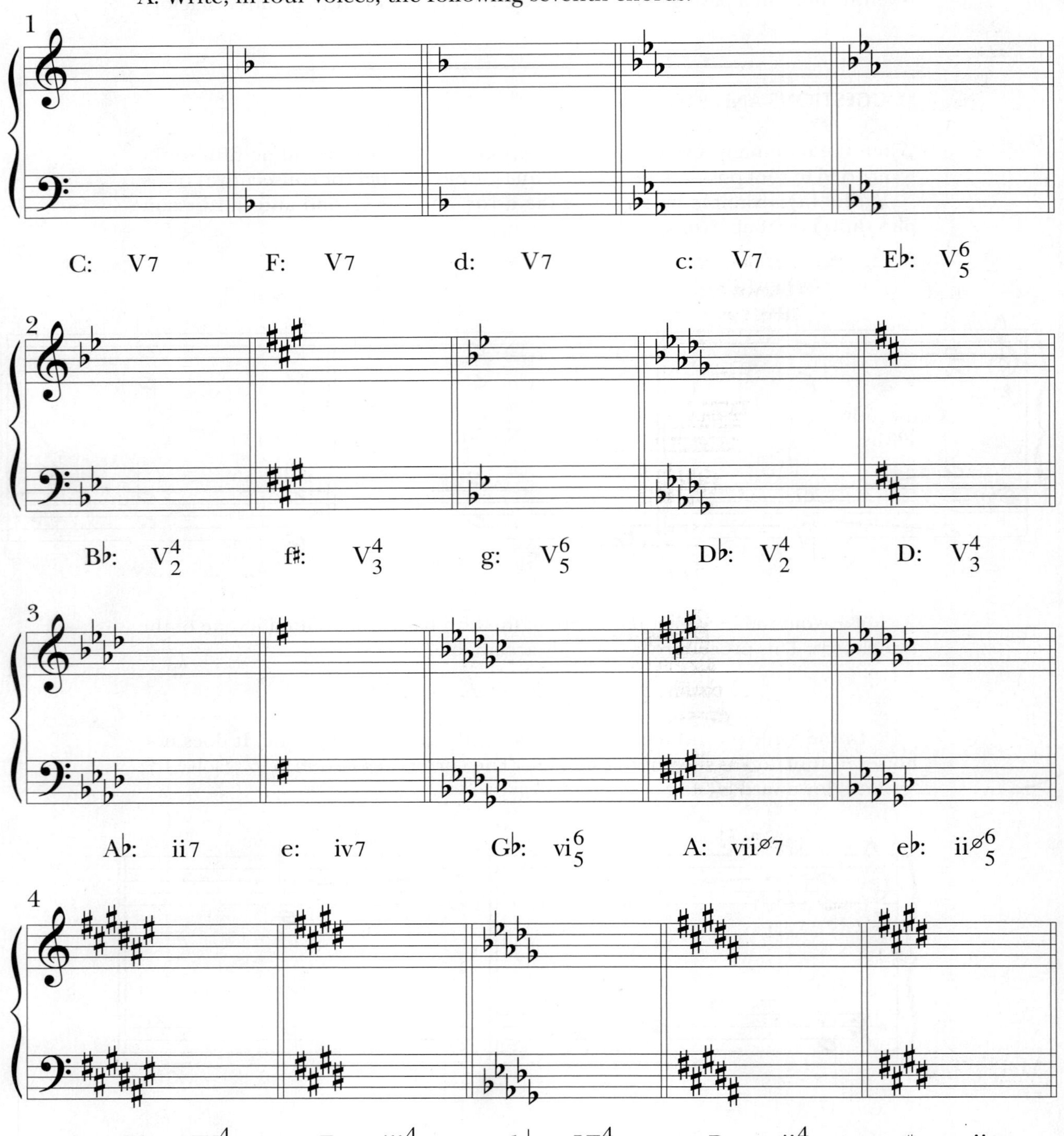

B. Write and resolve, in four voices, the following seventh chords.

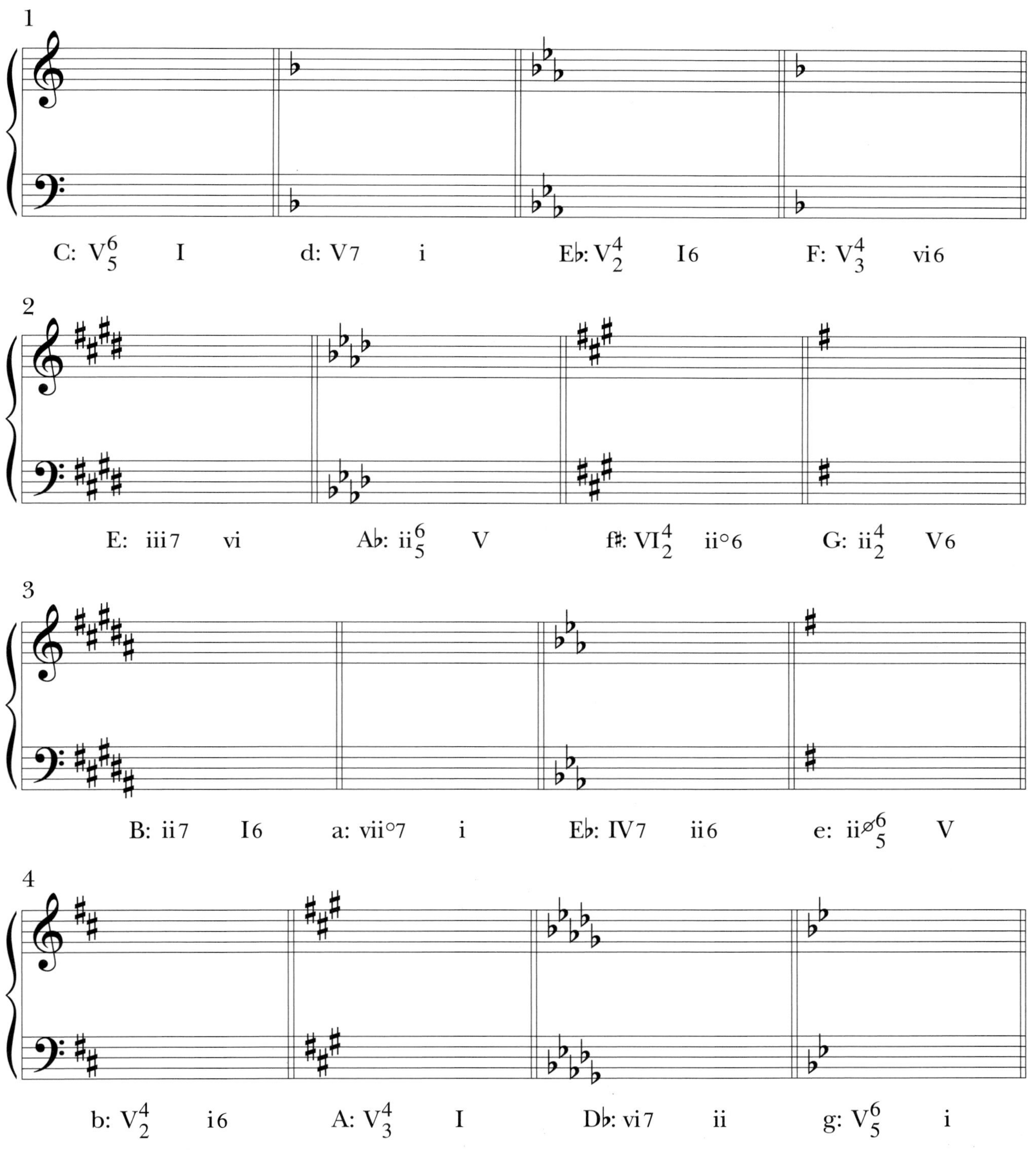

C. Add parts for alto and tenor.

D. Add parts for soprano, alto, and tenor.

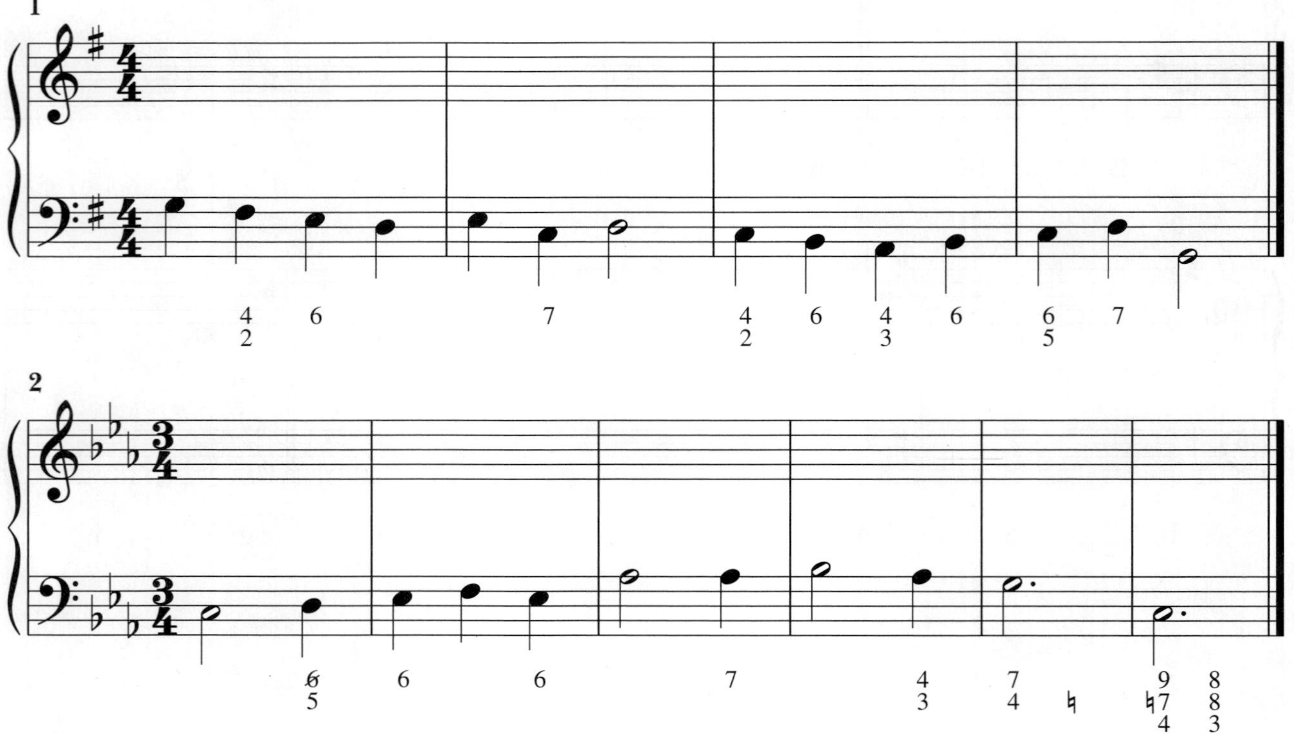

E. Harmonize the following melodies, using seventh chords.

1

2

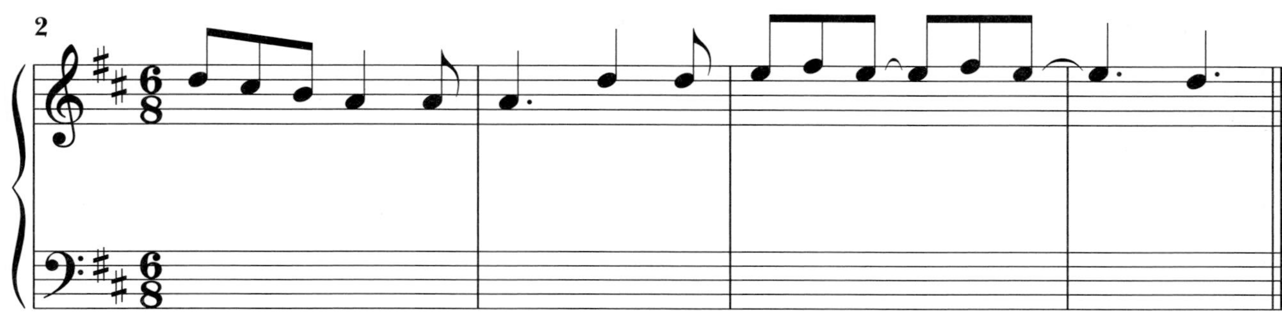

3

4

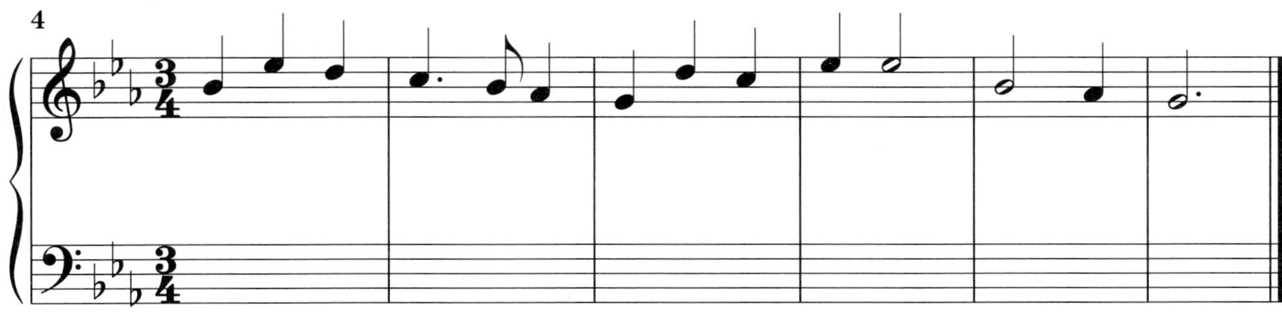

5

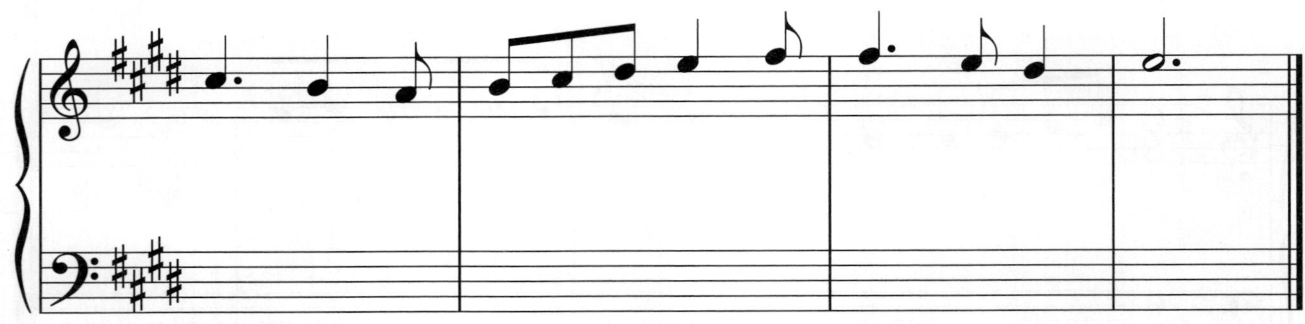

6

F. Using the given progressions, invent four-measure phrases for soprano, alto, tenor, and bass. The harmonic rhythm is given.

G. Make a complete harmonic analysis of the following phrases.

16
The Harmonization of Melodies II

In Chapter 12, the first to address the harmonization of melodies, it was shown how a student could reach an effective solution by systematically applying six steps. These steps are, in essence,

1. The determination of the key.
2. The identification of phrases and cadences.
3. The identification of the harmonic activity leading to each cadence.
4. The identification of the harmonic activity that sets each phrase in motion.
5. The construction of an appropriate bass line.
6. The addition of the inner voices.

The application of these six steps is equally relevant in this chapter, with one important addition—the melodies to be harmonized contain nonchord tones. This added variable forces the student to consider, before completing steps 3 through 6, which of the pitches in a melody should or should not be harmonized. An awareness of typical melodic patterns, and the nonchord tones that may be suggested by them, goes a long way toward facilitating this process.

The following pages exemplify some of the more commonly encountered patterns and how they may be identified in diatonic melodies.

In the patterns exemplified below, the white notes represent chord tones, and the black notes, nonchord tones.

PASSING TONE PATTERNS [P]

Note:

a. Although single passing tones are the most commonly encountered, two or more are by no means rare.

b. The white notes are more likely to be accented than the black ones.

NEIGHBORING TONE PATTERNS [N]

Note:

a. Changing tones are included in this category.

b. Again, the white notes are more typically accented than the black notes.

SUSPENSION PATTERNS [Sus]

Note:

a. The black notes are typically accented.

b. The last example shows the beginning of a chain of suspensions. This repetitive pattern may easily unfold over several measures of music.

APPOGGIATURA PATTERNS [Ap]

Note:

a. This group of patterns involves a leap followed by a step with or without a change of direction.

b. The black note is frequently (though not always) accented in each of these patterns.

ESCAPE TONE PATTERNS [ET]

Note:

a. This group of patterns involves a step followed by a leap with or without a change of direction.

b. The black note is frequently (though not always) unaccented in each of these patterns.

ANTICIPATION PATTERNS [An]

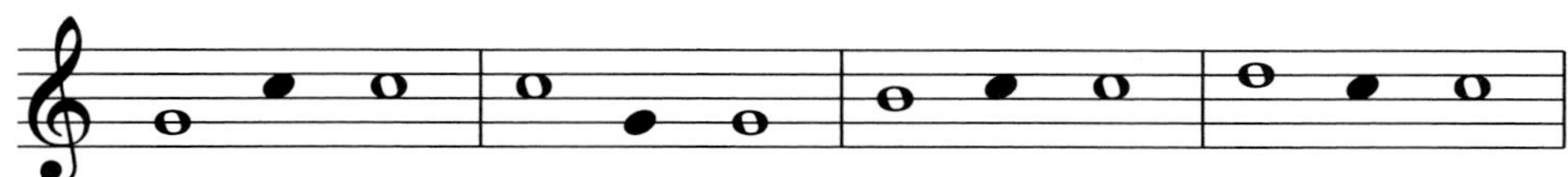

Note:

a. The black note is the result of a step or leap in either direction.

b. The black note is much more frequently unaccented than accented in this group of patterns.

Study the following examples carefully. The melody alone is first shown with the nonchord tone patterns bracketed above it and with a suggested harmonic progression below it. Then a complete harmonization is given.

Note:

a. The last beat of measure 3 is tied to the first of measure 4. This kind of suspension pattern is widely used at cadence points.

b. The harmonization of the first phrase is very simple, and the harmony changes only on the first beat of each measure.

c. In the second phrase, there are more frequent changes of harmony. It is quite common for the rate of change of harmony to accelerate as the final cadence is approached.

d. The term *harmonic rhythm* is used to describe changes in harmony. Thus, the harmonic rhythm is *slower* in the first phrase than in the second.

Note:

a. Throughout, the harmonic rhythm is faster in this example than in the previous one.

b. The tonality is clearly established in the first measure by the movement from the tonic to the dominant and back again.

c. The second half of measure 2 is harmonized with the supertonic triad. The C♯ therefore, is properly treated as an escape tone rather than a leading tone.

d. Because of the change in harmony on the third beat of measure 3, the chord tones are separated by adjacent passing tones.

e. The deceptive resolution of the dominant at the end of measure 6 allows for a very strong harmonic movement through the circle of fifths in measures 7 and 8.

In both examples, the procedures described in Chapter 12 and itemized at the beginning of this chapter were followed. The melodic phrase structure in each suggested a half cadence at the end of the first phrase and an authentic cadence at the end. The bass line in the first example is very simple, because the melody allows it to be so. In the second example, however, the sequential structure of the second and third measures of the melody implies a more elaborate harmonization. Finally, the complete harmonizations follow established voice-leading principles.

EXERCISES

A. Harmonize the following one-phrase melodies.

B. Harmonize the following two-phrase melodies.

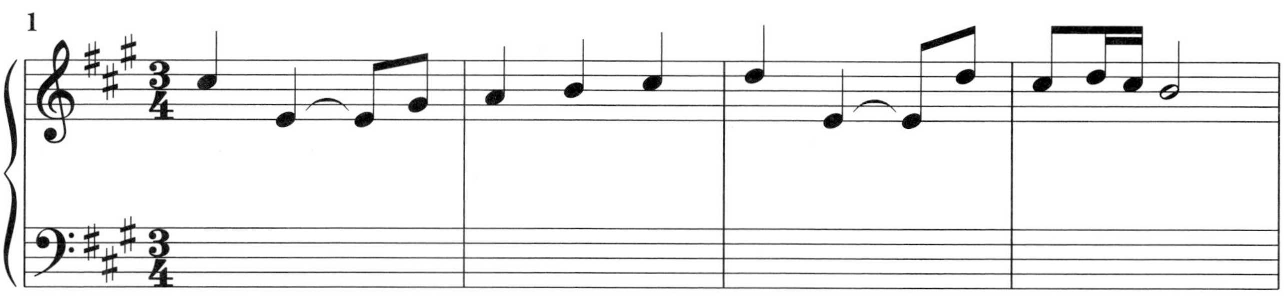

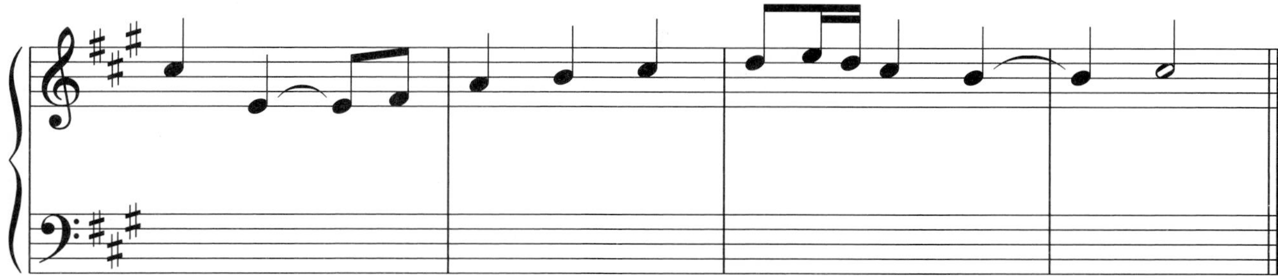

2
3

17
Writing for the Piano

One of the best ways to demonstrate a good understanding of the use of harmony in music is through composing for the piano, a single instrument that can be melodic, harmonic, and contrapuntal all at the same time. This chapter will incorporate melodic practices and counterpoint in discussing how to compose for piano.

Melodic writing involves a balance between steps, leaps, repeated notes, and rests. In tonal music, the melody must take shape within the key, and needs to agree with the harmony. Rhythm also plays a major part in the shape of the melody. A good place to start is to examine a series of melodies with critical commentary provided.

Bad—poor contour combined with constant rhythm.

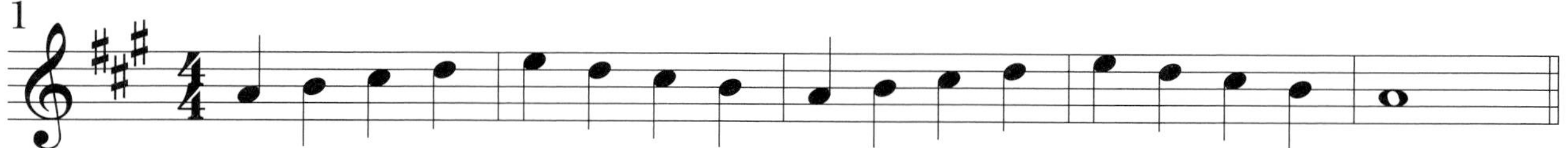

Avoid writing melodies that go up, down, up, down, etc., with the same distance up as down, and all the same rhythm.

Better—change rhythm to counteract the poor contour.

Rhythmic variety helps. The highest and lowest notes are not always on the downbeat.

Good shape

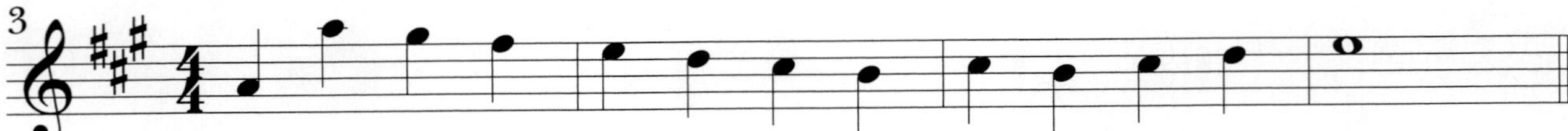

Rhythm can be constant if there is variety in direction and variety in the use of leaps and steps. Generally, a large leap should be followed by steps in the opposite direction.

Good shape

Repeating a motive but switching the order of the notes provides continuity as well as variety.

Good shape

The use of rests and repeated notes can also provide variety without disturbing the basic melodic contour.

Counterpoint is note against note, reflecting the linear (horizontal) movement of two or more melodies and how they relate to one another. Harmony is the vertical alignment of notes that form chords. Melody with accompaniment is primarily harmonic in nature; counterpoint does exist, but is not emphasized. You need to be sensitive to both vertical and horizontal relationships. Study the following examples carefully.

When all parts move in the same rhythm, the counterpoint is classified as 1:1. All tones are generally in agreement with each other. Nonchord tones may be used, but they need to be consonant with the other pitches.

The acceptable single line 1:1 example consists of broken chords in both hands. The seventh interval is part of the dominant-seventh and is therefore acceptable. The poor single line 1:1 example contains passing tones in the right hand that form too many consecutive dissonances against the left hand, and thus is not acceptable. The suspensions in the first chordal 1:1 example are quite common and are acceptable. The hands do not agree harmonically with each other in the second chordal 1:1 example, and therefore this is a poor example.

Movement involving two notes to one is classified as 2:1. Either of the moving notes may be dissonant to the harmony but, with the exception of passing tones, generally both are not dissonant.

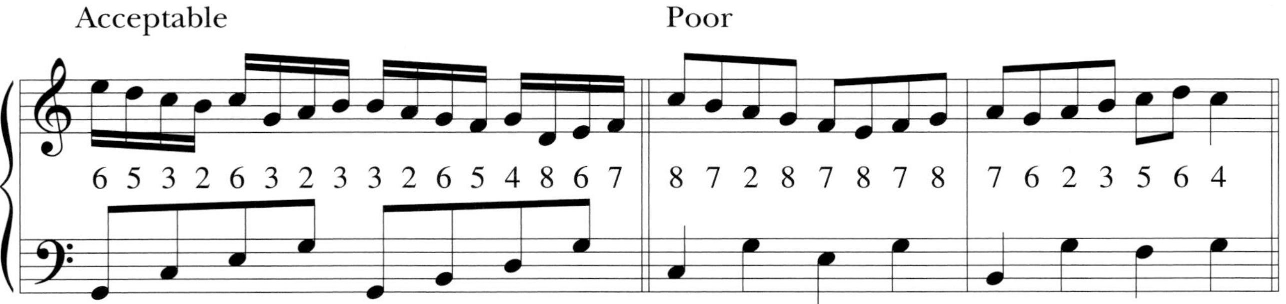

All of the nonchord tones in the acceptable 2:1 example are treated properly. In the poor 2:1 example, there are too many dissonances on consecutive beats, creating a disconnect between the implied harmonies of each hand.

Rhythmic movement that incorporates three or more notes to one note can be all harmonic or use two or more nonchord tones. With the exception of multiple passing tones, each nonchord tone needs to be surrounded by chord tones.

The preceding example is typical of piano music that incorporates a broken chord pattern in the left hand and melodic activity in the right hand. Notice that the majority of the notes in the melody are harmonic.

Let us also briefly address the nature of piano music, which is wide in its variety of styles. The hands work together but independently as well. Writing mistakes made by students often include too many independent lines for each hand, chord structures exceeding a typical pianist's reach, limiting the hands to narrow ranges, and cross voicing between the hands. Understanding voicing in piano music is also difficult to grasp—what looks like a single line often consists of two or more parts.

Since this book is primarily about harmony, the student is encouraged to first concentrate on presenting the harmonic structures in a clear fashion, and then determining appropriate melodic lines.

FOUR-PART CHORDAL STYLES

Relatively little piano music is written in a four-part, quasi-choral style. Such writing is not particularly idiomatic for the instrument because, compared with a choir, the piano has a very limited capacity for sustaining the sound of a chord. Besides this fact, the piano's considerable range (over seven octaves) and the ability of the hands to execute a wide variety of configurations give composers for the piano an enormous number of ways to express their musical ideas.

Piano writing has two basic four-part chordal styles, from which a number of more elaborate configurations may be derived. The former involves the playing of a three-part chord in the left hand and a single note in the right hand (A), and the latter, precisely the reverse (B).

The following pages exemplify how the two previous examples above may be converted into more elaborate settings for the piano.

A1 **Andante**

A2 **Allegretto**

A3 **Moderato**

A4 **Semplice**

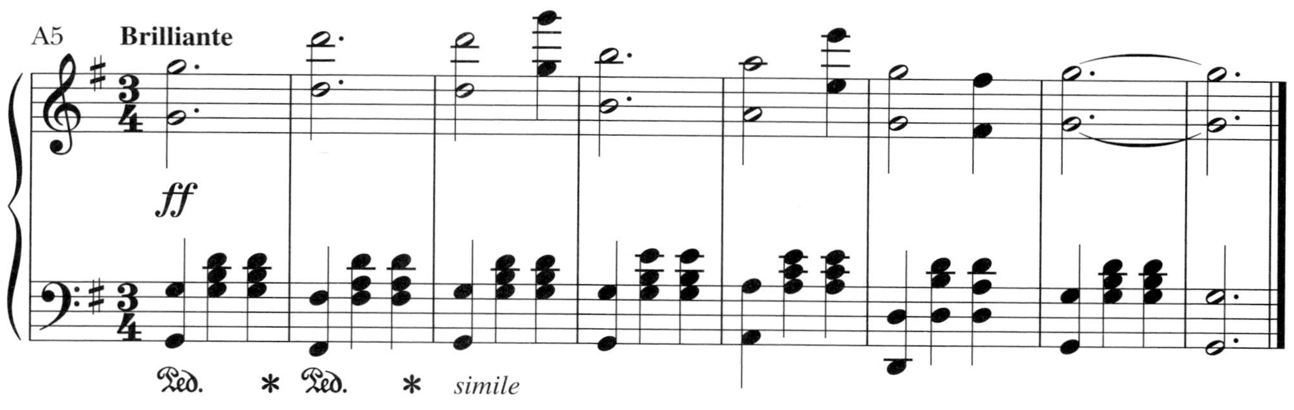
A5
Brilliante
ff
Ped. * Ped. * simile

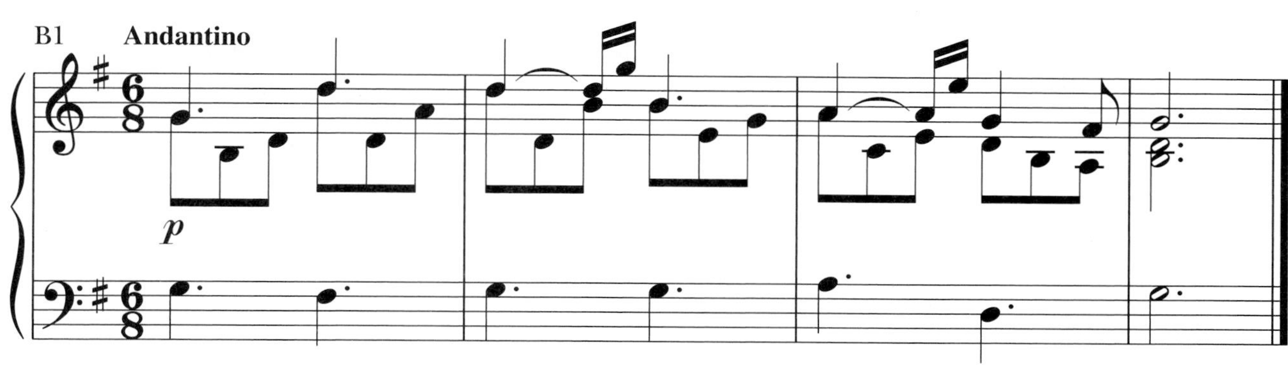
B1
Andantino
p

B2
Alla marcia
f

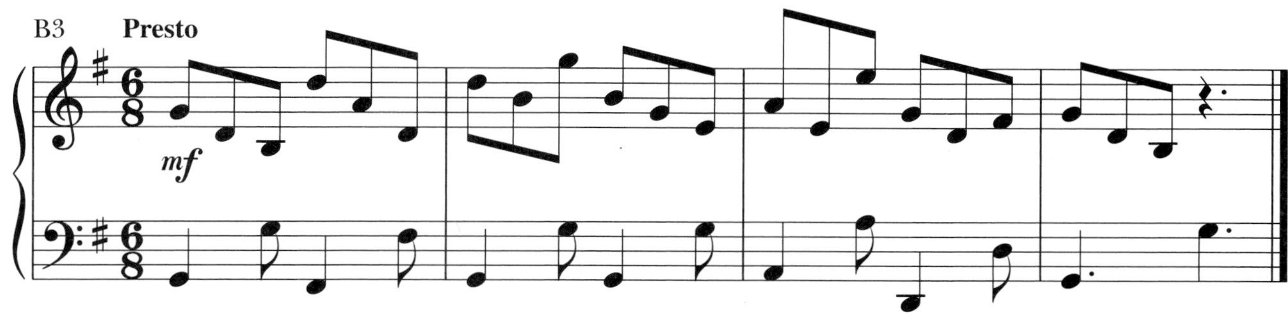
B3
Presto
mf

Note:

a. Although all of the elaborations of the two basic chordal styles demonstrate considerable freedom in handling parts, the basic principles of voice leading are not violated.

b. Each configuration fits the hands well. This is an important consideration in writing piano music.

c. A general direction as to tempo and character (e.g., Brilliante) is placed above the meter signature, and the dynamic markings are placed between the staves.

d. Two examples make use of the sustaining pedal. When the hand cannot be in continuous contact with the keys (as in the case of the left hand in A3 and A5), the sustaining pedal is used if it is desirable to sustain the sound.

e. The figuration in the left hand in A2 is known as an *Alberti bass.* It is named after the composer Domenico Alberti, who used it excessively in his piano music.

The exercises that follow are related to the materials on pages 197–203. The piano accompaniment is covered on pages 207–208.

SUGGESTIONS AND STRATEGIES

Whether you are working from a given accompaniment pattern, a given melody, a given harmonic progression, or creating your own piece, the following strategies are useful:

1. Determine/choose the key;
2. Identify/choose the phrase and cadence structure;
3. Decide what harmonies to use/have been used as you approach the cadence;
4. Decide/determine what harmonies to use/have been used to set the phrases in motion;
5. Invent an effective bass/melody line;
6. Add any necessary inner voices.

Pay attention to styles suggested by given melodies or accompaniment patterns. Be sensitive to harmonic rhythm, melodic contours, and rhythmic structures. Feel free to elaborate on the accompaniments given on the previous pages, or even emulate passages in piano music with which you are familiar. Your goal is to create a logical, cohesive piece for the piano.

EXERCISES

A. Add a right hand part to complete the piece.

B. Add a left hand part to complete the piece.

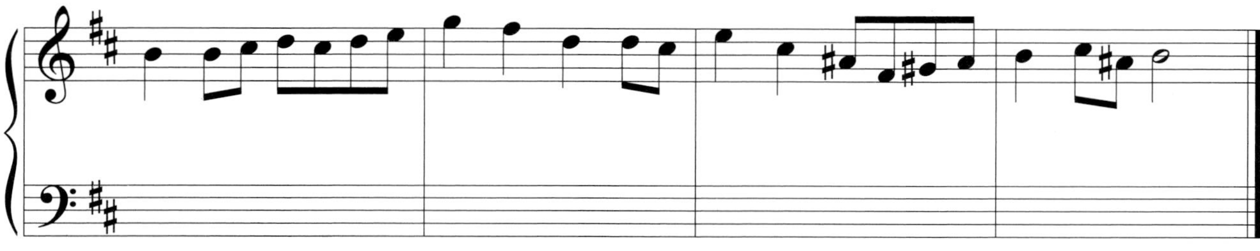

C. Create a two-phrase piano piece using the following progression:

I - vi - ii6 - V - I6 - ii6 - I^6_4 - V - I - IV - V - vi - ii - V - I

You choose key, meter, harmonic rhythm, and style.

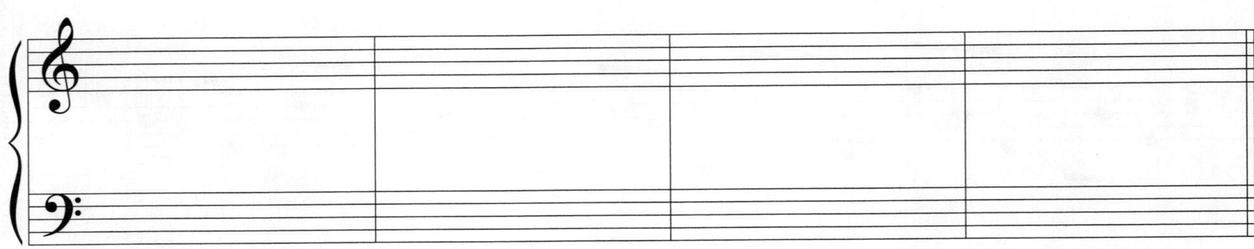

D. Create a two-phrase piano piece. All parameters are of your own choosing.

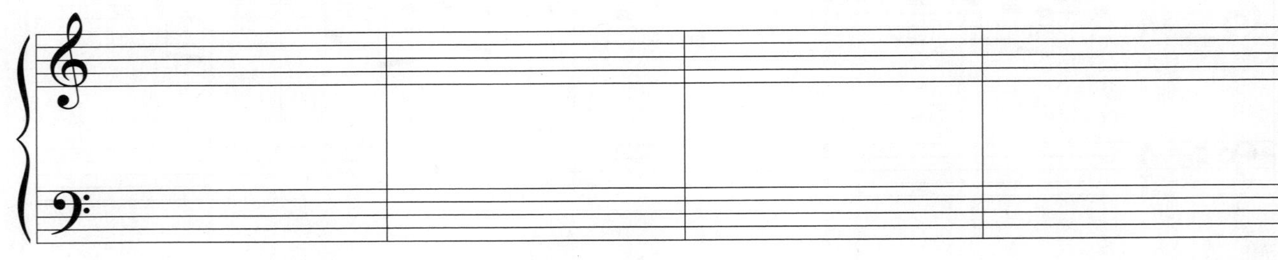

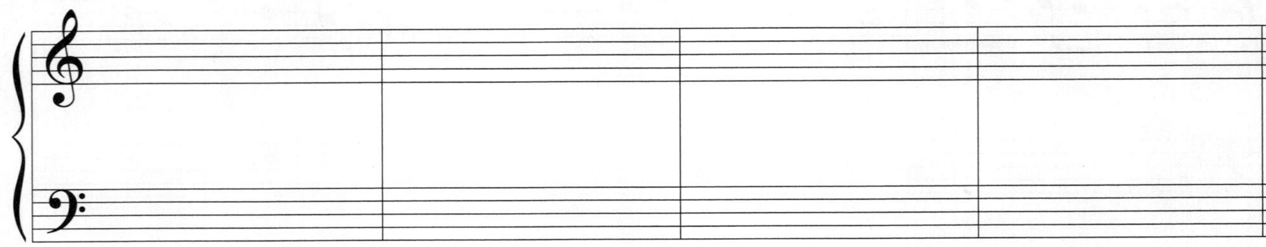

THE PIANO ACCOMPANIMENT

When the piano is used to accompany another instrument, the composer is not compelled to write the melody in the piano part. As a result, piano accompaniments display a wide variety of configurations. Typically, the piano part will accomplish the following:

1. Supply the harmony through an established accompaniment pattern.
2. Supply the harmony and a countermelody.

The following examples are based upon some of the settings in the previous section. They should be studied carefully, with particular attention to the function of the right hand.

Note:

a. The bar lines for the solo instrument are separated from those for the piano to facilitate reading.

b. Dynamic markings are given for both the piano and solo instrument. They are placed beneath the staff for the latter.

c. In A3, the countermelody in the right hand violates no voice-leading principles either with reference to the melody or to the accompaniment.

Sometimes both the piano and solo instrument are given the melody, as the following example shows:

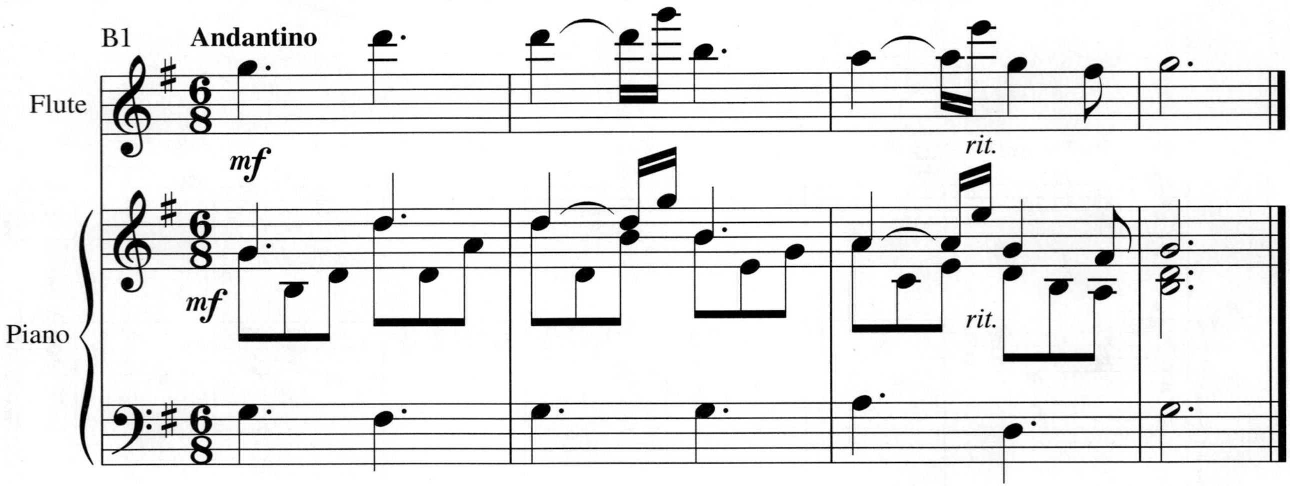

In all exercises that involve a solo instrument with piano accompaniment, students are advised to:

1. Equip themselves with manuscript paper.
2. Harmonize the melody according to the six procedures described in Chapters 11 and 16.
3. Decide upon an accompaniment that would seem to suit the character of the melody.
4. Write a countermelody when possible.

EXERCISES

Invent piano accompaniments for the following melodies.

Molto moderato
for violin
2

PART THREE

HARMONY IN COMMON PRACTICE
The Chromatic Vocabulary

18
Secondary Dominants

It is always possible to precede a major or minor triad with a chord that can be analyzed as its dominant. For instance, if a G major triad is written, then a D major triad written before it could be considered a V chord, and indeed it is one, provided that G is a I chord.

If, however, G is not a tonic chord but, for example, the dominant chord in the key of C, then D is no longer a V chord. Yet its relationship to G is still that of a dominant to a tonic. Under these circumstances, the D major triad is called a *secondary dominant*, and in the key of C is known as V of V (written V/V).

A secondary dominant of G might not always be a V/V. If G is not the dominant, then the V of G will be V/X, with X representing whatever G is in the key.

From the explanation provided, it follows that a major or minor triad on each scale degree can be preceded by a chord that stands in a dominant relationship to it.

Study the following examples carefully:

Note:

a. Secondary dominants are always chromatic chords; in other words, each contains at least one pitch that is not diatonic.

b. Secondary dominants are commonly used with the addition of the minor seventh and thus become major-minor seventh chords (V7/X).

c. As seventh chords, secondary dominants are used in all inversions.

d. The resolution of a secondary dominant seventh is the same as that of a dominant seventh (leading tone up by step, seventh down by step).

e. Observe the doubling at the asterisk. You normally would double the root or scale degree one, but this alternate doubling creates a smoother voice leading.

f. A secondary dominant may resolve to another secondary dominant rather than to a diatonic chord. For instance, a V7/ii may resolve to a V7/V, which is a secondary dominant built on the ii chord.

THE FUNCTION OF SECONDARY DOMINANTS

Secondary dominants have the effect of strengthening the harmonic movement to the chords that follow them. In addition to the root movement of a descending fifth, this strengthening effect is produced first by the resolution of the *secondary leading tone* to the root of the subsequent chord, and second, if the seventh is present, by its resolution to the third of that chord. The secondary dominant, then, allows the major or minor triad that follows it to sound like a temporary (or fleeting) tonic. The latter chord is said to be *tonicized*, and the process is known as *tonicization*. The function of the secondary dominant, therefore, is very similar to that of the dominant.

The following two examples represent phrases that terminate with a half cadence. Except for the chromatic pitches in measures 2 and 3, they are identical.

Note:

a. In the second example, the movement to IV is strengthened by the alteration of I^6_5 to V^6_5/IV, and the movement to V is similarly strengthened by changing ii^6_5 to V^6_5/V.

b. The half cadence in the second example creates a greater sense of repose than that in the first, because V is preceded by its dominant.

The exercises that follow are related to the materials introduced on pages 211–213. Deceptive resolutions of secondary dominants are covered on page 222.

SUGGESTIONS AND STRATEGIES

The accurate notation of secondary dominants depends upon the logical application of a few simple steps described below.

Preparation

When Roman numerals with figures are given, try following these procedures:

1. Use the formula V/X or V7/X.
2. For all resolutions in this group of exercises, determine the root of the X chord.
3. Determine the root of the chord that is a *perfect fifth above* (or a perfect fourth below), the X chord, and jot down the chord's letter names (e.g., C E G B).

4. Add accidental(s) to make the chord a major triad or a major-minor seventh chord. [There will always be at least one accidental on the third, fifth, or seventh of the chord.]
5. Notate the *bass,* and proceed with the exercise.

Part Writing

When you resolve the secondary dominants, make sure that:

1. The seventh resolves *downward by step.*
2. The secondary leading tone (the third of the chord) resolves *upward by step.* This resolution will involve motion to the root of the tonicized chord.

An example is given.

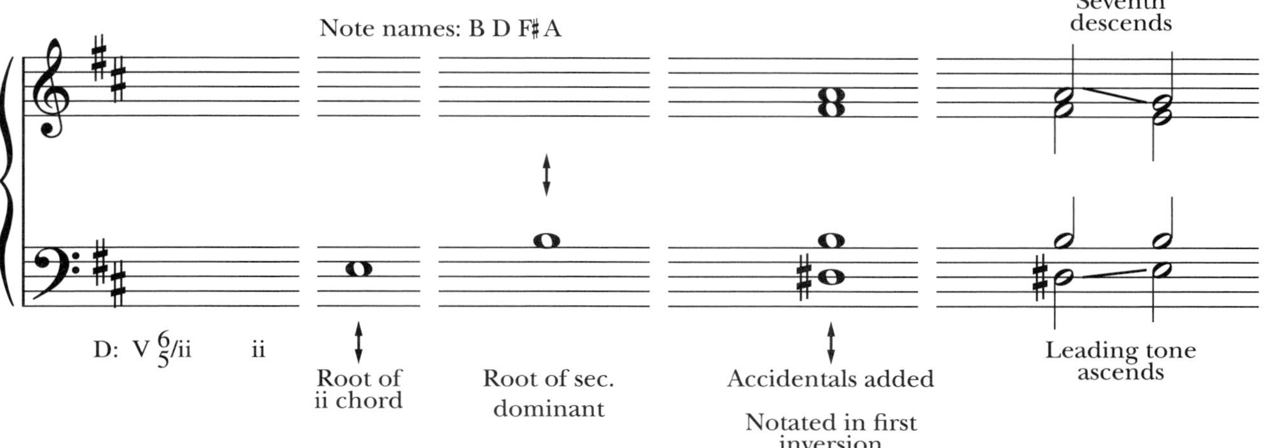

Preparation

When the figured bass symbols are given, the procedures are slightly different from the ones described above:

1. Identify bass notes that have been chromatically altered, or that have figures that show chromatic alterations. In major keys, these are the secondary dominants. (In minor keys, the same applies, except that the leading tone *always*, and the sixth scale degree *sometimes*, have chromatic alterations that do not represent secondary dominants.)
2. Determine the root of the chord that follows the chromatic chord, and on what scale degree it is built (e.g., ii, iii, IV, etc.).
3. The chord that precedes this chord is its secondary dominant.
4. Make a harmonic analysis of the entire phrase, and then follow the steps described previously.
5. Chromatic alterations are always given in the figured bass or as chromatic bass notes. Do not add accidentals that are not indicated.

SECONDARY DOMINANTS PRELIMINARY EXERCISE

The following exercise has two parts—a top line with no key signature (not in the context of a key), and a piano score with a key signature for SATB format (working in the context of a given key).

For the top line, precede each given note with a note that is a P4th below or a P5th above (a dominant relationship to the given not). Using that dominant relationship note as the root, write a major triad or a major-minor seventh chord. Then in the piano score area, in SATB fromat, using those exact pitches (placing accidentals where necessary), write and resolve the seondary dominants in the context of the given keys. The first measure of each system has been done as an example.

EXERCISES

A. Write, and resolve, the following secondary dominants.

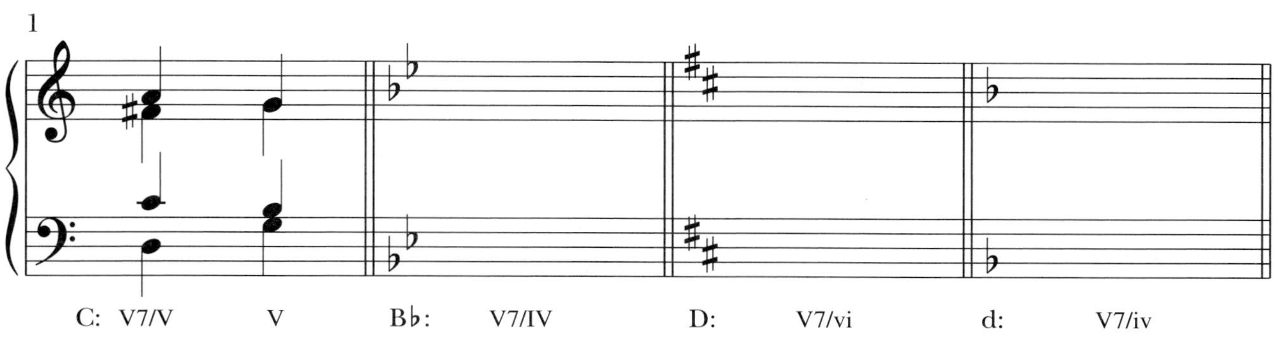

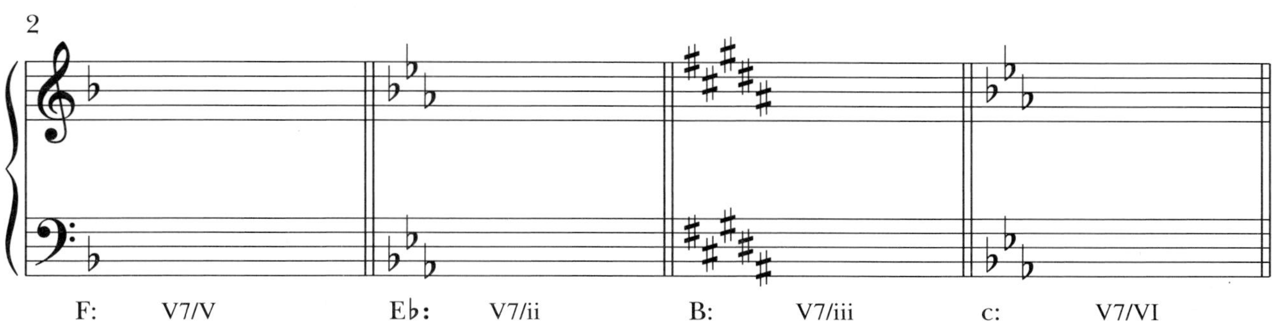

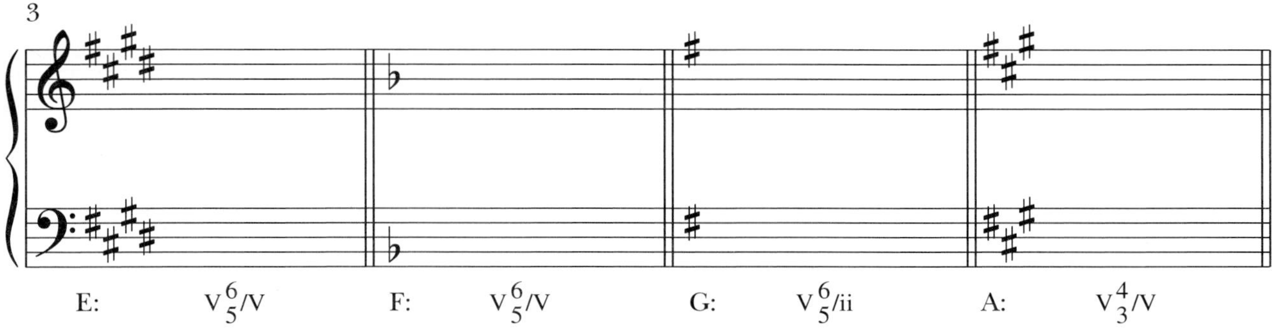

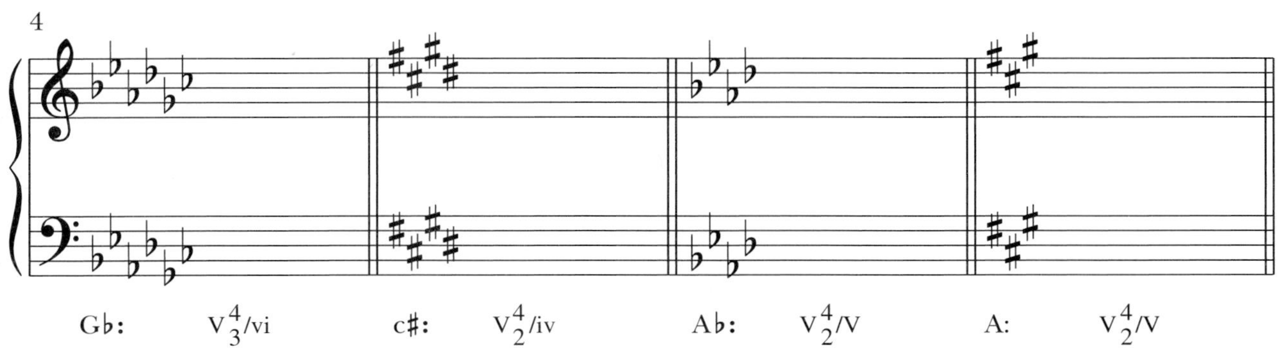

B. Add parts for alto and tenor.

C. Add parts for soprano, alto, and tenor.

D. Harmonize the following in open score.

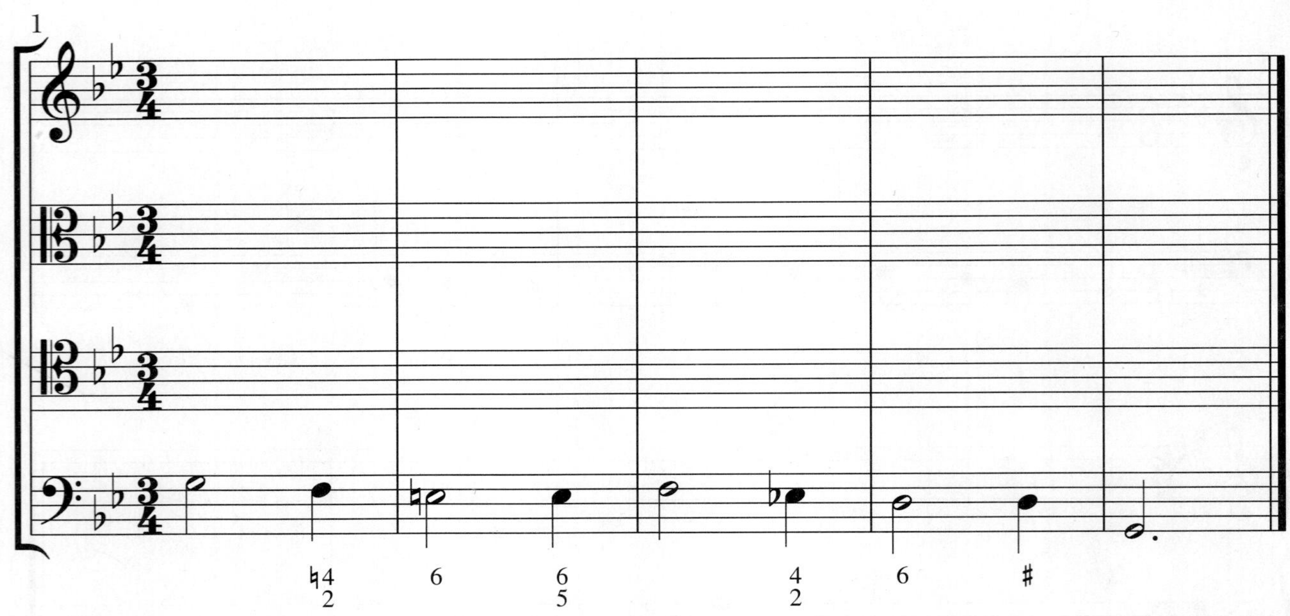

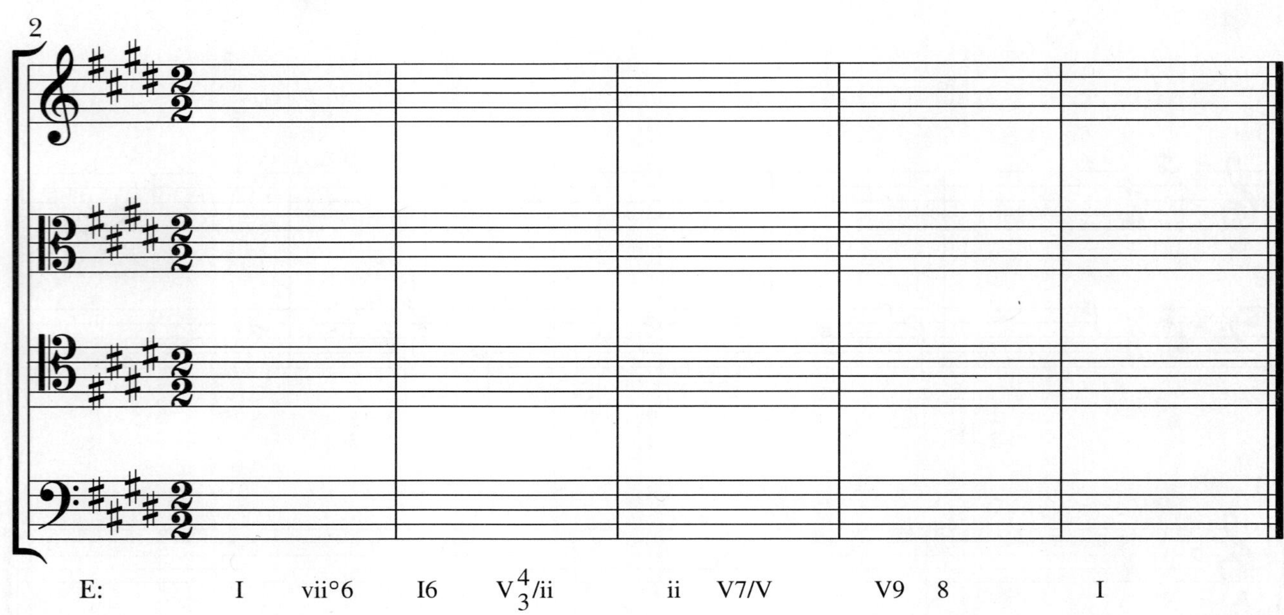

E. Add parts for alto, tenor, and bass.

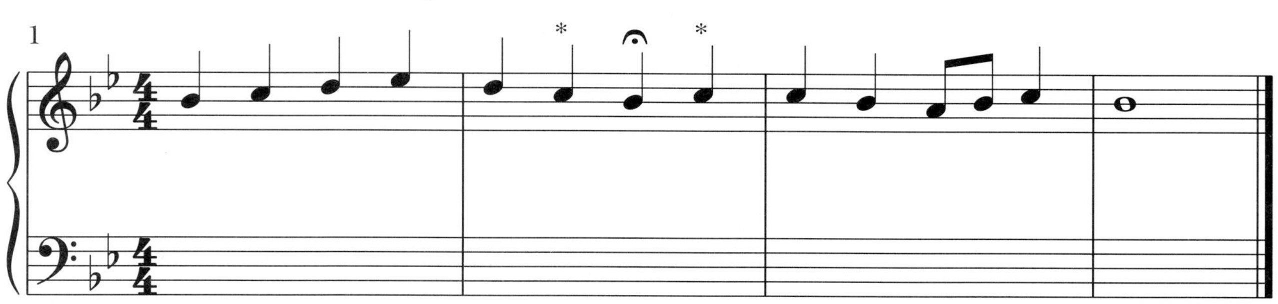

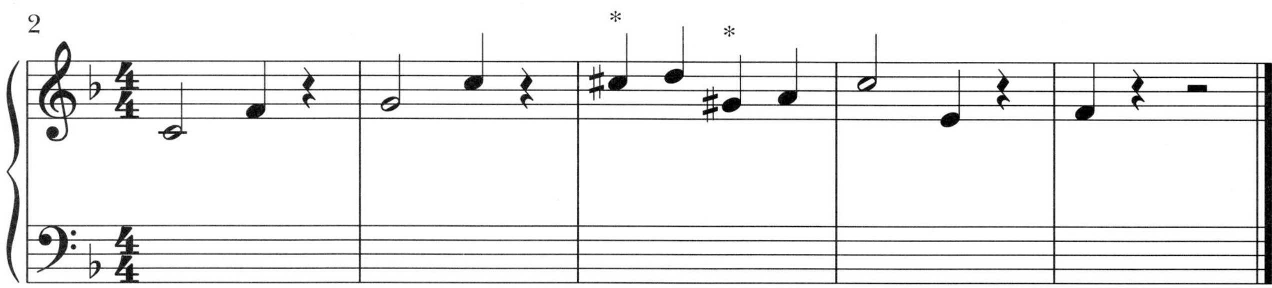

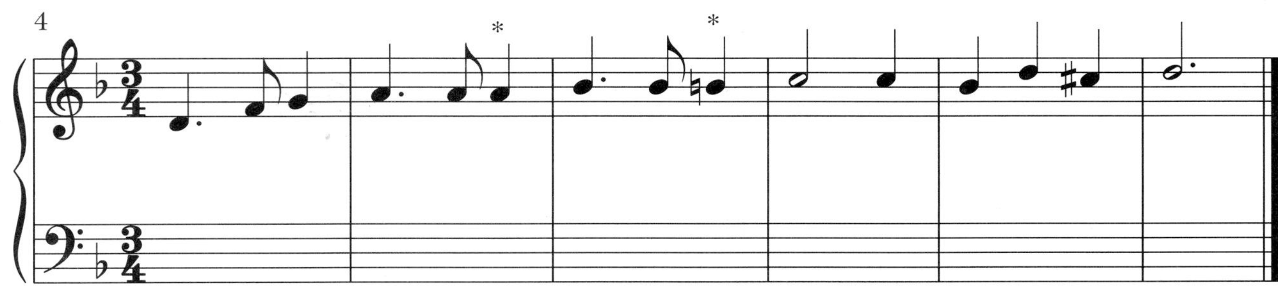

* indicates that a secondary dominant should be used

DECEPTIVE RESOLUTIONS OF SECONDARY DOMINANTS

The most natural resolution of V7 is to I, as in the authentic cadence. V7, however, frequently resolves to vi, a harmonic motion that occurs in the deceptive cadence. In the former progression, the root motion is a perfect fifth downward; in the latter, a second (major or minor, depending on the mode) upward.

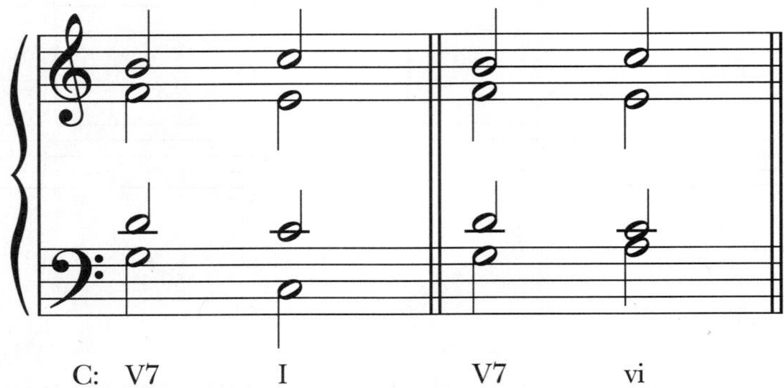

Similarly, the secondary dominant naturally resolves to a chord whose root is a perfect fifth below its own. It may, however, resolve *deceptively* (in the manner of an ordinary dominant) by root motion ascending by step.

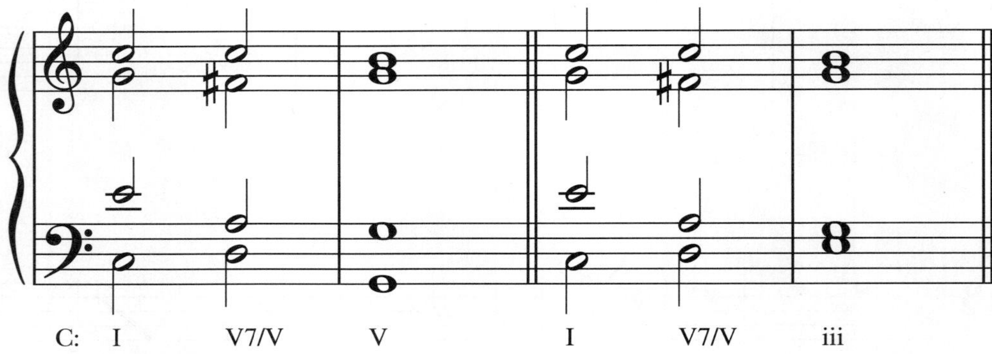

Notice that the third of the secondary dominant, which has a leading tone function, still resolves upward by step in the deceptive resolution.

The two root movement progressions shown below will help clarify the spelling of secondary dominants and their resolutions.

The first progression uses the root movement of fifths:

I – IV – VII – III – VI – II – V – I.

Use this progression to determine which chord is to be altered to become the V/X. Locate chord X, back up one chord, and turn that chord into a major triad or a major-minor seventh chord. For example, to spell V/V, the chord that precedes V in the fifths progression is II. Add accidentals to the II chord to make it a major triad or a major-minor seventh chord, turning it into the V/V.

The second progression uses the root movement of seconds:

I – II – III – IV – V – VI – VII – I.

Use this progression to determine the chord that follows the secondary dominant when V/X resolves deceptively. Locate the root of the V/X in the progression of seconds, then move one chord to the right. For example, the V/V is built on the II chord. A deceptive resolution of V/V will therefore move to the III chord.

EXERCISES

A. Using the given progressions, invent four-measure phrases for soprano, alto, tenor, and bass. The harmonic rhythm is given.

19
Secondary Diminished Seventh Chords

A diminished seventh chord is constructed by adding to a diminished triad a pitch that is a diminished seventh above its root (vii°7 in the minor key is a diatonic diminished seventh chord). The result is a sonority with four pitches stacked in minor thirds.

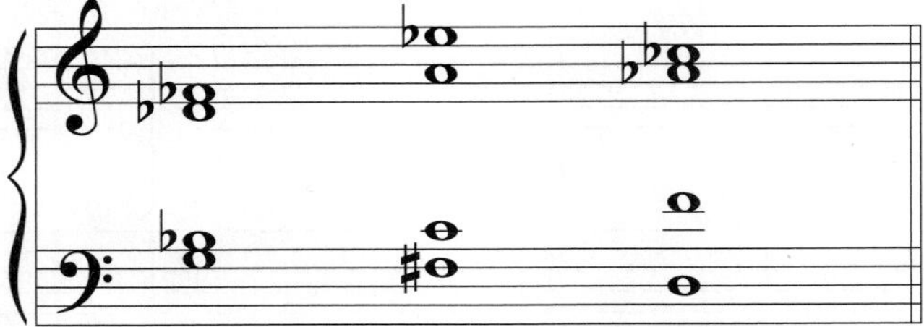

Example 7 (p. 180) in Chapter 15 shows a vii°7 resolving to i. In that resolution, the chord functioned as a dominant.

Since V7–i may be substituted by vii°7–i without causing a change in harmonic function, it follows that, for example, V7/V–V may similarly be substituted by vii°7/V–V. Thus, secondary diminished seventh chords may be used as secondary dominants.

Study the following examples carefully:

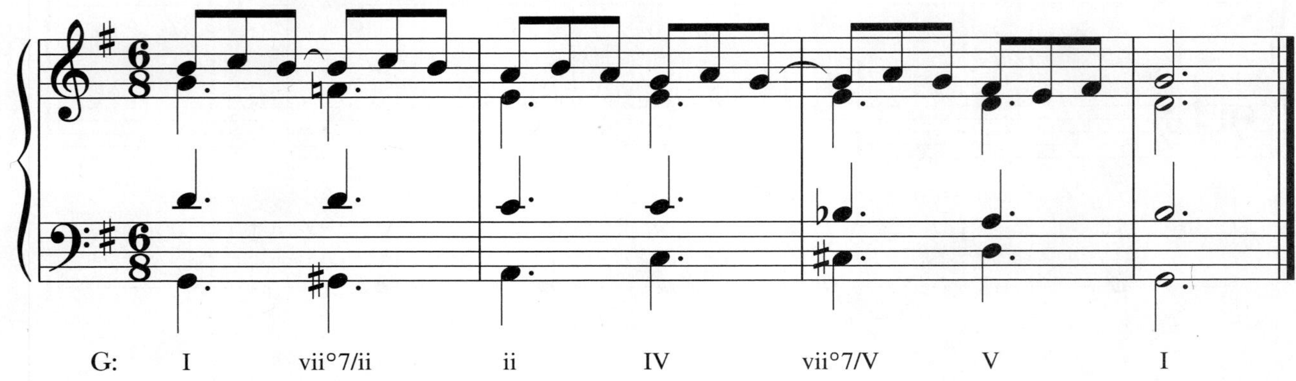

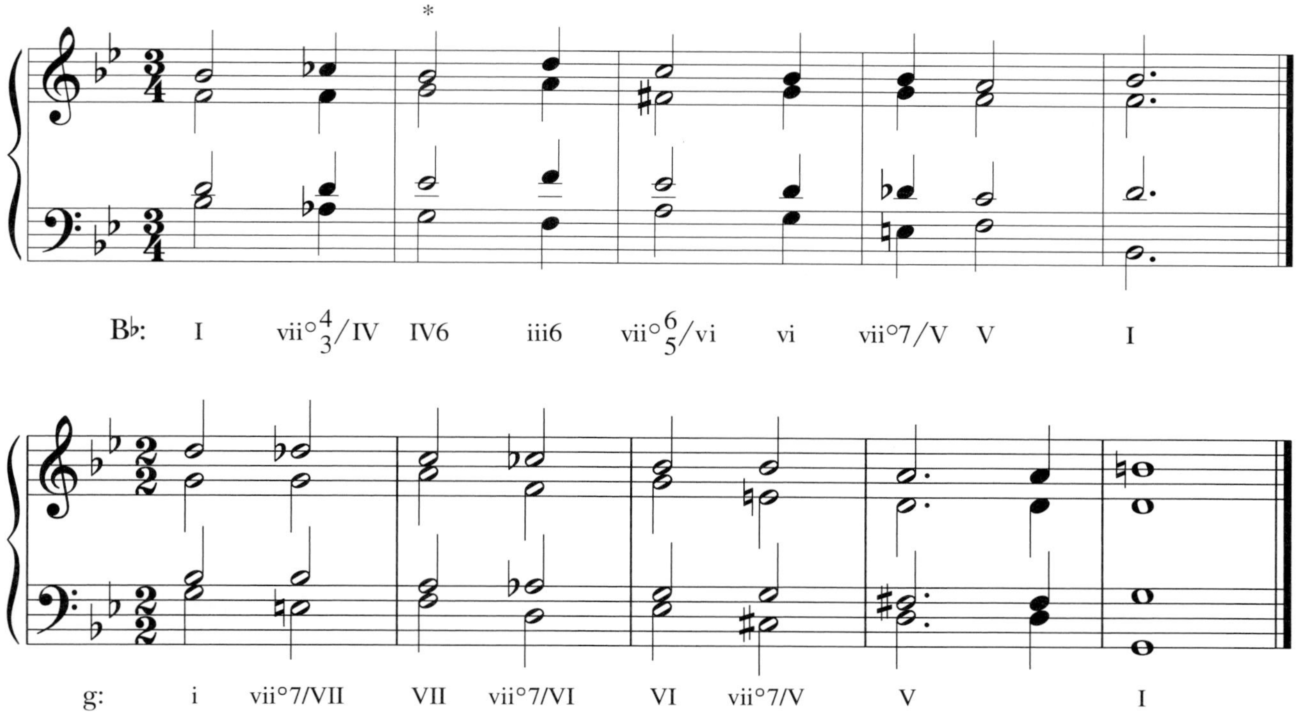

Note:

a. Each diminished seventh chord is built on a root that is a *minor second* below the root of its chord of resolution. Thus, each diminished seventh chord is in a leading tone relationship with its successor.

b. In resolution, the root of the diminished seventh chord moves *upward* by step, and its seventh moves *downward* by step. The remaining pitches resolve in either of the following ways:

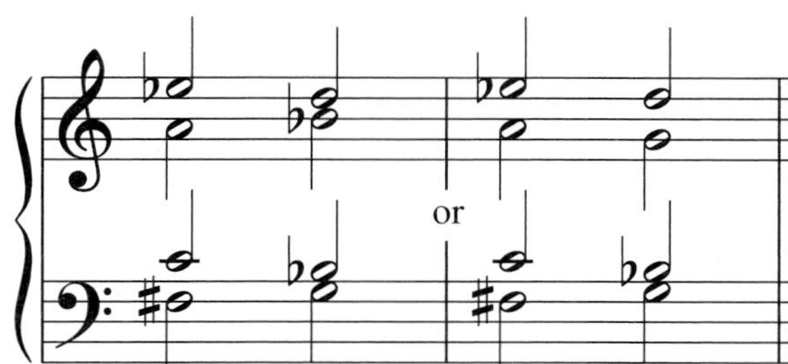

Of the two resolutions, the first is stronger in terms of line, because the two diminished fifths are more naturally resolved. The second, however, gives a better doubling in the successive chord. The movement from a diminished fifth to a perfect fifth is not considered to be parallel fifths.

c. Observe the doubling at the asterisk. You normally would double the root or scale degree one, but the alternate doubling creates a smoother voice leading.

d. Diminished seventh chords are used freely in root position, first inversion, and second inversion. The third inversion is less frequently used because it normally resolves to a $^6_4$ chord. (As a means of modulation this resolution will be found to be valuable.)

e. These examples are variants of those on pages 212–213 ("Secondary Dominants") and should be compared to them.

THE FUNCTION OF SECONDARY DIMINISHED SEVENTH CHORDS

Like secondary dominants, secondary diminished seventh chords have the effect of strengthening the harmonic movement to the chords that follow them. They produce this effect first by the resolution of the secondary leading tone to the root of the subsequent chord, and second, by the resolution of the seventh to the fifth of that chord. Thus, secondary diminished seventh chords also tonicize major or minor triads that follow them and may be said to have a dominant function.

The two examples below, variants of the examples on page 214 of the previous chapter, represent phrases that terminate with a half cadence. Once again, they are identical with the exception of the chromatic pitches in measures two and three in the second example.

Note:

a. In the second example, the movement to IV is strengthened by the alteration of iii7 to vii°7/IV, and the movement to V is similarly strengthened by changing IV7 to vii°7/V.

b. The half cadence in the second example creates a greater sense of repose than that in the first, because V is preceded by its secondary diminished seventh, which has a dominant function.

The exercises that follow are related to the materials introduced on pages 224–226. Irregular resolutions of secondary diminished seventh chords are covered on page 234.

SUGGESTIONS AND STRATEGIES

The accurate notation of secondary diminished seventh chords depends upon the logical application of steps that are very similar to those described in the previous chapter.

Preparation

When Roman numerals with figures are given, try following these procedures:

1. Identify the secondary diminished seventh chords (vii°7/X).
2. For all resolutions in this group of exercises, determine the *root* of the X chord.
3. Determine the root of the chord that is a *minor second below* the X chord (e.g., if the root of X is D, then the note a minor second below D is C sharp). Jot down the chord's letter names, C E G B.
4. Add accidental(s) to make the chord a diminshed seventh. [There will always be at least one accidental on the root, third, fifth, or seventh of the chord.]
5. Notate the *bass*, and proceed with the exercise.

Part Writing

When you resolve the secondary dimished sevenths, make sure that:

1. The root (secondary leading tone) resolves *upward by half step.*
2. The seventh resolves *downward* by step.
3. The third and fifth resolve by step (or half step) to the appropriate notes in the chord that follows.

When a figured bass is given, the chromatic alterations could indicate either secondary diminished sevenths or secondary dominants.

The procedures for determining what they are, however, follow the same patterns.

1. Identify bass notes that have been chromatically altered, or that have figures that show chromatic alterations.
2. Determine the root of the chord that follows the chromatic chord, and on what scale degree it is built (e.g., ii, iii, IV, etc.).
3. The chord that precedes this chord is either its secondary diminished seventh or secondary dominant. The structure of the chromatic chord—dd or Mm—gives you the information.
4. Make a harmonic analysis of the entire phrase, and then follow the steps described previously.

PRELIMINARY EXERCISE

The following exercise has two parts—a top line with no key signature (not in the context of a key) and a piano score with a key signature for SATB format (working in the context of a given key).

For the top line, precede each given note with a note that is a minor second below (a leading tone relationship to the given note). Using that leading tone relationship note as the root, write a fully diminished seventh chord. Then in the piano score area, in SATB format, using those exact pitches (placing accidentals where necessary), write and resolve the secondary diminished sevenths in the context of the given keys. The first measure of each system has been done as an example.

2 vii$^{\circ 6}_{5}$/X
F: vii$^{\circ 6}_{5}$/ii ii
g: vii$^{\circ 6}_{5}$/iv iv
E♭: vii$^{\circ 6}_{5}$/vi vi
A: vii$^{\circ 6}_{5}$/iii iii
3 vii$^{\circ 4}_{3}$/X
D: vii$^{\circ 4}_{3}$/IV IV
d: vii$^{\circ 4}_{3}$/iv iv
C: vii$^{\circ 4}_{3}$/ii ii6
E: vii$^{\circ 4}_{3}$/vi vi6

EXERCISES

A. Write, and resolve, the following secondary diminished sevenths.

B. Add parts for alto and tenor.

C. Add parts for soprano, alto, and tenor.

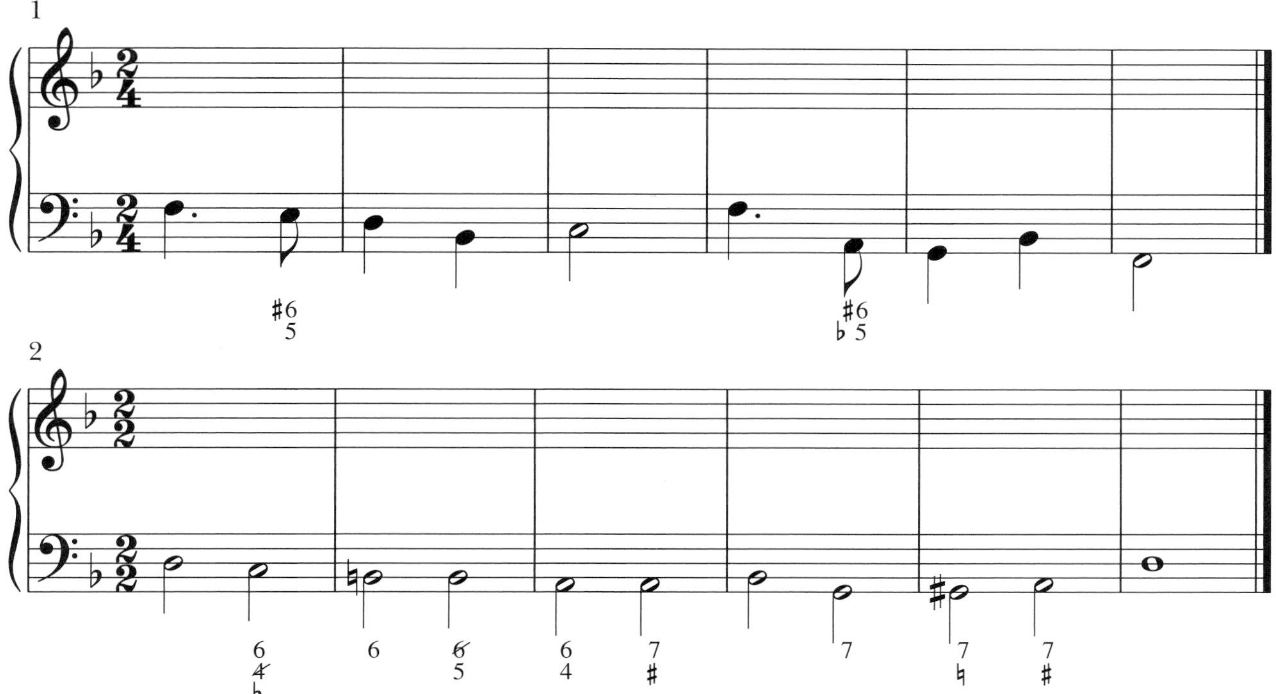

D. Harmonize the following phrases in open score.

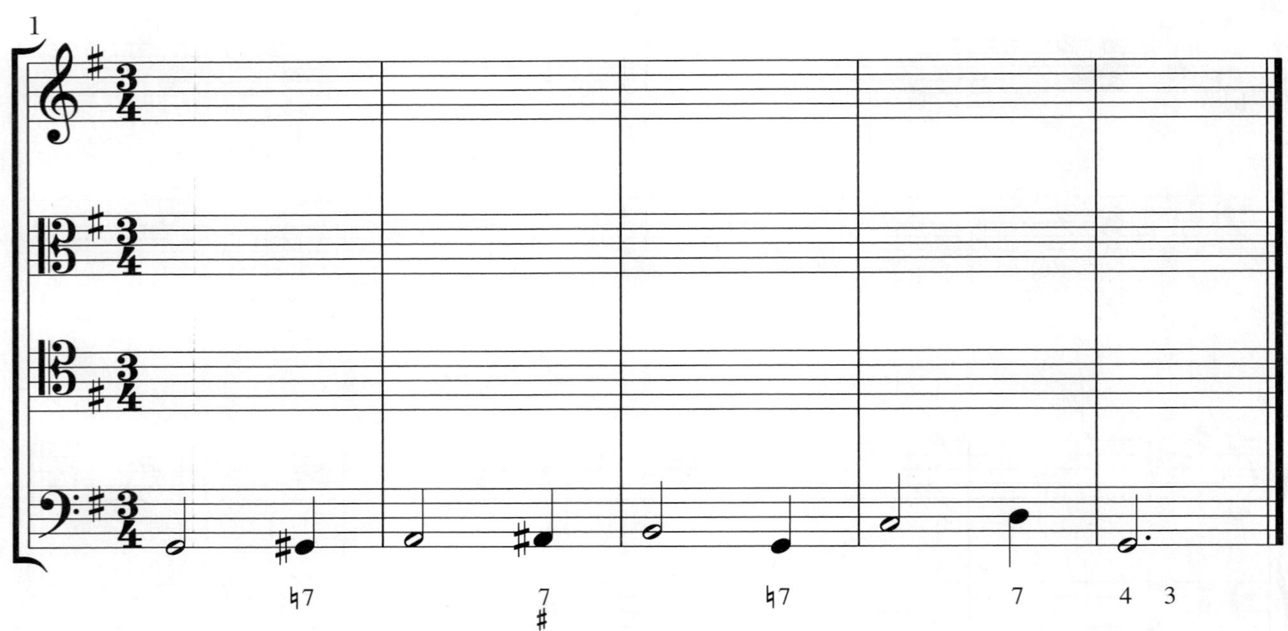

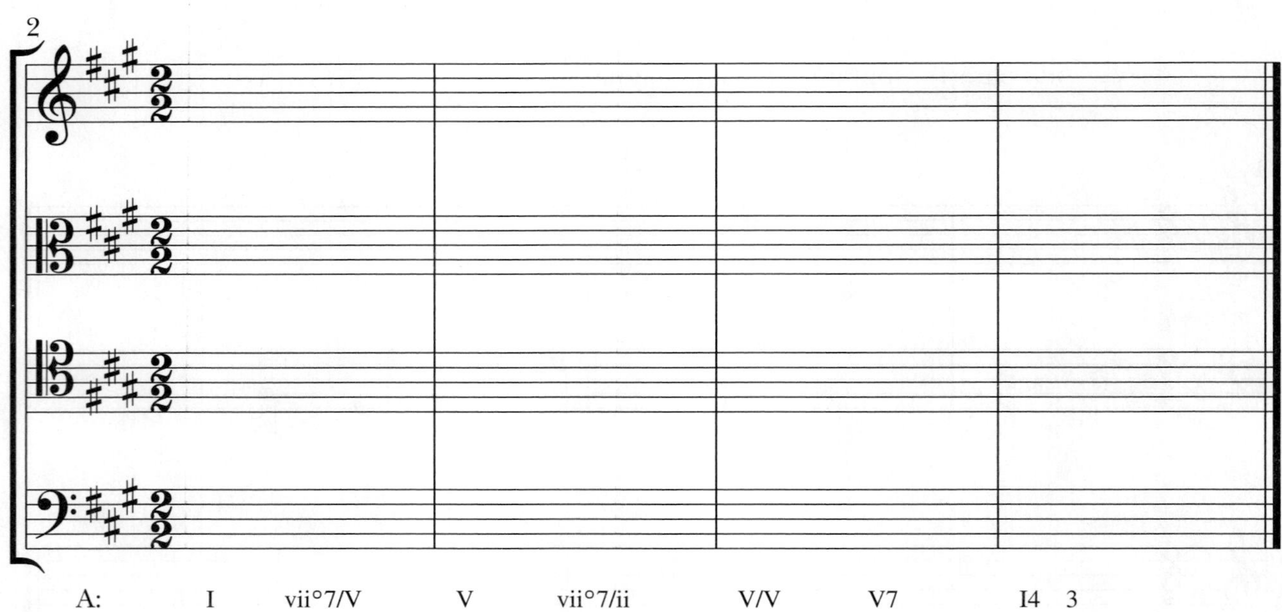

E. Add parts for alto, tenor, and bass.

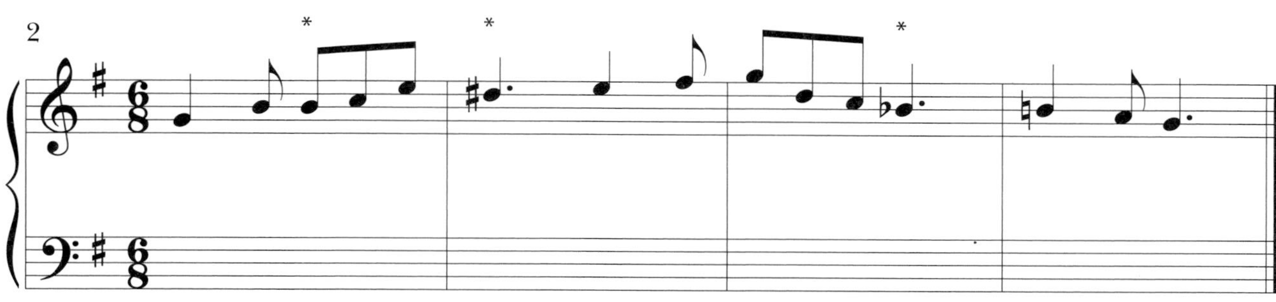

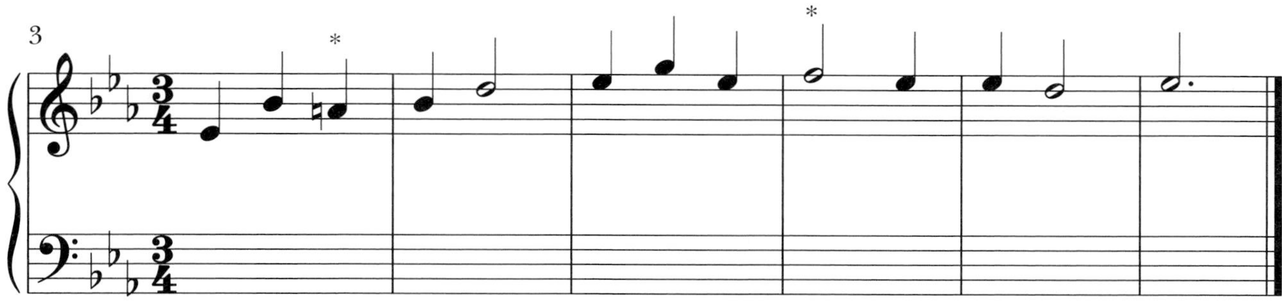

* indicates that a secondary diminished seventh should be used

IRREGULAR RESOLUTIONS OF DIMINISHED SEVENTH CHORDS

Any resolution of the diminished seventh chord that does not exploit the chord's dominant function may be called irregular. The two most common uses of the chord in this respect are:

1. The resolution of a diminished seventh chord to another diminished seventh chord.

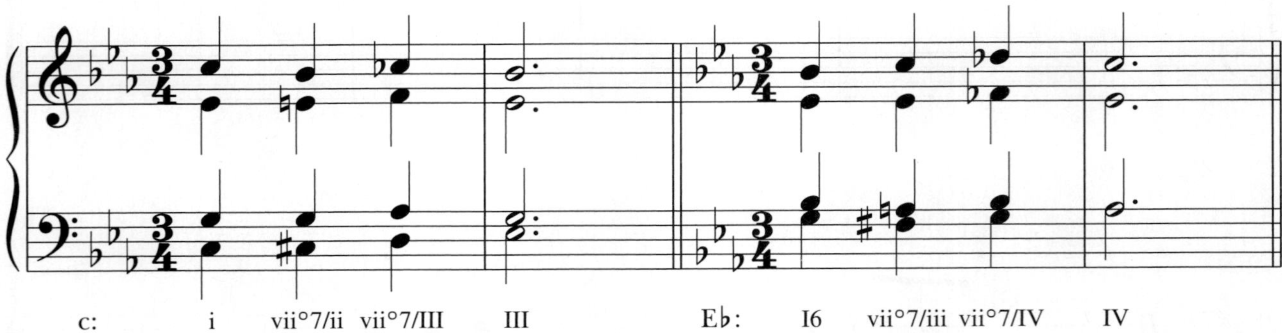

Note:

The movement from one diminished seventh to another involves similar motion of all voices by half steps, unless changing inversions.

2. The diminished seventh chord as a "passing" chord.

Note:

In this example, the resolution of the seventh of the diminished seventh chord is passive.

EXERCISES

A. Add parts for soprano, alto, and tenor.

B. Using the given progressions, invent four-measure phrases for soprano, alto, tenor, and bass. The harmonic rhythm is given.

20
Augmented Sixth Chords

The progressions below show the three common approaches to the dominant in the key of a minor.

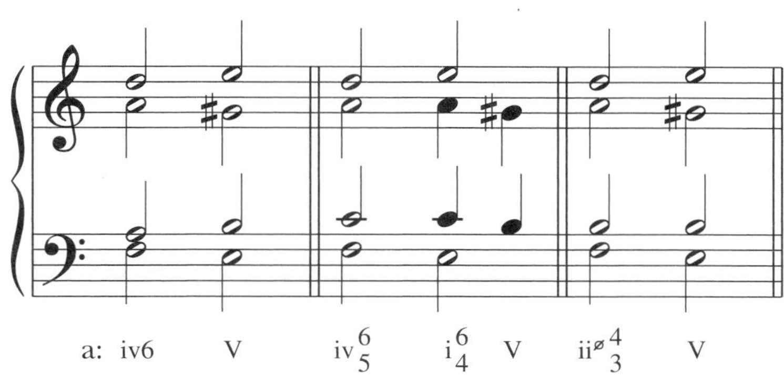

In each of these progressions, the movement to V can be strengthened by rewriting d^2 as $d\sharp^2$, so that there is a melodic movement of only a half step to the dominant pitch. The progressions will now be

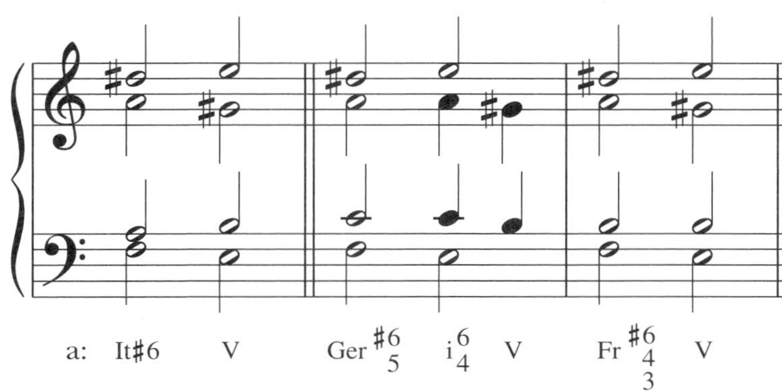

Each of the chords that precedes V is known as an augmented sixth chord, because in each case there exists an interval of an augmented sixth between the bass and soprano voice. The first is the *Italian sixth,* an altered iv6 chord; the second is the German sixth, an altered iv^{6}_{5} chord; the third is the French sixth, an altered $\text{ii}^{\varnothing 4}_{3}$ chord.

Note:

a. The interval of the augmented sixth resolves outward to the octave in each progression.

b. In the Italian sixth, the fifth is doubled.

c. All three of the augmented sixth chords contain a pitch that is a *major third above the bass.*

d. The German sixth also contains a pitch that is a *perfect fifth above the bass.*

e. The French sixth also contains a pitch that is an *augmented fourth above the bass.*

f. The intervallic construction of the augmented sixth chords from *root* up is: Italian—d3, M3; German—d3, M3, m3; French—M3, d3, M3.

Study the following examples carefully. They show the augmented sixth chords in different settings in both major and minor keys.

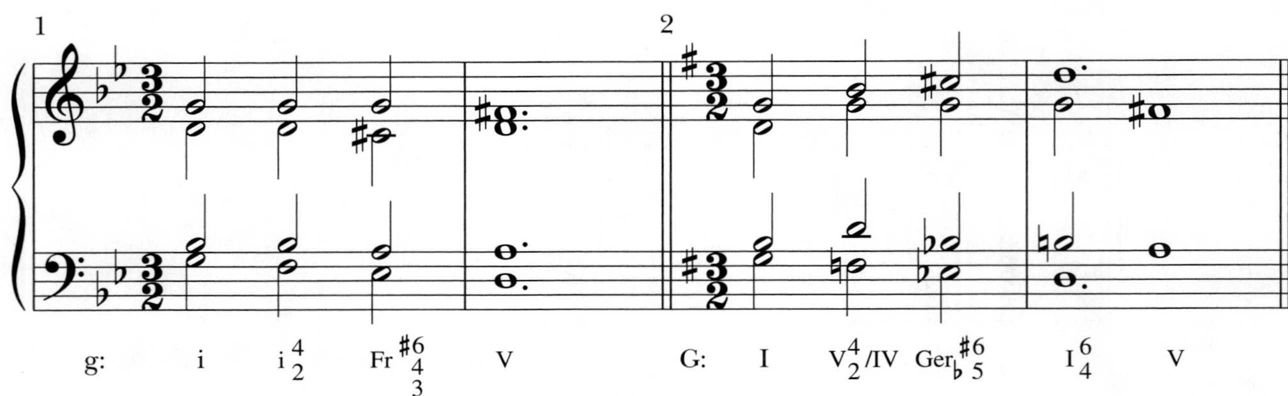

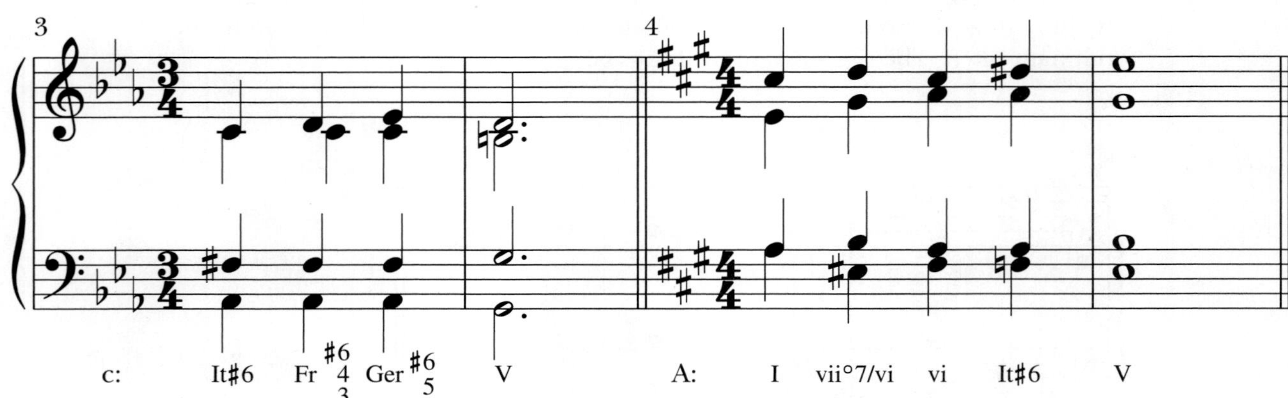

Note:

a. The interval of the augmented sixth may occur between the bass and any upper voice.

b. The direct resolution of the German sixth to V involves parallel fifths (see 3). This is an exceptional, but accepted, procedure.

c. In example 6, the German sixth is respelled with an A♯ instead of a B♭ (see *) so that the tenor's resolution to b is more natural.

d. Augmented sixth chords are used in both major and minor keys.

e. The seventh of the German sixth and French sixth resolves down by step.

THE FUNCTION OF AUGMENTED SIXTH CHORDS

The diatonic scale degrees (2 and 4) from which the augmented sixth chords are derived give information about the chords' predominant function. A comparison of the augmented sixth chords with secondary dominants and diminished sevenths helps to reveal their true role in the chromatic vocabulary.

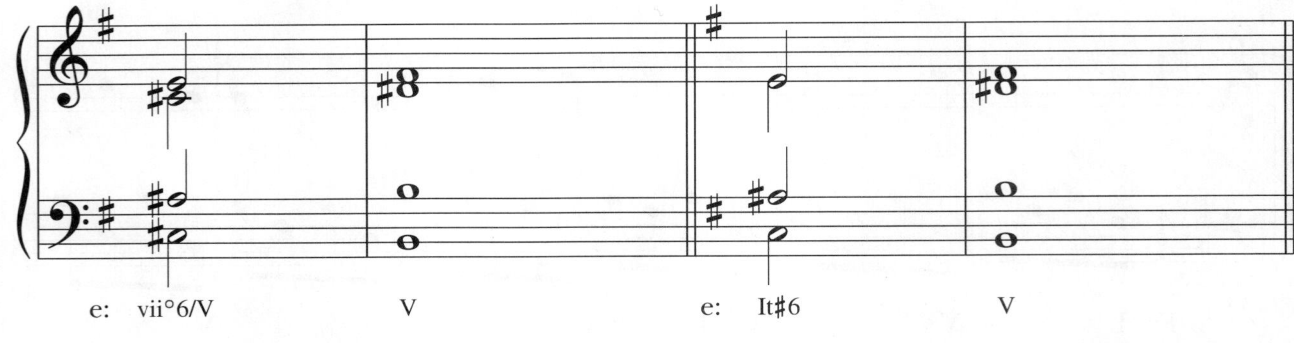

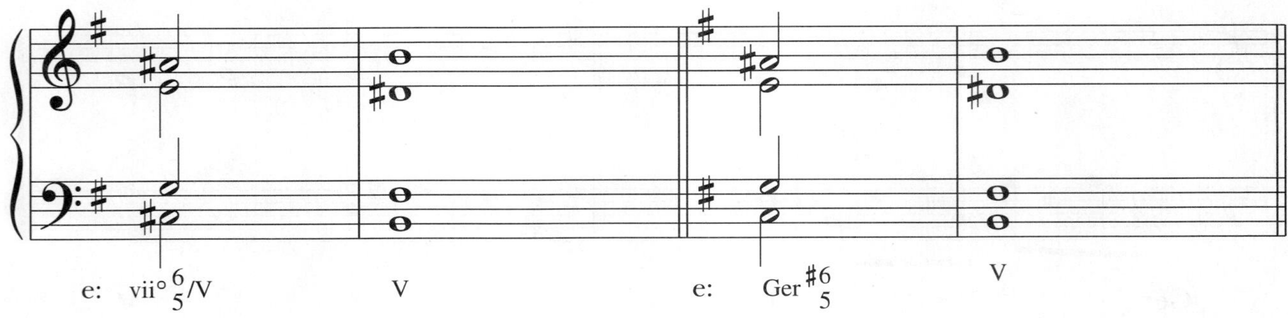

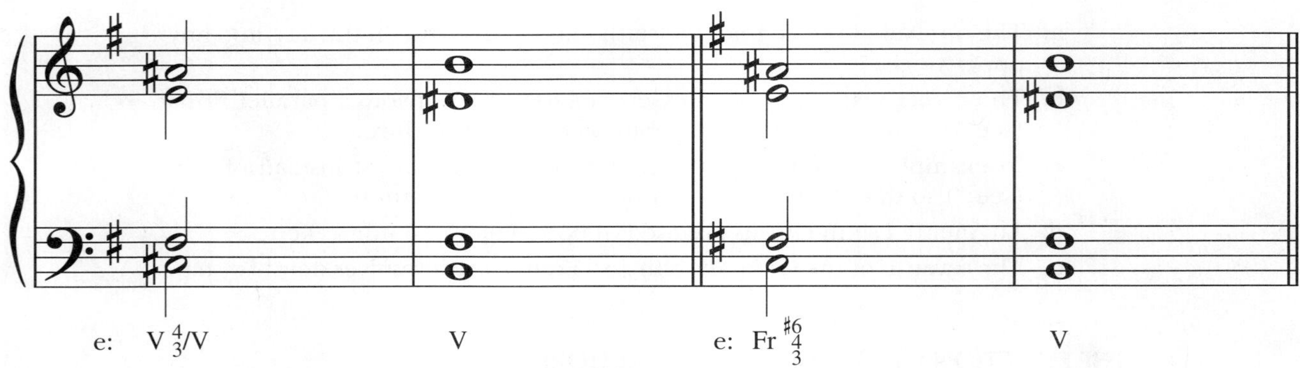

Note:

a. The Italian sixth may be viewed as vii°6/V with a lowered third.

b. The German sixth may be viewed as vii°$^{6}_{5}$/V with a lowered third.

c. The French sixth may be viewed as V$^{4}_{3}$/V with a lowered fifth.

d. In each case, the augmented sixth chord contains those pitches that give the secondary dominants and secondary diminished sevenths their dominant function, that is, root, leading tone, and seventh. The augmented sixth chords, therefore, are functionally very similar to secondary dominants and secondary diminished sevenths.

Other uses of augmented sixth chords are covered on pages 249–250.

SUGGESTIONS AND STRATEGIES

Since augmented sixth chords virtually always precede the dominant, strategies for construction and resolving them are quite easily created.

When Roman numerals with figures are given:

Work backwards!

1. Identify the key, and its dominant.
2. Write the dominant's *root* in the bass, and double the root at least an octave higher in another voice.
3. Create the augmented sixth interval by writing a note that is a *minor second above* the dominant note in the bass, and a note that is a *minor second below* the other dominant note.
4. Check that the resulting interval is an augmented sixth.
5. **a.** For an Italian sixth, add notes that are both a *major third* above the bass.
   b. For a German sixth, add notes that are a *major third* and a *perfect fifth* above the bass.
   c. For a French sixth, add notes that are a *major third* and an *augmented fourth* above the bass.

An example is given.

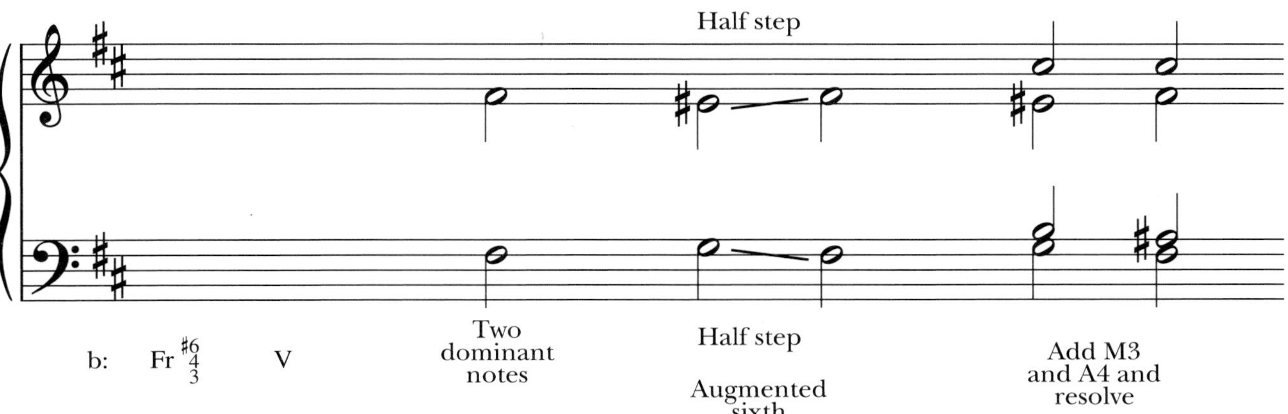

When the figured bass is given:

1. Look for bass notes on the *lowered sixth scale degree.* These notes are diatonic in minor keys, and are preceded by naturals or flats in major keys.
2. If the figure under the bass is:

♯6; the chord is an Italian augmented sixth;

♯6 ♭5; the chord is a German augmented sixth;

♯6 4 3; the chord is a French augmented sixth.

Resolution:

In each of the augmented sixth chords, the interval of the augmented sixth resolves outward by half step to the octave (the dominant note).

1. Italian sixth—the remaining two voices form either a unison or an octave and resolve to the third and the fifth of the dominant triad.
2. German sixth—the remaining two voices move down by step (one of these voices is the seventh of the chord and its natural tendency is to move down by step). This movement creates the parallel fifth mentioned on page 239, Note b. German sixths often resolve to I(i) $^6_4$ before moving to V. This progression eliminates the parallel fifths. In a major key, the movement to I $^6_4$ then to V, the seventh would have a chromatic inflection before moving down by step, and the remaining voice would stay the same before stepping down. Refer to Example 2 on page 238.
3. French sixth—the seventh resolves down by step and the remaining voice stays the same.

PRELIMINARY EXERCISE

Measure 1 of each system has been completed as an example:

1. For each given key, provide the notes of the augmented sixth interval followed by the octave on the dominant pitch.

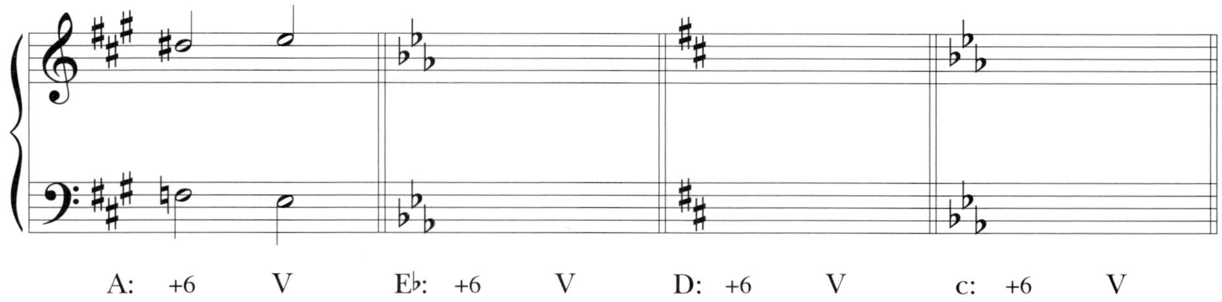

2. Copy the notes from system 1, add the tonic note, and double it. This is the Italian sixth. To resolve, each tonic note moves by step, one goes to the leading tone, and one goes to scale degree 2.

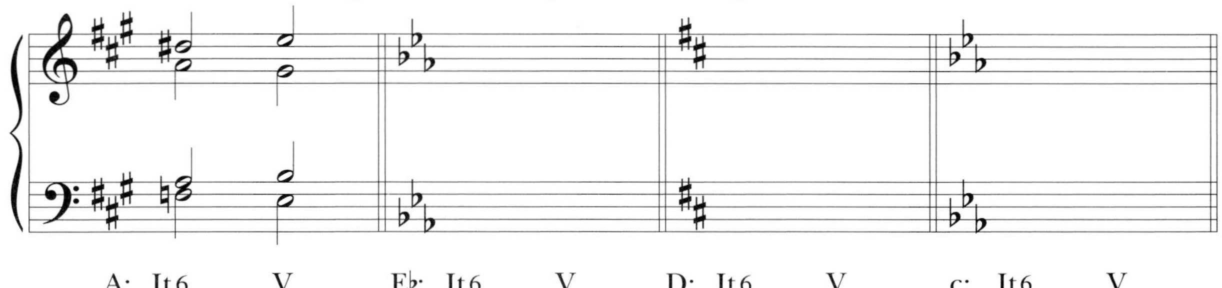

3. For the German sixth, remove one tonic note and add a perfect fifth above the bass. To resolve, the P5 above the bass steps down, and the tonic note moves down to the leading tone.

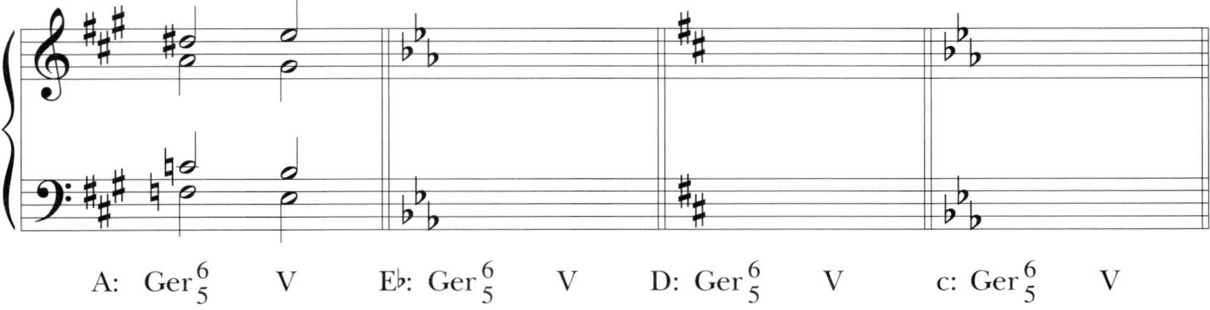

4. For the French sixth, remove the P5 above the bass and add scale degree 2. To resolve, scale degree 2 stays the same.

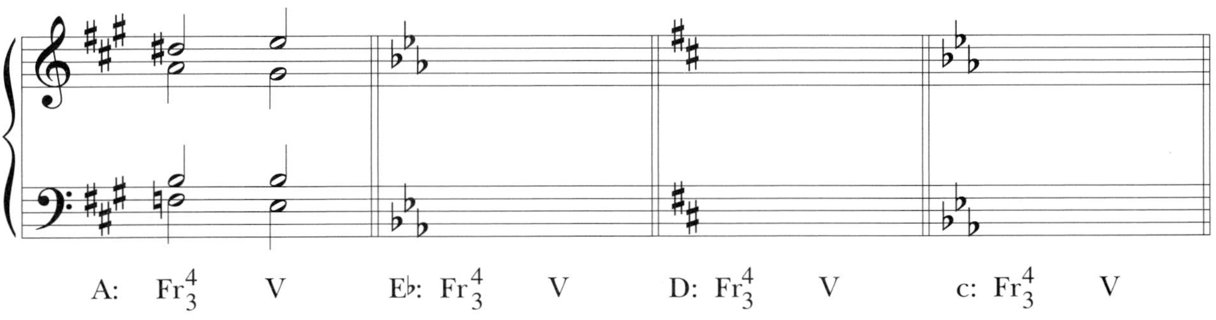

EXERCISES

A. Write, and resolve to V, the following augmented sixth chords.

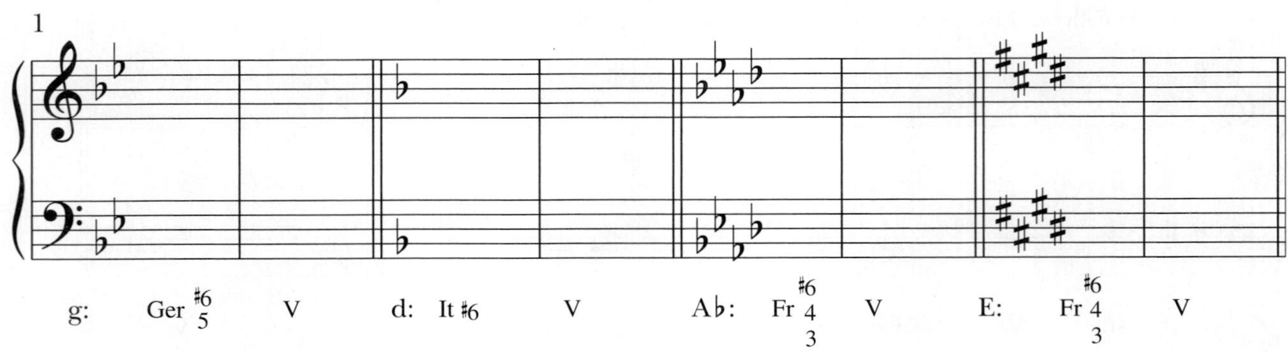

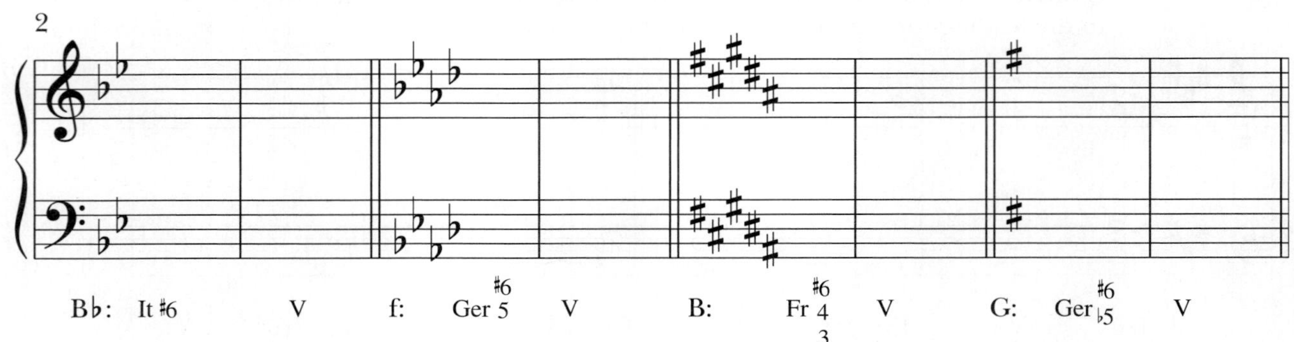

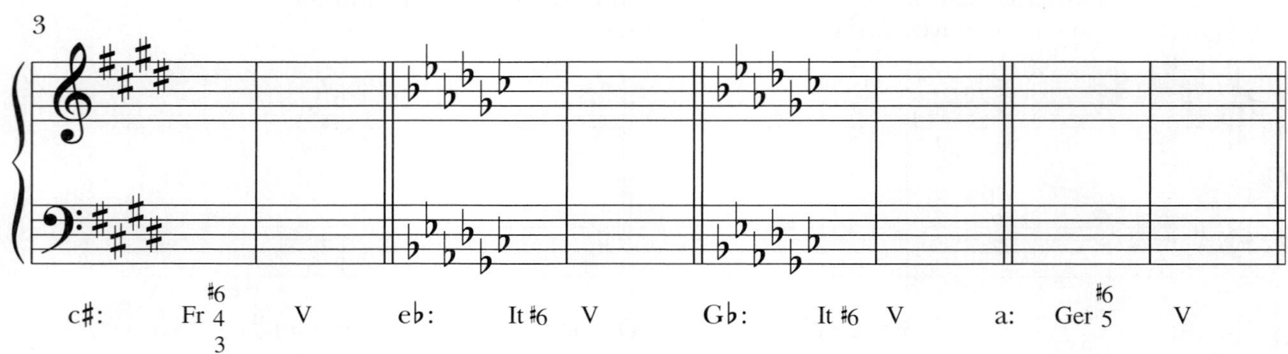

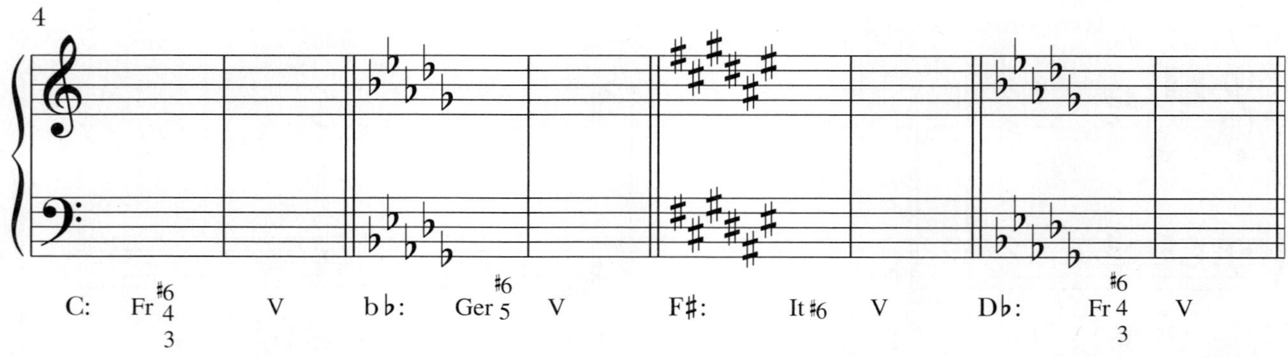

B. Add parts for alto and tenor.

C. Add parts for soprano, alto, and tenor.

D. Harmonize the following phrases in open score.

1

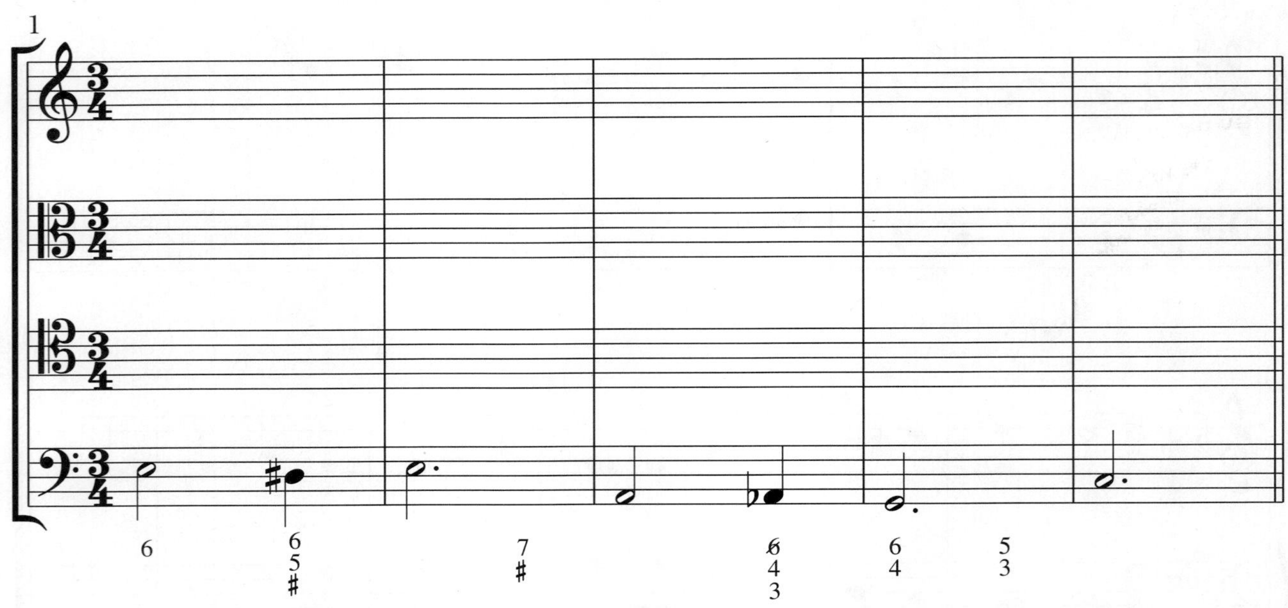

2

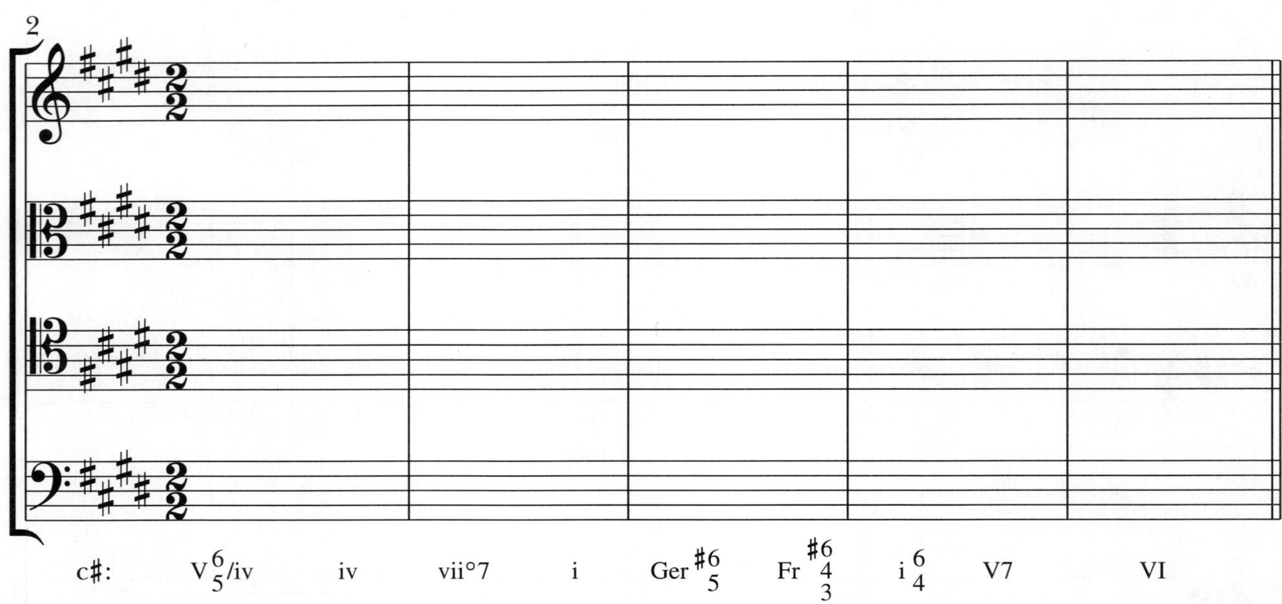

E. Add parts for alto, tenor, and bass.

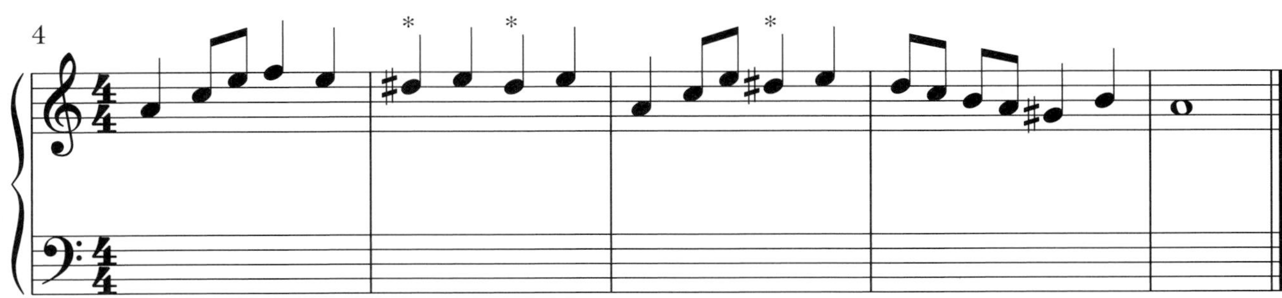

* indicates that an augmented sixth chord should be used

F. Using the given progressions, invent four-measure phrases for soprano, alto, tenor, and bass. The harmonic rhythm is given.

OTHER USES OF AUGMENTED SIXTH CHORDS

Although augmented sixth chords usually occur as predominant sonorities, they may also be used to precede major triads on other degrees of the scale. (They very rarely resolve to minor triads.) Under these circumstances, the augmented sixth chords are obviously no longer altered forms of iv and ii; instead, their analysis depends upon the scale degree of the chord of resolution.

If an augmented sixth chord does not resolve to V, it is most commonly used in resolution to I as an altered chord with a dominant function, a pre-secondary dominant sonority, or possibly as a secondary dominant substitution.

The following examples show some of these uses:

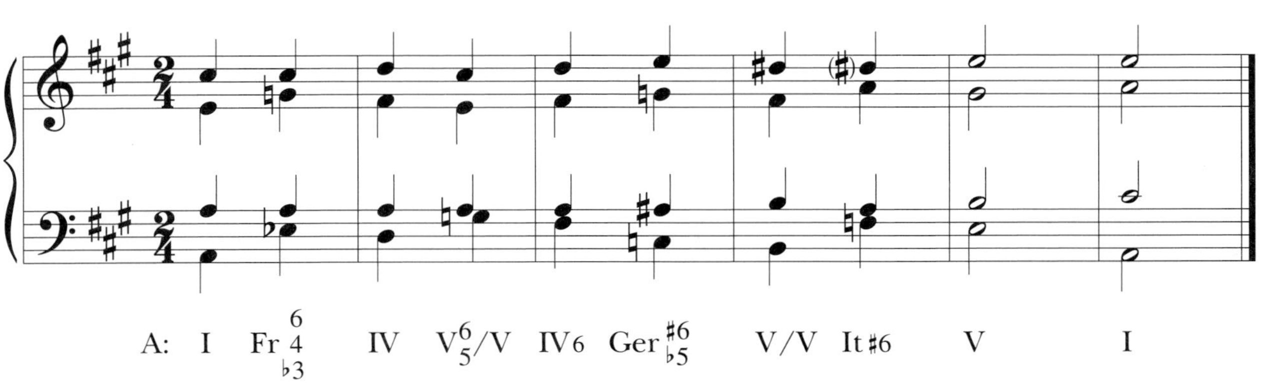

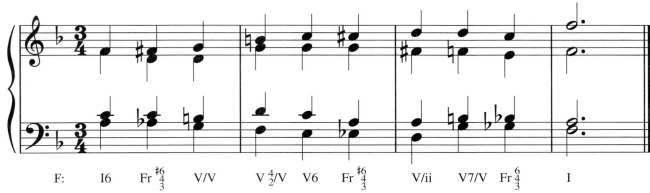

Note:

a. The Italian sixth in the first example is built on the seventh scale degree and therefore has a dominant function.

b. In the second example, the three French sixth chords are built on the sixth, third, and fifth scale degrees, respectively. The first two French sixth chords function as pre-secondary dominants while the last functions as a dominant.

c. In the third example, the French sixth functions as a secondary dominant substitution; the German sixth functions as a pre-secondary dominant; the Italian sixth has a regular pre-dominant function.

d. Regardless of the scale degree, the resolution of augmented sixth chords does not change.

EXERCISES

A. Add parts for soprano, alto, and tenor.

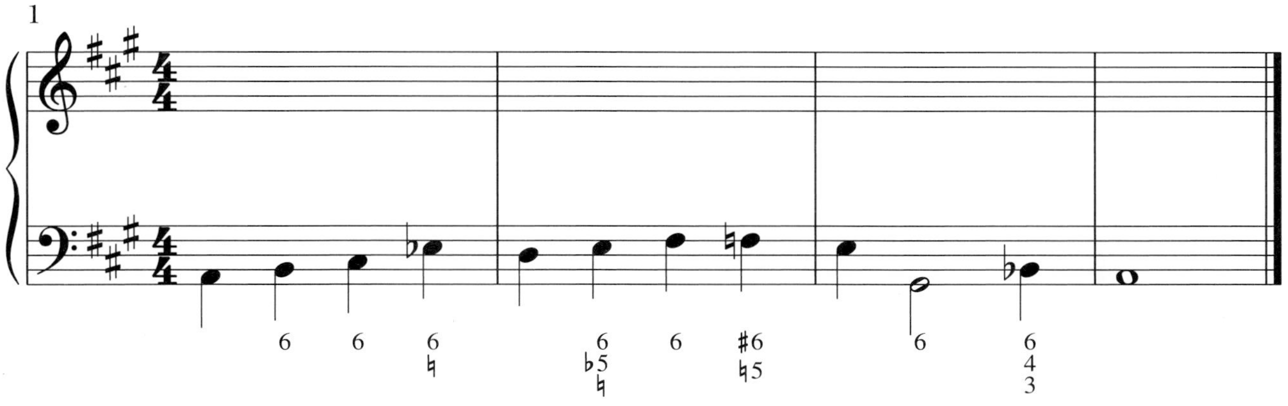

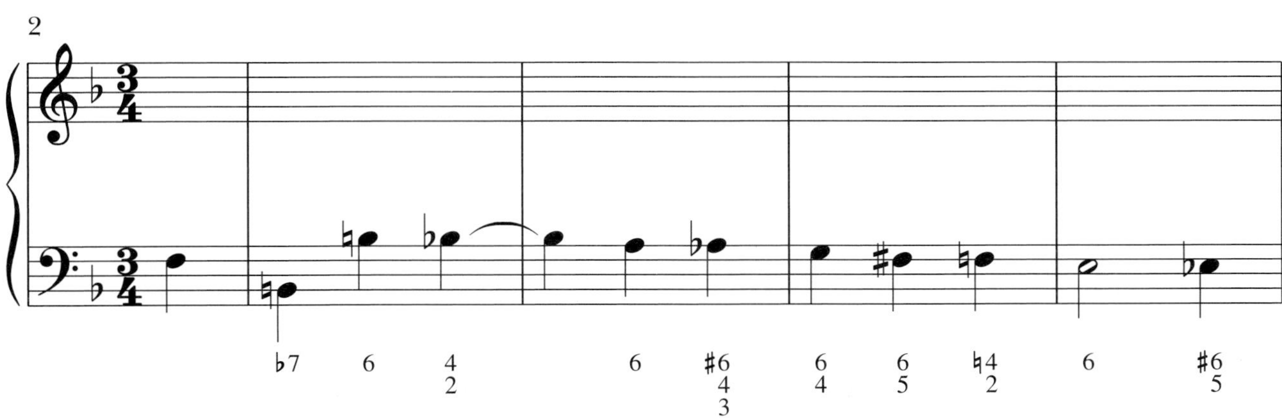

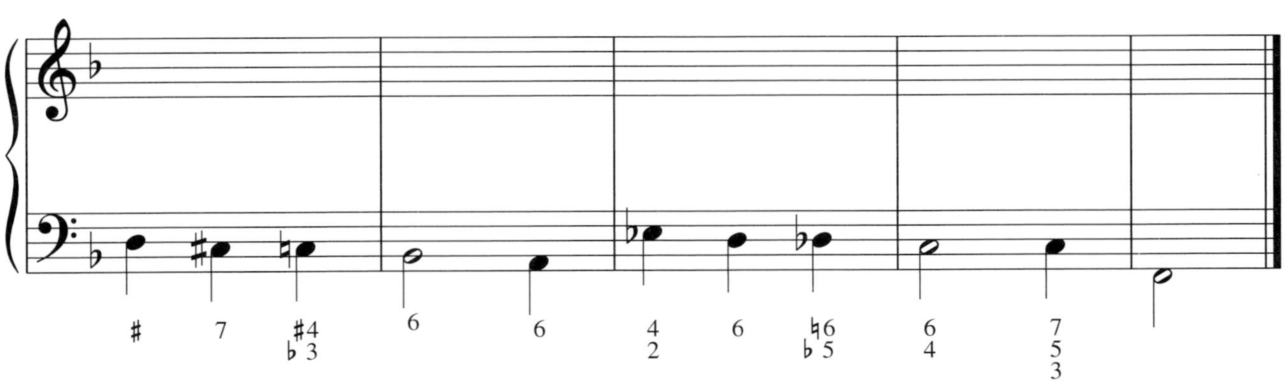

21 Borrowed Chords

All of the chromatic chords that have so far been encountered have been functional in nature. In other words, they have been used to complete a specific harmonic task, usually that of tonicizing a major or minor triad, or emphasizing a movement to the dominant.

Some chromatic chords, however, are used for the purpose of creating harmonic color and thus are said to be coloristic rather than functional. These

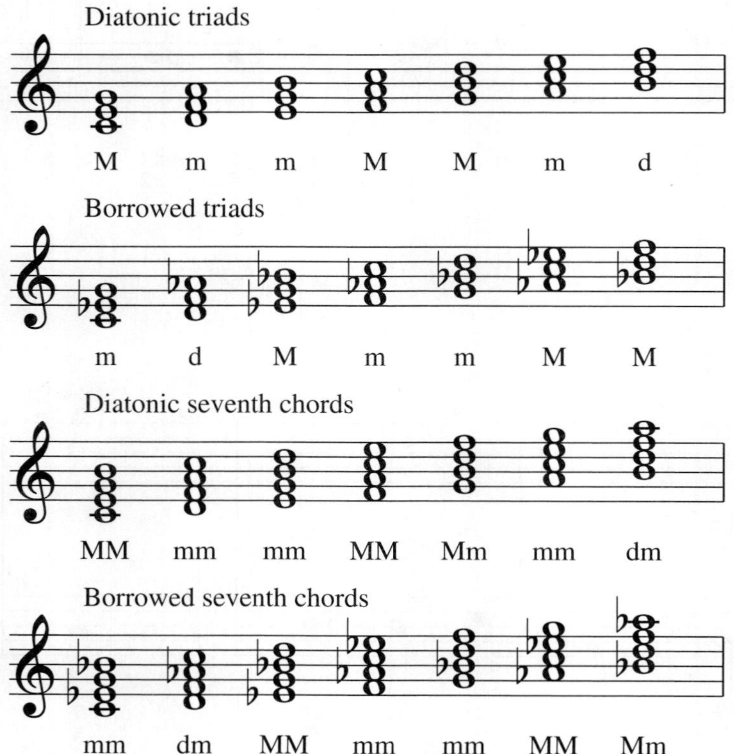

chords nearly always appear in the major key and come from the parallel minor. They are referred to as *borrowed chords.*

The previous example shows the triads and seventh chords on each of the degrees of the major scale, and their equivalents in the parallel minor. In a chromatic idiom, harmonic variety may be achieved by using chords from the minor mode in place of the diatonic ones, as the examples below show:

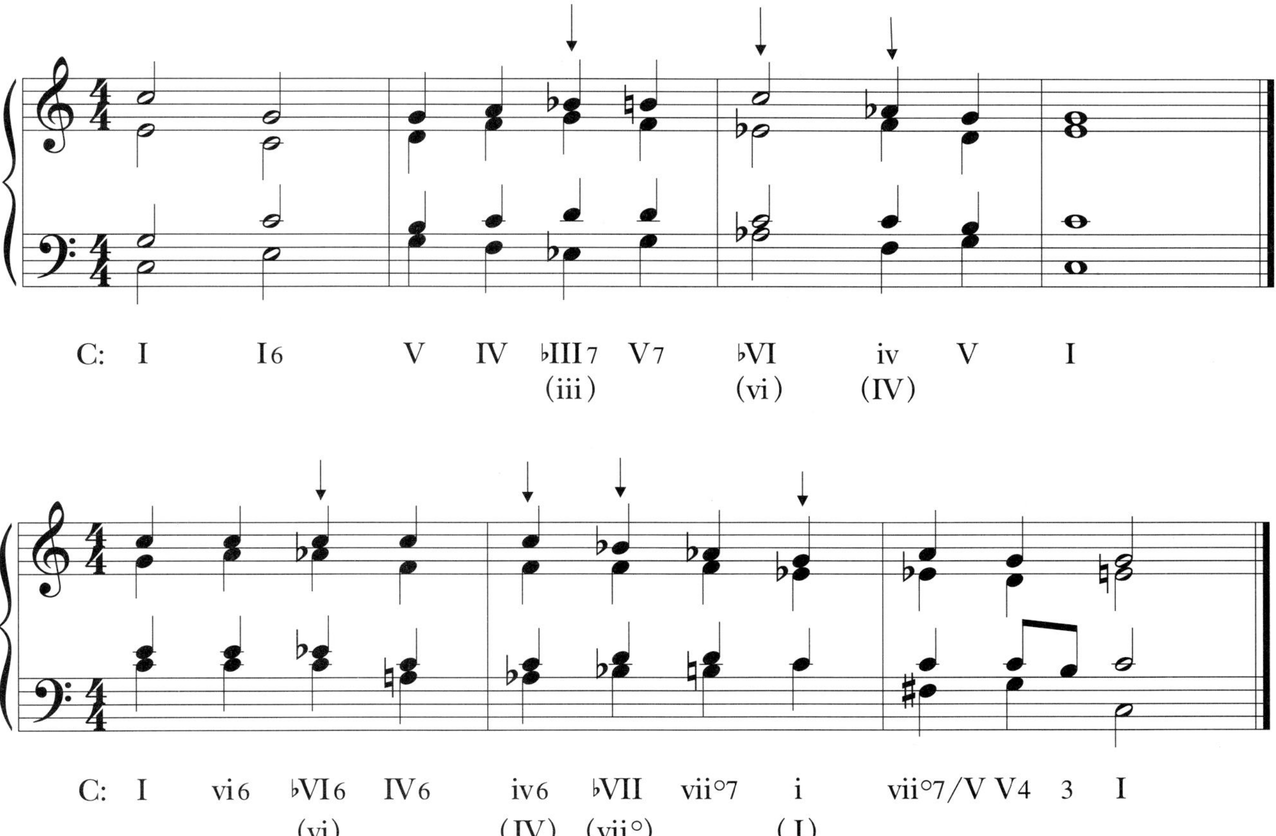

Note:

a. Each borrowed chord is either preceded by, or used directly in place of, its diatonic equivalent. Observe the change in harmonic quality, and in the case of chords built on scale degrees three, six, and seven, the use of a flat in front of the Roman numeral to indicate the lowering of the root.

b. Typically one would double an unaltered note in a borrowed chord; however, the root may be doubled if that produces better voice leading.

c. Notice the deceptive resolution of V to ♭VI in the first example. The use of the borrowed submediant after the dominant heightens the deceptive movement by creating root movement of a half step rather than a whole step.

The borrowed supertonic, a diminished triad, contains a tritone and thus may be viewed in a functional as well as coloristic capacity. In the example below, the movement to the cadence is enhanced by the borrowed dissonant supertonic seventh. The dissonance of the augmented fourth between the tenor and the alto would, of course, be absent if the diatonic chord were employed.

D: I V4/3 vii°4/3/vi vi6 iiø6/5 V I

EXERCISES

A. Write the following chords.

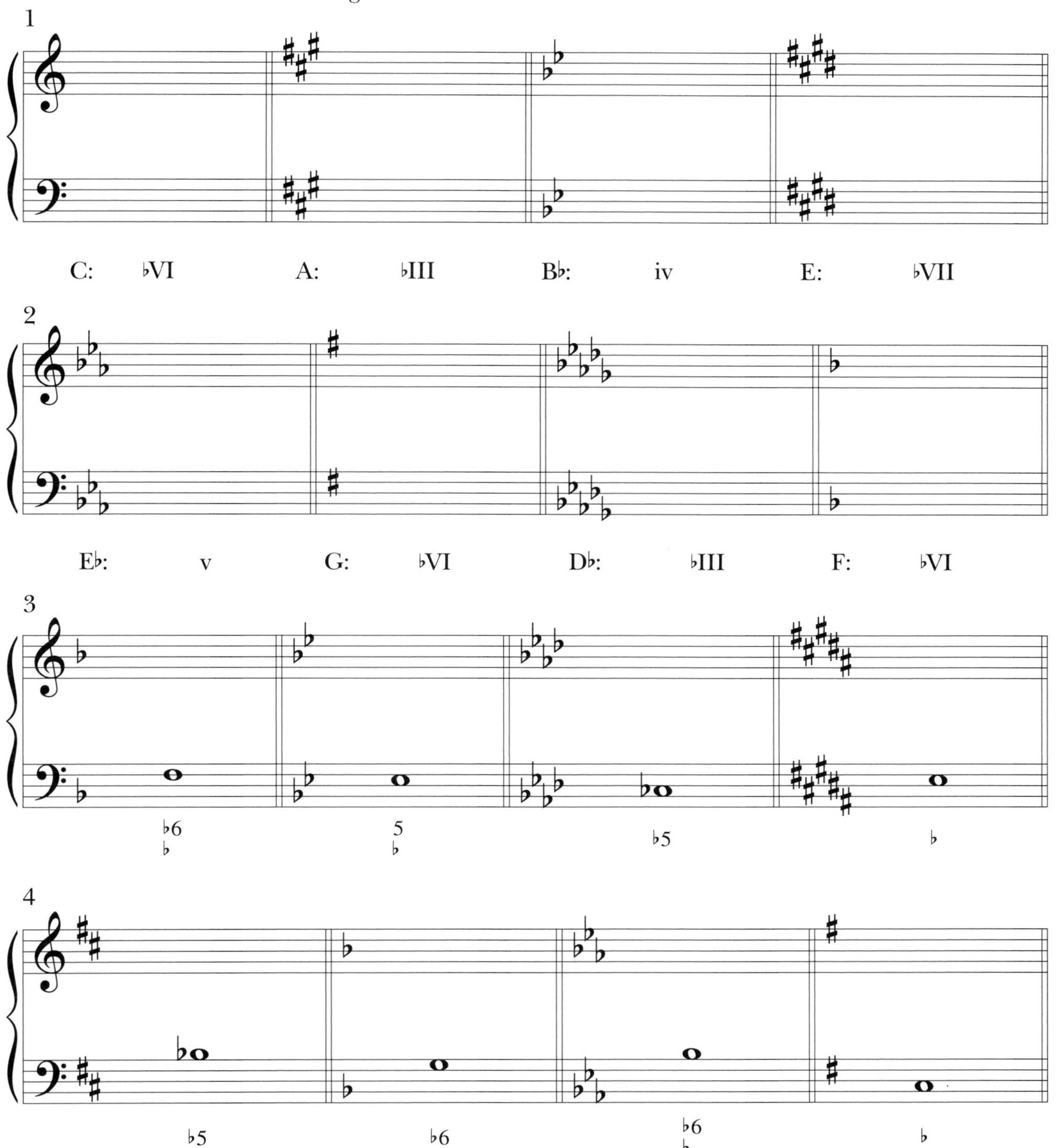

B. Add parts for alto and tenor.

C. Add parts for soprano, alto, and tenor.

D. Add parts for alto, tenor, and bass, making use of borrowed chords.

22
The Neapolitan

The major triad built on the lowered second degree of the scale is known as the *Neapolitan.* Because it is diatonic in neither the major nor the parallel minor mode, it may not be considered a borrowed chord. Although it is clearly derived from ii°, it is used in both major and minor keys.

THE NEAPOLITAN SIXTH CHORD

The Neapolitan is used far more frequently in first inversion than in root position and is thus described as the *Neapolitan sixth chord.*

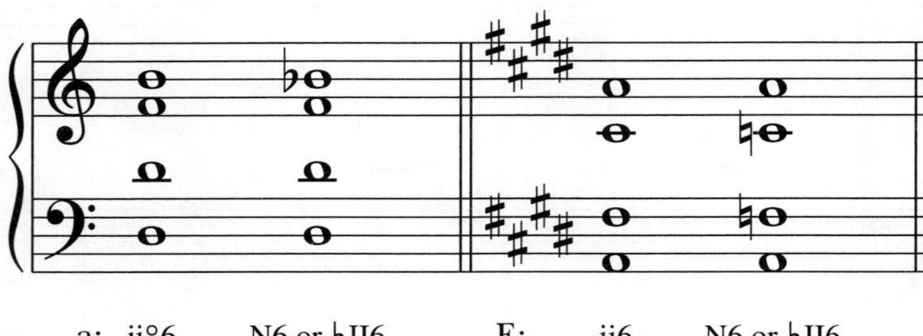

a: ii°6 N6 or ♭II6 E: ii6 N6 or ♭II6

Study the following examples carefully:

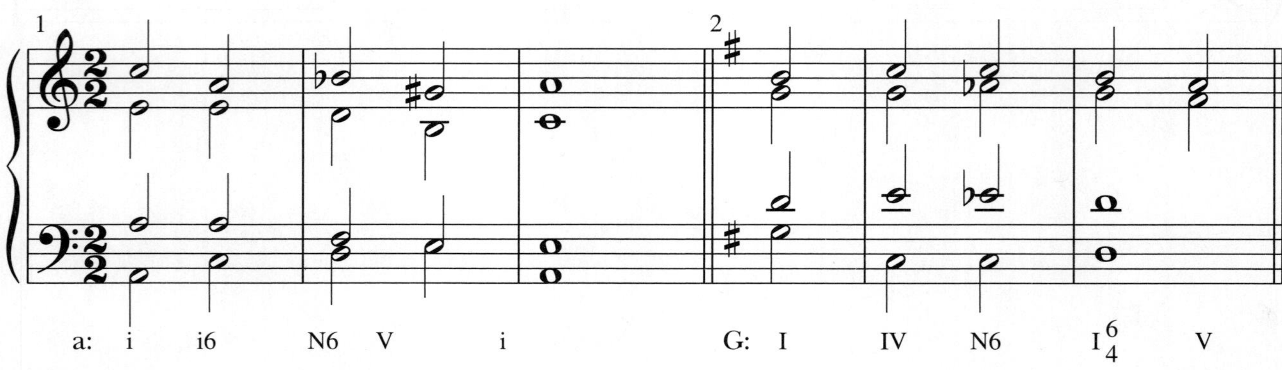

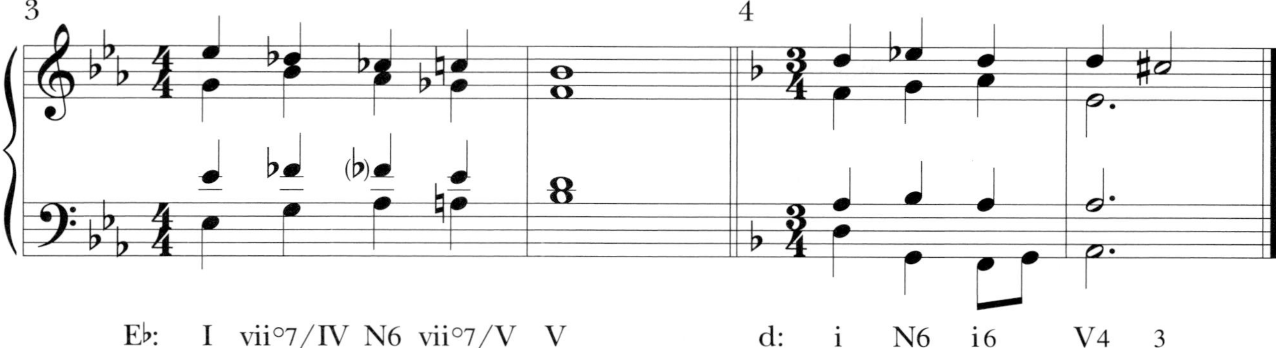

Note:

a. The *bass* of the Neapolitan sixth is doubled (third of the chord).

b. The root of the Neapolitan resolves *downward* to the closest pitch in the subsequent chord.

THE FUNCTION OF THE NEAPOLITAN SIXTH

In the four examples above, it may be observed that the Neapolitan sixth chord either directly precedes the dominant or is followed by a chord that precedes the dominant. The bass movement is from the subdominant note to the dominant note. In fact, as the example below shows, if the root of the Neapolitan sixth were lowered a half step, a subdominant triad (with its root doubled) would be formed.

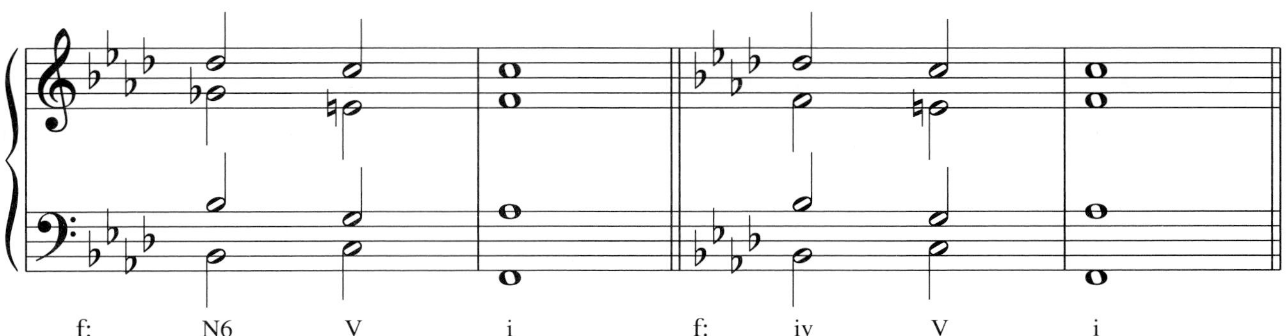

Because of the close similarity between the Neapolitan sixth and the subdominant, the chord is often used in place of the subdominant and is said to have a *subdominant function.*

THE NEAPOLITAN IN ROOT POSITION

The Neapolitan is occasionally used in root position. In this case, the chord follows procedures common to all major triads in root position—the root is usually doubled.

Note:

a. The Neapolitan is a part of a progression common to harmonic activity preceding a cadence—root movements in descending fifths: VI–II–V–I.

b. In the second measure in the bass, the lowered second scale degree creates a descending diminished fifth between the supertonic and dominant.

SUGGESTIONS AND STRATEGIES

Take care to avoid parallel fifths when you resolve the Neapolitan to the tonic $\frac{6}{4}$ chord. They will occur if the root of the Neapolitan is below the fifth.

By inverting the soprano and alto parts, the inadmissible parallel fifths become admissible parallel fourths.

PRELIMINARY EXERCISE

The following exercise has two parts—a top line with no key signature (not in the context of a key) and a piano score with a key signature for SATB format (working in the context of a given key).

For the top line, precede each given note with a note that is a minor second above (lowered scale degree two relationship). Using that lowered two relationship note as the root, write a major triad. Then in the piano score area, in SATB format, using those exact pitches (placing accidentals where necessary), write the chord in first inversion with the bass note doubled. Resolve the bass note to the dominant pitch, and resolve the root of the Neapolitan to the leading tone of the key. The first measure of each system has been done as an example. The arrow points from the root of the Neapolitan to the leading tone of the key.

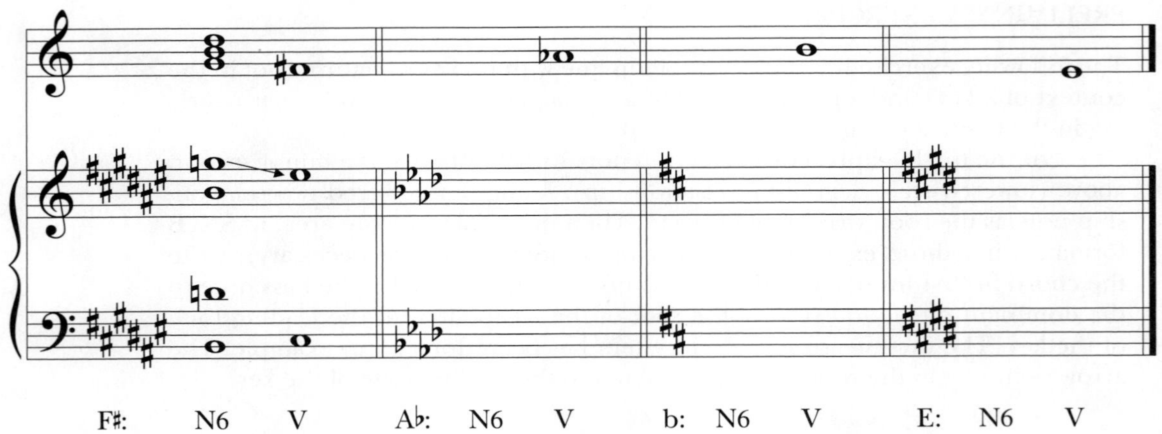
F♯: N6 V
A♭: N6 V
b: N6 V
E: N6 V

EXERCISES

A. Write and resolve the following Neapolitan sixth chords as directed.

B. Add parts for alto and tenor.

C. Add parts for soprano, alto, and tenor.

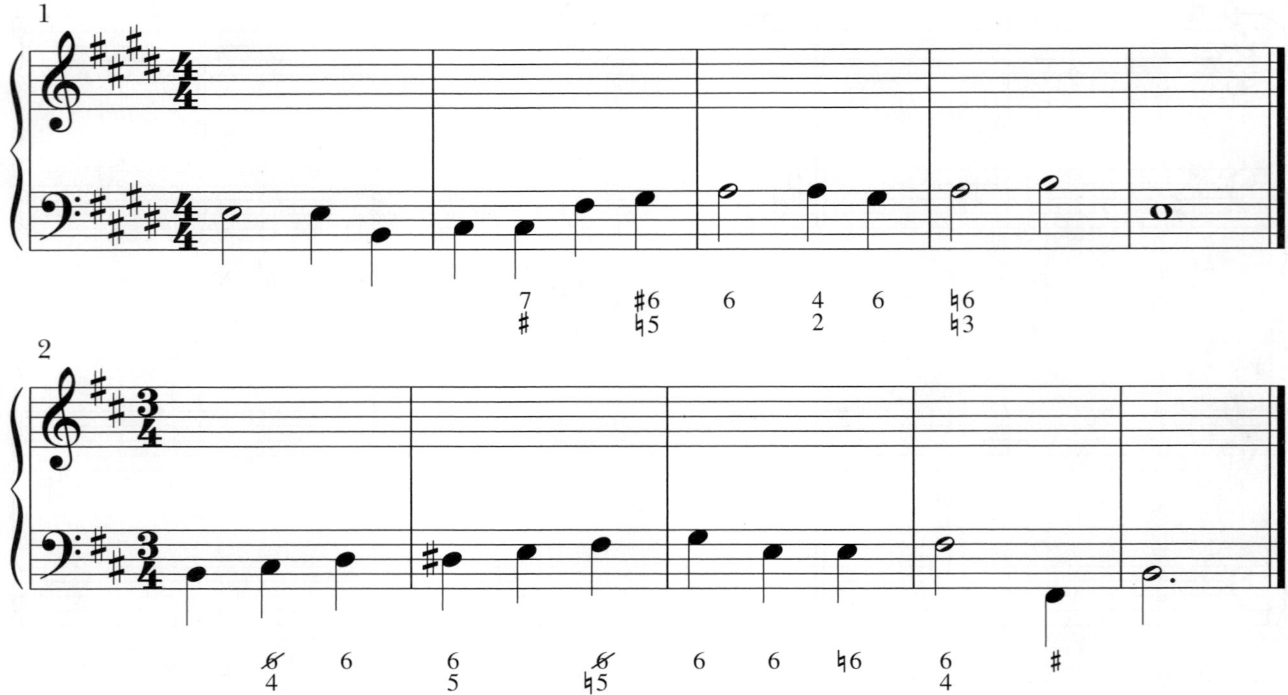

D. Harmonize the following phrases in open score.

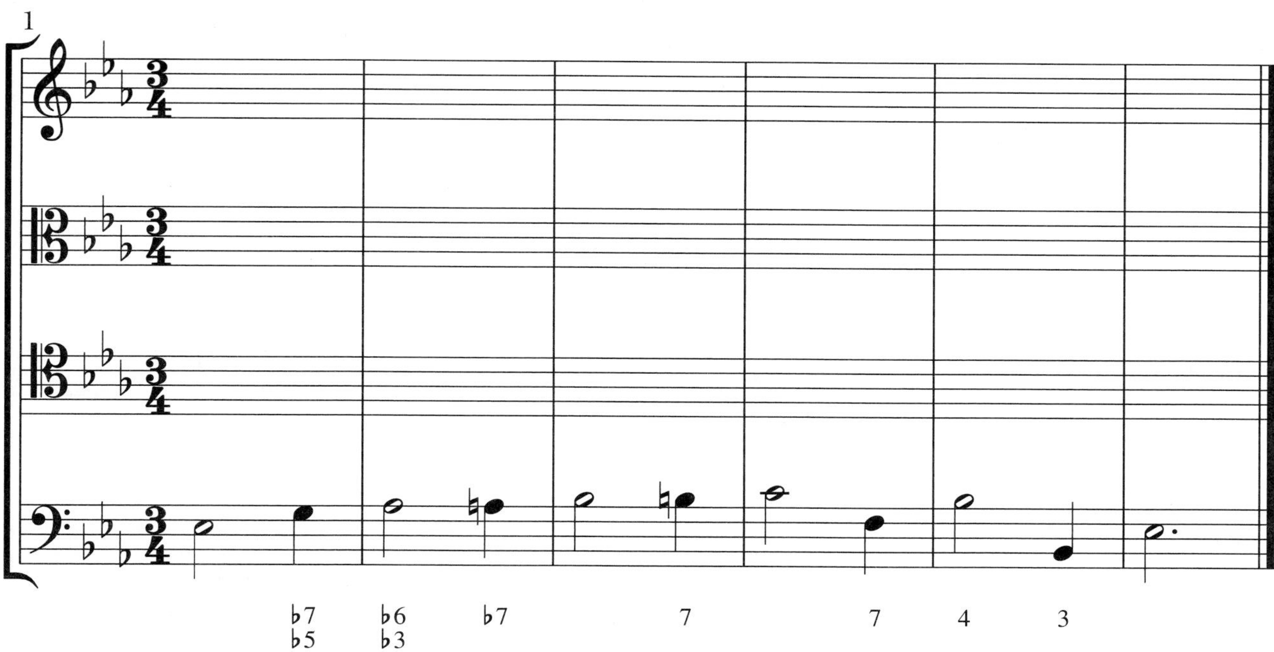

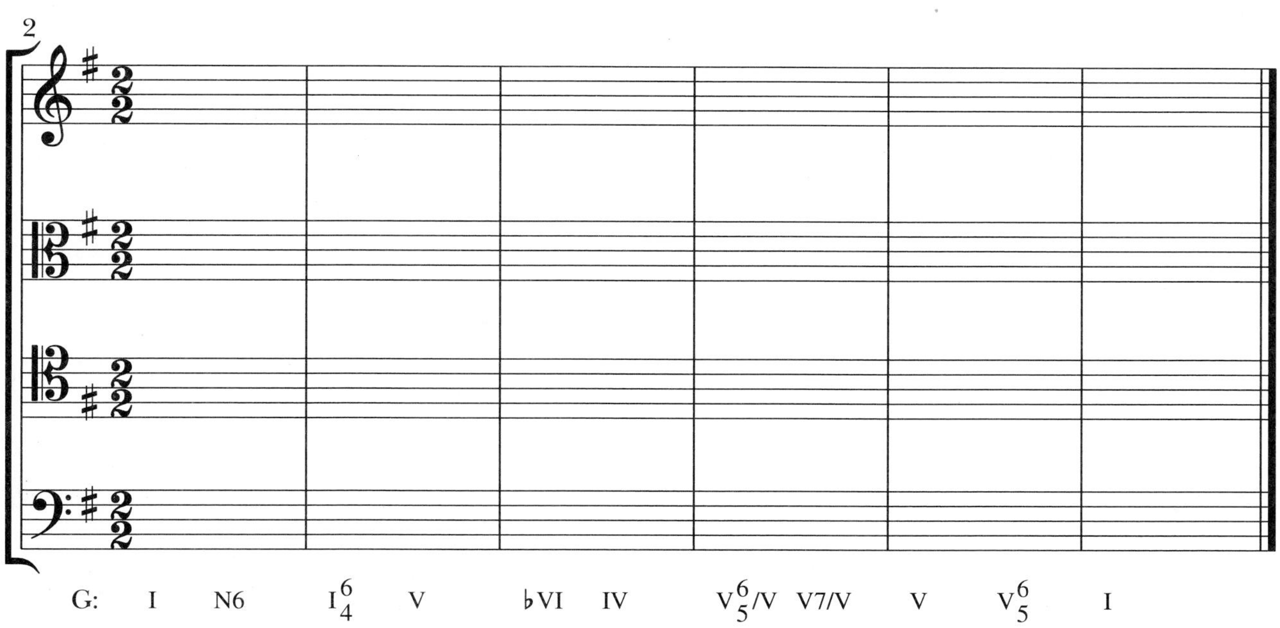

E. Add parts for alto, tenor, and bass.

F. Using the given progressions, invent four-measure phrases for soprano, alto, tenor, and bass. The harmonic rhythm is given.

23
Common Chord Modulation

Modulation may be defined as the process of moving from one key to another. Although all keys are related, the degree of relationship is a function of their relative positions in the circle of fifths.

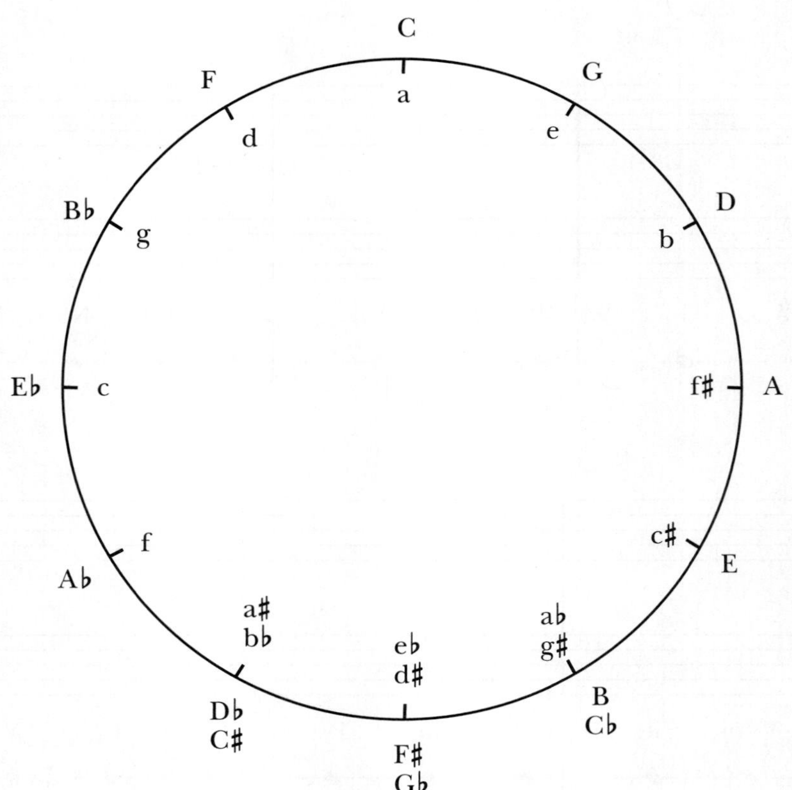

The diagram shows that if C is the tonic, then, after a minor, the keys of G and F and their relative minors would be the most closely related to C because G and F, respectively, are a perfect fifth above and below C.

Similarly, D and B♭ and their relative minors would follow in terms of close relationship; and F♯/G♭ and their relative minors would be the most remote keys.

The essence of modulation lies in the appropriate writing of a chord that suggests a new key as a result either of the presence of a pitch (or pitches) foreign to the established key, or of the subsequent musical activity, or of both. In simple modulation, this chord, the *modulating chord,* almost always has a dominant function in the new key, for example, V, V7, vii°, vii°7, or I_4^6 in a cadential situation. In more complex modulation, however, the function of the modulating chord is less predictable. In any event, the new key is established by the harmonic progression that follows the modulating chord. A change of modality—major to minor, minor to major—without a change of tonic is not a modulation.

Common chord modulation may be effected only between keys that have diatonic chords in common. (The C major triad, for instance, is I in C, VI in e, IV in G, V in F, III in a, and VII in d.) This kind of modulation is usually employed to modulate from a given key to a *closely related key,* although it may be used for more distant modulations as well. The term *closely related* serves to describe keys that are no more than one step removed in the circle of fifths from a given key (plus or minus one in a key signature). Another method to name the keys that are closely related is to identify the dominant and subdominant of the current key, and their respective relative keys, along with the relative key of the tonic. Such keys have several chords in common with one another. For example, common chord modulation may easily be effected from A to f♯ E, c♯ D, and b.

Study the following examples carefully:

Note:

a. The common chord directly precedes the first appearance of a chord with dominant function in the new key.

b. The common chord is analyzed as a diatonic chord in both keys.

c. The common chord is the "pivot" of the modulation. At this point, the harmonic analysis expresses the last event in the established key and the first event in the new key.

The exercises that follow are related to the materials on pages 268–269. Abrupt and enharmonic modulation are covered on pages 281–284.

SUGGESTIONS AND STRATEGIES

In preparation for realizing the given progressions in Exercise B, make note of the differences between the two keys. Then determine the accidental(s), or lack thereof, that will be needed for the second key.

In preparation for harmonizing the melodies in Exercise C, you may find the following steps useful:

1. Play through the melody and make a note of the key at the beginning, as well as the key at the end.
2. Jot down the five chords (V, V7, etc.) that have dominant function in the new key, and spell them out.

3. Study the melody, and try to determine: a) in what measure (or part of a measure) dominant harmony in the new key is first suggested, and b) whether the melodic activity continues in the new key from that point. If both conditions are satisfied—
4. The melodic activity immediately preceding should be able to support a harmony that is diatonic in both keys (i.e., the common chord).
5. Harmonize the melody according to the procedures described in Chapters 12 and 16.

Note:
With the exclusion of the common chord, these suggestions are applicable for Exercise E following the text on *Abrupt and Enharmonic Modulation.*

In preparation for completing the given incipits in Exercise D, you may find the following steps useful:

1. List the chords that are common to both keys.
2. Make a harmonic analysis of the given fragment to try to identify a harmonic pattern that may be helpful in extending the composition. Each incipit ending implies a harmony to immediately follow. Determine this harmony and what needs to follow to arrive at the first cadence point.
3. Make a rough harmonic draft of the entire composition, including the common chord, modulating chord, and subsequent activity in the new key.
4. Make use of the given melodic, rhythmic, and (possibly) harmonic motives throughout, to create unity and continuity in the composition.

Note:
Again, with the exclusion of the common chord, these suggestions are applicable for Exercise F, in Chapter 24, following the text on *Abrupt and Enharmonic Modulation.*

EXERCISES

A. The column on the left is a triad. Write the diatonic function of that triad in five different keys.

1.	C	C: I	a: III	G: IV	F: V	e: VI
2.	A♭	______	______	______	______	______
3.	E♭	______	______	______	______	______
4.	g	______	______	______	______	______
5.	f♯	______	______	______	______	______
6.	D	______	______	______	______	______
7.	B♭	______	______	______	______	______
8.	a	______	______	______	______	______
9.	e	______	______	______	______	______
10.	F♯	______	______	______	______	______
11.	F	______	______	______	______	______
12.	c	______	______	______	______	______

B. Using the given progressions, invent four-measure phrases for soprano, alto, tenor, and bass. The harmonic rhythm is given.

4

g: i i6 V 6/5/iv iv vii° 4/3/III III6
d: VI6 i 6/4 V4 3 i

5

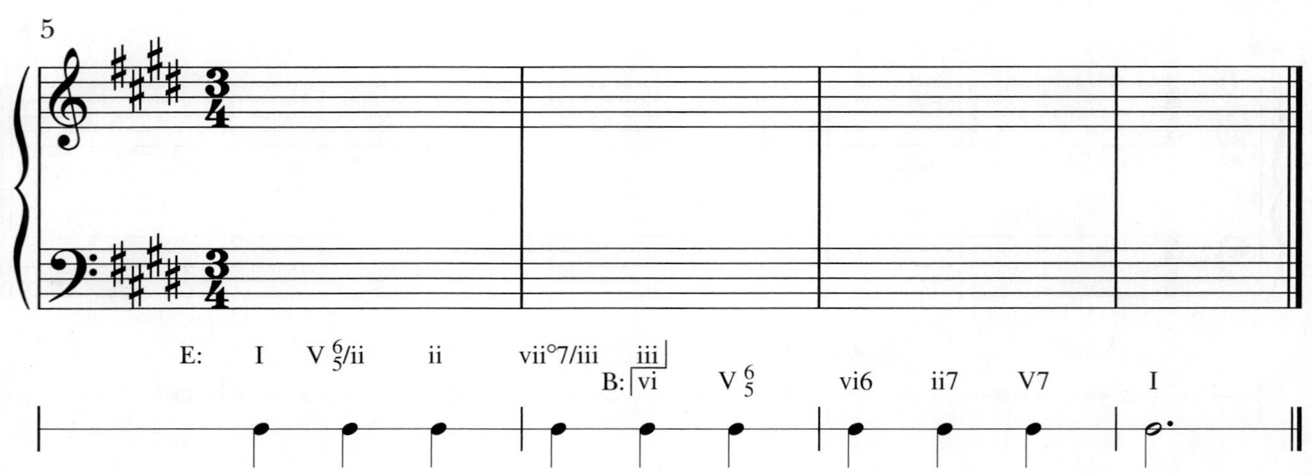
E: I V 6/5/ii ii vii°7/iii iii
B: vi V 6/5 vi6 ii7 V7 I

6

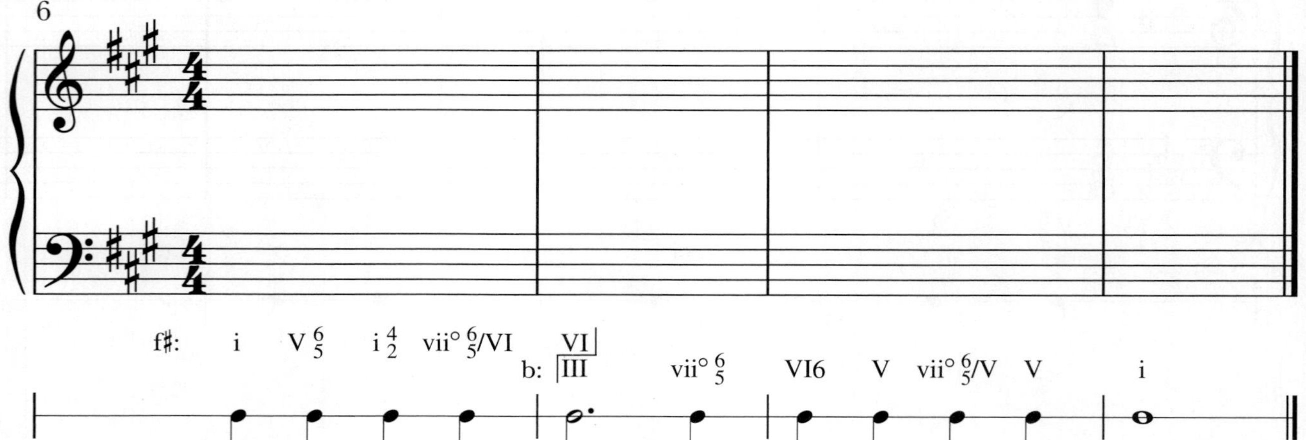
f♯: i V 6/5 i 4/2 vii° 6/5/VI VI
b: III vii° 6/5 VI6 V vii° 6/5/V V i

C. Harmonize the following melodies and set them for piano using a left-hand chordal style (refer to Chapter 17, page 201, example A).

2 **Alla breve**

3
Andante pastorale

D. Complete the following pieces for piano in the style suggested by the beginning of each. They should be between eight and sixteen measures in length and should modulate as indicated.

2

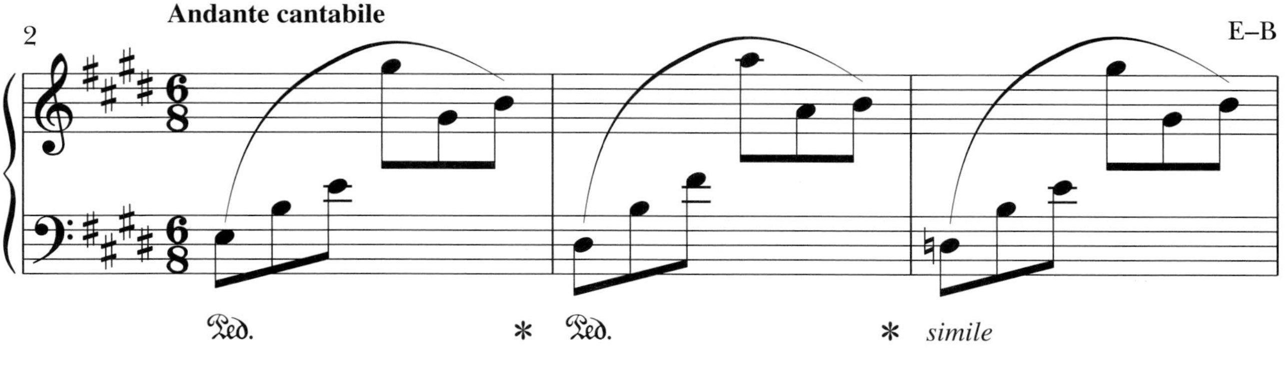

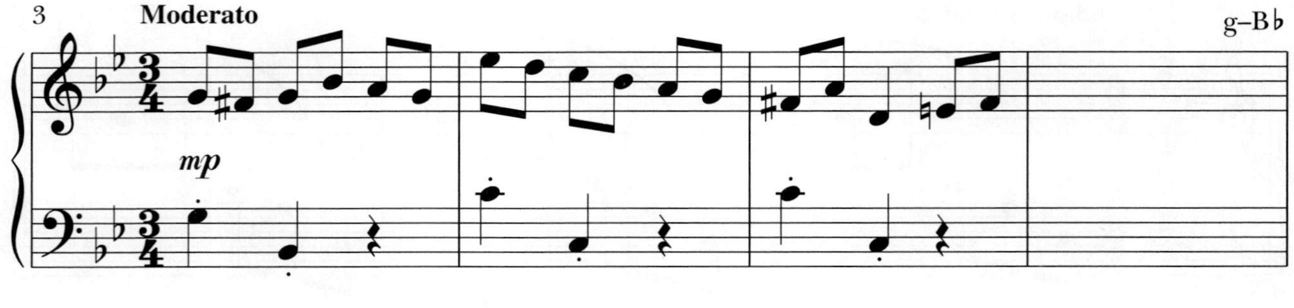
3
Moderato
g–B♭
mp

24 Abrupt and Enharmonic Modulation

ABRUPT MODULATION

Abrupt modulation occurs when the chord that precedes the modulating chord is *not diatonic* in the new key. The emphasis, therefore, in this type of modulation is upon the modulating chord itself.

In the previous section, the modulating chord was identified as a chord with dominant function in the new key. The examples below, which should be studied carefully, show that in abrupt modulation the modulating chord may or may not be one with dominant function and may be either diatonic or chromatic in the new key.

1. Modulating chord *diatonic* in new key—dominant type:

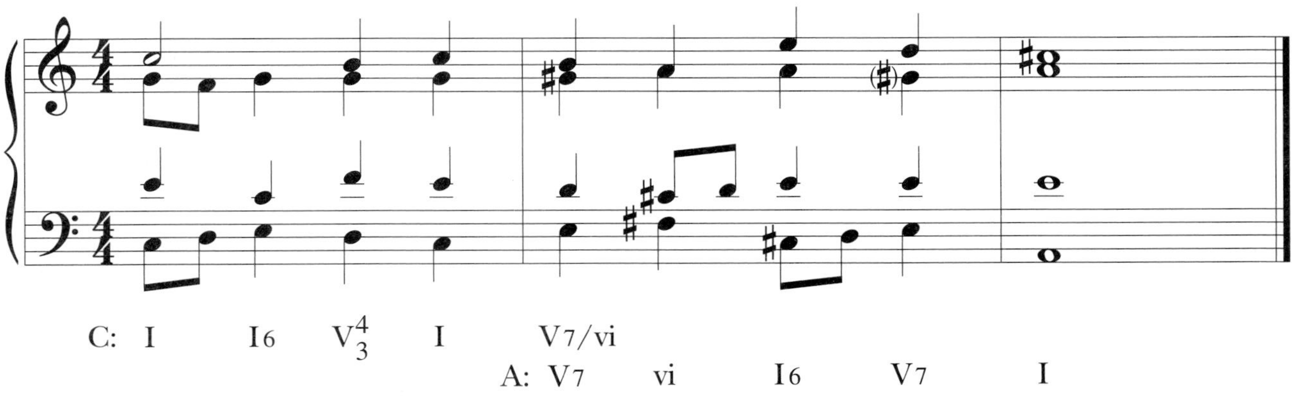

Note:

The modulating chord, the secondary dominant seventh of the submediant in the established key, becomes the dominant seventh in the new key.

2. Modulating chord *diatonic* in new key—nondominant type:

Note:

The modulating chord, the lowered submediant in the established key, becomes the subdominant in the new key.

3. Modulating chord *chromatic* in new key—dominant type:

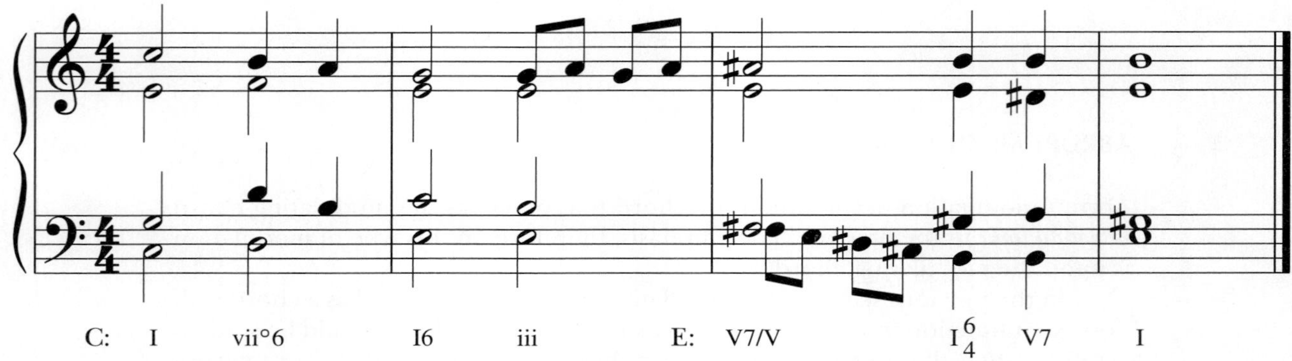

Note:

The modulating chord, which has a very obscure function in the established key, is the secondary dominant seventh of the dominant in the new key.

4. Modulating chord *chromatic* in new key—nondominant type:

Note:
The modulating chord, which in the established key is borrowed from f minor, is the Neapolitan sixth chord in the new key.

ENHARMONIC MODULATION

The word *enharmonicism* is used to describe the respelling of a pitch, or pitches, to produce a new harmonic function. In an enharmonic modulation, therefore, the modulating chord is respelled and, as a result, performs an appropriate function in the new key.

Enharmonic modulations by their very nature tend to be dramatically abrupt, as the following examples show.

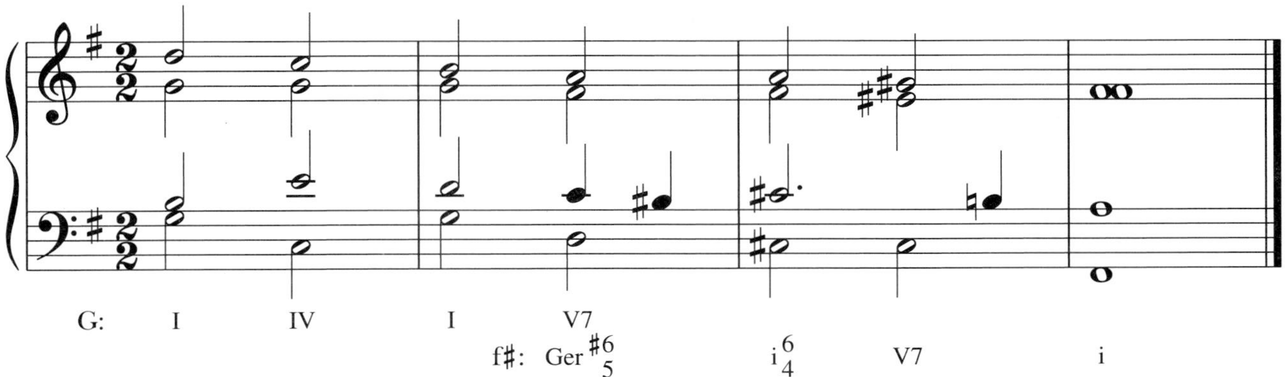

Note:
The modulating chord *sounds* as the dominant seventh in the established key, but by respelling the C♮ as a B♯ a German sixth chord is formed in the new key, and thus the modulation is effected.

Note:

In this example, the respelled diminished seventh chord resolves naturally to a cadential tonic six-four in the new key. Such a resolution is typically employed to establish tonality.

In fact, with respect to modulation, the diminished seventh chord is an extremely versatile sonority, since, with the exception of the augmented triad, it is the only tertian chord that retains its identity under inversion. In other words, it is impossible *by ear* to tell whether a diminished seventh chord is in root position. By way of illustration, the diminished seventh chord extracted from the example above is respelled and revoiced to produce another two modulations that are effective.

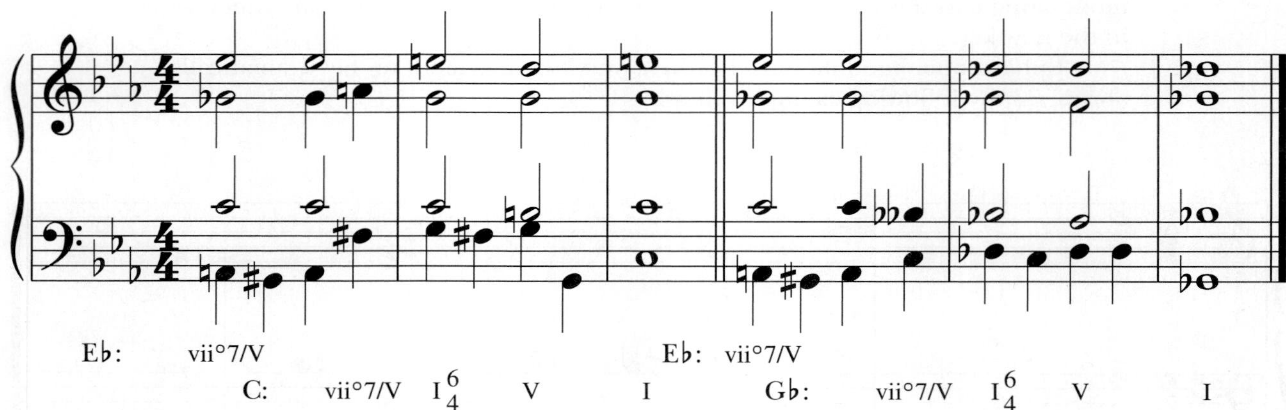

Note:

Modulation has been defined here as the process of moving from one key to another, and the mechanics of this process have been described and exemplified. Key change does occur, however, without the presence of a modulating chord. For example, a half or authentic cadence at the end of a phrase or period is frequently followed by musical activity in another key. Under these circumstances it makes no musical sense to designate any particular chord as a pivot between the two keys because the termination of activity in one key is not linked to the beginning of activity in another. Thus, key change occurs with the omission of the process of modulation.

EXERCISES

A. For each given chord, indicate a key and chromatic function, and then indicate a key and diatonic function. Supply a key signature for each key and appropriate accidentals where needed.

1

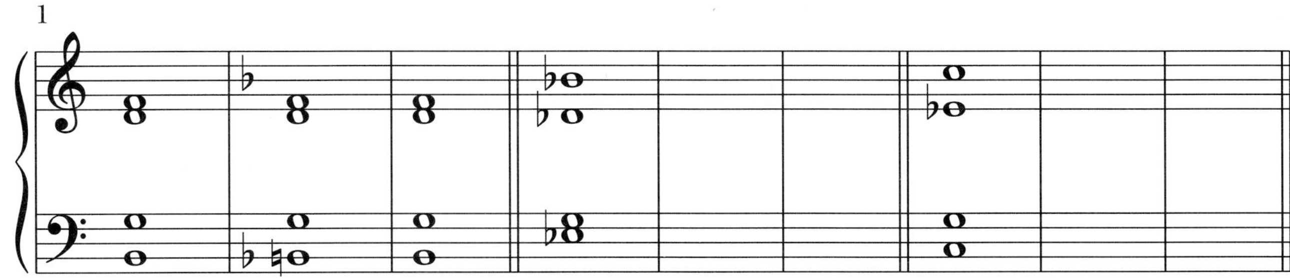

F: V^6_5/V C: V^6_5

2

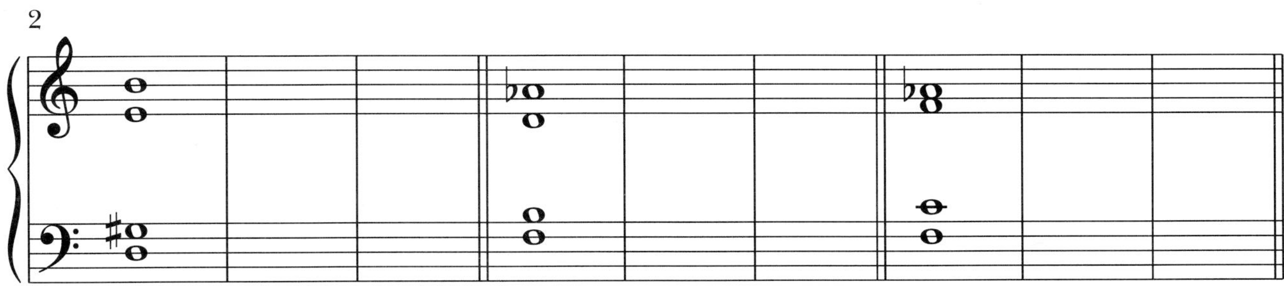

3

4

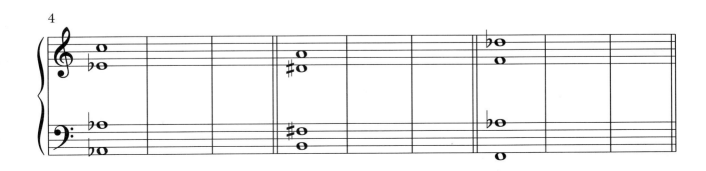

B. Identify the key for the given V7 chords. Then rewrite the chord as a German sixth and identify that key.

1

F(f) E(e)

2

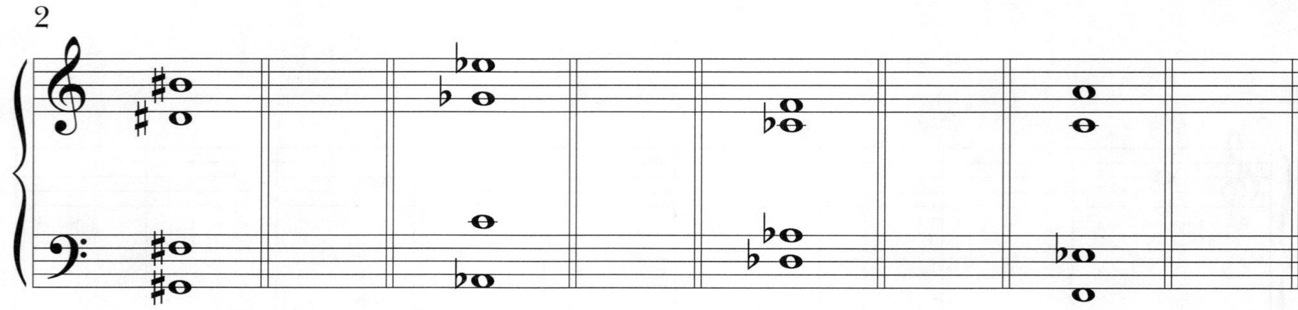

Identify the key for the given Ger 6 chords. Then rewrite the chord as a V7 and identify the key.

3

4

C. Respell and revoice the given diminished seventh chords in two keys, so that they would resolve naturally to I(i) $^{6}_{4}$ or to V.

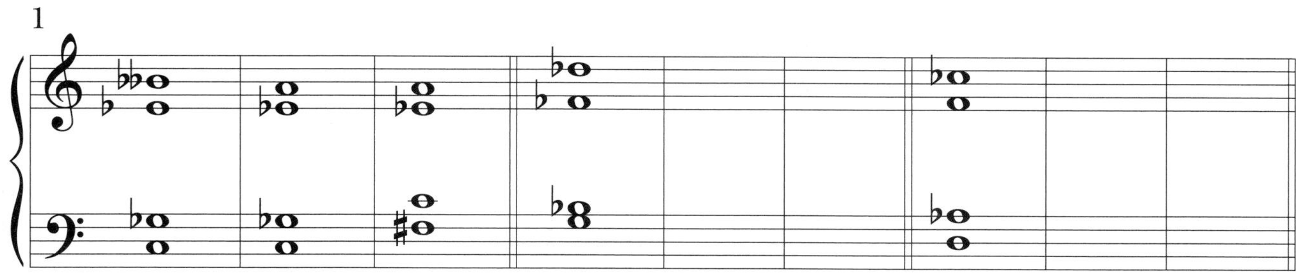

E♭: vii°$^{6}_{5}$/V c: vii°7/V

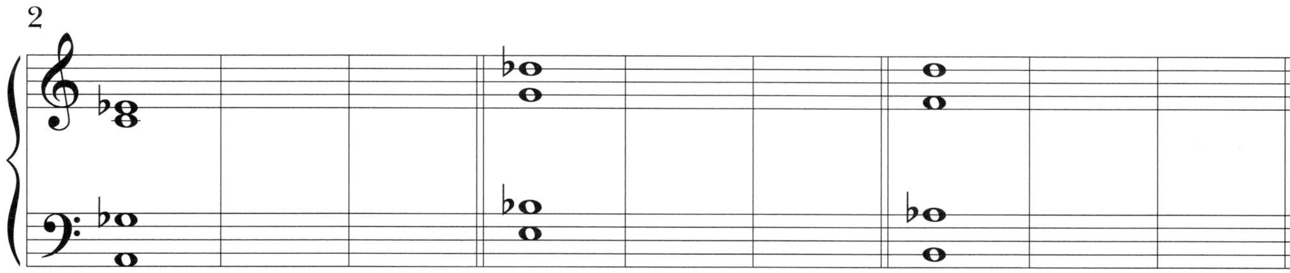

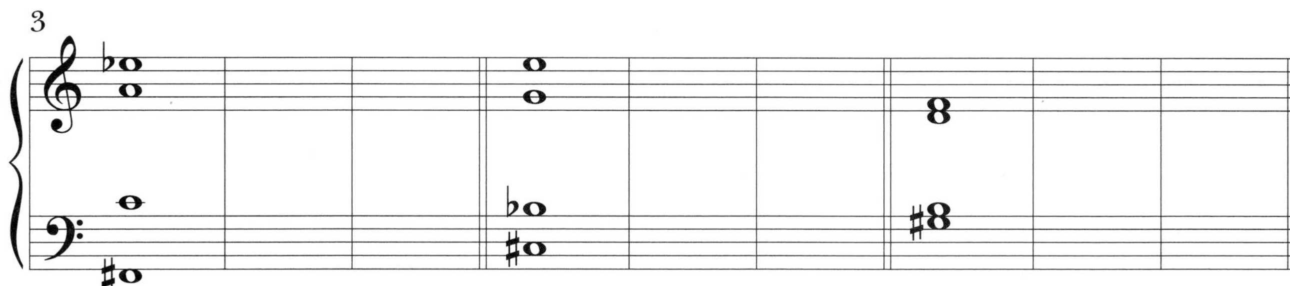

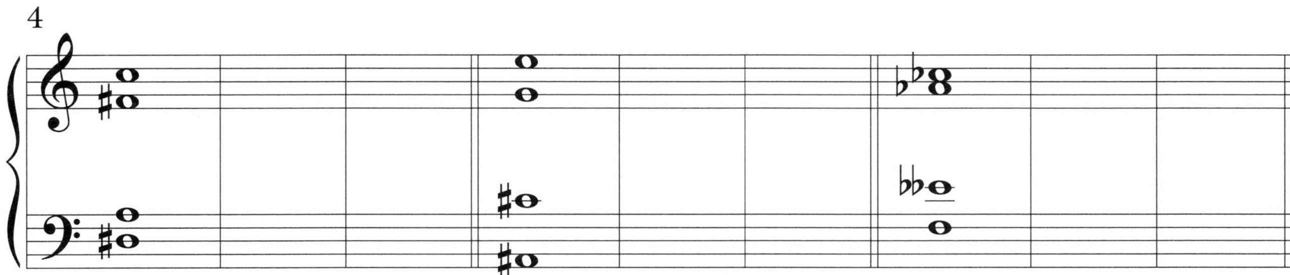

D. Using the given progressions, invent four-measure phrases for soprano, alto, tenor, and bass. The harmonic rhythm is given.

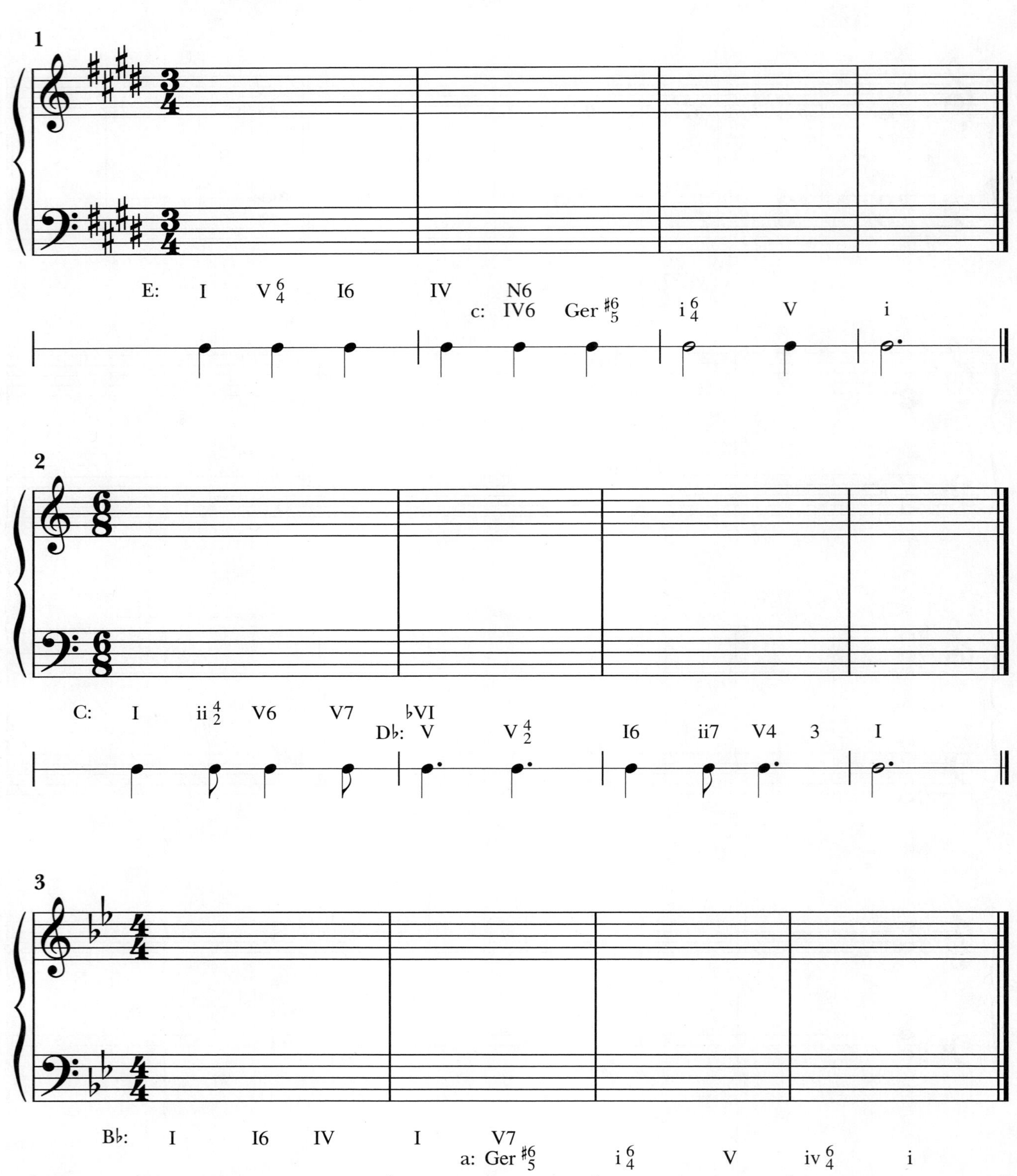

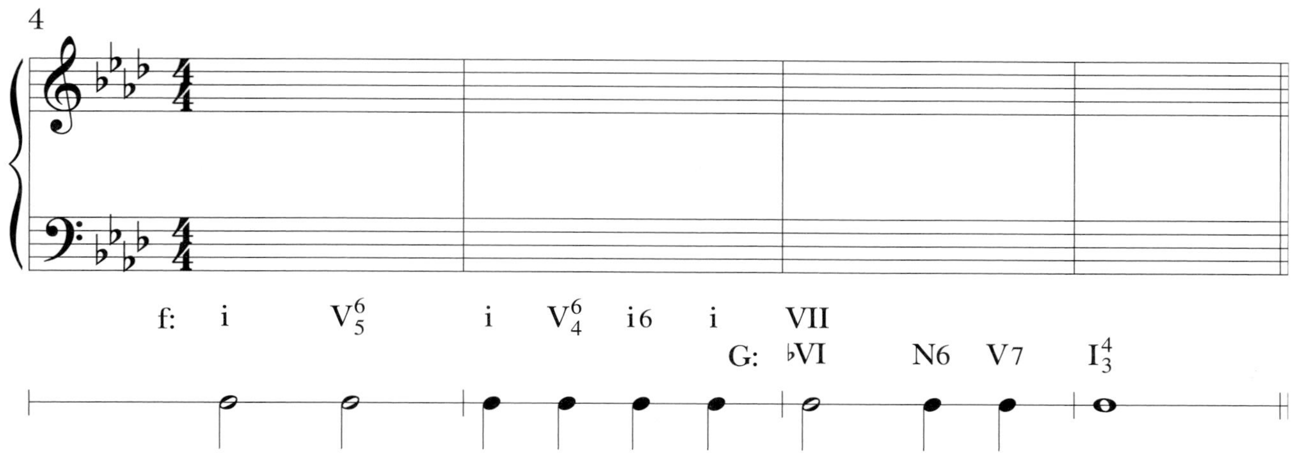
4
f: i V6 5 i V6 4 i6 i VII
G: ♭VI N6 V7 I4 3

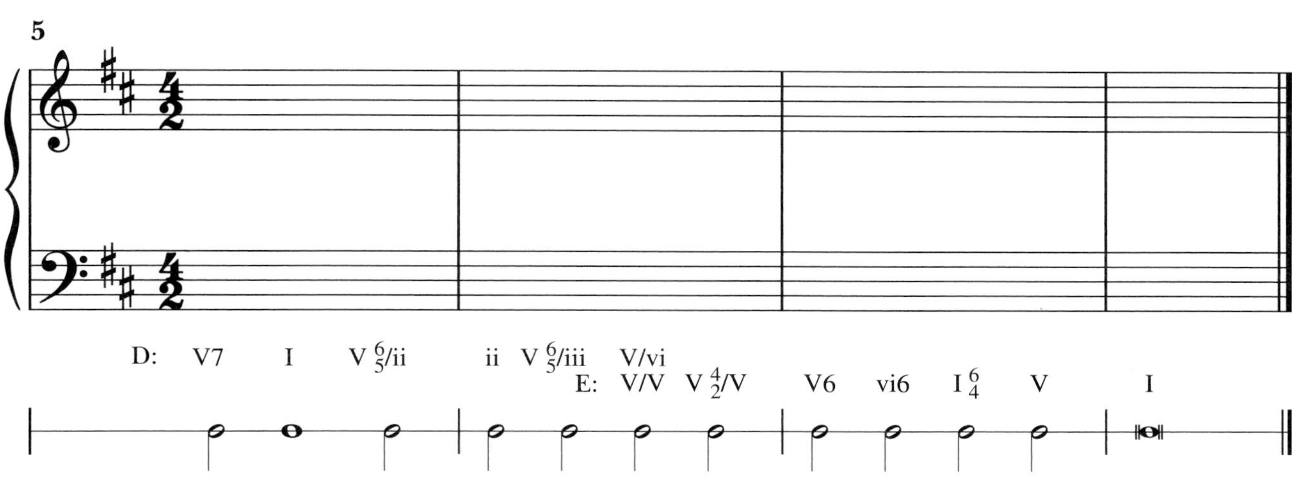
5
D: V7 I V6 5/ii ii V6 5/iii V/vi
E: V/V V4 2/V V6 vi6 I6 4 V I

6
G: I V V6 5/vi vi vii°7/V vii°4 3/V
B♭: vii°6 5/V I6 4 V I

E. Harmonize the following melodies and set them for piano, using a left-hand chordal style.

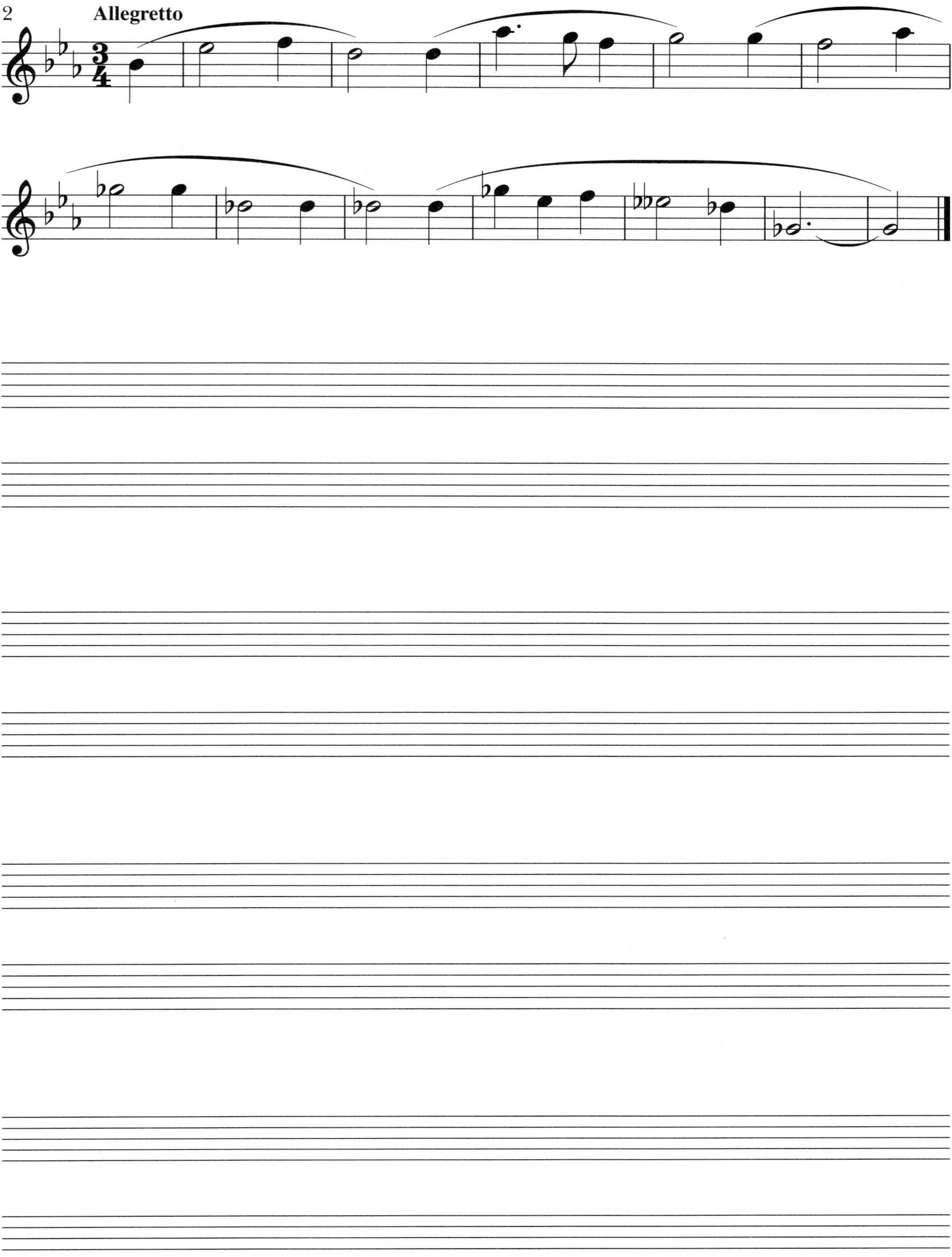
2
Allegretto

F. Complete the following pieces for piano in the style suggested by the beginning of each. They should be between twenty-four and thirty-two measures in length and should modulate at least once before returning to the original key. Refer to Chapter 17 for phrase models.

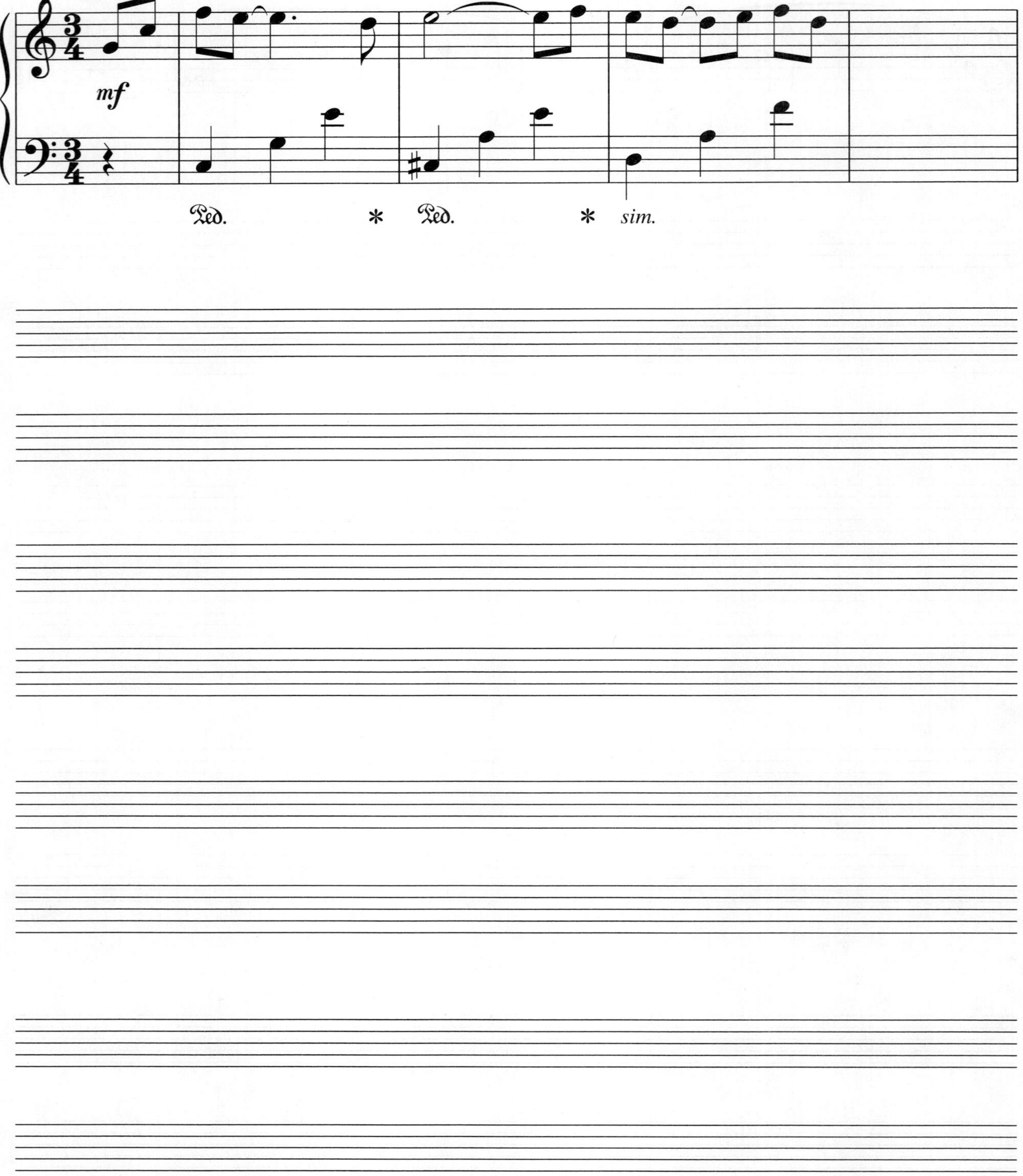

2
Moderately and simply
p

3
Allegro con brio
mp
f

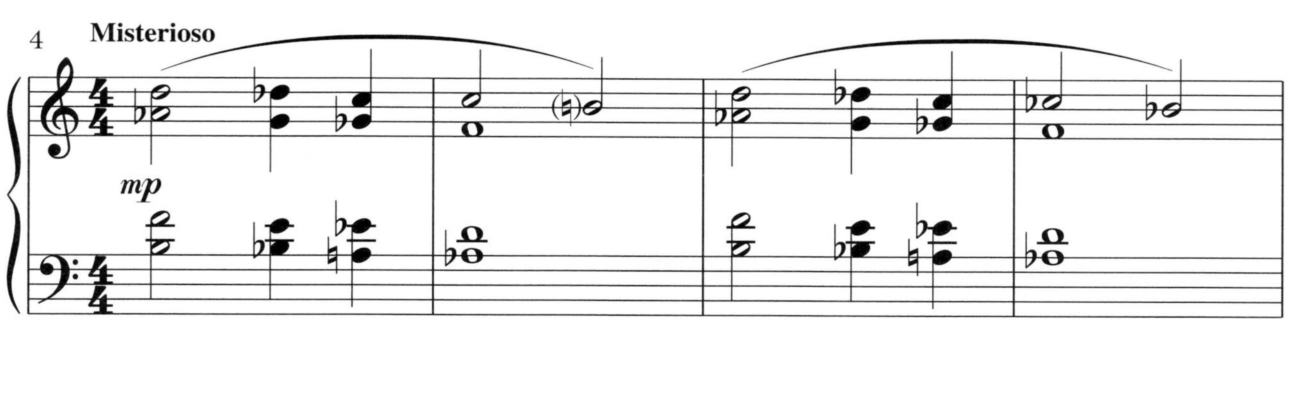
4
Misterioso
mp

PART FOUR

POST–COMMON PRACTICE HARMONY

25

Ninth, Eleventh, and Thirteenth Chords

Since the latter part of the nineteenth century, composers have expanded the tertian vocabulary by the use of multivoiced structures. Although these structures have been treated both conventionally and unconventionally with regard to part-writing and harmonic function, they enjoy wide usage largely as elaborations, or extensions, of seventh chords. Ninth, eleventh, and thirteenth chords may be employed on all scale degrees. In practice, however, they most frequently occur as extensions of the Mm7 chord and are exemplified below mainly in that role.

A seventh chord is constructed by adding to a triad a pitch that is a seventh above its root. Similarly, a ninth chord is constructed by adding to a seventh chord a pitch that is a ninth above its root. The logical extension of this procedure accounts for the eleventh and thirteenth chords, as shown by the examples below.

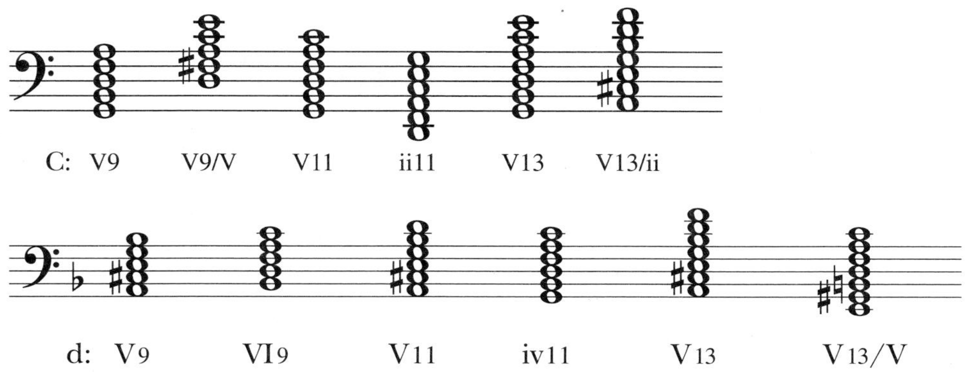

Note:
Each chord is designated by a single number.

NINTH CHORDS

1. In four voices:

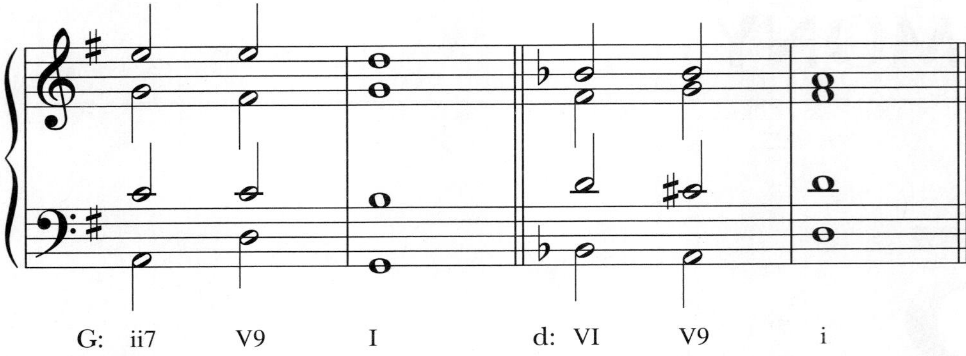

Note:

a. The fifth is omitted.

b. The ninth resolves downward by step.

2. In five voices:

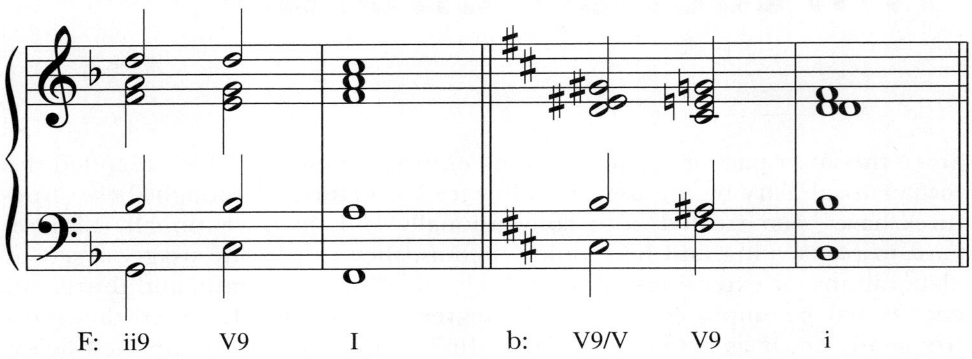

Note:
In the resolution of the dominant ninth to the tonic, the fifth is resolved upward by step to avoid parallel fifths.

PERFECT ELEVENTH CHORDS

1. In four voices:

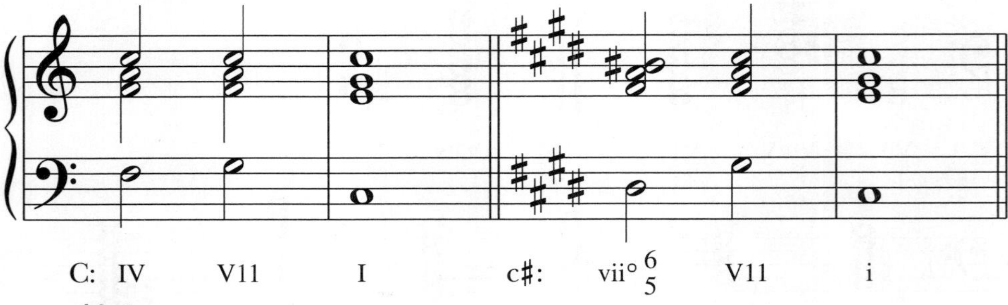

Note:

a. The third and fifth are omitted.

b. The eleventh is resolved passively.

c. The sonority has characteristics of both dominant and subdominant harmony.

2. In five voices:

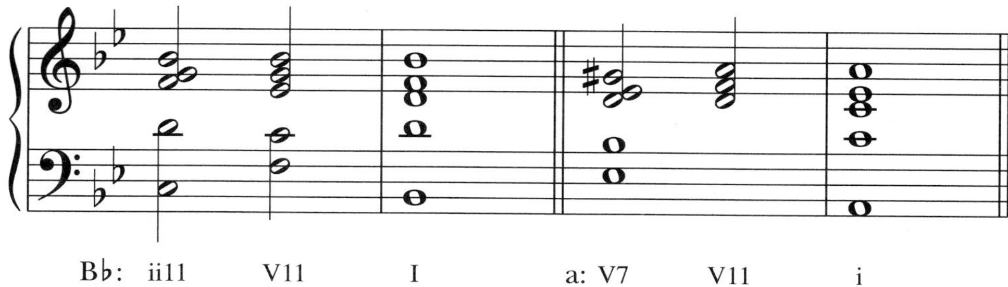

Note:

a. The third is omitted.

b. In the resolution of the dominant eleventh to the tonic, the fifth is resolved upward by step to avoid parallel fifths.

3. In six voices:

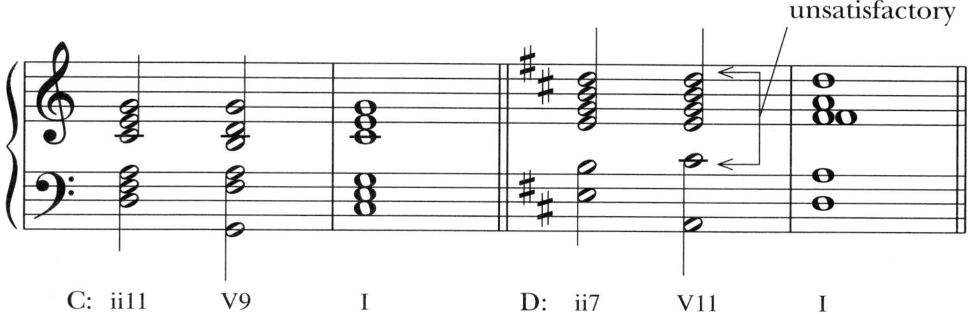

Note:
Because the complete dominant perfect eleventh includes both the leading tone and the tonic note, the chord is very rarely used.

AUGMENTED ELEVENTH CHORDS

1. In four voices:

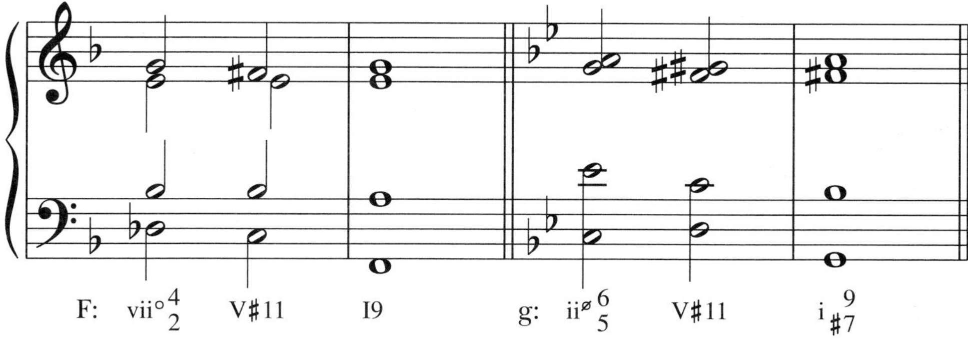

Note:

a. The fifth and ninth are omitted.

b. The eleventh resolves upward by a half step.

c. The third is resolved passively.

d. I9 is a dissonant sonority. The use, therefore, of the dominant augmented eleventh is restricted to musical styles in which this kind of activity is tolerated, for example, jazz and popular music, and in the works of many composers of the impressionist period through the present.

2. In five voices:

Note:

a. The fifth is omitted.

b. The resolution of the dominant augmented eleventh is a complete tonic ninth.

3. In six voices:

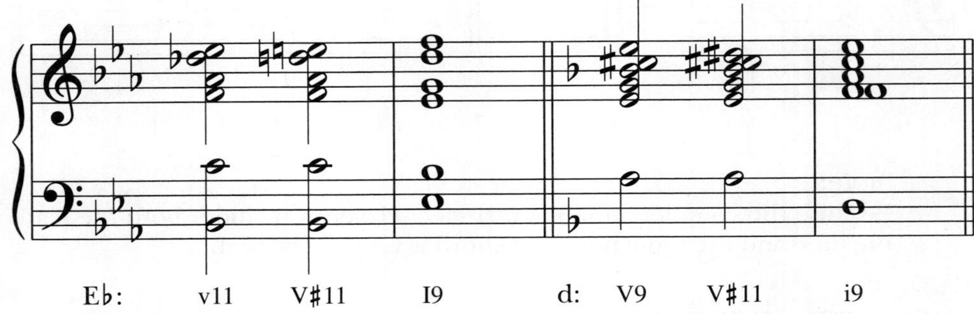

Note:
The fifth is resolved upward by step when doing so is necessary to avoid parallel fifths.

THIRTEENTH CHORDS

1. In four voices:

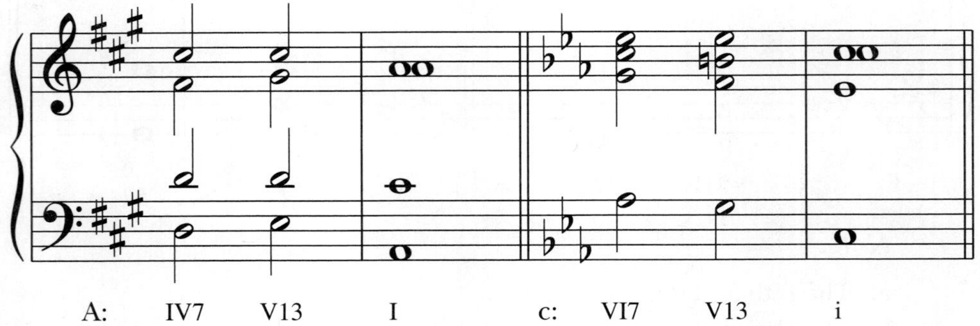

Note:

a. The fifth, ninth, and eleventh are omitted.

b. The thirteenth resolves downward by a third to the tonic note.

2. In five voices:

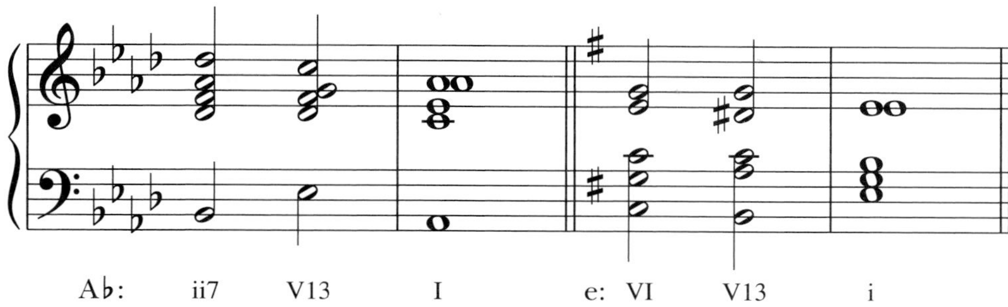

Note:
The fifth and the eleventh are omitted.

3. In six voices:

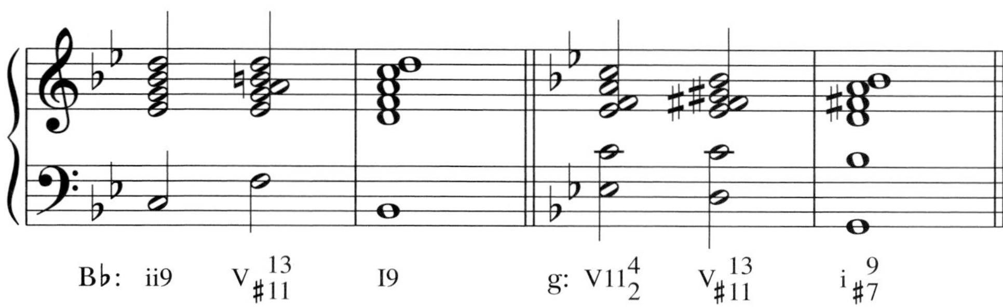

Note:

a. The fifth is omitted.
b. The augmented eleventh is used.
c. The thirteenth is usually resolved passively to avoid crossing voices.
d. The third is resolved passively.

4. In seven voices:

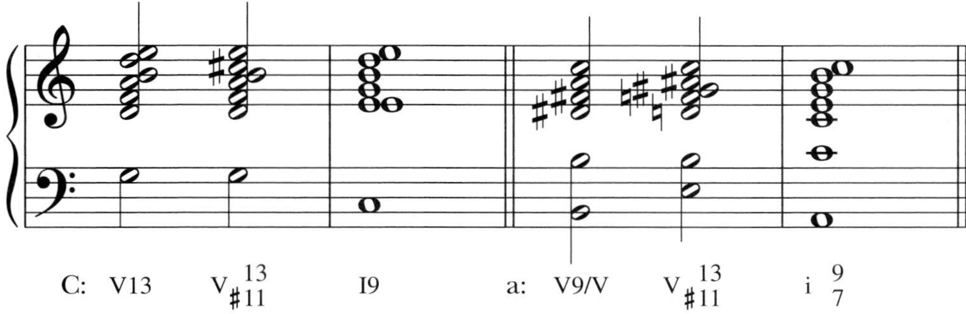

Note:
The fifth is resolved upward to avoid parallel fifths.

NINTH, ELEVENTH, AND THIRTEENTH CHORDS IN COMBINATION

The two musical examples that follow, one for piano and one for SATB, show how these extended chords may be used within the framework of functional tertian harmony. Careful study of the examples will reveal some minor irregularities in voice leading. The addition of ninths, elevenths, and thirteenths to seventh chords frequently creates problems for which no "correct" solutions exist. Under such circumstances, one resolves the problems as smoothly as the situation allows.

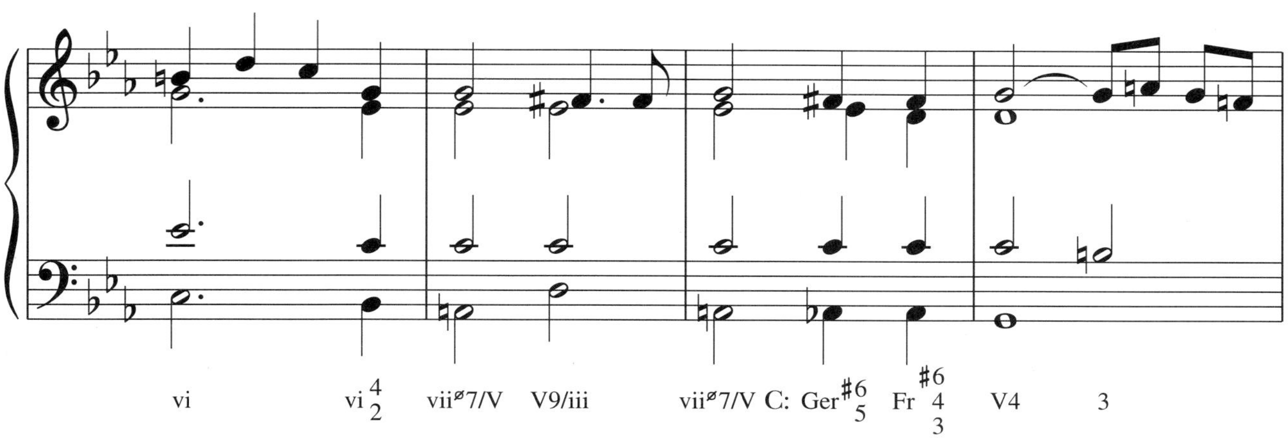
vi
vi 4 2
vii⌀7/V
V9/iii
vii⌀7/V
C: Ger♯6 5
Fr ♯6 4 3
V4
3

I7
V9/IV
IV7
V7
ii7
V13
V6 5/vi
vi
vi7
V♭9/V

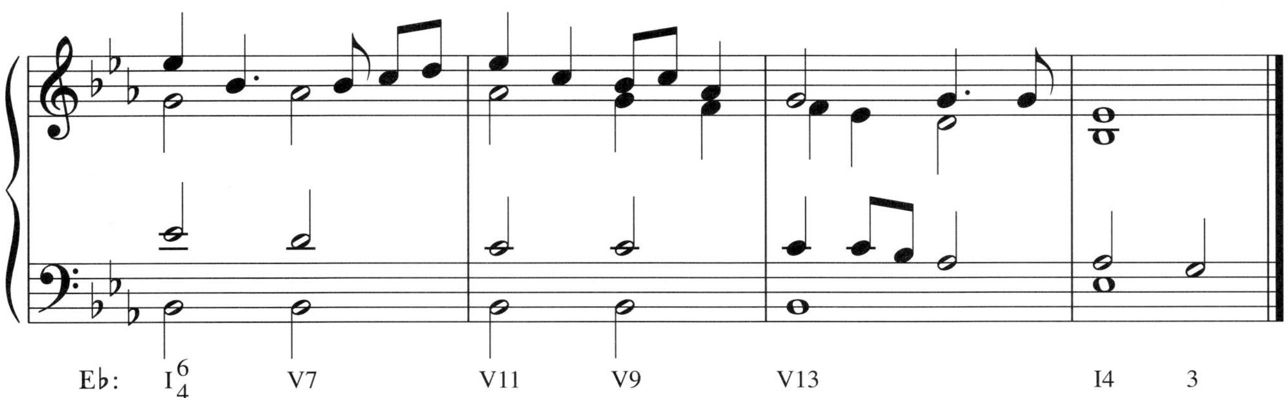
E♭: I6 4
V7
V11
V9
V13
I4
3

EXERCISES

A. Write and resolve the following chords in four voices.

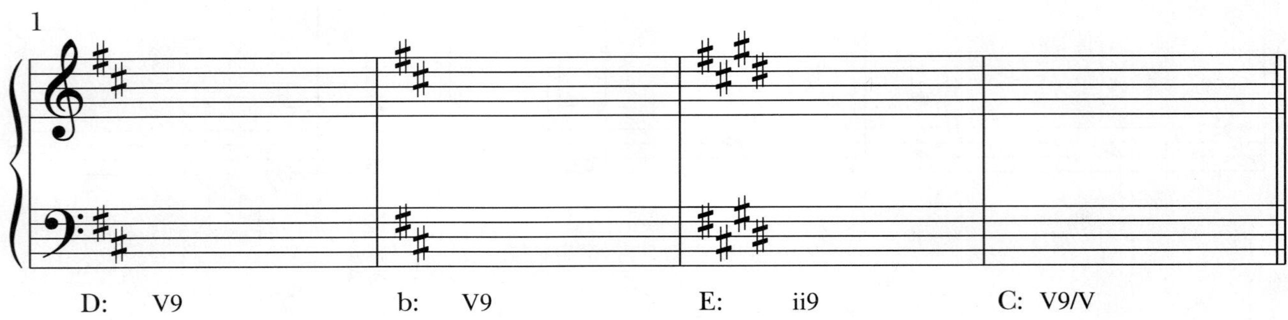

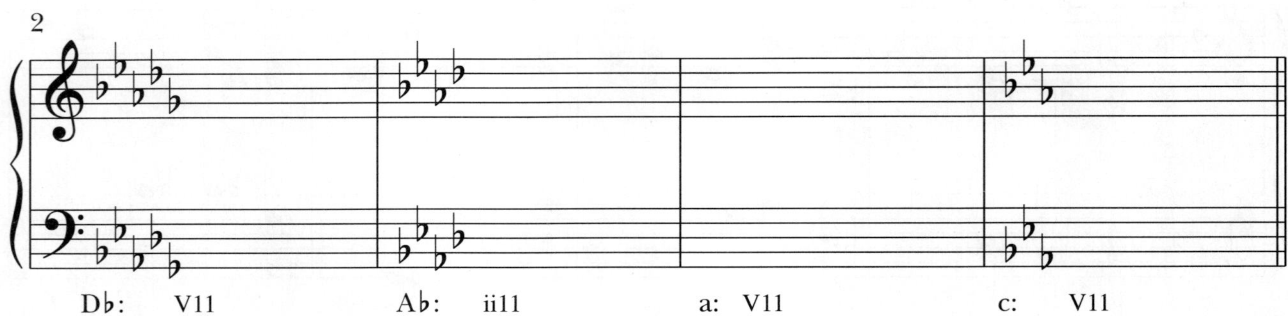

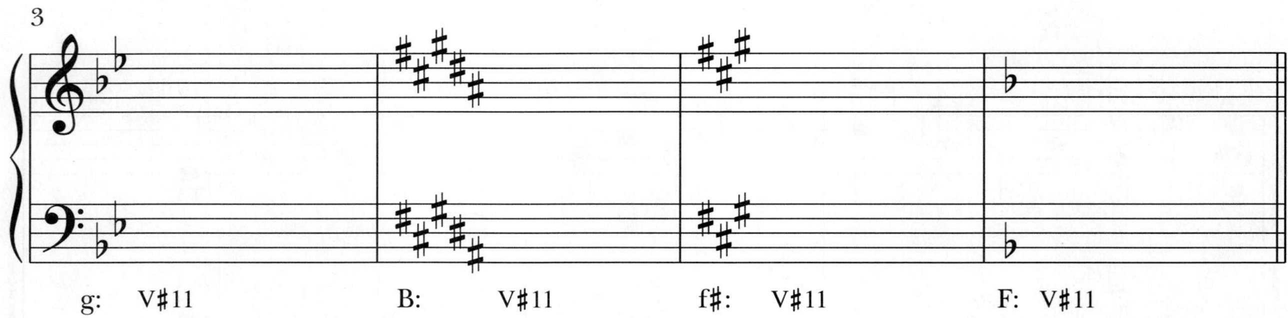

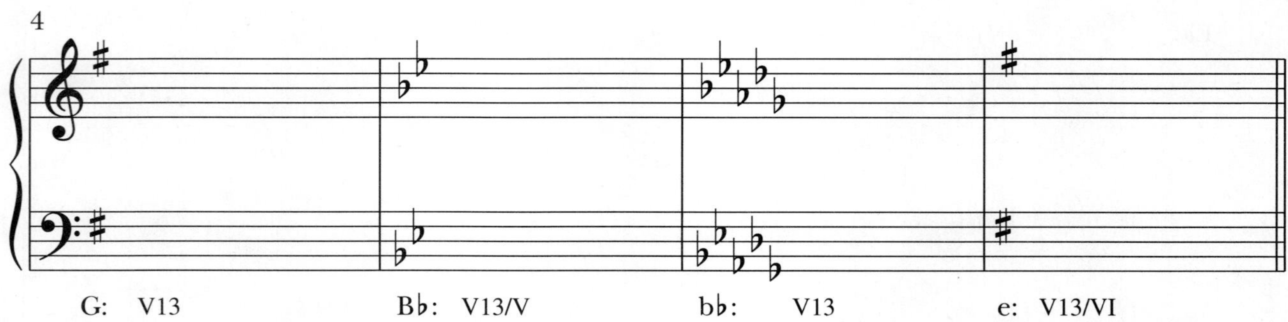

B. 1. Make a harmonic analysis of the piece below.
2. Reduce it to a four-voice structure by crossing out all the unessential pitches.

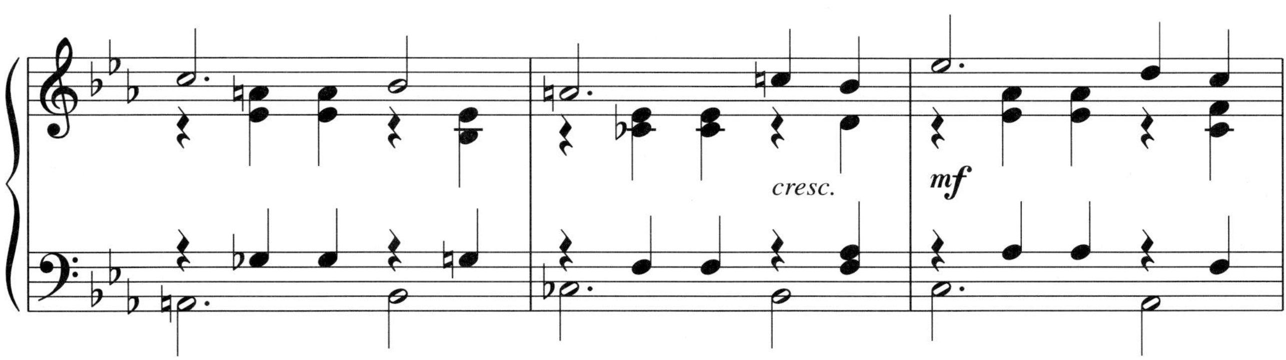

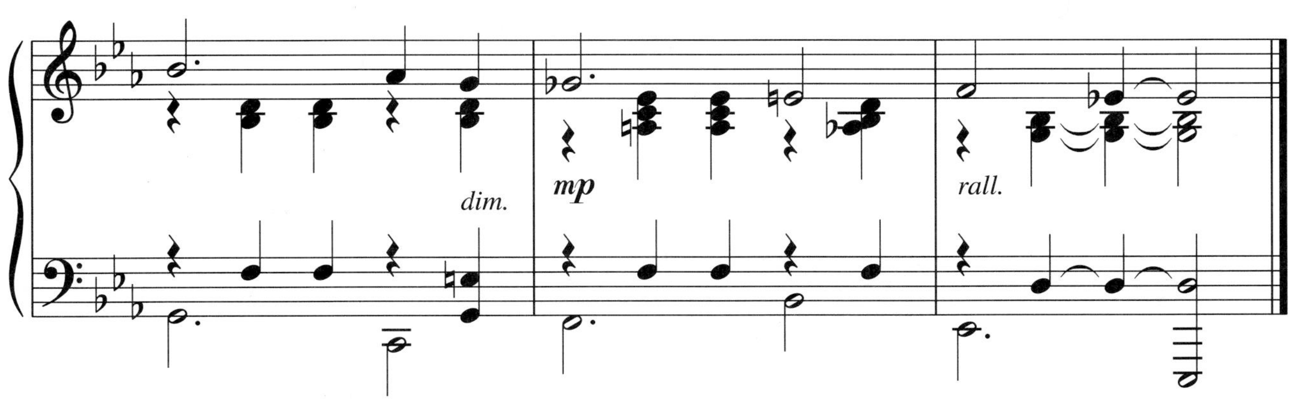

C. Harmonize the following in open score, making appropriate use of nonchord tones.

1

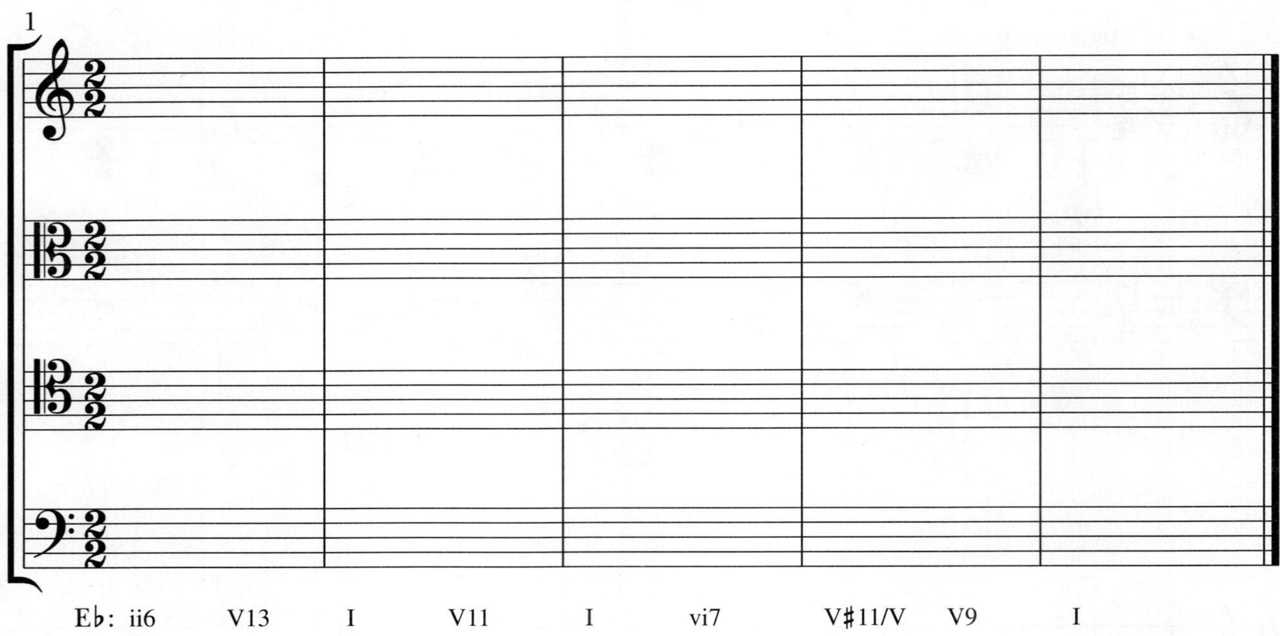

2

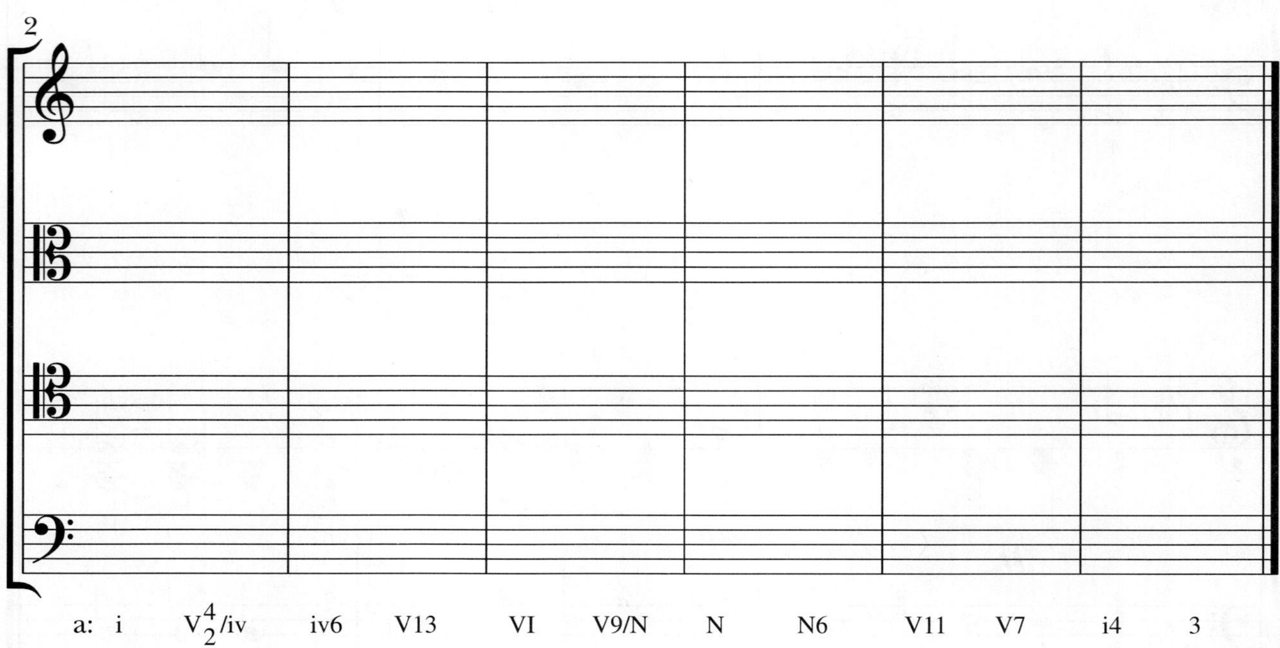

D. Complete the following pieces for piano in the style suggested by the beginning of each. They should be no more than sixteen measures in length.

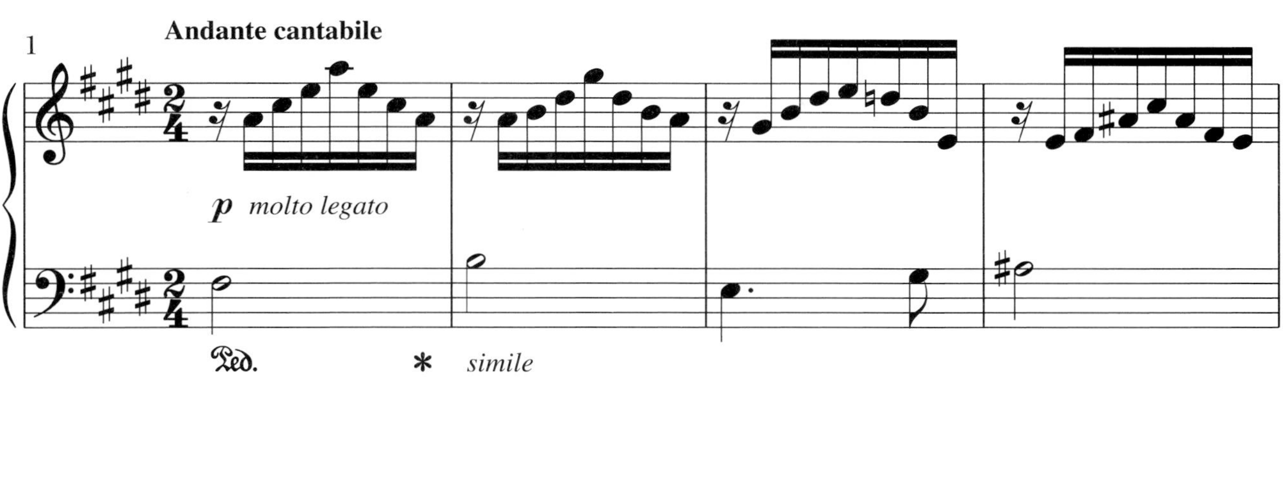

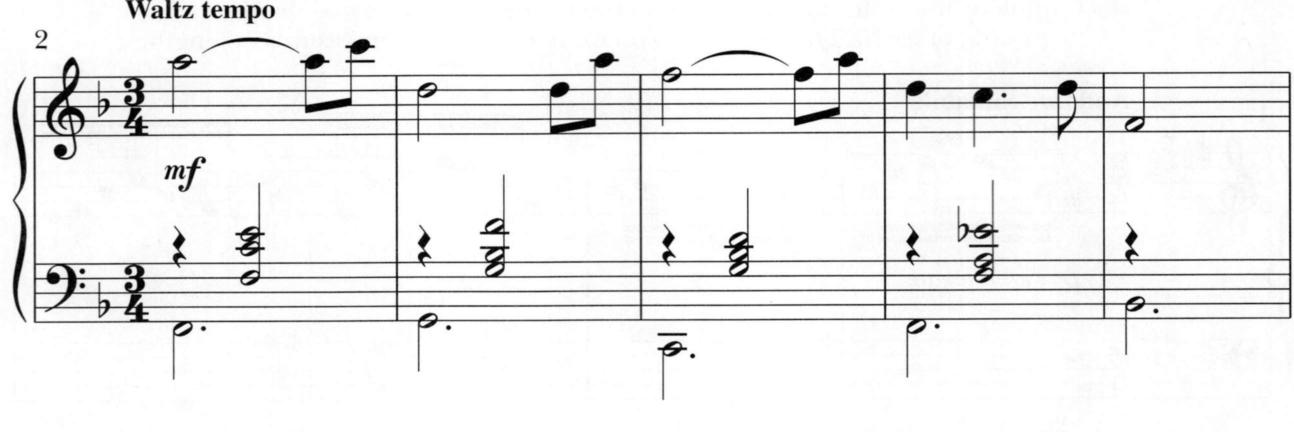
Waltz tempo
2
mf

EXERCISES FOR HARMONIC ANALYSIS

Wagner, Richard

Prelude to and opening of Act I from *Tristan und Isolde*
Prelude to and opening of Act III from *Tristan und Isolde*

Beethoven, Ludwig van

Piano Sonata no. 9 in E major, op. 14 no. 1, I

Schubert, Franz

Originaltänze, op. 9 no. 29

Chopin, Frédéric

Nocturne in C-sharp minor, op. 27 no. 1

Wolf, Hugo

"Der Mond hat eine schwere Klag' erhoben" ("The moon has been seriously complaining") from *Italienisches Liederbuch*
"Er ist's" from *Gedichte von Eduard Mörike*

Ravel, Maurice

Menuet from *Le Tombeau de Couperin*

Ives, Charles

The Housatonic at Stockbridge (1921)

1. Analyze the key scheme of each example.
2. Identify all chords with dominant (or secondary dominant) function, and label the resolution of each one as normal (N) or deceptive (D).
3. Identify all extended harmonies.

26
Chord Symbols

In Chapter 9, figured bass was introduced and shown to be a musical shorthand to save composers' time; with the addition of Roman numerals representing the seven scale degrees, it has become a useful analytical tool. With a change in emphasis from bass to soprano (or melody), a similar shorthand has developed. Commonly found in lead sheets of popular music is a melody line under (or above) which chord symbols are written. These symbols (which, unlike the combination of Roman numerals and figured bass, give no specific information about harmonic function and voice leading) allow performers both to harmonize the melody and, depending upon their expertise, to improvise upon it. In addition, chord symbols are printed above the vocal line in published sheet music and are used by performers who either cannot play the written-out piano part or prefer to invent their own accompaniment based upon the given harmonies.

The symbols below are those understood and used by most performers and composers of jazz and popular music.

SYMBOL	QUALITY	NOTATION
C	major triad	
Cm or C-	minor triad	
C° or Cdim	diminished triad	
C+ or Caug	augmented triad	
C6	major triad with added major sixth	
Cm6	minor triad with added major sixth	
C7	major-minor seventh (dominant seventh)	

CM7 or Cmaj7	major-major seventh
Cm7 or C-7	minor-minor seventh
C°7 or Cdim7 (or C° or Cdim)	diminished-diminished seventh
C9	dominant ninth
Cm9	minor-minor seventh with added ninth
C11	dominant eleventh
C13	dominant thirteenth

Note:

a. The symbol for the diminished triad is also used when a diminished seventh chord is intended.

b. There is no simple symbol for a half-diminished seventh chord, but its equivalent is given below.

Chromatic alterations and more complex chords are indicated in the following manner:

An inversion is indicated by writing the name of the bass note either below or to the right of the chord symbol, thus:

$\frac{\text{C7}}{\text{E}}$ or C7/E

A pedal bass note may be written similarly:

$\frac{\text{Cm7}}{\text{F}}$ or Cm7/F

The two examples below are lead sheet, and therefore approximate, reductions of the examples of combined ninth, eleventh, and thirteenth chords in the previous chapter. Compare the two versions carefully, and make note of the translation of the Roman numeral analysis into chord symbols.

Moderately
Bm7 Bm11+9 Em7 Em9 Am7 Am11 D7 D7+11
GM7 G7 CM7+11 Am6 D13+11 G9

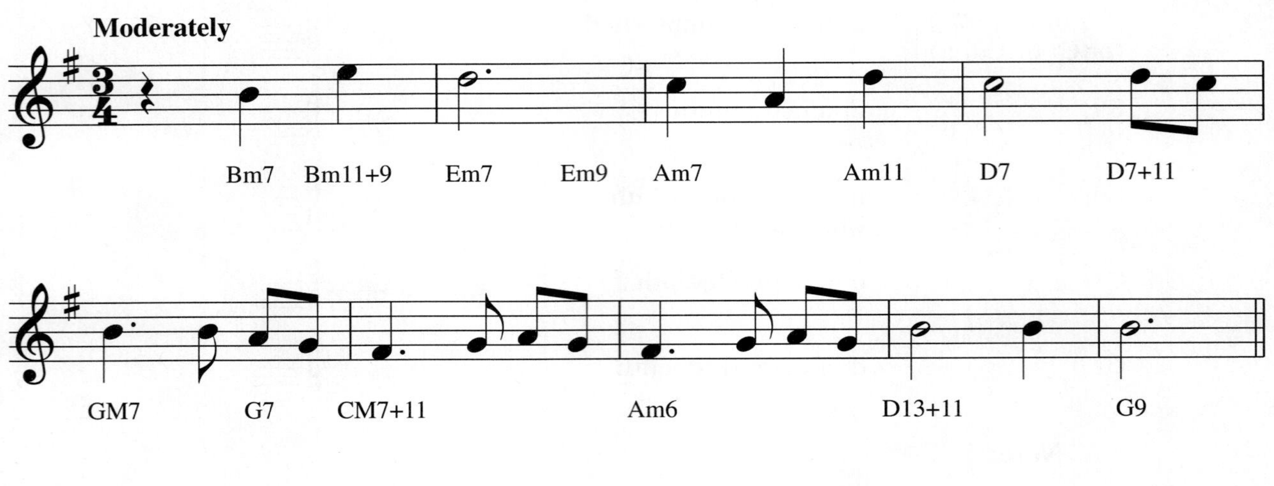

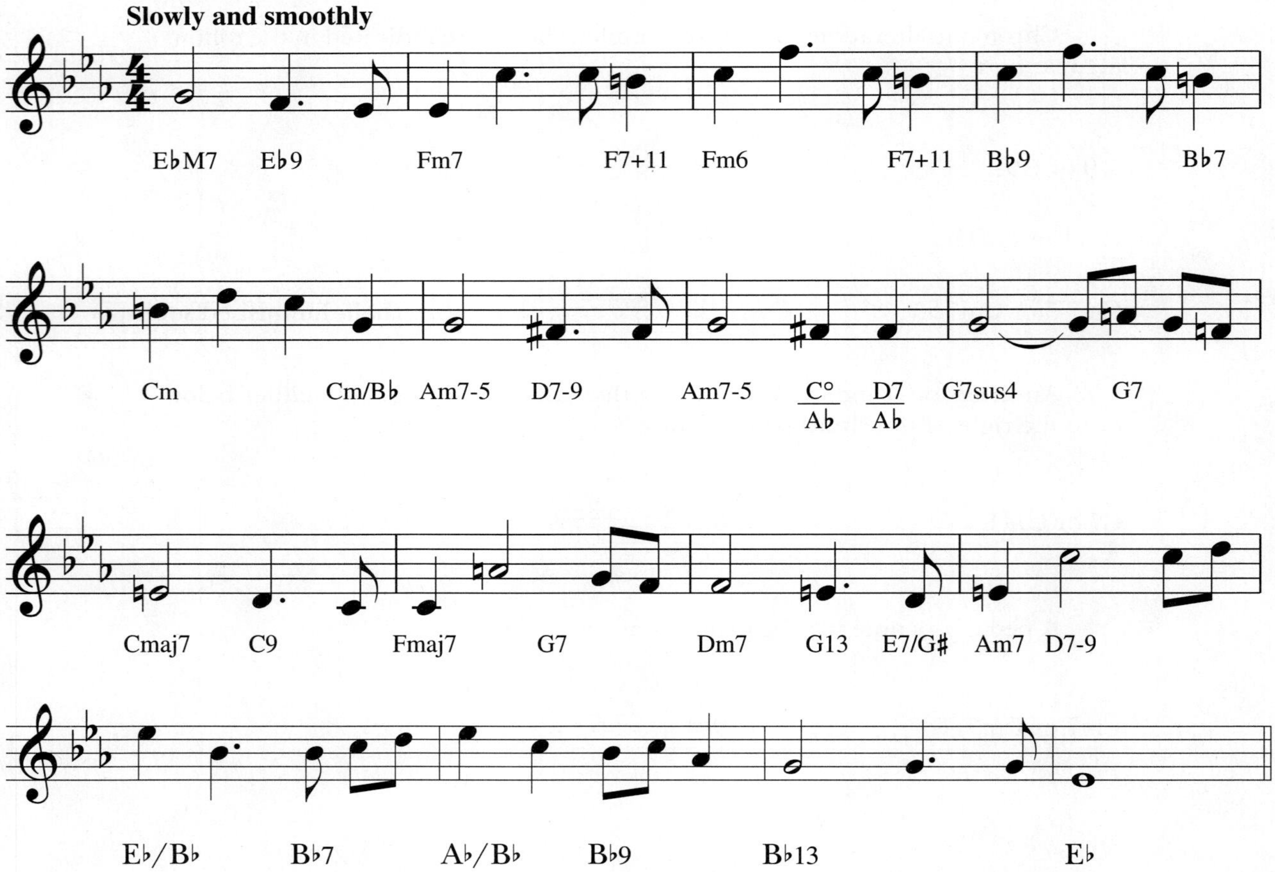

Slowly and smoothly
E♭M7 E♭9 Fm7 F7+11 Fm6 F7+11 B♭9 B♭7
Cm Cm/B♭ Am7-5 D7-9 Am7-5 C°/A♭ D7/A♭ G7sus4 G7
Cmaj7 C9 Fmaj7 G7 Dm7 G13 E7/G♯ Am7 D7-9
E♭/B♭ B♭7 A♭/B♭ B♭9 B♭13 E♭

TRITONE SUBSTITUTION

In jazz and popular music, a dominant-type chord (e.g., G7, G9, etc.) is often replaced in a progression by a dominant-type chord whose root is a diminished fifth above (or augmented fourth below) it. Such a replacement is called a *tritone substitution.* The substitution is effective because both chords enharmonically share two important chord members, the third and seventh, which themselves form the interval of a tritone. The following examples show how the substitution works:

Note:

In these progressions, there are irregularities in voice leading, including parallel fifths and unconventionally resolved leading tones. These irregular procedures are commonly encountered in popular music and jazz.

EXERCISES

A. Assign symbols to the following chords.

B. 1. Write out the indicated chords using a combination of 3-7 voices.

2. Determine an accompaniment pattern that complements the melody and complete the piece for either solo piano or piano plus melodic instrument.

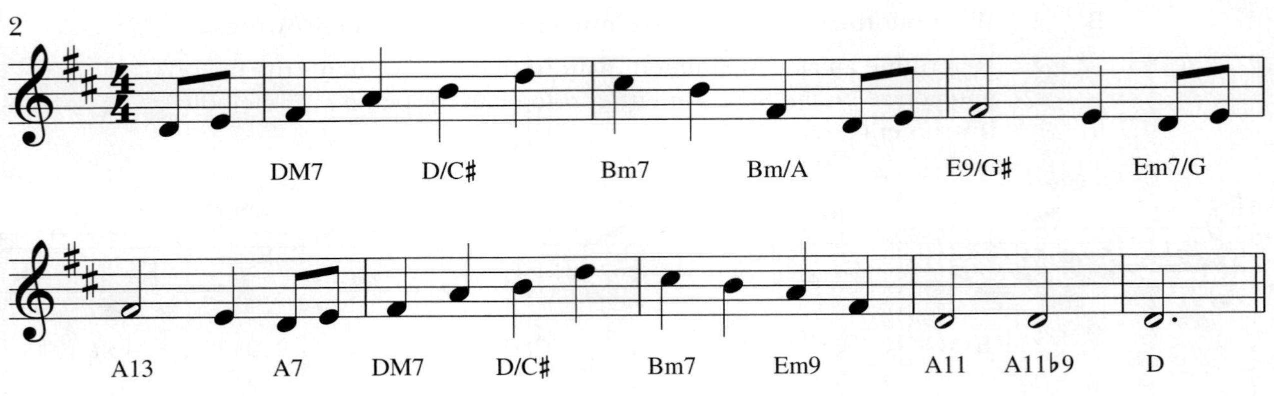
2
DM7
D/C♯
Bm7
Bm/A
E9/G♯
Em7/G
A13
A7
DM7
D/C♯
Bm7
Em9
A11
A11♭9
D

C. Provide an analysis of the given incipits. Using chord symbols, create a progression of up to sixteen measures and complete the following pieces for piano in the style suggested.

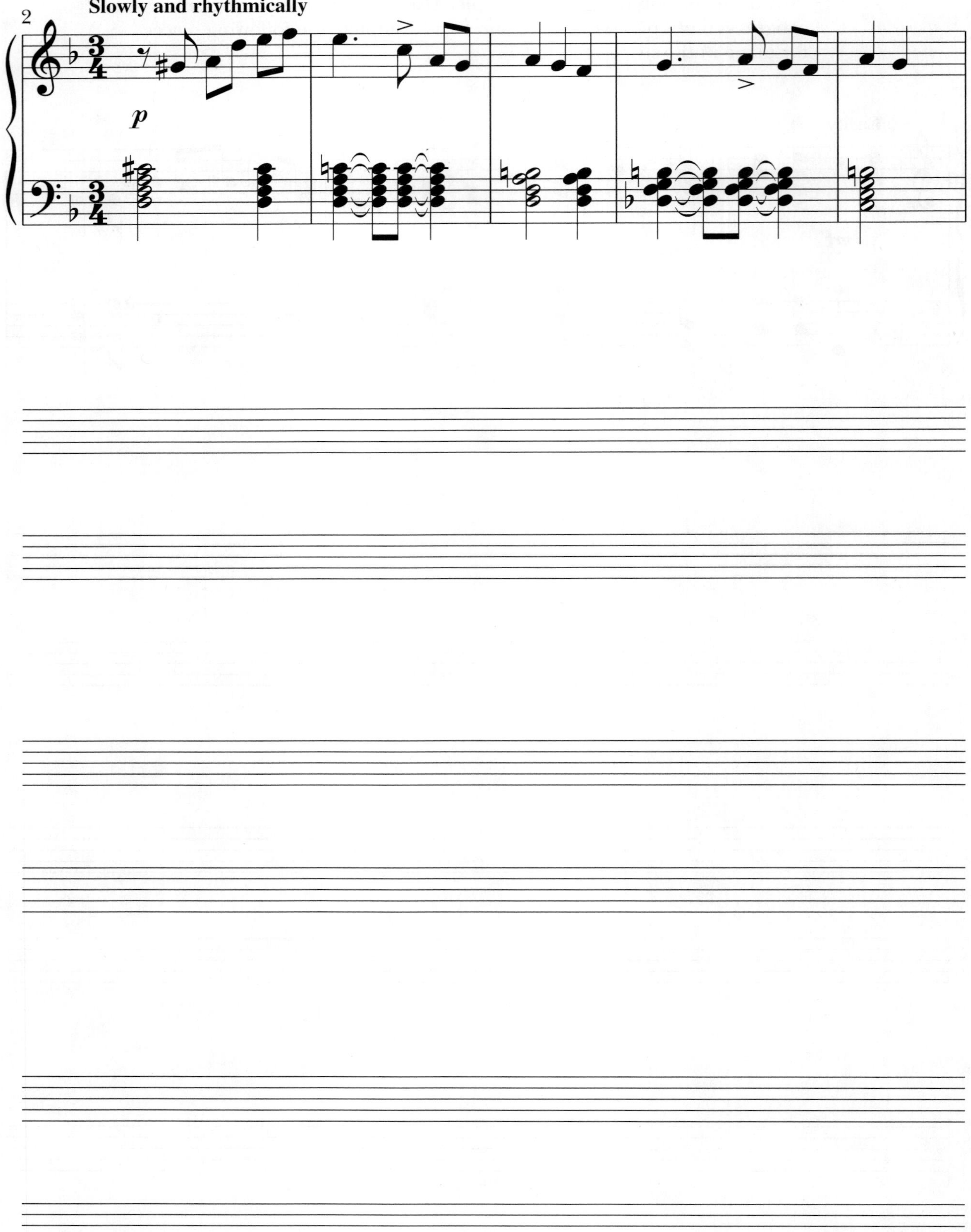
2
Slowly and rhythmically
p

27
Modal Harmony

MODES

Despite the wealth of resources offered by the major-minor scale system, toward the end of the nineteenth century some composers began to seek out alternative scale patterns from which to build their compositions. As a result of these endeavors, the so-called Greek modes, which predate the major-minor scale system by several centuries, enjoyed a renaissance as the basis for both melodic and harmonic activity.

There are seven of these modes, each of which may be constructed by beginning upon a different degree of the major scale:

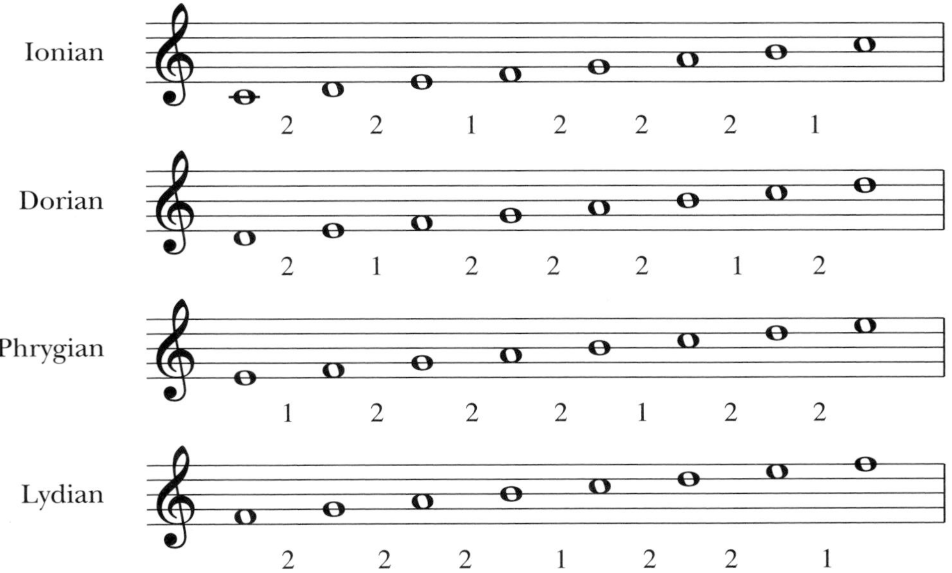

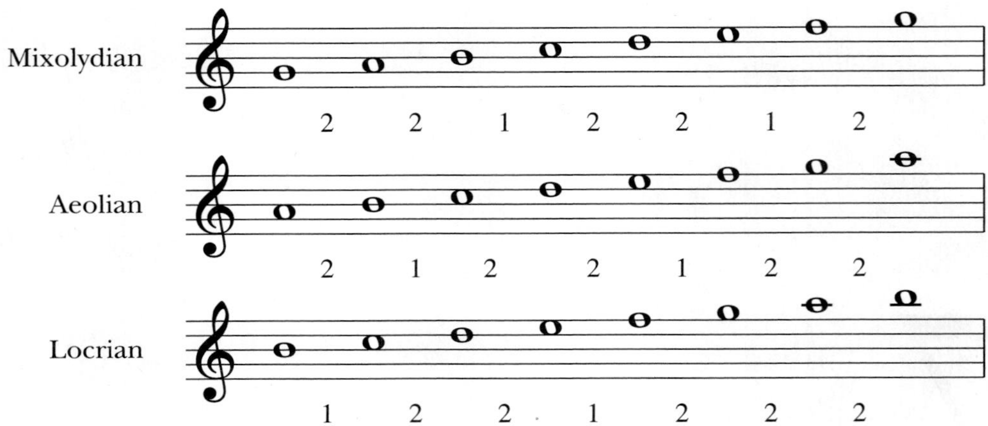

It can be seen that, because of its starting point, each mode has an individual intervallic organization which gives it its particular character.

There are, however, three logical groupings of the modes, based upon the qualities of the "tonic" triads.

1. *Major modes:*

   Ionian—The same as the major scale.

   Lydian—The major scale with a *raised fourth* degree.

   Mixolydian—The major scale with a *lowered seventh* degree.

2. *Minor modes:*

   Dorian—The natural minor scale with a *raised sixth* degree.

   Phrygian—The natural minor scale with a *lowered second* degree.

   Aeolian—The same as the natural minor scale.

3. *Diminished mode:*

   Locrian—The natural minor scale with a *lowered second* and *lowered fifth* degree. The only mode without a dominant-tonic relationship.

The first six measures of "America" are set below in each of the seven modes. Study the examples carefully, and make note of how they differ one from another.

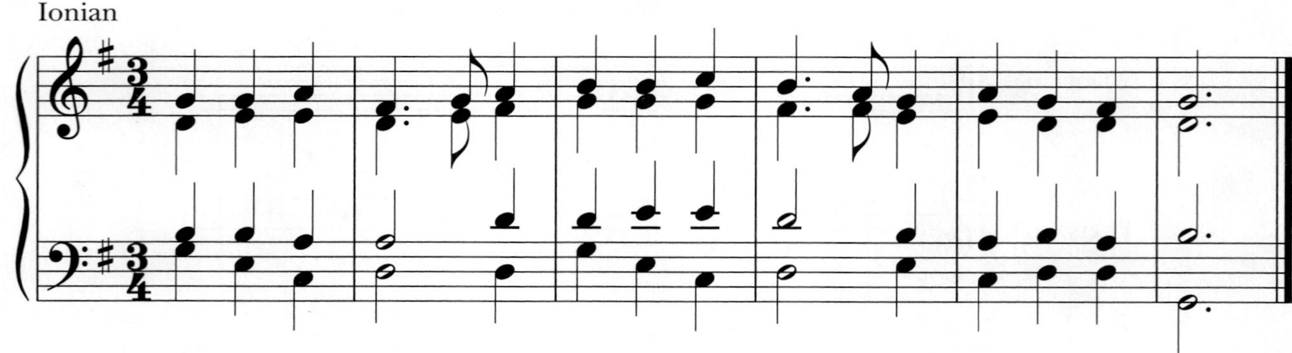

Note:
Since the Ionian mode is the same as the major scale, this is a simple diatonic setting of the melody.

Lydian

Note:

a. The Lydian mode is built upon the fourth degree of the major scale. Since G is the fourth degree of the D major scale, G Lydian has the same key signature as D major.

b. The soprano $c\sharp^2$ at the end of the third measure has a strong tendency to resolve to d^2. For this reason, the melody is subsequently transferred to the alto voice.

c. Although G is emphasized throughout as a tonic, the presence of the leading tone to V creates a certain tonal ambiguity. This is a feature to exploit in harmonizing Lydian melodies.

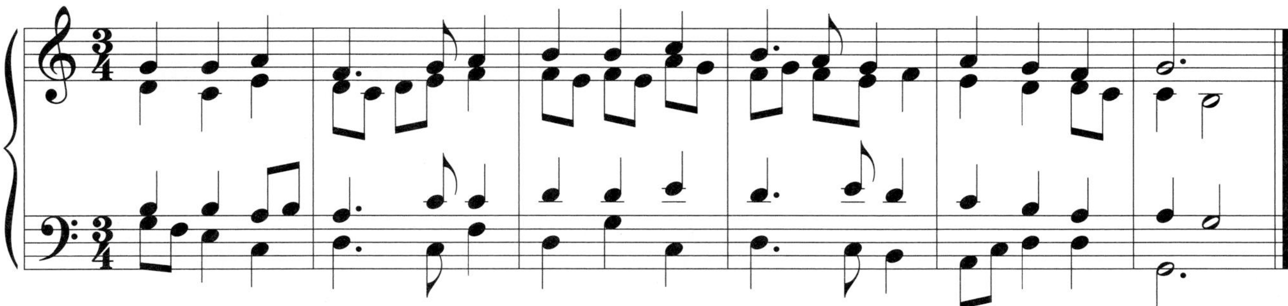

Note:

a. The Mixolydian mode is built upon the fifth degree of the major scale. Since G is the fifth degree of the C major scale, G Mixolydian has the same key signature as C major.

b. The tonal center of G is reinforced by a strong cadence and a scarcity of C major chords.

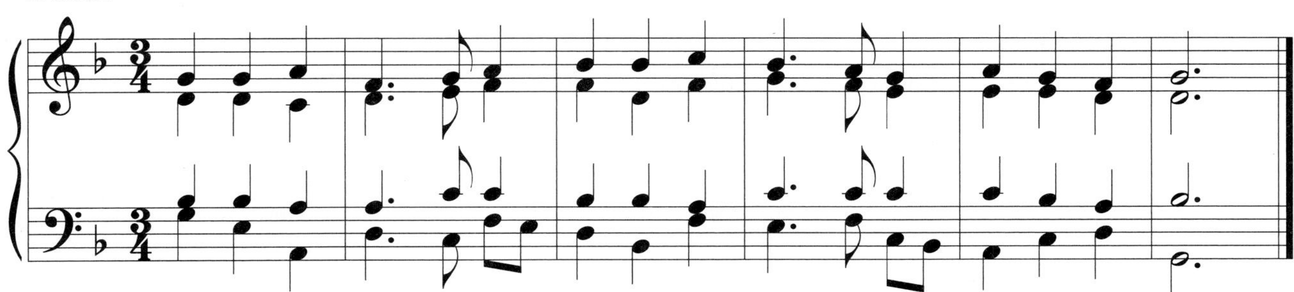

Note:

a. The Dorian mode is built upon the second degree of the major scale. Since G is the second degree of the F major scale, G Dorian has the same key signature as F major.

b. This setting tends to gravitate toward F major, largely due to the structure of the melody in this mode. The deceptive resolution of the C7 chord at the cadence aids in reaffirming G as tonic.

Phrygian

Note:

a. The Phrygian mode is built upon the third degree of the major scale. Since G is the third degree of the E♭ major scale, G Phrygian has the same key signature as E♭ major.

b. This setting typically concludes with the so-called Phrygian cadence, which, in this case, gives a strong impression of a half close in c minor.

Aeolian

Note:

a. The Aeolian mode is built upon the sixth degree of the major scale. Since G is the sixth degree of the B♭ major scale, G Aeolian has the same key signature as B♭ major.

b. This setting is an elaboration of the one in the Ionian mode but placed, of course, in the parallel natural minor. The two should be compared.

Note:

a. The Locrian mode is built on the seventh degree of the major scale. Since G is the seventh degree of the A♭ major scale, G Locrian has the same key signature as A♭ major.

b. The unstable diminished triad on G is no more than a theoretical tonic, and the setting concludes with a half cadence in A♭ major. The Locrian mode, in fact, is seldom used within the framework of functional harmony because a satisfactory conclusion on the tonic is almost impossible to achieve.

No chromatic pitches were used in any of the seven settings. Although such pitches are not prohibited, they should be handled with great care so that the flavor of the mode is not destroyed. For example, the excessive use of a raised seventh degree in a Mixolydian setting would negate the reason for using the Mixolydian mode in the first place.

THE PENTATONIC SCALE

An ancient scale with a number of modal connotations is the *pentatonic* scale. It contains five different pitches whose intervallic organization corresponds to the black keys on the piano. Although, technically, any one of its notes may be considered a tonic, the two forms given below are the most common since they alone allow the construction of a tonic triad.

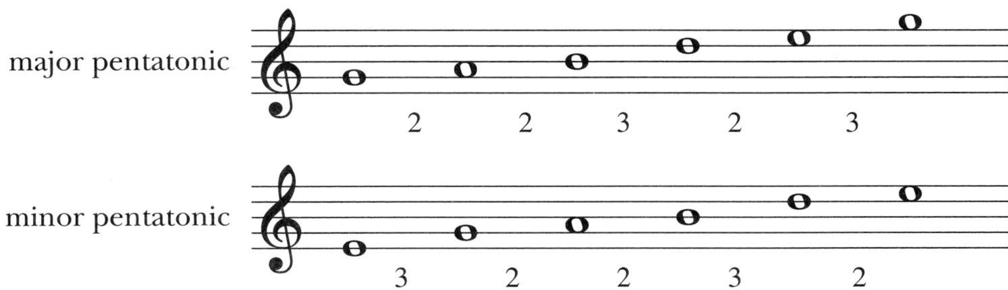

Note:

a. The scales are made up entirely of major seconds and minor thirds.

b. Neither scale contains a dominant triad. As a result, pentatonic harmonizations tend to have a modal flavor.

SUGGESTIONS AND STRATEGIES

You may find the following procedures helpful in identifying a mode when the key signature and the mode's tonic are given (Exercise A):

1. Always assume that the key signature is major (e.g., 2 sharps = D major).
2. If the mode's tonic is, for example, A, determine what scale degree A represents in D major.
3. Because A is the fifth scale degree in D major, it must be the tonic of the *Mixolydian* mode.

Similarly, if the key signature has four flats, and the mode's tonic is C:

1. The key signature is that of A♭ major.
2. The mode's tonic, C, is the third scale degree.
3. The mode built on the third scale degree is the *Phrygian* mode.

When you are preparing to harmonize a melody in a given mode (Exercise B), consider the following:

Harmony

1. Follow the same general procedures as you would in harmonizing a melody according to tonal principles (see Chapters 12 and 16).
2. Use the "tonic-dominant" relationships to establish the mode's quality—major, minor, or diminished.
3. Observe, to the extent that it is possible, normal voice-leading procedures. Avoid awkward intervals, parallel fifths and octaves, and so on.

When you are preparing to write and harmonize a melody (Exercise C), consider the following in addition to the above harmony statements:

Melody

1. Make sure that the mode's tonic appears prominently, particularly at the beginning and end of the melody.
2. Design the melody so that it has a clearly defined antecedent/consequent phrase structure.
3. Exploit the mode's characteristic scale degree(s). For example, a Lydian melody should feature the raised fourth scale degree.
4. If you add chromatic pitches, do so with caution. An excess of chromaticism has the effect of obscuring the identity of the mode.

EXERCISES

A. The key signature and the tonic are given. Identify the mode.

B. Harmonize the given melodies in SATB format.

C. Write two melodies using two different modes and each consisting of two four-measure phrases. Then determine a harmonization and arrange for piano.

MUSIC FOR ANALYSIS

Debussy, Claude

"Pagodes" from *Estampes*
"Canope" from *Préludes Book II,* no. 10
"Sarabande" from *Pour le Piano*
"Nuages" from *Nocturnes*

Stravinsky, Igor

"Spring Rounds" from *Le Sacre du printemps*

Bartók, Béla

Nos. 59 and 128 from *Mikrokosmos*

The use of pentatonic and modal scales may be found in the above pieces.

1. Identify the sections that seem to be modal.
2. To each modal section, assign a tonal center.
3. To each tonal center, assign a mode.
4. Identify the sections that use the pentatonic scale.
5. Determine what types of harmonies are used with the pentatonic scales.

28 Nonfunctional Harmony

Tertian harmony may be described as nonfunctional under one, or both, of the following conditions:

1. The renunciation of the hierarchy of root relationships associated with the major-minor key system.
2. The violation of the principles governing voice leading, with particular reference to sensitive pitches and intervals.

Music that demonstrates a conscious exploitation of either of these two conditions is not necessarily extremely complex from an analytical standpoint, nor even modern anymore, but nonetheless very much at odds with the "common practice" tradition.

ROOT MOVEMENTS BASED ON THE CHROMATIC SCALE

The following example, constructed in two four-measure phrases, begins and ends with a C major triad and may reasonably be said to have C as a tonal center. It exhibits very few harmonic progressions, however, that one would normally associate with the key of C.

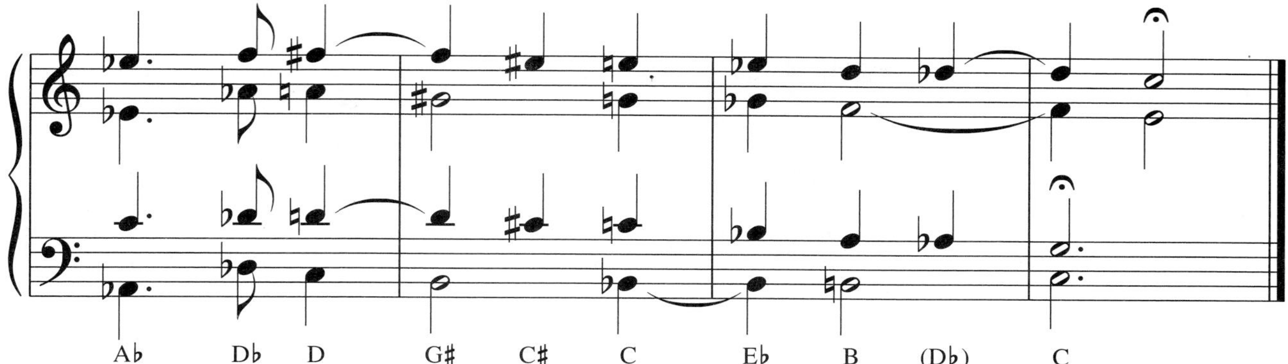

Note:

a. The dominant of C is avoided.

b. With the exception of E and G, chord roots occur on every degree of the chromatic scale.

c. The example consists largely of chromatic root movements, including those of the tritone.

d. In spite of the chromaticism, the voice leading is quite logical.

PARALLELISM

Parallelism describes the activity of a chain of chords whose voices proceed in parallel motion. The result usually contributes to a complete breakdown of traditional voice-leading procedures, and instead the emphasis shifts to the production of a "thickened" melodic line. "Real" parallelism involves a series of exact transpositions of a given chord; "tonal" parallelism involves the rewriting of a chord type (for example, triad, seventh chord) upon different degrees of a scale so that changes in quality may occur.

Note:

a. The example is based upon a chain of complete dominant ninth chords.

b. Neither the voice leading nor the root relationships are treated functionally.

Note:

a. The example is written in the Mixolydian mode on G.

b. Unlike the previous example, the quality of each chord is determined by the scale degree upon which it is built. The motion is, nonetheless, parallel throughout.

CHORDS OF ADDITION

A chord of addition is formed by adding a nonchord tone (or tones) to a tertian structure. This tone is usually a second, fourth, or sixth above the root of the chord.

Consider the following sonority and its use in the examples that follow:

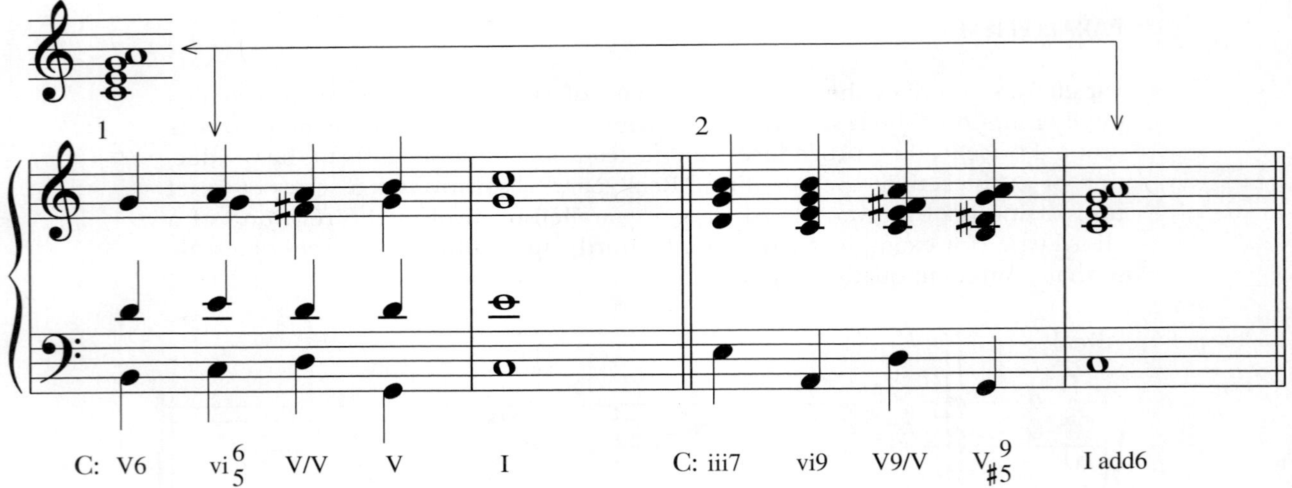

In Example 1, a¹ is the root of the submediant $^6_5$ chord. In Example 2, by contrast, there is no doubt that C is the root and that a¹ is simply "added" to the chord.

Thus, chords of addition tend to be used to create harmonic color:

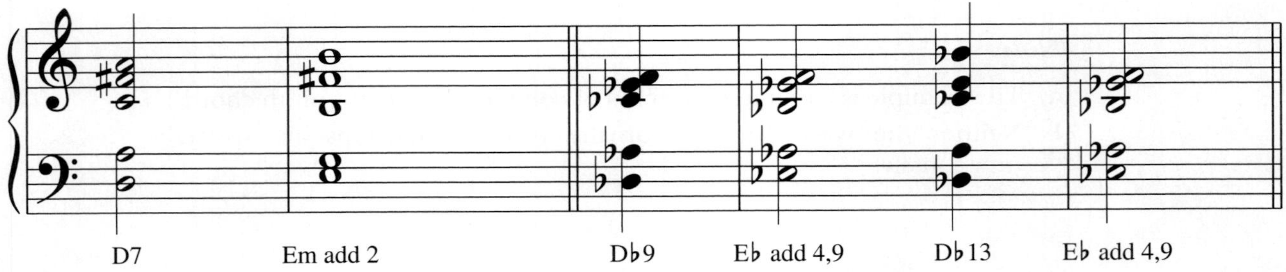

POLYCHORDS

A polychord is formed by superimposing one tertian structure upon another with a different root.

Thus:

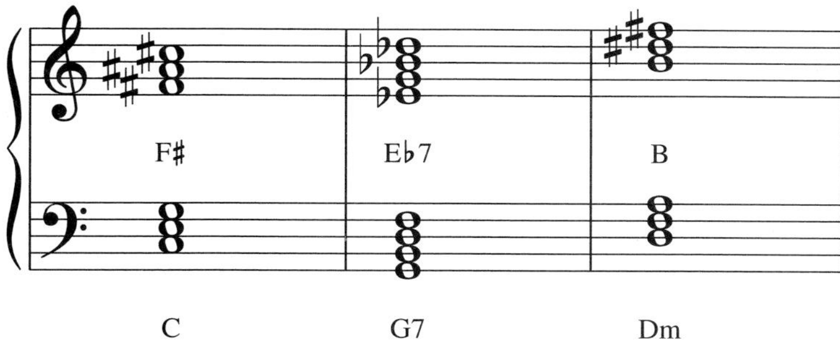

are polychords because in each case clearly distinguishable pairs of roots can be identified.

Care must be taken not to mistake polychords for extended single-root tertian sonorities.

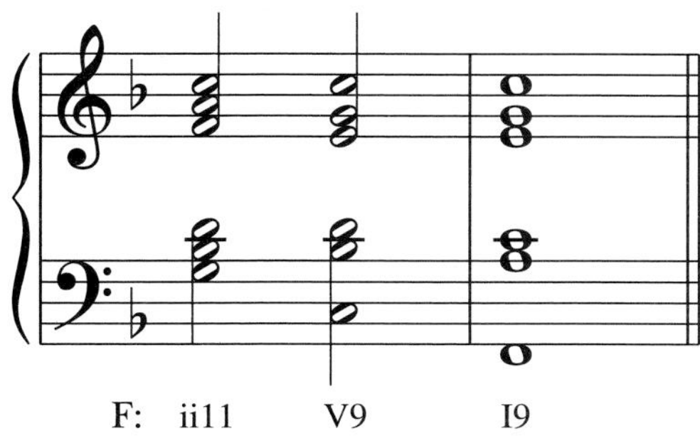

In the example above, for instance, the first chord is obviously a supertonic eleventh in F major, even though the bottom and top three notes form g minor and F major triads, respectively.

The following examples represent typical uses of polychords. Study them carefully.

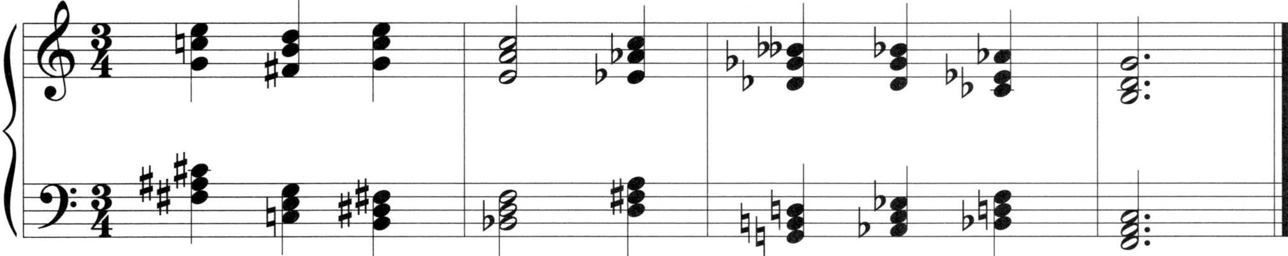

Note:

a. The right-hand part consists of alternating major and minor triads.

b. The left-hand part consists of only major triads. Each triad, however, contains a pitch that is related to the top line by a whole step (i.e., D–E, E–F♯, C–D, etc.).

Note:
The example is constructed entirely from pairs of Mm7 chords that move in contrary motion.

BITONALITY

Music in which two tonal centers simultaneously coexist is said to be *bitonal.* For such music to be comprehensible to the listener, the two tonalities are usually set in different registers or, in the case of instrumental music, allotted to instruments of contrasting timbres.

The term *polytonality,* which in theory refers to an unspecified number of simultaneous tonalities, is used synonymously with bitonality. In practice, music with more than two concurrent tonal centers is rarely encountered.

In the examples that follow, within each tonality the harmonic and melodic treatment is functional. The sense of function, however, is largely destroyed by the choice of tonal combinations.

PANDIATONICISM

Music that is the result of the free use of the diatonic rather than the chromatic scale is said to be *pandiatonic.* Implicit in the term is the organization of diatonic materials (major or minor) in a nonfunctional manner with respect both to chord progression and voice leading.

Although pandiatonic compositions are usually based upon tertian harmony, the linear movement "stretches" the chords so that conventional harmonic analysis is impossible. Chords tend to be implied, not stated, as the following example shows:

Note:

a. There are no chromatic pitches. The piece consists entirely of notes played on the white keys of the piano.

b. The harmonic motion evolves from the linear motion.

c. The final cadence on to the tonic, C, is voiced traditionally to achieve a sense of conclusion.

EXERCISES

A. Using the given chord roots, invent four-measure phrases for soprano, alto, tenor, and bass. The chords may be major or minor, and freely inverted. The harmonic rhythm is given.

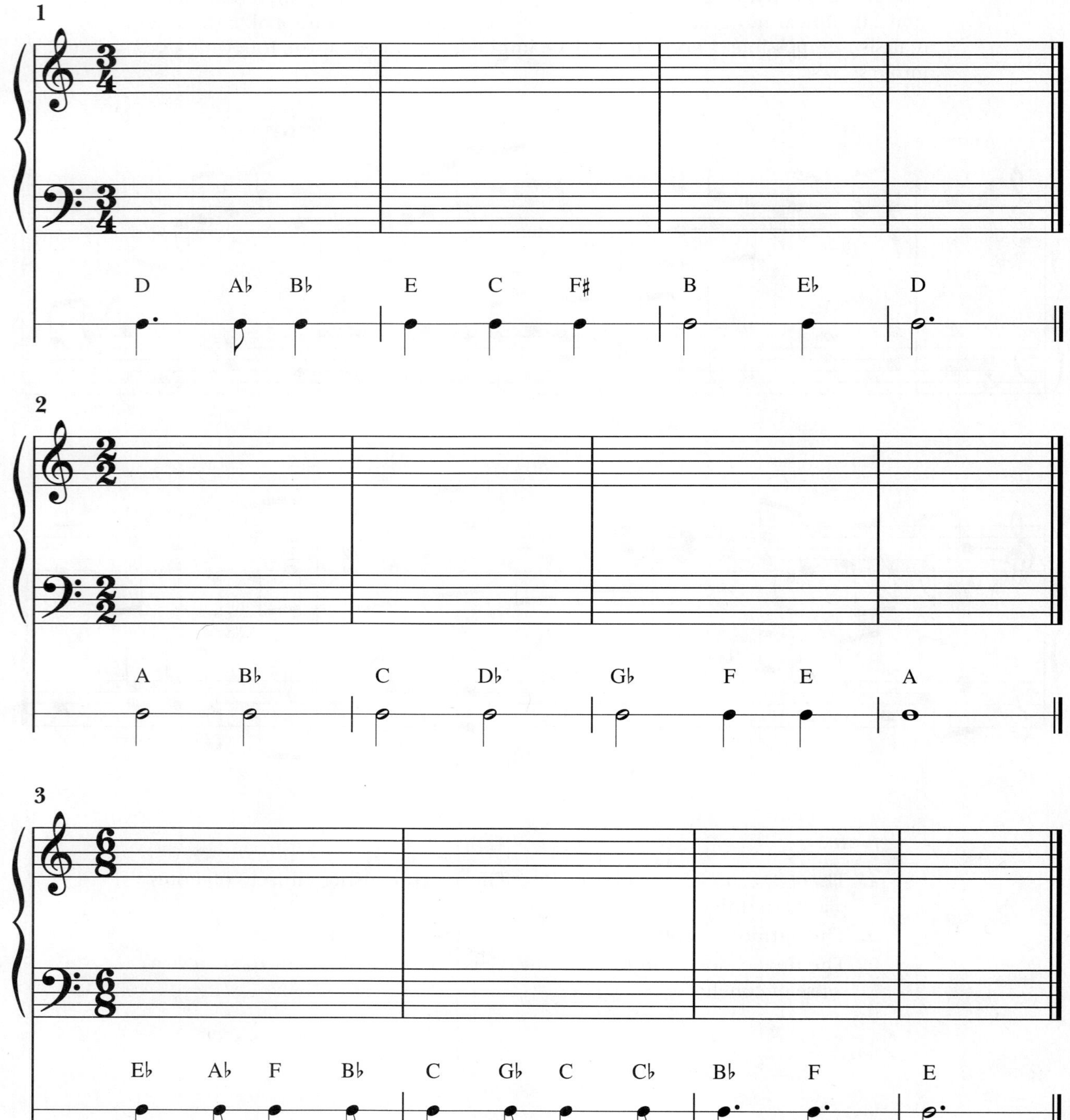

B. Continue the following in parallel motion as indicated.

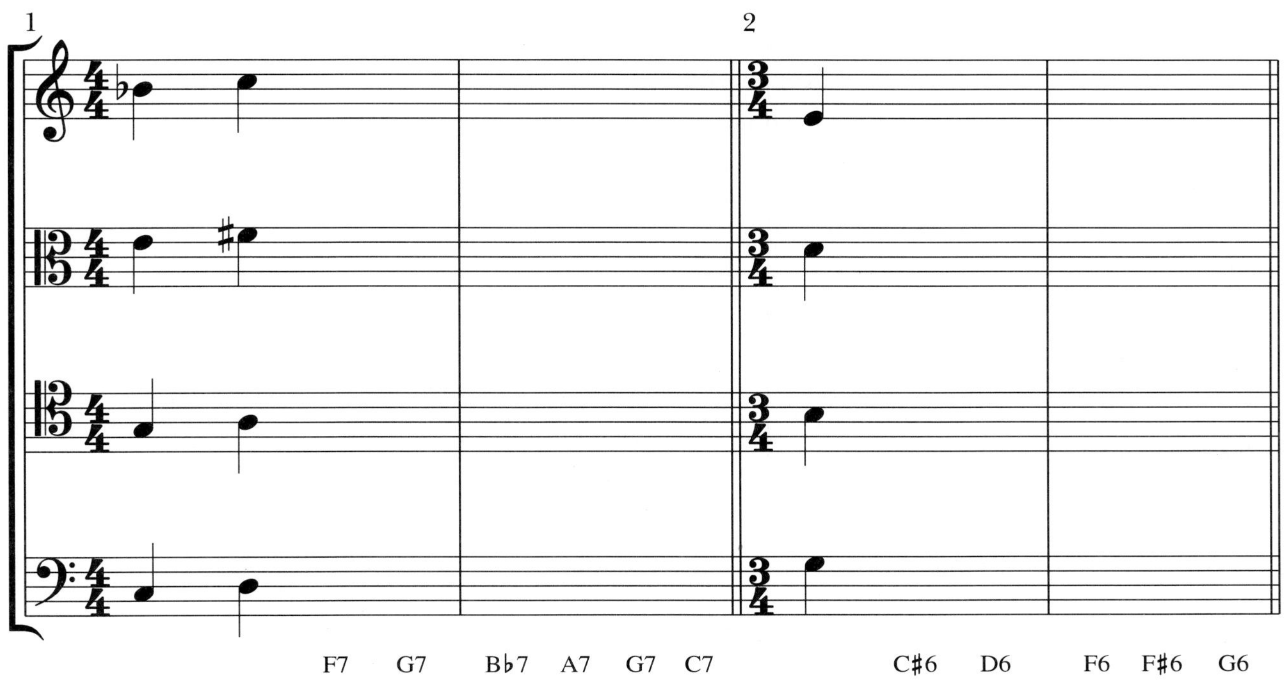

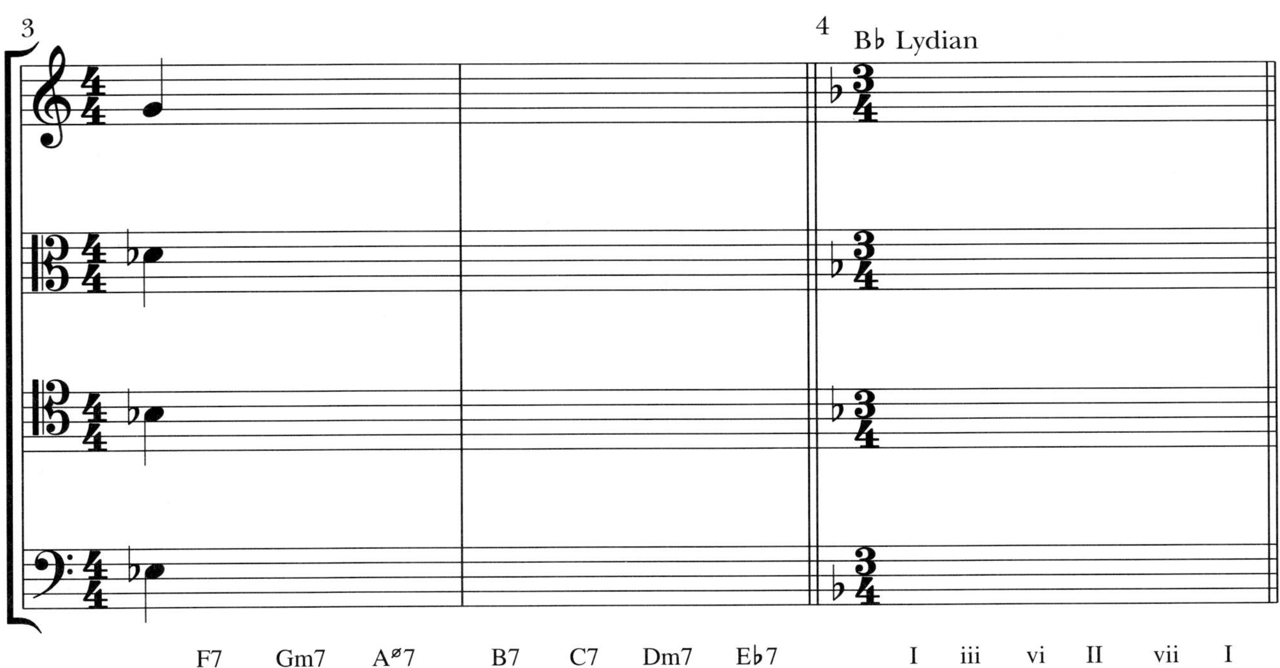

C. Beginning with the four given polychords, write a twelve-measure piece for piano made up of three four-measure phrases.

Phrase 1: Minor triads in the right hand, major triads in the left.
Phrase 2: Major triads in the right hand, minor triads in the left.
Phrase 3: Major triads in both hands.

Each polychord should have one, but not more than one, common note.

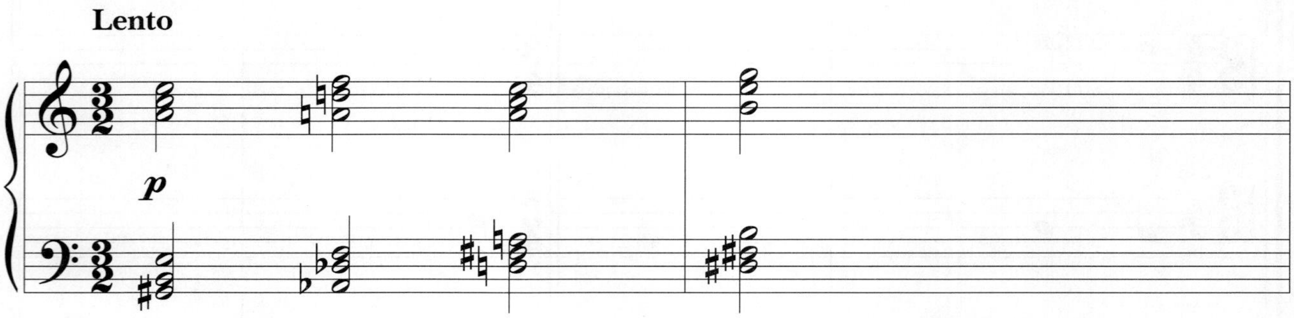

Lento

p

D. Harmonize the given two-phrase melody using a nonfunctional progression. Maintain a logical voice leading.

E. Using a free diatonic style, create a bass line to accompany the given melody. Then add an inner voice to fill out the suggested harmony that could be either the right hand of a piano part or another melodic instrument.

MUSIC FOR ANALYSIS

Identify and describe all uses of parallelism.

Debussy, Claude

"Sarabande" from *Pour le Piano*
"Nuages" from *Nocturnes*
"La Cathèdrale engloutie" from *Préludes Book I*, no. 10
"Canope" from *Préludes Book II*, no. 10

a. Identify the roots and qualities of the triads of which the polychords are constructed.
b. Try to determine the logic behind the construction of the polychords.

Debussy, Claude

"La puerta del Vino" from *Préludes Book II*, no. 3

Stravinsky, Igor

"Danses des Adolescentes" from *Le Sacre du printemps.* Rehearsal number 13

Ives, Charles

"Mists" from *114 Songs*, no. 57

These movements contain some of the compositional techniques discussed in this chapter. Identify and describe as many of them as you can.

Ives, Charles

Piano Sonata no. 2 (*Concord*), III (*The Alcotts*)

Hindemith, Paul

Piano Sonata no. 2, I

This *Tema* may be described as pandiatonic.

a. Identify all vertical structures of three or four pitches.
b. Divide the structures into those that are obviously tertian sonorities and those that are not so clearly tertian sonorities.
c. Determine the extent to which the clear tertian sonorities play a functional role in the music.

Dello Joio, Norman

Piano Sonata no. 3, I (Theme and Variations)

29
Artificial Scales

A scale that does not conform to a traditional pattern is said to be *artificial.* Although the possibilities for the construction of artificial scales are enormous, composers have tended to use those scales that possess an intrinsic mathematical logic, or scales from which unusual harmonic relationships may be derived.

Two artificial scales are in common use.

THE WHOLE TONE SCALE

The whole tone scale is constructed entirely of whole steps:

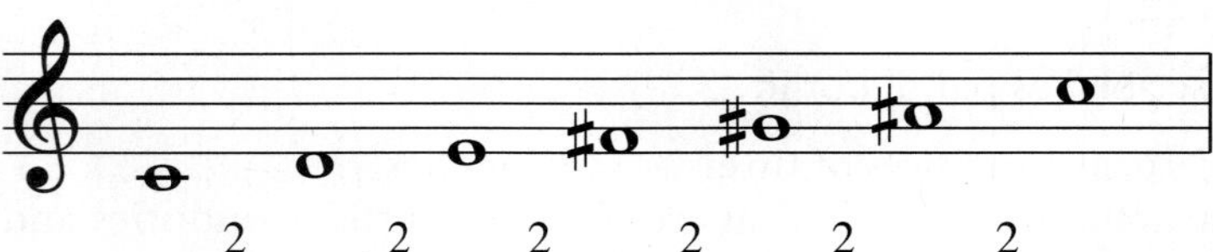

Derived tertian sonorities:

Note:

a. As a result of its construction, any note of the scale may be chosen as a tonic; the intervallic organization is unchanged.

b. The only transposition of the scale that allows a different pitch collection is that of a half step up or down. Thus, with reference to pitch, there are two distinct whole tone scales.

c. No stable tertian structures can be derived from the whole tone scale.

THE OCTATONIC (OR DIMINISHED) SCALE

The octatonic scale, made up of alternating half steps and whole steps, exists in two forms:

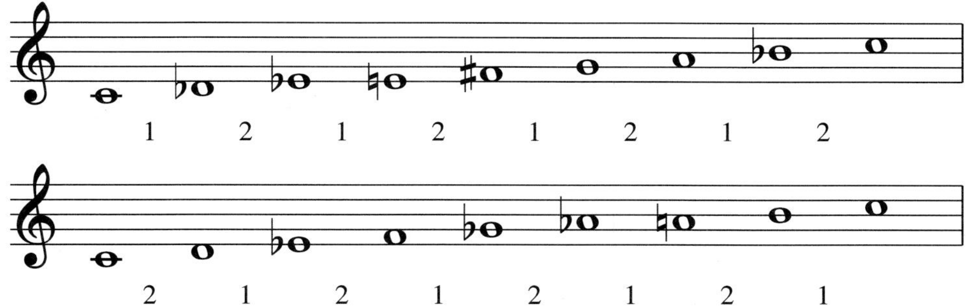

Derived tertian sonorities:

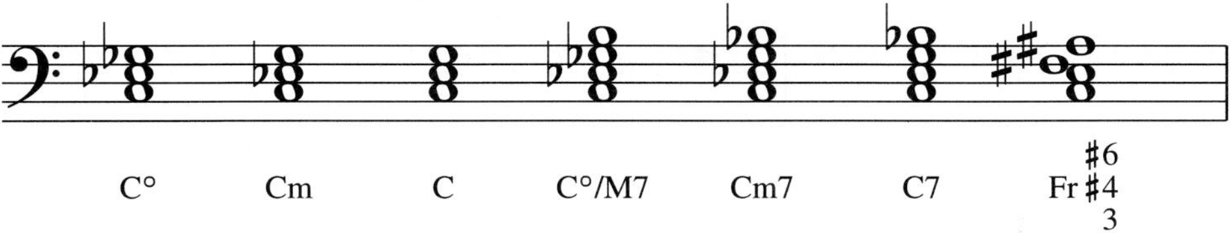

Note:

a. As a result of its construction, the first, third, fifth, and seventh note of either scale form may be chosen as tonics; the intervallic organization is unchanged.

b. Each form may be transposed up or down a half step *twice* before the pitch content and the intervallic organization are duplicated. Thus, for each form, three distinct octatonic scales exist. (It is not accidental that each of the forms consists of two interlocking diminished seventh chords, for it is the symmetrical property of these sonorities that explains the limited number of distinct transpositions of the scale.)

c. The scale abounds with bitonal implications because major and minor triads that are obscurely related to one another can be formed on four of the eight scale degrees:

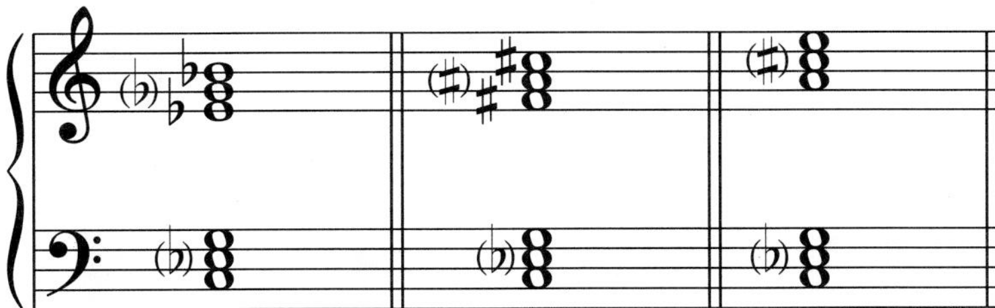

The two examples that follow are based upon the whole tone and octatonic scales, respectively. Although the tonal resources of the latter are richer, notice how in both

1. The interval of the tritone predominates, particularly melodically.
2. The tertian harmony is treated nonfunctionally.

EXERCISES

1. Invent a symmetrical artificial scale between six and eight notes.
2. From the scale, derive all the possible tertian structures, triads as well as extended harmonies.
3. Using the untransposed scale and tertian structures, write a piece for piano of not more than sixteen measures.

MUSIC FOR ANALYSIS

Bartók, Béla

"From the Island of Bali" from *Mikrokosmos*, no. 109
"Diminished Fifth" from *Mikrokosmos*, no. 101

Ives, Charles

"Evening" from *114 Songs*, no. 2

Messiaen, Olivier

"Liturgie de crystal" from *Quartuor pour la fin du temps*, I, clarinet and cello parts

Debussy, Claude

"Les sons et les parfums tournent dans l'air du soir" from *Préludes Book I*, no. 4
Syrinx for solo flute
"Soirée dans Grenade" from *Estampes*
"Jardins sous la pluie" from *Estampes*
"Nuages" from *Nocturnes*

Scriabin, Alexander

Five Preludes, op. 74, no. 1

Locate any use of the whole tone or octatonic scale in the given pieces.

30
Nontertian Harmony

This chapter will serve to introduce the student to a number of harmonic procedures of the twentieth century that are not based on the interval of the third. The contents of Chapters 28 and 29 exemplified how tertian structures could be manipulated despite a departure from functional root relationships. With the abandonment of the third as the governing interval, harmonic procedures are obviously perceived as even further removed from common practice in the traditional sense. Composers have been experimenting with nontertian harmony since the first decade of the last century. It is interesting to observe, however, that after four generations no single harmonic system has evolved that can reasonably be said to represent a new common practice.

NONTERTIAN PROJECTIONS

The tertian harmonic system is, by implication, founded on the projection of the interval of the third from a given series of pitches. On the basis of this implication one may always determine the root of a chord, however the pitches are arranged, by discovering which member of the chord allows the remaining pitches to be stacked in thirds upon it. Thus, a nonchord tone is definable, in a general sense, as a pitch that is not a member of a projection from a given chord root.

Similar systems may be developed by projecting intervals other than the third. The resulting sonorities of the systems are commonly described by the organizing interval (secundal, quartal, quintal, etc.) and by the number of pitches (triad, tetrad, pentad, etc.). A three-note chord built in fourths, therefore, is said to be a *quartal triad*; a five-note chord built in seconds is a *secundal pentad*, and so on.

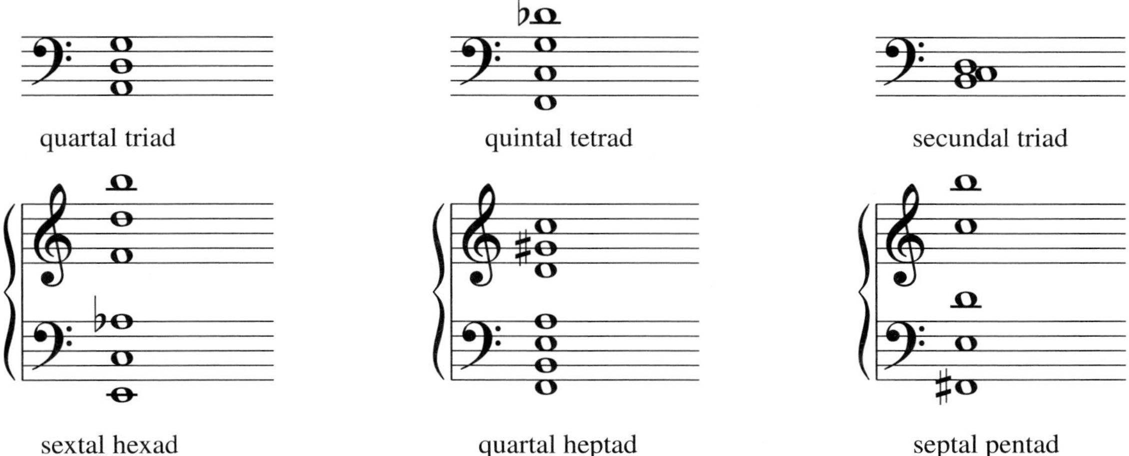

Provided that the generating interval is known, chord roots may be identified when the sonorities are inverted.

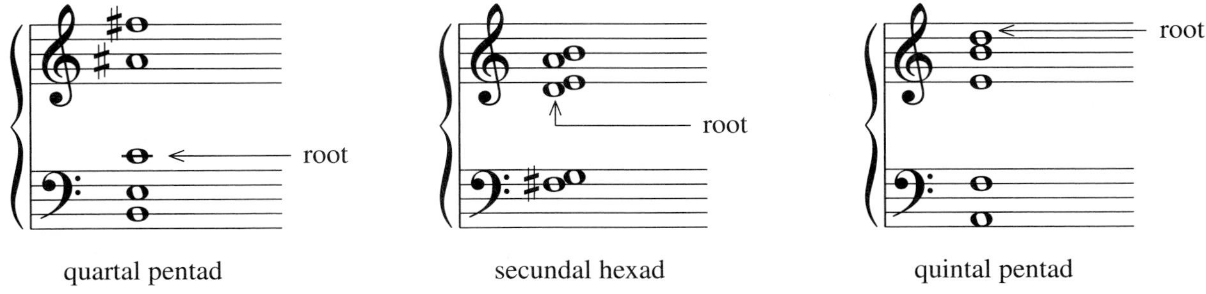

Unlike the tertian system, there is no universally accepted common practice involving chords built upon other intervals. In fact, relatively few well-known works demonstrate the *systematic* projection of any single interval other than the third. Thus, voice-leading procedures and root relationships are assumed to be the prerogatives of the individual composer.

The following chorale exemplifies the use of *quintal tetrads*. The student should analyze each chord with a view to determining its root.

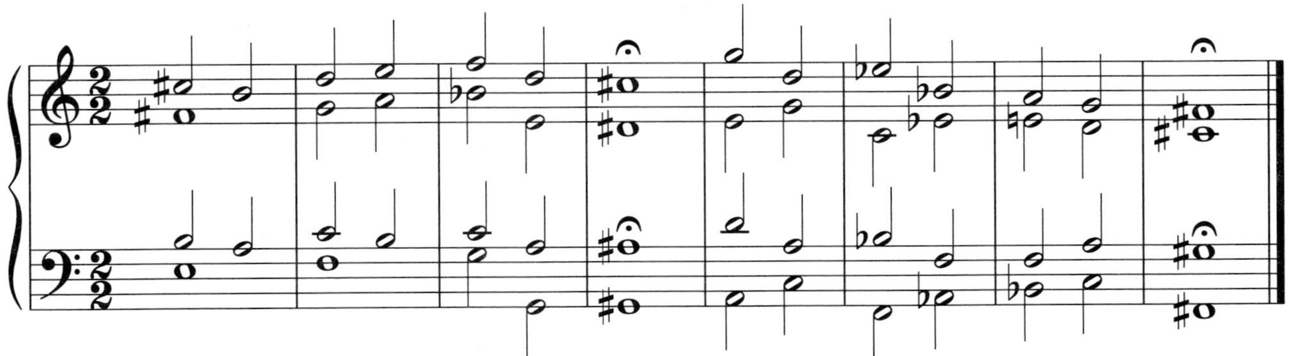

FREELY FORMED HARMONIC STRUCTURES

The final break with the common practice harmonic tradition occurs when one conceives of a chord as a set of pitches constructed not by intervallic projection but by free intervallic selection. Thus, any set of pitches sounded simultaneously can be the harmonic basis for all or part of a composition. With the elimination of a single interval as an organizing agent, the concept of inversion ceases to have any real meaning. A chord, therefore, may be more conveniently identified by its *interval content* than by its pitch structure.

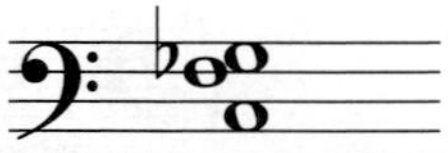

The three-note chord above has no clear root, and so it makes little sense to single out one of its pitches by which to designate it. The chord does, however, contain a perfect fourth (C–F), a diminished fifth (C–G♭), and a minor second (F–G♭). Furthermore, when the chord is transposed,

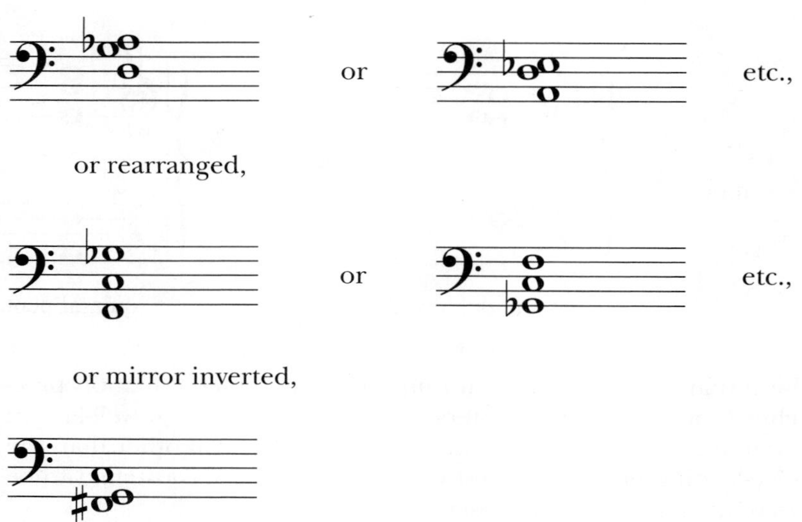

the same interval content prevails.

This interval content is effectively described by the *interval vector,* a structure that allows one to determine how many and what intervals a chord contains. The interval vector is based upon two assumptions. First, all intervals can be reduced to a span of a tritone or less by the process of inversion. Thus, the major seventh is equivalent to the minor second, the minor seventh to the major second, the major sixth to the minor third, and so on. Second, a note name (C, D♭, D, E♭, etc.) or its enharmonic equivalent is counted only once in a chord. A major triad, for example, written in four voices, is considered to be a three-note chord.

The chord C–F–G♭, along with its various transpositions, rearrangements, and mirror inversions, therefore, is classified by its interval vector as 100011. The first entry gives the number of minor seconds, the second gives the number of major seconds, the third gives the number of minor thirds, the fourth gives the number of major thirds, the fifth gives the number of perfect fourths, and the sixth gives the number of tritones.

Further examples follow:

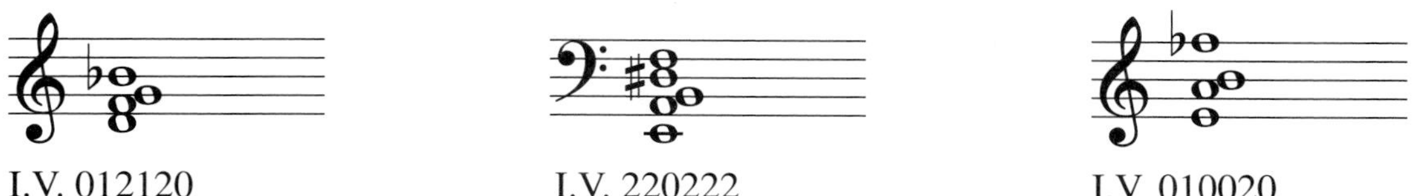

Whereas there are four tertian triads, there are twelve freely constructed three-note chords that have different interval contents; compared with the five or six seventh chords in common usage, the complete set of four-note chords is represented by twenty-eight different interval vectors. The composer's potential harmonic resources, therefore, are dramatically expanded. Typically, these resources are kept under control by:

1. The exploitation of a small number of predetermined chord types in a given movement or work.
2. The derivation of vertical (chordal) from horizontal (melodic) structures.

The two examples for piano that follow should be studied carefully.

1. This example is based upon the following four-note chord:

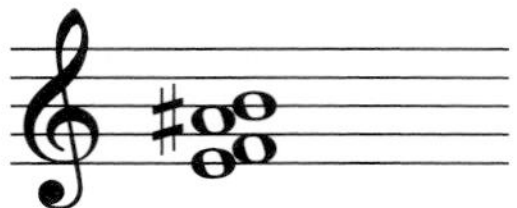

I.V. 200022

Note:

a. Eleven four-note chords have the same interval content.

b. The first chord is never restated at its original pitch level. Instead, it is transposed and revoiced to create variety.

2. This example is based upon the following two melodic fragments:

Note:

a. The accompaniment in measures 2, 3, and 8 is derived from the melody in measure 1.

b. The accompaniment in measures 4, 5, 6, and 7 is derived from the melody in measure 2.

c. The entire melody can be derived from the two four-note fragments.

SUGGESTIONS AND STRATEGIES

When finding the interval vector of a chord (Exercise C), it is useful to know how many intervals that chord contains. The answer is found by using the following simple formula:

$$N = [n \times (n - 1)]/2$$

where N is the total number of intervals, and n is the number of different pitch classes in the chord.

Thus, if a chord has five different pitch classes, the total number of intervals, N, is:

$$(5 \times 4)/2 = 10$$

And so a five-note chord contains ten intervals.

You should also be very systematic about finding the intervals. Start with the lowest note in the chord, and measure the interval between that note and each of the chord members above it. Then repeat the procedure with the next to the lowest note, and so on.

Study the example below.

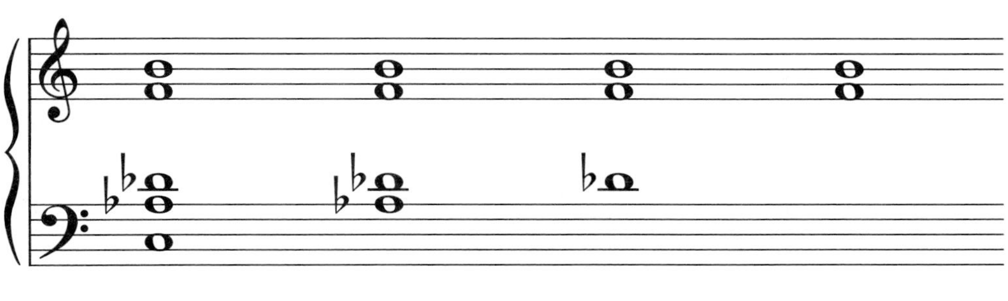

C - A♭ = M3	A♭ - D♭ = P4	D♭ - F = M3	F - B = T
C - D♭ = m2	A♭ - F = m3	D♭ - B = M2(d3)	
C - F = P4	A♭ - B = m3		
C - B = m2			

m2 = 2

M2 = 1

m3 = 2 **The interval vector is: 212221**

M3 = 2

P4 = 2

T = 1

EXERCISES

A. Project intervals from the given pitches as indicated.

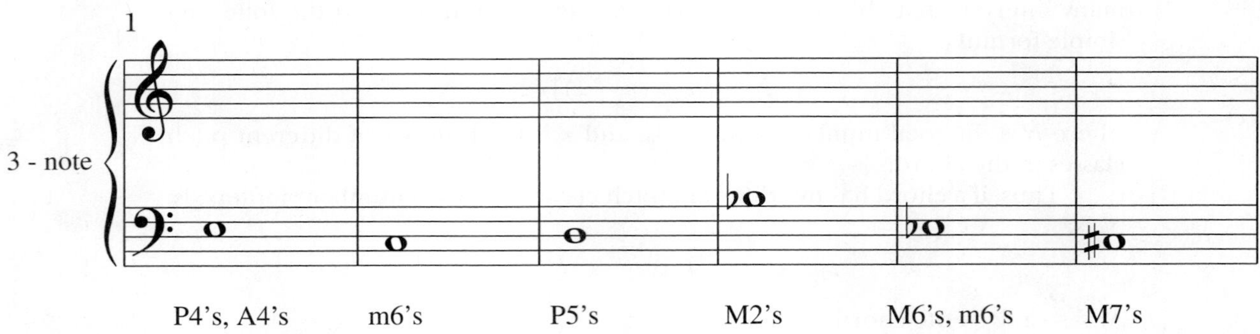

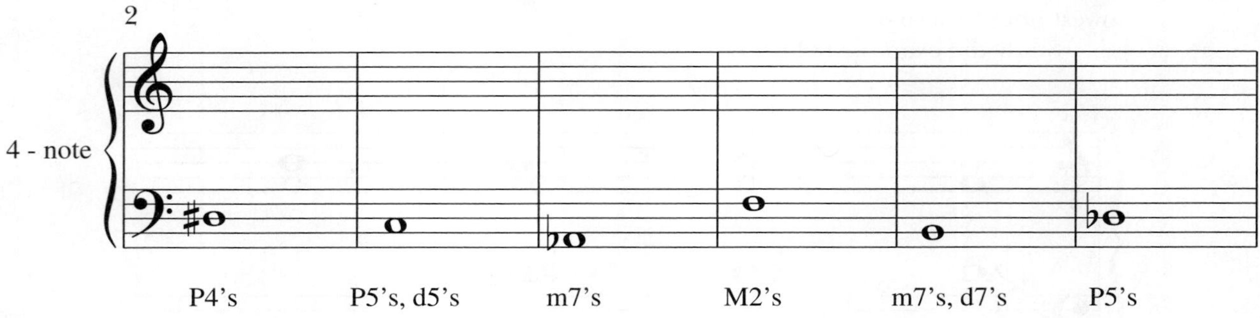

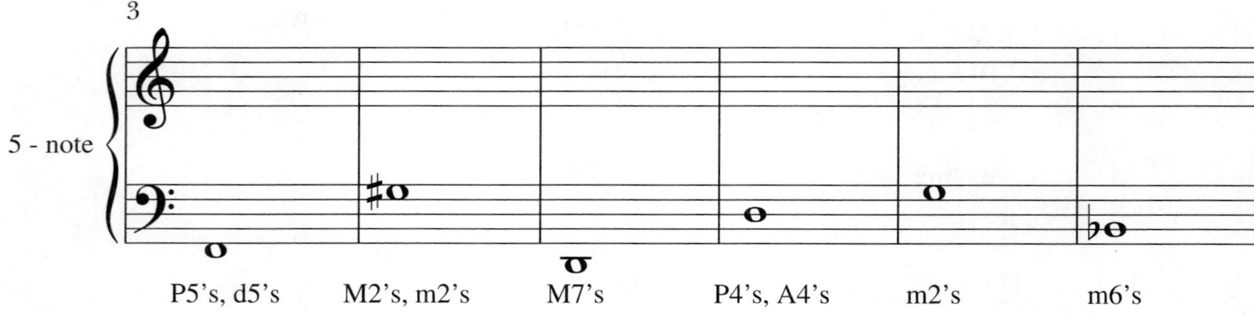

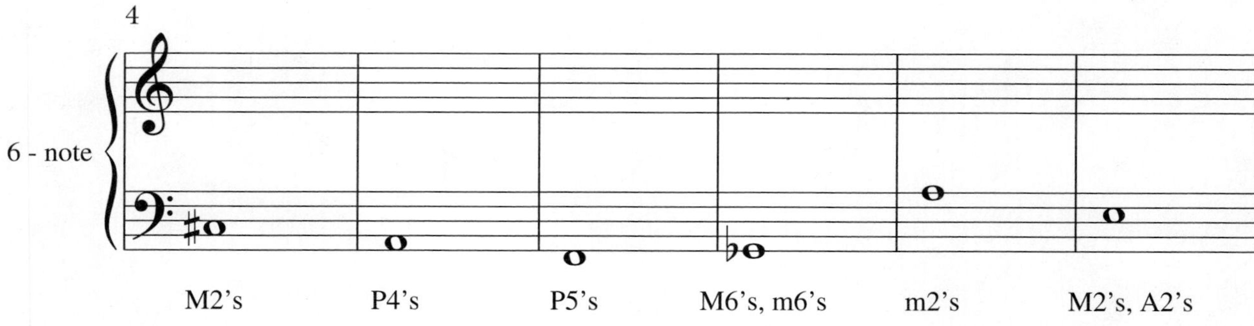

B. Harmonize the given chorale melody in quartal tetrads.

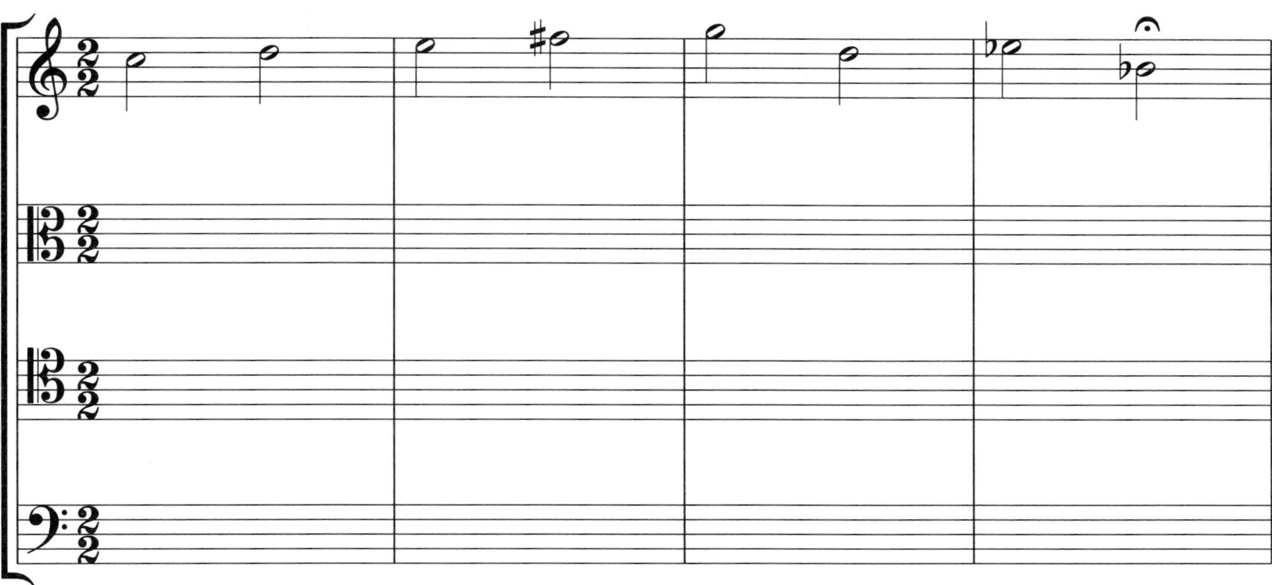

C. Find the interval vector of each of the following chords.

1

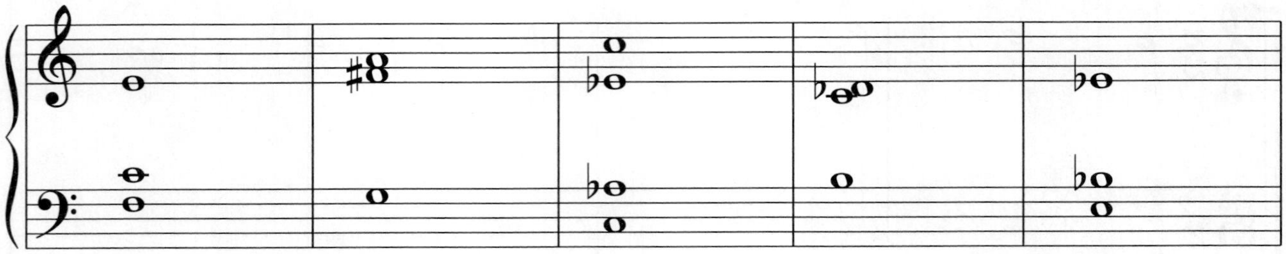

2

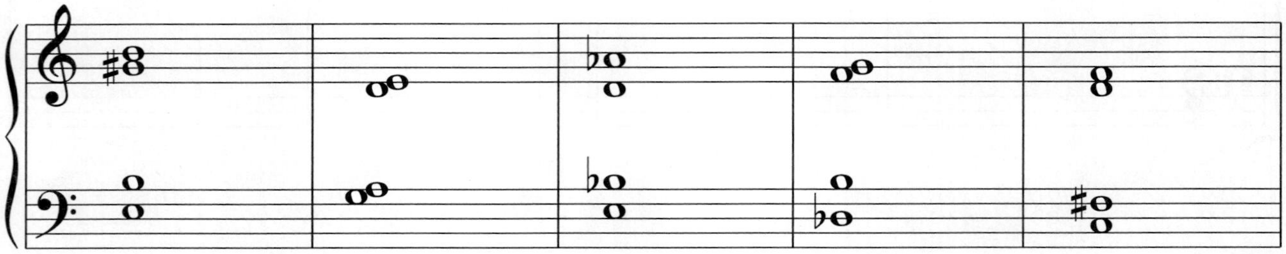

3

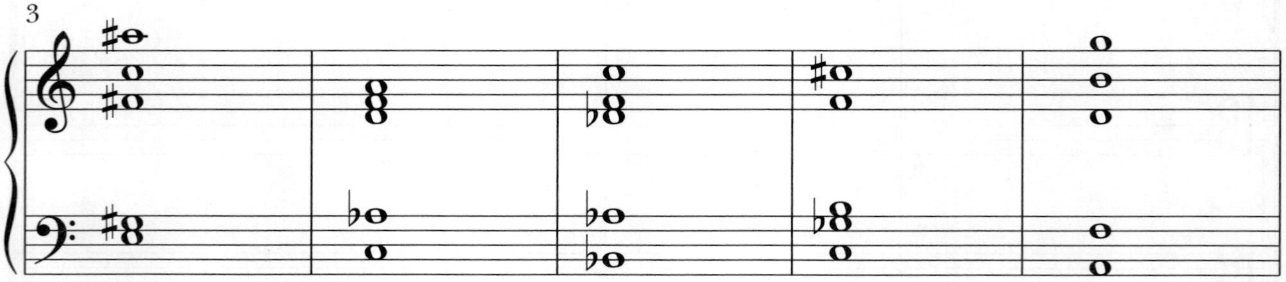

4

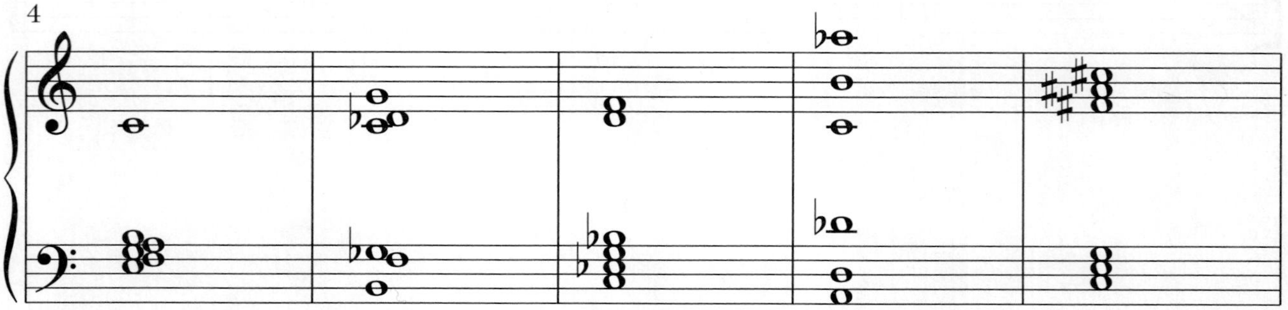

D. Choose two of the four-note chords from C2, and write a short piece for piano based upon some of the transpositions and inversions of these chords.

MUSIC FOR HARMONIC ANALYSIS

Schoenberg, Arnold

Sechs kleine Klavierstücke op. 19, no. 6
Klavierstücke op. 33a

Hindemith, Paul

"Un Cygne" from *Six Chansons*

Ives, Charles

"The Cage" from *114 Songs*, no. 64

1. Identify all *clearly stated* three- and four-note chords.
2. Make an interval vector analysis of all of them.
3. As a result of this analysis, is it possible to arrive at some conclusions about the nature of the sonorities the composer used?

31 Harmonic Procedures in Twelve-Tone Serialism

INTRODUCTION

Serial composition is based on the construction of a series of pitch classes (see page 2) that is designated as the *basic set*. The basic set may be expressed in four different forms—the *prime*, the *inversion* (upside down), the *retrograde* (backwards), and the *retrograde-inversion* (backwards and upside down). Furthermore, the notation may be expressed conventionally or through *pitch class integers*, as the example below shows:

Prime

Inversion

0 8 2 6 4 9 11 10 5 3 7 1

Retrograde

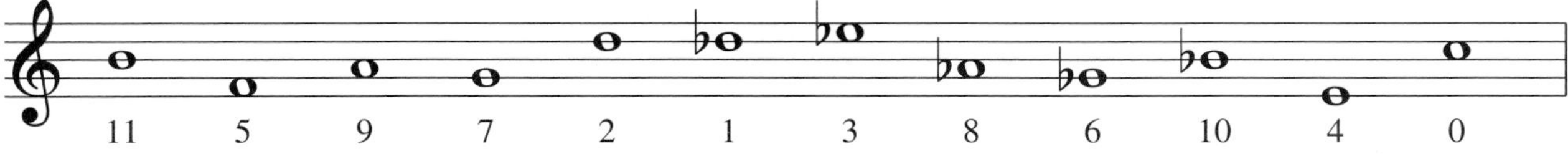

Retrograde-inversion

1 7 3 5 10 11 9 4 6 2 8 0

Note:

a. The prime (P) is constructed of all twelve of the pitch classes of the chromatic scale. There is no duplication. For the notation in pitch class integers, 0 is assigned to the first pitch class (C), 1 to D♭, 2 to D, 3 to E♭, 4 to E, and so on.

b. The inversion (I) begins with the same pitch class as the prime; subsequently, all of the intervals are inverted. The notation in pitch class integers clearly shows the process of *complementation.* 0 to 8 is the inversion of 0 to 4 (8 + 4 = 12); 8 to 2 (difference of 6) is the inversion of 4 to 10 (difference of 6) (6 + 6 = 12); 2 to 6 (difference of 4) is the inversion of 10 to 6 (difference of 8 – count up to 6 from 10) (4 + 8 = 12), and so on. (An interval plus its inversion adds up to twelve.)

c. The retrograde (R) is derived from the writing of P in reverse order.

d. The retrograde-inversion (RI) is derived from the writing of I in reverse order.

Because the process of transposition allows each form of the basic set to begin on any one of the twelve pitch classes in the chromatic scale, forty-eight different permutations are possible. The following matrix displays the options for the given row.

	I0	I4	I10	I6	I8	I3	I1	I2	I7	I9	I5	I11	
P0	C	E	B♭	G♭	A♭	E♭	D♭	D	G	A	F	B	R0
P8	A♭	C	G♭	D	E	B	A	B♭	E♭	F	D♭	G	R8
P2	D	F#	C	A♭	B♭	F	D#	E	A	B	G	C#	R2
P6	F#	A#	E	C	D	A	G	G#	C#	D#	B	F	R6
P4	E	G#	D	B♭	C	G	F	F#	B	C#	A	E♭	R4
P9	A	C#	G	E♭	F	C	B♭	B	E	F#	D	A♭	R9
P11	B	D#	A	F	G	D	C	C#	F#	G#	E	B♭	R11
P10	B♭	D	A♭	E	F#	C#	B	C	F	G	E♭	A	R10
P5	F	A	E♭	B	C#	G#	F#	G	C	D	B♭	E	R5
P3	E♭	G	D♭	A	B	F#	E	F	B♭	C	A♭	D	R3
P7	G	B	F	C#	D#	A#	G#	A	D	E	C	F#	R7
P1	D♭	F	B	G	A	E	D	D#	A♭	B♭	G♭	C	R1
	RI0	RI4	RI10	RI6	RI8	RI3	RI1	RI2	RI7	RI9	RI5	RI11	

Alternatively, numbers may be used to represent pitch classes, where C=0.

	↓ I0	I4	I10	I6	I8	I3	I1	I2	I7	I9	I5	I11	
→ P0	0	4	10	6	8	3	1	2	7	9	5	11	R0 ←
P8	8	0	6	2	4	11	9	10	3	5	1	7	R8
P2	2	6	0	8	10	5	3	4	9	11	7	1	R2
P6	6	10	4	0	2	9	7	8	1	3	11	5	R6
P4	4	8	2	10	0	7	5	6	11	1	9	3	R4
P9	9	1	7	3	5	0	10	11	4	6	2	8	R9
P11	11	3	9	5	7	2	0	1	6	8	4	10	R11
P10	10	2	8	4	6	1	11	0	5	7	3	9	R10
P5	5	9	3	11	1	8	6	7	0	2	10	4	R5
P3	3	7	1	9	11	6	4	5	10	0	8	2	R3
P7	7	11	5	1	3	10	8	9	2	4	0	6	R7
P1	1	5	11	7	9	4	2	3	8	10	6	0	R1
	RI0 ↑	RI4	RI10	RI6	RI8	RI3	RI1	RI2	RI7	RI9	RI5	RI11	

Note:

a. The prime is read horizontally from left to right.

b. The inversion is read vertically from top to bottom.

c. The retrograde is read horizontally from right to left.

d. The retrograde-inversion is read vertically from bottom to top.

e. The naming is designated by its form (P, I, R, or RI) and, for the P and I forms, by the number of half steps it has been *raised* above the 0 transposition. For example, P7 begins with the pitch class G (=7) because it is a perfect fifth (or interval 7) above P0. Similarly, I9 begins with the pitch class A (=9) because it is a major sixth (or interval 9) above I0. The R and RI forms use the number of their ending pitch. For example, R7 (last pitch G) is the retrograde of P7, and RI9 (last pitch A) is the retrograde of I9.

f. The tables show only pitch classes and pitch class integers; the specific octave is not indicated. In serial composition, it is important to understand that, after the basic set has been established, the pitches may be written *in any octave.* Thus, as an example, I8 may be notated as

or, indeed, in thousands of other ways.

g. Enharmonic spellings are routinely employed with a view to producing the most logical and readable notation.

THE CONSTRUCTION OF THE BASIC SET

The intervallic organization of the basic set plays a significant part in determining the tonal character of the subsequent composition. Although the number of possible twelve-tone series exceeds 479 million, basic sets tend to fall into two types—those with and those without obvious tonal implications. For instance, the series

suggests that the pitches B and F are tonal centers around which the other pitches are organized. By contrast,

gives no clear indication of a tonal center.

The idea of basing a composition upon a twelve-tone series originated (with Arnold Schoenberg) in an attempt to write extended movements without tonal centers. Composers, however, have since used the twelve-tone technique in such a wide variety of ways that the treatment of tonality, or the absence thereof, is only one of several considerations that have to be made in the construction of a serial work.

THE HARMONIC BASIS

Vertical structures in twelve-tone music are commonly formed by the segmentation of the basic set into three, four, or six parts and by the consequent notation of the segments as chords.

The musical examples below, based on the basic set presented at the beginning of this chapter, clearly illustrate the principles of segmentation.

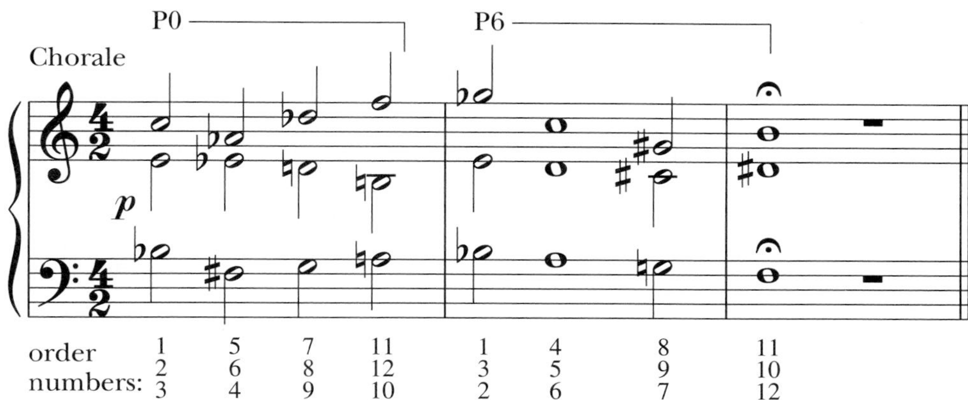

Note:

a. The chorale phrase is constructed exclusively from P0 and P6.

b. The position (order number) of each pitch in P0 and P6 is indicated beneath the example. The sets are thus segmented (or partitioned) into four three-note groups. Furthermore, the pitches are voiced freely within each group, so that the precise order of the basic set is not evident.

c. The individual lines are notated as far as possible to conform with traditional voice-leading procedures.

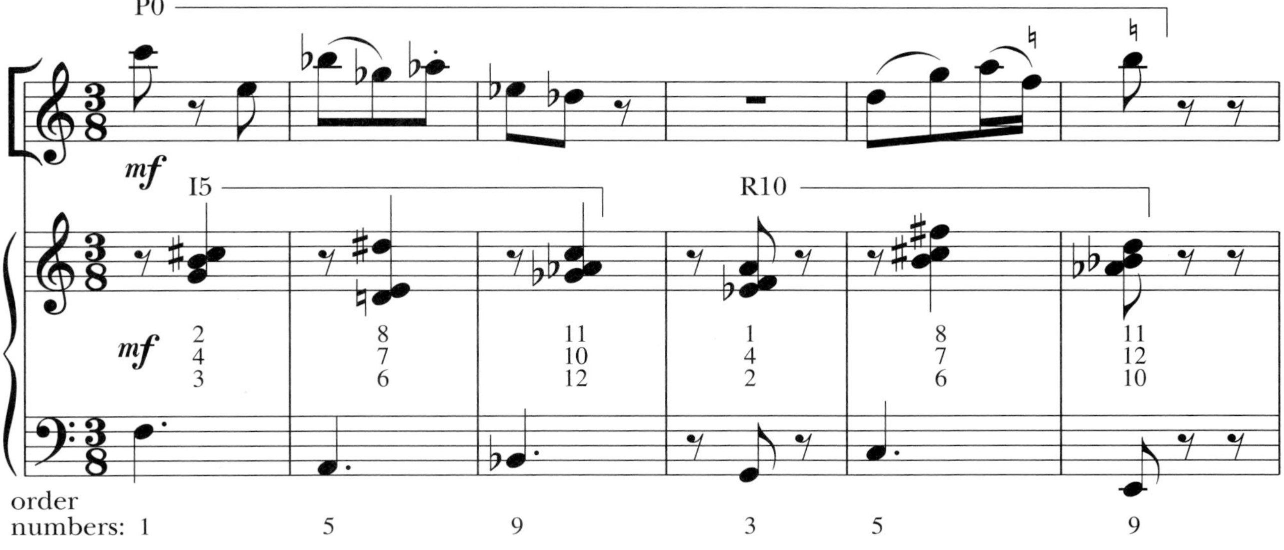

Note:

a. The solo part (P0) is constructed from a different form of the set than the accompaniment.

b. The accompaniment is based upon I5 and R10, which are both segmented into four-note groups.

c. A certain harmonic homogeneity is achieved by the presence of a major second in each chord.

d. At no time does a pitch in the accompaniment sound simultaneously with the same pitch, or its transposition by one or more octaves, in the solo part. Generally speaking, octave duplication in serial works is avoided; unison duplication is more frequently encountered.

The approach to harmony in twelve-tone writing varies dramatically from composer to composer, so that the realizations of vertical events occur as a result of a large number of techniques, many of which are highly complex.

As a final illustration, the series used in the examples above is manipulated so that the projection of the interval of the perfect fifth (see Chapter 30) is employed for all vertical structures.

Note:

The three voices are in *canon*; they display the same melodic and rhythmic organization.

EXERCISES

A. Write the inversions of the given prime forms.

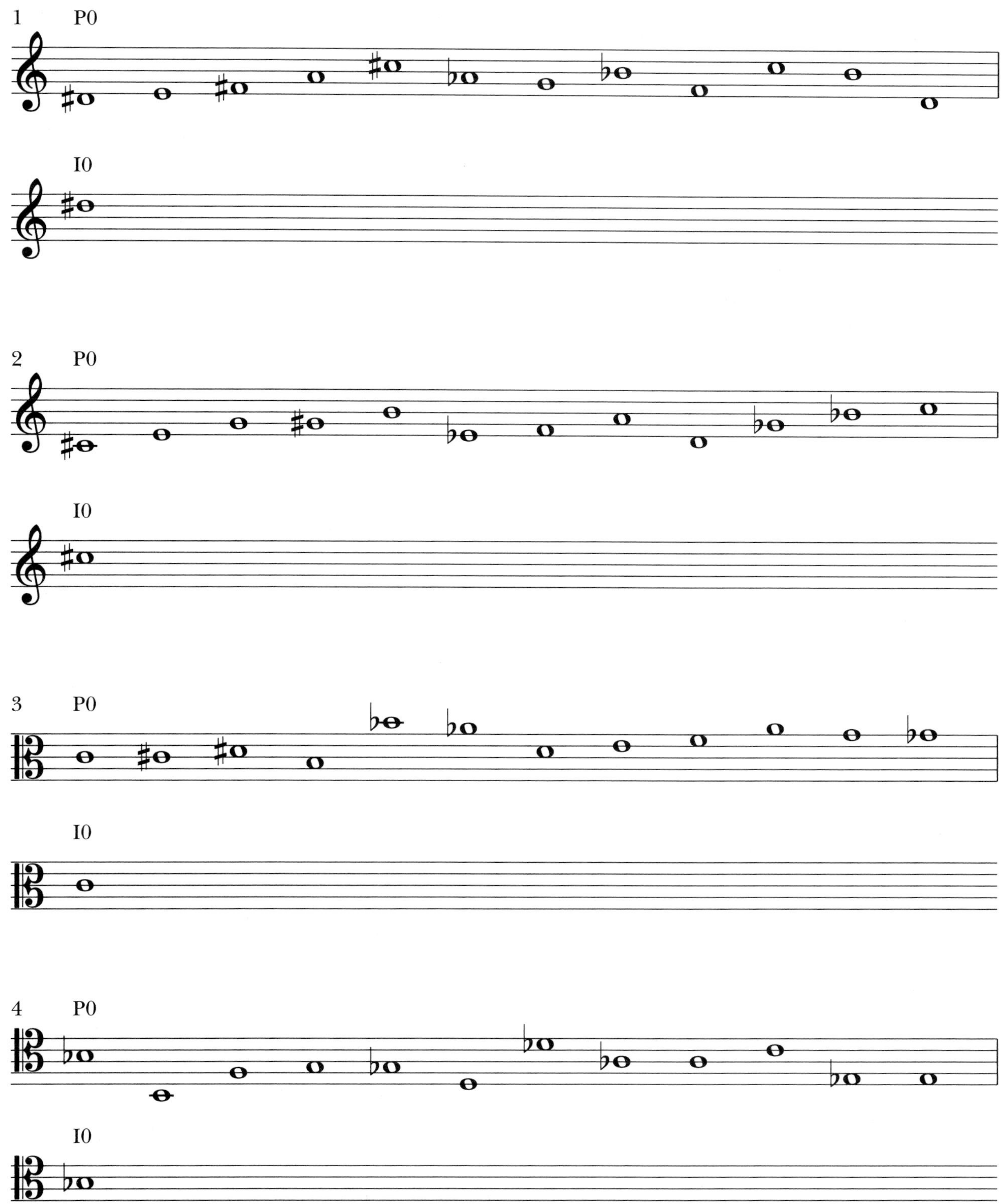

B. Invent three basic sets, and, for each, notate P0 and I0. In the space provided, fill in each matrix as demonstrated on pages 360 and 361.

1

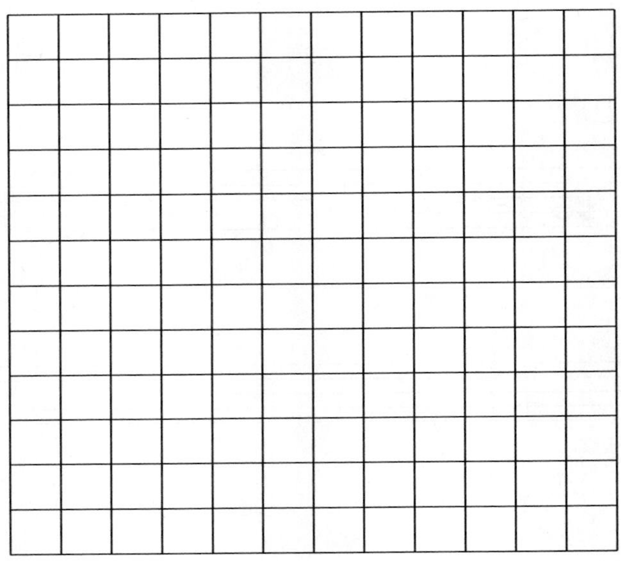

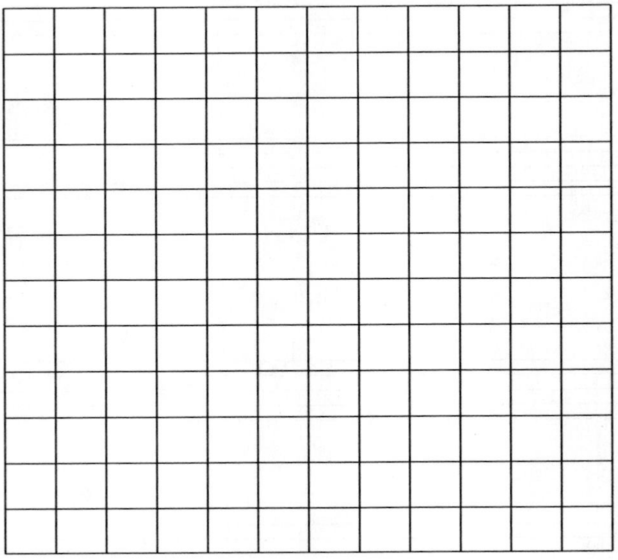

2

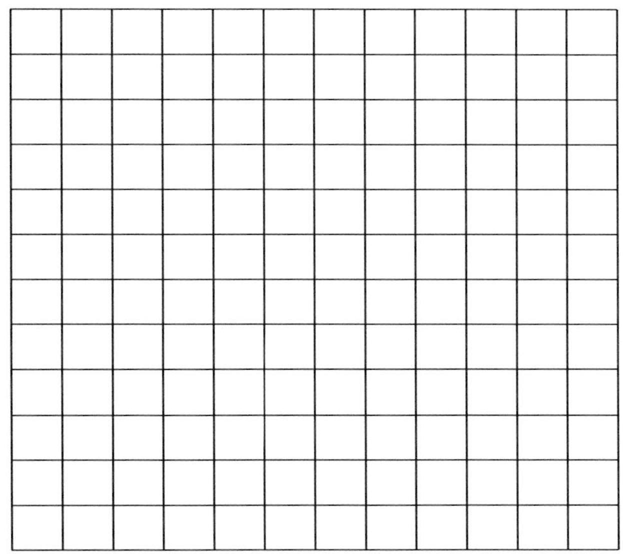

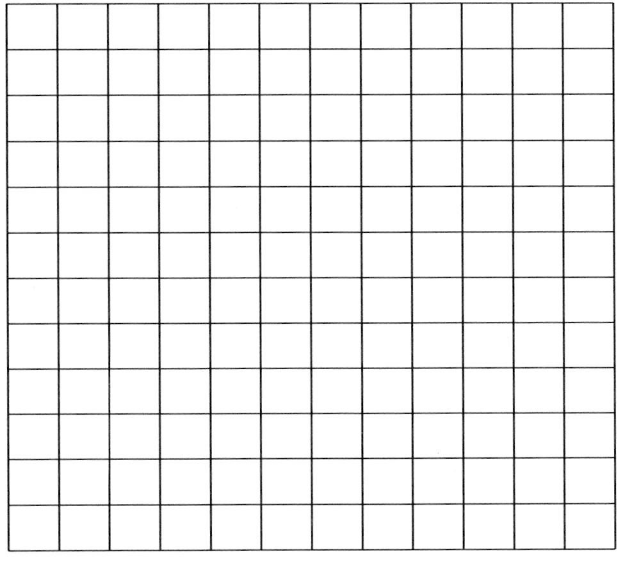

3

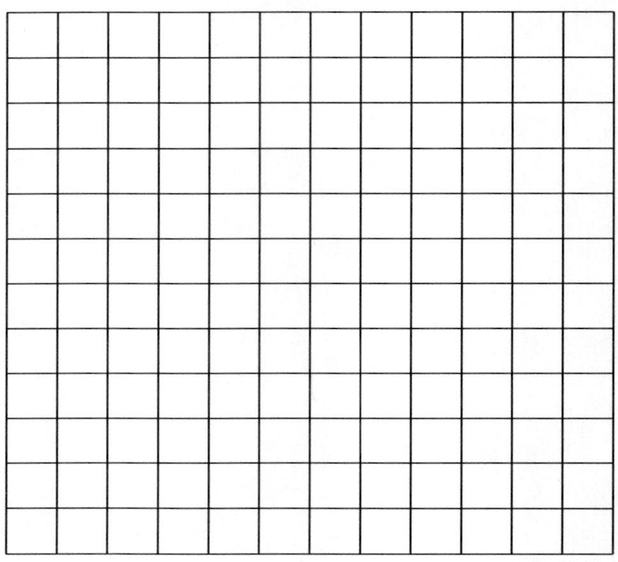

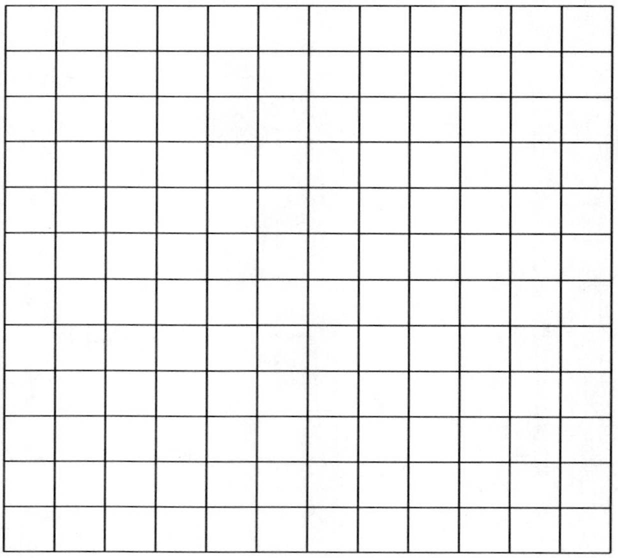

C. Choose one of the series from B and create four phrases exploiting four-note segmentation.

D. Turn the progressions from C into an accompaniment pattern, and add a melodic line to create a piece for piano.

MUSIC FOR ANALYSIS

Schoenberg, Arnold

Klavierstücke, op. 33a
"Tot" from *Three Songs*, op. 48 no. 2

Berg, Alban

Schliesse mir die Augen beide (Close my eyes at parting), version B
Lyric Suite for string quartet, I

Webern, Anton

Concerto for Nine Instruments, op. 24, I and III

Dallapiccola, Luigi

Quaderno musicale di Annalibera, nos. 4, 5, and 6
"Die sonne kommt!" from *Goethe Lieder*

Babbitt, Milton

Semi-Simple Variations
No. 1 from *Three Compositions for Piano*

Spies, Claudio

Times Two

1. Determine precisely how each statement of the series is constructed.
2. Where applicable, investigate the degree to which there is a systematic approach to harmony.

Appendix A

CHAPTERS 7–22 POSSIBLE ANSWERS FOR SELECTED EXERCISES

The following answers should serve as reference points only. Part-writing is not absolute; there are voice-leading alternatives to almost every exercise. Chord spelling, however, is absolute, and these answers do provide proper spelling.

CHAPTER 7—FOUR PART VOCAL WRITING—EXERCISE A

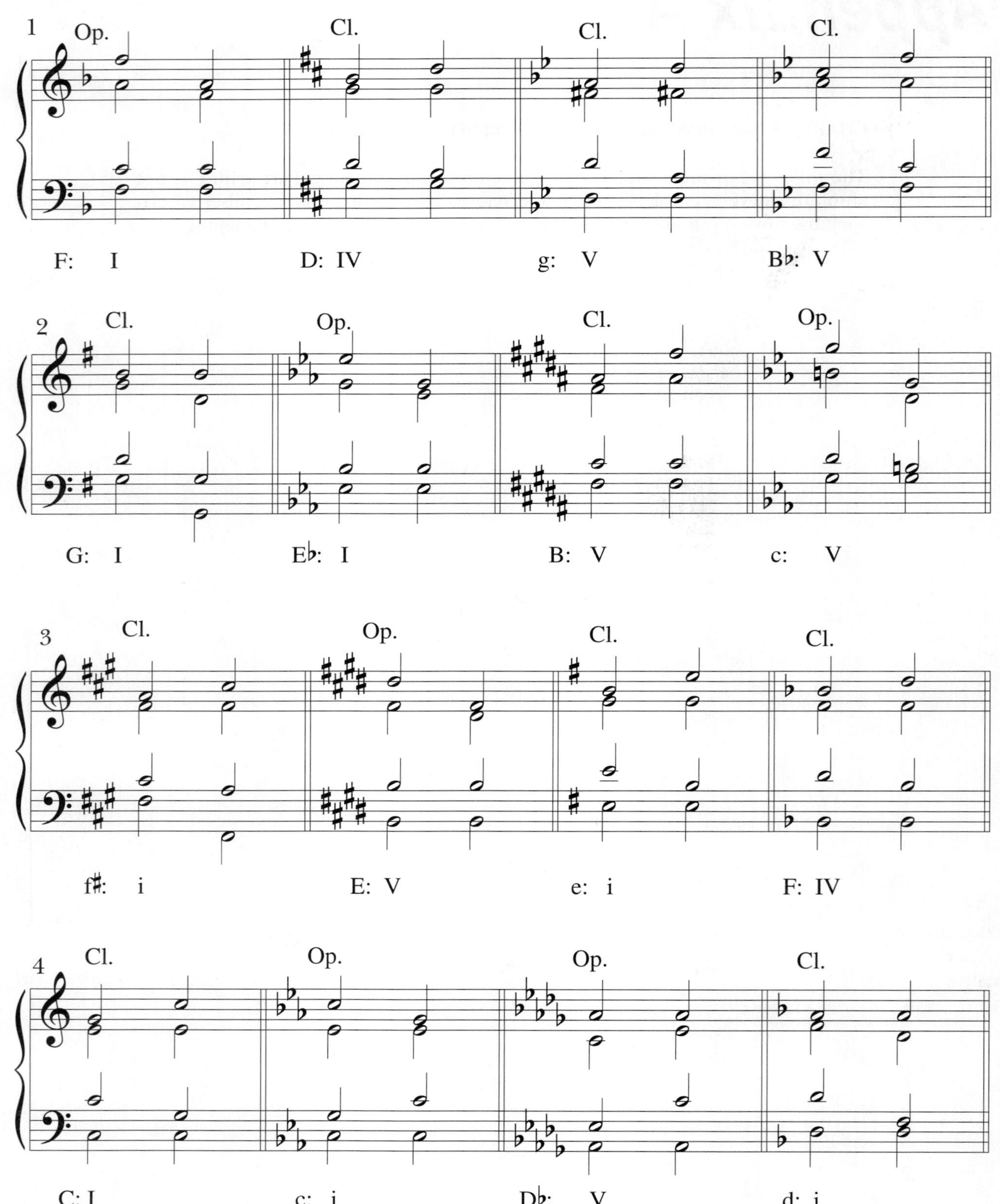

CHAPTER 8—PRIMARY TRIADS IN ROOT POSITION—EXERCISE A

CHAPTER 8—PRIMARY TRIADS IN ROOT POSITION—EXERCISE H

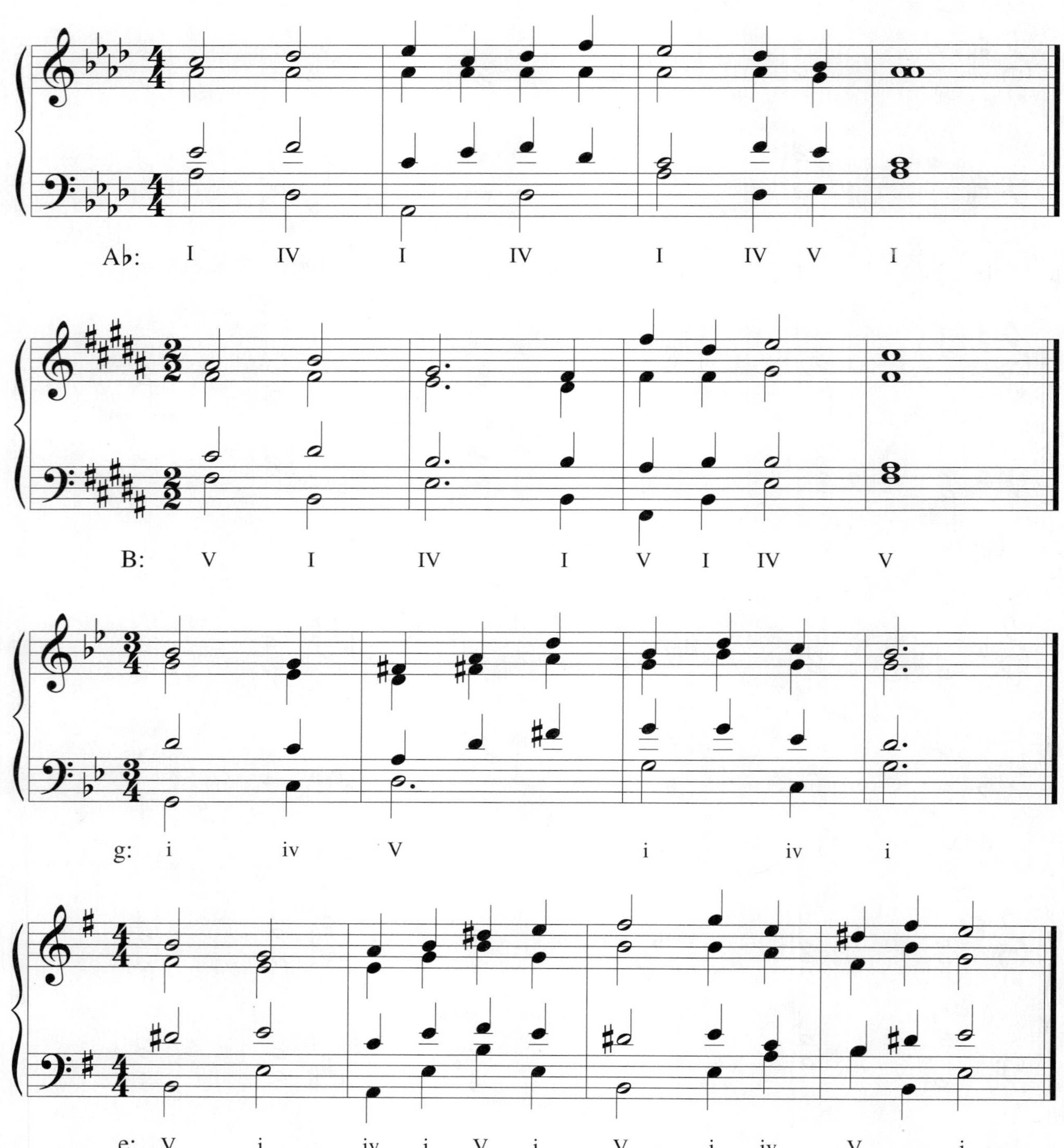

CHAPTER 9—PRIMARY TRIADS IN FIRST INVERSION—EXERCISE A

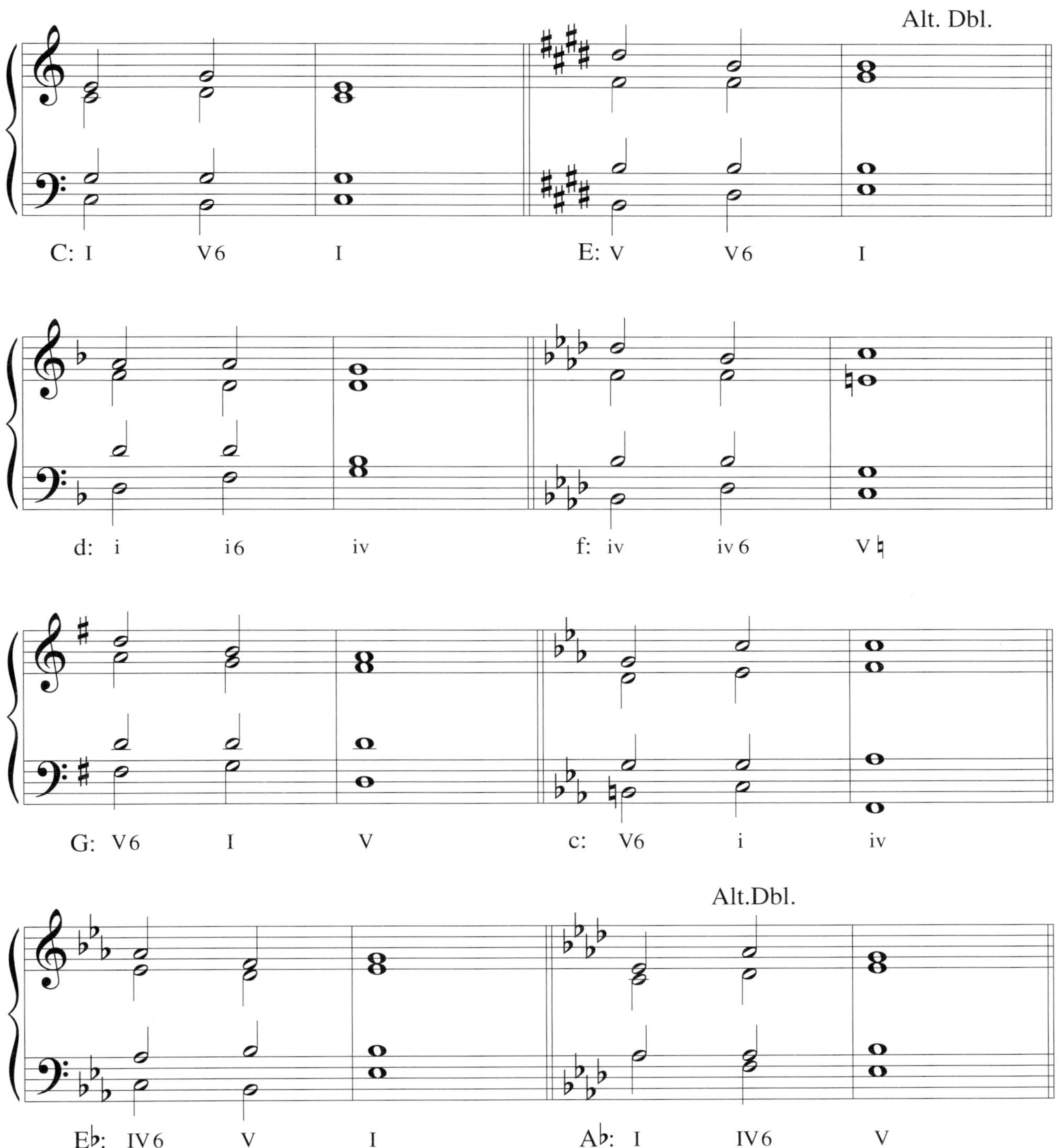

CHAPTER 9—PRIMARY TRIADS IN FIRST INVERSION—EXERCISE H

CHAPTER 10—PRIMARY TRIADS IN SECOND INVERSION—EXERCISES A AND B

CHAPTER 11—SECONDARY TRIADS—PRELIMINARY EXERCISE

Root movement of a fourth or fifth

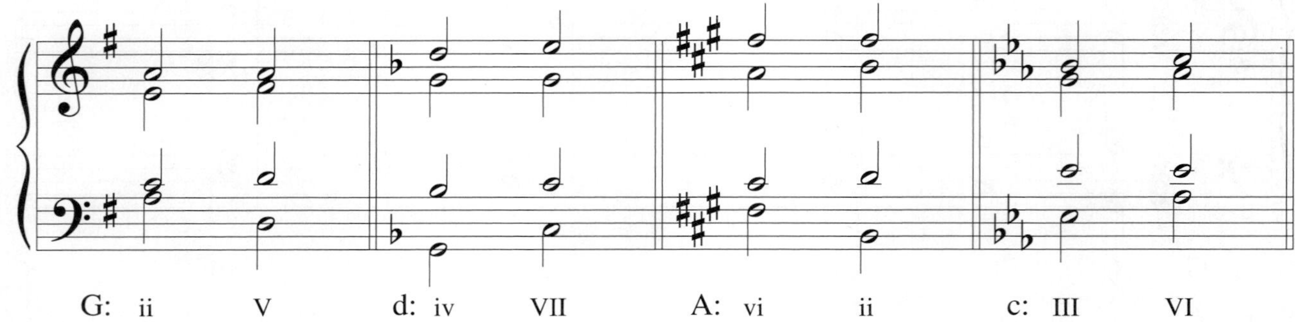

Root movement of a second

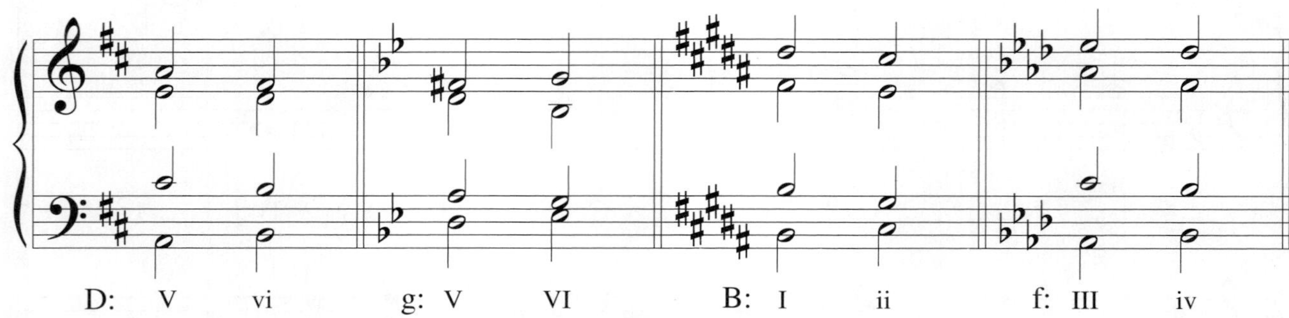

Root movement of a third

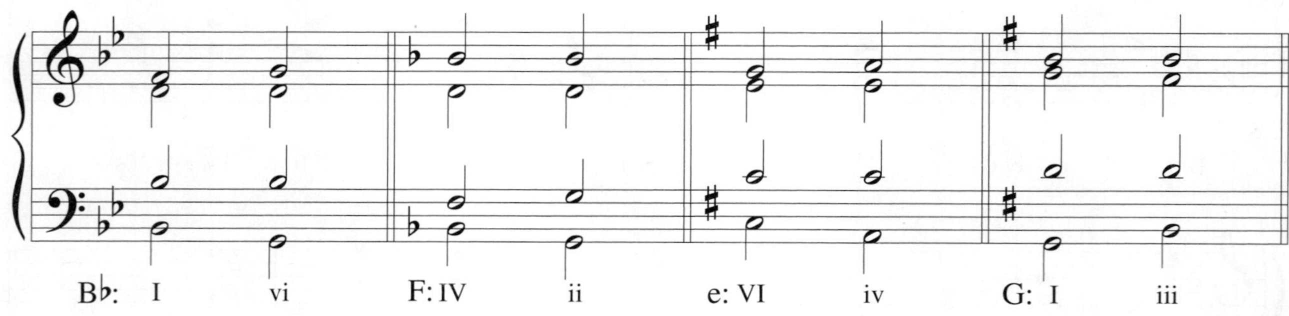

Use of first inversion

CHAPTER 12—THE HARMONIZATION OF MELODIES I—EXERCISE A

CHAPTER 15—DIATONIC SEVENTH CHORDS—EXERCISE A

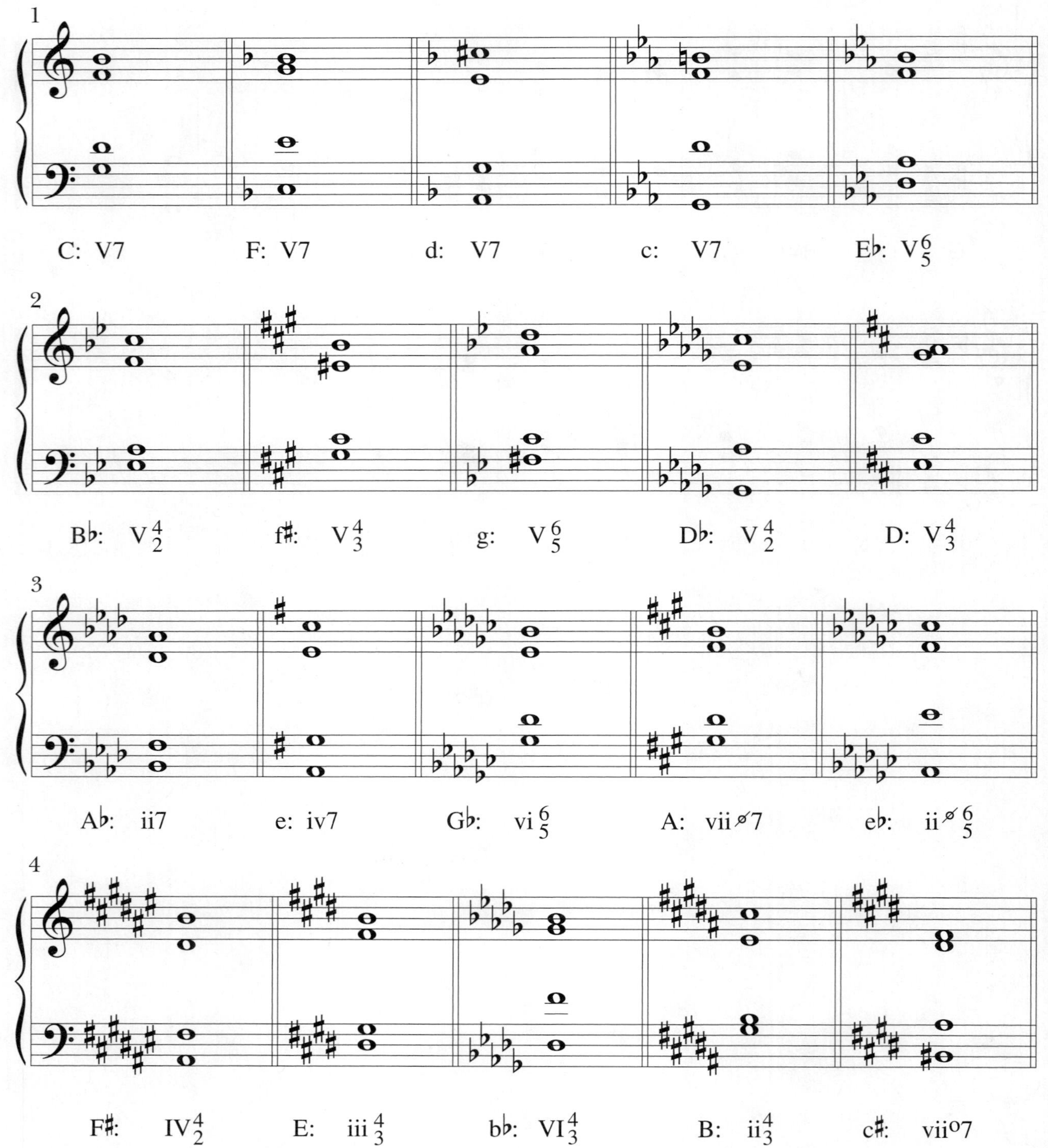

CHAPTER 18—SECONDARY DOMINANTS—PRELIMINARY EXERCISE

CHAPTER 19—SECONDARY DIMINISHED SEVENTH CHORDS—EXERCISE A

CHAPTER 20—AUGMENTED SIXTH—PRELIMINARY EXERCISE

1. For each given key, provide the notes of the augmented sixth interval followed by the octave on the dominant pitch.

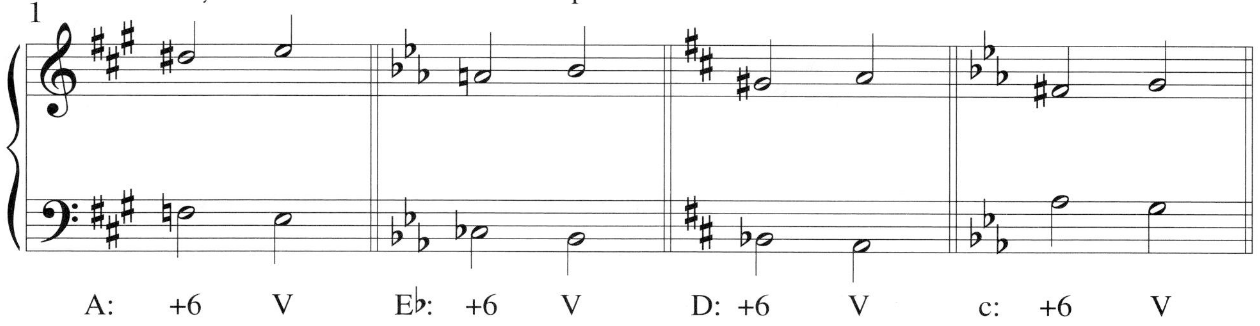

2. Copy the notes from system 1, add the tonic note, and double it. This is the Italian sixth. To resolve, each tonic note moves by step—one goes to the leading tone, and one goes to scale degree 2.

3. For the German sixth, remove one tonic note and add a perfect fifth above the bass. To resolve, the P5 above the bass steps down, and the tonic note moves down to the leading tone.

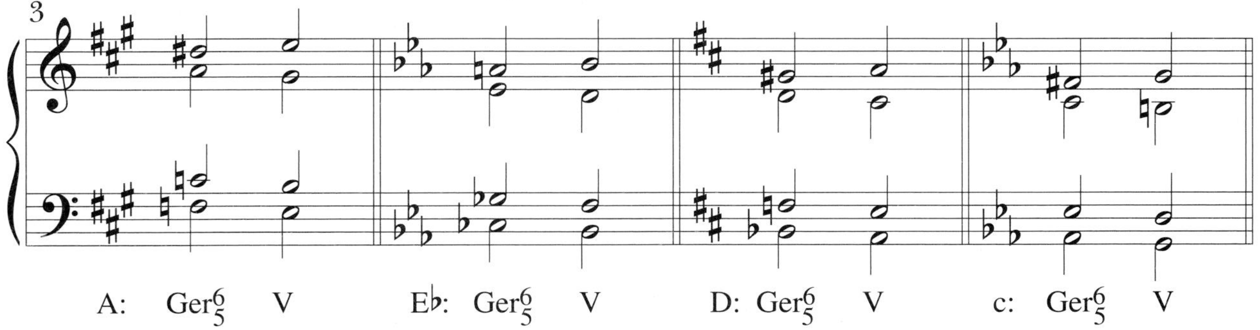

4. For the French sixth, remove the P5 above the bass and add scale degree 2. To resolve, scale degree 2 stays the same.

CHAPTER 21—BORROWED CHORDS—EXERCISE A

CHAPTER 22—THE NEAPOLITAN—PRELIMINARY EXERCISE

Appendix B

The study of harmonic practices includes realization of figured bass, melodic harmonization, creation of original works, and analysis of music. This appendix provides an analysis study guide, a guided analysis of two short excerpts, and a list of music for analysis.

STUDY GUIDE FOR ANALYSIS

Items to determine:

Key(s)

Chords

Nonchord tones

Points to consider when determining key:

Key signature

Accidentals—functional, not decorative

Opening harmonic gestures

Closing harmonic gestures

Points to consider when determining chords:

Patterns

Vertical presentations (verticalization of patterns)

Repetition of patterns including those at different pitch levels (sequences)

Harmonic rhythm

Right hand and left hand agree harmonically

Points to consider when determining nonchord tones:

Nonchord tones are notes that are not part of the harmony.

Nonchord tones are decorative notes.

Nonchord tones are usually melodic in nature.

Nonchord tones are surrounded by chord tones.

Nonchord tones are dissonant to the harmony.

A note cannot simultaneously be a nonchord tone and part of the harmony.

Harmonies exist in a wide variety of patterns. The simplest is the vertical chordal pattern that contains just notes of the harmony. Generally, all notes in a vertical structure belong to the harmony. Horizontal patterns range from a simple Alberti bass to complex arpeggiations that include nonchord tones. The key to determining the chord structure is to recognize the pattern and filter out the nonchord tones. Begin by looking at four measures. Where is the melody? How is the harmony presented. What is the pattern? Disregard notes that are decorative.

Passacaglia

from *Suites de Pieces,* 1st Collection
No. 7, HWV 432, IV, meas. 1-12

George Frideric Handel

GUIDED ANALYSIS—HANDEL—*PASSACAGLIA*, MEASURES 1–12

Try analyzing the music with the steps below and then look at the analysis provided.

Step 1—Determine the key. The key signature is that of two flats—possible keys are B-flat major or g minor. The excerpt is from the beginning of the piece, so the key is probably that of the key signature. The first and last chords are both g minor, and there are prominent F-sharps.

Step 2—Identify patterns and vertical structures in both hands. Look for a harmonic pattern. (This is one you want to remember!) Look for harmonic repetitions (the skinny double bars are there for a reason). Determine the harmonic rhythm. The left hand in measures 5–8 is moving primarily step wise; there will be passing tones. The left hand in measures 9–12 is more of a "walking" bass line; each note is not the bass note. Verticalize notes in the left hand to determine the bass note of the chord.

Step 3—Once you have observed the patterns, you can determine the harmonies and identify nonchord tones. Enter the Roman numeral analysis, then circle all the notes that do not fit the designated harmony and label them accordingly.

Passacaglia

from *Suites de Pieces,* 1st Collection
No. 7, HWV 432, IV, meas. 1-12

George Frideric Handel

Piano Sonata, K. 457, III

measures 167 - 183

W. A. Mozart

GUIDED ANALYSIS—MOZART—PIANO SONATA, K. 457, III, MEASURES 167–183

For purposes of this analysis, the score is numbered measures 1–17.

Try analyzing the music with the steps below and then look at the analysis provided.

> ***Step 1***—Determine the key. The key signature is three flats—possible keys are E-flat major or c minor. The first given measure has the notes of the c minor chord; the last given measure is a G major chord (notice the right hand is in the bass clef here). There are prominent B-naturals.
>
> ***Step 2***—Identify patterns that could be verticalized into chord structures. Who has the accompaniment? Who has the melody? Notice that in measures 1–9, the first note of each measure in the left hand is the same. Pay attention to the descending bass line from measure 9 to measure 13. The B-flat in measure 10 starts the descent; this note is a sensitive pitch within the chord structure and needs a particular resolution. The E-natural in measure 10 (chromatic to the key) is part of the broken chord accompaniment pattern, and thus is a chord tone. The F-sharp in measure 12 is an important chordal note, not a nonchord tone. To what pitch do the F-sharp and A-flat in measure 12 resolve? Observing repeated accompaniment patterns and when/how those patterns change will aid in determining the harmonic rhythm, which will help to determine a chord structure, particularly when that chord is spread over several measures.
>
> ***Step 3***—Once you have provided the Roman numeral analysis, you can proceed to identifying the nonchord tones. While long notes tend to be part of the chord, first notes of measures are not always chord tones. Mozart frequently uses downbeat dissonances—that's a hint for measure 5. Measure 7 has both an F-sharp and F-natural—one is decorative, one is not.

Piano Sonata, K. 457, III

measures 167 - 183

W. A. Mozart

The list of music for analysis (Chapters 8–24) consists primarily of piano music. The list is not coordinated with any particular anthology, although many of the pieces can be found in one or more anthologies.

MUSIC FOR ANALYSIS

Primary Triads in Root Position (Chapter 8)

Beethoven, Ludwig van

1. "Für Elise" from *Klavierstück*, mm. 1–8
2. Seven Country Dances, no. 7
3. Trio in B-flat for Violin (Clarinet), Cello and Piano, Finale, mm. 1–8
4. Sonata no. 8 for Violin and Piano in G major, op. 30 no. 3, I, mm. 1–8

Chopin, Frédéric

1. Mazurka in B-flat major, op. 17 no. 1, mm. 1–8
2. Etude in E major, op. 10 no. 3, mm. 1–5
3. Waltz in G-flat major, op. 70 no. 1, mm. 1–8
4. Prelude in C-sharp minor, op. 28 no. 10, mm. 1–5

Haydn, Franz Joseph

1. String Quartet in E-flat major, op. 33 no. 2, III (Trio), mm. 35–42
2. String Quartet in D major, op. 64 no. 6, III (Trio), mm. 37–44
3. Sonata in E major, Hob. XVI: 13, III, mm. 15–22

Mozart, Wolfgang Amadeus

1. Piano Sonata in F major, K. 332, III, mm. 15–22
2. Piano Concerto no. 21 in C major, K. 467, II, mm. 23–29
3. Piano Sonata in A major, K. 331, III, mm. 97–109
4. String Quartet in d minor, K. 173, III, mm. 1–4

Puccini, Giacomo

1. "Sola perduta" from *Manon Lescaut,* Act IV, mm. 1–20

Rossini, Gioacchino

1. "Largo al Factotum" from *Il barbiere di Siviglia,* Act I:4, mm. 236–53

Schubert, Franz

1. Impromptu in A-flat major, op. 90 no. 4, D. 899, mm. 47–50
2. *Wiegenlied,* op. 98 no. 2, D. 498, mm. 1–4

Schumann, Robert

1. "Scherzino" from *Faschingsschwank aus Wien,* op. 26 no. 3, mm. 86–93
2. "Hasche-Mann" from *Kinderscenen,* op. 15 no. 3, mm. 1–8
3. "Reiterstück" from *Album für die Jugend,* op. 68 no. 23, mm. 1–8

Verdi, Giuseppi

1. "Libiamo ne' lieti calici" from *La traviata,* Act I, no. 3, mm. 22–42

Weber, Carl Maria von

1. Theme from *Variations on "Vien' qua Dorina bella,"* op. 7, mm. 1–12

Primary Triads Add First Inversion (Chapter 9)

Mozart, Wolfgang Amadeus

1. Piano Sonata in B-flat major, K. 570, I, mm. 1–20
2. Piano Sonata in D major, K. 311, III. mm. 33–40

Hasse, Johann Adolf

1. Trio Sonata no. 1 in e minor for two Flutes and Basso Continuo, I, mm. 1–6

Beethoven, Ludwig van

1. Seven Peasant Dances, No. 4, WoO 168, mm. 1–8

Schubert, Franz

1. Piano Sonata in A major, op. 120, I, mm. 1–4 (includes dominant seventh in inversion)

Clementi, Muzio

1. Sonatina in G major, op. 36 no. 2, I, mm. 1-4; III, mm. 1–8

Chopin, Frédéric

1. Waltz in D-flat major, op. 64 no. 1, mm. 1–8

Bach, Carl Philipp Emanuel

1. Wurttemberg Sonata no. 1 in a minor, I, mm. 1–3

Primary Triads Add Second Inversion (Chapter 10)

Mozart, Wolfgang Amadeus

1. Piano Sonata in C major, K. 545, I, mm. 1–4
2. Piano Sonata in G major, K. 283, I, mm. 1–10
3. Piano Sonata in C major, K. 330, I, mm. 1–12

Beethoven, Ludwig van

1. Piano Sonata no. 17 in d minor, op. 31 no. 2 (*Tempest*), I, mm. 1–5
2. Piano Sonata no. 3 in C major, op. 2 no. 3, III (Trio), mm. 1–3
3. Piano Sonata no. 1 in f minor, op. 2 no. 1, II, mm. 1–4

Scarlatti, Dominico

1. Toccata in d minor, L. 422, mm. 10–18
2. Sonata in C major, L. 457, mm. 1–5

Schumann, Robert

1. "Wilder Reiter" from *Album für die Jugend*, op. 68 no. 8, mm. 1–4
2. Grand Sonata no. 1 in F-sharp minor, op. 11, I, mm. 1–5

Secondary Triads (Chapter 11)

Handel, George Frideric

1. "Air" from *Suites de Pièces*, 2nd Collection, no. 1, HWV 434, III
2. "Passacaglia" from *Suites de Pièces*, 1st Collection, no. 7, HWV 432, IV, mm. 1–12

Bach, Johann Sebastian

1. Prelude no. 21 in B-flat major from *Well-Tempered Clavier, Book I,* BWV 866, mm. 1–3 (sequence)

Bach, Carl Philipp Emanuel

1. Piano Sonata no. 4 from *6 Sonaten für Kenner und Liebhaber,* I, mm. 1–12

Haydn, Franz Joseph

1. Piano Sonata in E-flat major, Hob. XVI:49, I, mm. 1–12
2. Piano Sonata in C major, Hob. XVI:35, I, mm. 1–16
3. String Quartet in f minor, op. 20 no. 5, I, mm. 1–5

Mozart, Wolfgang Amadeus

1. Piano Sonata in G major, K. 283, III, mm. 1–24
2. Sonata for Violin and Piano in B-flat major, K. 372, I, mm. 30–48
3. Piano Sonata in C major, K. 545, I, mm. 5–8; mm. 18–28
4. Piano Sonata in a minor, K. 310, I, mm. 1–8
5. Piano Sonata in A major, K. 331, I, mm. 1–8
6. Piano Sonata in D major, K. 284, III, mm. 1–4; Var. XI mm. 1–4
7. Piano Sonata in B-flat major, K. 281, I, mm. 1–8
8. Piano Sonata in C major, K. 279, III, mm. 120–124 (consecutive first inversion)
9. Rondo in F major, K. 494, mm. 51–54

Mendelssohn, Felix

1. *Lieder ohne Worte,* op. 53 no. 3, mm. 88–103

Chopin, Frédéric

1. Nocturne in g minor, op. 15 no. 3, mm. 89–96
2. Mazurka in D major, op. 33 no. 2, mm. 1–8

Beethoven, Ludwig van

1. Piano Sonata no. 31 in A-flat major, op. 110, I, mm. 1–4
2. Sonata no. 5 for Violin and Piano in F Major, op. 24 (*Spring*), I, mm. 1–10
3. Piano Sonata no. 18 in E-flat major, op. 31 no. 3, II, mm. 1–9
4. Piano Sonata no. 23 in f minor, op. 57 (*Appassionata*), II, mm. 9–16
5. Piano Sonata no. 3 in C major, op. 2 no. 3, III, mm. 81–88
6. Piano Sonata no. 1 in f minor, op. 2 no. 1, II, mm. 1–8; III, mm. 59–68
7. Piano Sonata no. 30 in E major, op. 109, I, mm. 1–4 (sequence)

Schubert, Franz

1. "Frühlingstraum" from *Winterreise,* op. 89 no. 11, D. 911, mm. 1–10
2. Impromptu in G-flat major, op. 90 no. 3, D. 899, mm. 1–4
3. Impromptu in A-flat major, op. 90 no. 4, D. 899, mm. 72–79

Schumann, Robert

1. Waltz from *Albumblätter,* op. 124 no. 4, mm. 17–28 (sequence)

Lennon, John and Paul McCartney

1. *Hello Little Girl*
2. *Misery*
3. *Not A Second Time*

Nonchord Tones (Chapters 13–14)

Beethoven, Ludwig van

1. Piano Sonata no. 4 in E-flat major, op. 7, III
2. Piano Sonata no. 12 in A-flat major, op. 26, III
3. Bagatelle in E-flat major, op. 33, mm. 1–32

Schumann, Robert

1. "Das ist ein Flöten und Geigen" from *Dichterliebe,* op. 48 no. 9, mm. 1–8 (contains secondary diminished sevenths)

Chopin, Frédéric

1. Mazurka in a minor, op. 17 no. 4, mm. 61–91
2. Nocturne in B-flat minor, op. 9 no. 1, mm. 1–4
3. Nocturne in D-flat major, op. 27 no. 2, mm. 1–9 (includes chromaticism)

Haydn, Franz Joseph

1. Piano Sonata in D major, Hob. XVI:37, III, mm. 1–4

Bach, Johann Sebastian

1. Prelude no. 1 in C major from *Well-Tempered Clavier, Book I,* BWV 846 (suspensions and pedal points; chromatic harmonies)
2. Little Prelude in C major, BWV 939 (pedal points and secondary dominants)

Schubert, Franz

1. Moment Musical in f minor, op. 94 no. 3, mm. 1–10

Mozart, Wolfgang Amadeus

1. Rondo in a minor, K. 511, mm. 1–8

Mussorgsky, Modest

1. "The Old Castle" from *Pictures at an Exhibition,* mm. 1–18

Diatonic Seventh Chords (Chapter 15)

Schubert, Franz

1. Impromptu in A-flat major, D. 935, mm. 1–8
2. "Ständchen" (Serenade) from *Schwanengesang,* D. 957, no. 4, mm. 1–10

Mozart, Wolfgang Amadeus

1. Sonata no. 25 for Violin and Piano in F major, K. 377, II, mm. 1–16
2. *Das Kinderspiel,* K. 598
3. Rondo in D major, K. 485, mm. 1–16

Kuhlau, Friedrich

1. Piano Sonatina in C major, op. 20 no. 1, I, mm. 1–8
2. Piano Sonatina in D major, op. 55 no. 5, II

Beethoven, Ludwig van

1. Piano Sonata no. 10 in G major, op. 14 no. 2, I, mm. 1–8
2. Piano Sonata no. 5 in c minor, op. 10 no. 1, I, mm. 1–30

Chopin, Frédéric

1. Waltz in b minor, op. 69 no. 2, mm. 9–16

Clementi, Muzio

1. Sonatina in G major, op. 36 no. 5, III, mm. 1–16

Writing for the Piano (Chapter 17)

Haydn, Franz Joseph

1. Piano Sonata in D major, Hob. XVI:37, I, mm. 1–16; III, mm. 61–80 (includes secondary dominant)

Mozart, Wolfgang Amadeus

1. Sonata in F major, K. 280, II, mm. 1–8
2. Sonata in D major, K. 284, I, mm. 1–9; III, mm. 1–4
3. Sonata in A major, K. 331 (*Turkish March*), I, mm. 1–18
4. Rondo in a minor, K. 511, mm. 1–8

Beethoven, Ludwig van

1. Piano Sonata no. 9 in E major, op. 14 no. 1, III, mm. 1–8
2. Piano Sonata no. 4 in E-flat major, op. 7, III, mm. 1–8
3. Piano Sonata no. 10 in G major, op. 14 no. 2, I, mm. 1–8

Schumann, Robert

1. "Valse noble" from *Carnaval*, op. 9 no. 4, mm. 1–8

Bach, Carl Philipp Emanuel

1. Sonata no. 3 in f Minor, I, mm. 1–13
2. Solfeggietto in c minor (sequences; secondary dominants; augmented sixth; modulations)

Brahms, Johannes

1. *Variations and Fugue on a Theme by Handel*, op. 24, mm. 1–16
2. Intermezzo in A major, op. 118 no. 2, mm. 1–8; mm. 49–56 (includes secondary dominants)
3. Ballade in g minor, op. 118 no. 3, mm. 1–10 (includes secondary dominants)
4. Capriccio in b minor, op. 76 no. 2, mm. 1–11 (includes chromaticism)
5. Intermezzo in C major, op. 119 no. 3, mm. 1–13 (includes chromaticism)

Schubert, Franz

1. Originaltänze, op. 9 no. 3, mm. 1–8; no. 14, mm. 1–8; no. 23, mm. 1–8
2. Impromptu in A-flat major, op. 142 no. 2, D. 935, mm. 1–8
3. Moment Musical in f minor, op. 94 no. 3, mm. 1–10
4. Impromptu in G-flat major, op. 90 no. 3, mm. 1–9

Chopin, Frédéric

1. Nocturne in B-flat minor, op. 9 no. 1, mm. 1–4
2. Nocturne in D-flat major, op. 27 no. 2, mm. 1–9 (includes chromaticism)

3. Mazurka in a minor, op. 17 no. 4, mm. 1–20 (includes chromaticism)
4. Etude in E-flat minor, op. 10 no. 6, mm. 1–8 (includes chromaticism)
5. Etude in C-sharp minor, op. 10 no. 4, mm. 1–5
6. Etude in C major, op. 10 no. 1, mm. 1–8 (includes chromaticism)
7. Etude in c minor, op. 10 no. 12, mm. 1–18 (includes chromaticism)

Grieg, Edvard

1. "Niels W. Gade" from *Lyric Pieces for the Piano,* op. 57 no. 2, mm. 1–8

Mussorgsky, Modest

1. "The Old Castle" from *Pictures at an Exhibition,* mm. 1–18

Secondary Dominants (Chapter 18)

Bach, Johann Sebastian

1. "Courante" from *Allemande and Courante in A,* BWV 838, mm. 12–27
2. Prelude no. 1 in C major from *Well-Tempered Clavier, Book I,* BWV 846, mm. 1–11

Haydn, Franz Joseph

1. String Quartet in C major, op. 33 no. 3 (*The Bird*), IV, mm. 1–22
2. Piano Sonata in C major, Hob. XVI:50, II, mm. 1–8 (irregular resolution)
3. Piano Sonata in D major, Hob. XVI:37, III mm. 1–20
4. Piano Sonata in E-flat major, Hob. XVI:52, I, m. 1

Beethoven, Ludwig van

1. "Ohne Liebe Leve" from *Eight Songs,* op. 52 no. 6
2. Piano Concerto no. 4 in G major, op. 58, II, mm. 1–13
3. Bagatelle, op. 126 no. 6, mm. 7–21 (irregular resolution)
4. "Die Ehre Gottes aus der Natur" from *Sechs Lieder von Gellert,* op. 48 no. 4 (also augmented sixth, borrowed, and dominants of borrowed)
5. Piano Sonata no. 8 in c minor, op. 13 (*Pathétique*), III, mm. 12–17; II, mm. 1–16
6. Piano Sonata no. 21 in C major, op. 53 (*Waldstein*), I, mm. 35–42 (deceptive resolution)
7. Piano Sonata no. 4 in E-flat major, op. 7, II, mm. 1–8
8. Piano Sonata no. 31 in A-flat major, op. 110, I, mm. 5–12
9. Piano Sonata no. 7 in D major, op. 10 no. 3, III, mm. 1–16

Mozart, Wolfgang Amadeus

1. *Die Zufriedenheit,* K. 349
2. Piano Sonata in F major, K. 332, I, mm. 1–12
3. Piano Sonata in D major, K. 311, III, mm. 207–22

Schubert, Franz

1. Originaltänze, op. 9 no. 3, mm. 9–16; no. 14, mm. 1–8; no. 16; no. 23, mm. 9–16
2. "Danksagung an den Bach" from *Die schöne Müllerin,* op. 25 no. 4, D. 795, mm. 1–18
3. Impromptu in A-flat major, op. 90 no. 4, mm. 39–46
4. *An die Nachtigall,* op. 98 no. 1, D. 497 (numerous examples)

Chopin, Frédéric

1. Prelude in F-sharp major, op. 28 no. 13, mm. 29–38
2. Waltz in b minor, op. 69 no. 2, mm. 73–80
3. Mazurka in g minor, op. 67 no. 2, mm. 17–32 (sequence of secondary dominants)

Schumann, Robert

1. "Grillen" from *Phantasiestücke*, op. 12 no. 4, mm. 1–16

Vivaldi, Antonio

1. "Laudamus Te" from *Gloria*, RV 589, III, mm. 92–109 (includes dominants of borrowed chords)

Lennon, John and Paul McCartney

1. *Ask Me Why*
2. *From Me to You*
3. *I Want to Hold Your Hand*
4. *I'll Be On My Way*
5. *I'll Get You*
6. *Little Child*
7. *Ringo's Theme* (*This Boy*)
8. *She Loves You*

Secondary Diminished Seventh Chords (Chapter 19)

Bach, Johann Sebastian

1. Prelude no. 1 in C major from *Well-Tempered Clavier, Book I*, BWV 846, mm. 12–24

Caldara, Antonio

1. *Come Raggio di Sol*, mm. 1–27

Schumann, Robert

1. "Die Rose, die Lilie" from *Dichterliebe*, op. 48 no. 3
2. "Ich Grolle Nicht" from *Dichterliebe*, op. 48 no. 7, mm. 1–19 (irregular resolution)
3. "Wichtige Begebenheit" from *Kinderscenen*, op. 15 no. 6, mm. 1–8
4. "Von fremden Ländern und Menschen" from *Kinderscenen*, op. 15 no. 1, mm. 1–8
5. "Arlequin" from *Carnaval*, op. 9 no. 3, mm. 17–29 (irregular resolution)
6. "Soldatenmarsch" from *Album für die Jugend*, op. 68 no. 2, mm. 1–8
7. "Du bist wie eine Blume" from *Myrten*, op. 25 no. 24, mm. 1–5

Brahms, Johannes

1. "Das Mädchen" from *Seven Songs*, op. 95 no. 1, mm. 37–66 (irregular resolution)

Mozart, Wolfgang Amadeus

1. Piano Sonata in C major, K. 309, III, mm. 213–33 (consecutive)
2. Piano Sonata in F major, K. 547a, I, mm. 169–83

Beethoven, Ludwig van

1. String Quartet in F major, op. 18 no. 1, I, mm. 1–20 (consecutive)
2. String Quartet in B-flat major, op. 18 no. 6, IV, mm. 1–44 (consecutive)
3. Piano Sonata no. 9 in E major, op. 14 no. 1, III, mm. 68–76
4. Piano Sonata no. 21 in C major, op. 53 (*Waldstein*), I, mm. 284–95
5. Piano Sonata no. 7 in D major, op. 10 no. 3, II, mm. 1–9

Schubert, Franz

1. Sonata for Violin and Piano in a minor, op. posth. 137 no. 2, D. 385, II, mm. 1–20 (consecutive)
2. Originaltänze, op. 9 no. 29, mm. 1–8
3. "Ungeduld" from *Die schöne Müllerin*, op. 25 no. 7, D. 795, mm. 9–26 (regular and irregular resolutions)
4. *Valses Nobles*, op. 77 no. 6, D. 969, mm. 1–16
5. *Schwanengesang*, op. 23 no. 3, D. 744, mm. 1–4

Augmented Sixth Chords (Chapter 20)

Beethoven, Ludwig van

1. Sonata no. 7 for Violin and Piano in c minor, op. 30 no. 2, IV, mm. 1–22
2. "Die Ehre Gottes aus der Natur" from *Sechs Lieder von Gellert*, op. 48 no. 4 (also secondary dominants, dominants of borrowed, and borrowed chords)
3. Piano Sonata no. 8 in c minor, op. 13 (*Pathétique*), I, mm. 9–27; III, mm. 1–8
4. Piano Sonata no. 1 in f minor, op. 2 no. 1, mm. 140–52 (also secondary dominant)
5. Piano Sonata no. 5 in c minor, op. 10 no. 1, III, mm. 1–12
6. Bagatelle, op. 119 no. 1, mm. 1–8
7. Piano Sonata no. 17 in d minor, op. 31 no. 2 (*Tempest*), I, mm. 1–6

Mozart, Wolfgang Amadeus

1. "Lacrimosa dies Illa" from *Requiem*, K. 626, mm. 1–8
2. Piano Sonata in F major, K. 332, I, mm. 31–40; III, mm. 50–57

Haydn, Franz Joseph

1. Piano Sonata in E-flat major, Hob. XVI:52, I, mm. 44–45

Schumann, Robert

1. "Three Little Pieces," III, from *Bunte Blätter*, op. 99, mm. 1–8 (also modulation and enharmonic spelling of augmented sixth)
2. Waltz from *Albumblätter*, op. 124 no. 4, mm. 1–8
3. "Am leuchtenden Sommermorgen" from *Dichterliebe*, op. 48 no. 12, mm. 1–8

Chopin, Frédéric

1. Etude in E major, op. 10 no. 3, mm. 1–21
2. Prelude in c minor, op. 28 no. 20, mm. 5–8

Schubert, Franz

1. *Die Liebe hat Gelogen*, D. 751, mm. 1–4 (also Neapolitan)
2. Piano Sonata in A major, D. 959, I, mm. 331–57 (secondary function)
3. "Am Feierabend" from *Die schöne Müllerin*, op. 25 no. 5, D. 795, mm. 1–4
4. Waltz in C major from *Valses sentimentales*, op. 50 no. 16, D. 779
5. "Pause" from *Die schöne Mullerin*, op. 25 no. 12, D. 795, mm. 40–45

6. Impromptu in A-flat major, op. 142 no. 2, D. 935, mm. 28–34
7. Moment Musical no. 6 in A-flat major, op. 94, D. 780, mm. 17–24
8. *An die Nachtigall,* op. 98 no. 1, D. 497, m. 35 (preparation for mm. 30–34)

Mendelssohn, Felix

1. "Help, Lord!" from *Elijah,* mm. 1–9

Wolf, Hugo

1. "Er ist's" from *Gedichte von Eduard Mörike,* mm. 26–33

Tartini, Giuseppe

1. Violin Sonata in g minor (*The Devil's Trill*), I, mm. 1–4

Borrowed Chords (Chapter 21)

Kuhlau, Friedrich

1. Piano Sonatina in C major, op. 20 no. 1, I, mm. 13–14; mm. 38–40

Beethoven, Ludwig van

1. Piano Sonata no. 9 in E major, op. 14 no. 1, I, mm. 102–7
2. Piano Sonata no. 21 in C major, op. 53 (*Waldstein*), I, mm. 8–13

Mussorgsky, Modest

1. "The Great Gate of Kiev" from *Pictures at an Exhibition,* mm. 156–62

Schumann, Robert

1. "Der Dichter spricht" from *Kinderscenen,* op. 15 no. 13, mm. 13–25
2. "Valse noble" from *Carnaval,* op. 9 no. 4, mm. 26–40
3. "Ich Grolle Nicht" from *Dichterliebe,* op. 48 no. 7, mm. 1–4

Schubert, Franz

1. *Schwanengesang,* op. 23 no. 3, D. 744 (numerous examples; secondary diminished sevenths)
2. Waltz in C major from *Valses sentimentales,* op. 50 no. 16, D. 779
3. Piano Sonata in A major, D. 959, III, mm. 80–87
4. Impromptu in c minor, op. 90 no. 1, mm. 46–55
5. *An die Nachtigall,* op. 98 no. 1, D. 497, mm. 30–34

Vivaldi, Antonio

1. "Laudamus Te" from *Gloria,* RV 589, III, mm. 92–109

Chopin, Frédéric

1. Mazurka in g minor, op. 67 no. 2, mm. 17–32
2. Nocturne in E-flat major, op. 9 no. 2, mm. 7–12
3. Waltz in E major, posthumous, mm. 1–20

Lennon, John and Paul McCartney

1. *Hey Jude*
2. *Hold Me Tight*
3. *I Call Your Name*
4. *I Saw Her Standing There*
5. *I'll Keep You Satisfied*
6. *It Won't Be Long*
7. *Love of the Love*
8. *P.S. I Love You*

The Neapolitan (Chapter 22)

Schumann, Robert

1. Waltz from *Albumblätter*, op. 124 no. 4, mm. 1–16 (augmented sixth)

Schubert, Franz

1. *Die Liebe hat Gelogen*, op. 23 no. 1, D. 751, mm. 1–4 (augmented sixth; whole piece has numerous chromatic harmonies and modulations)
2. Piano Sonata in A major, D. 959, I, mm. 331–57 (secondary function); III, mm. 38–43
3. *An Mignon*, op. 19 no. 2, D. 161 (numerous examples)
4. "Der Müller und der Bach" from *Die schöne Müllerin*, op. 25 no. 9, D. 795, mm. 1–26
5. *Erlkönig*, op. 1, D. 328, mm. 146–48 (final cadence)

Bach, Johann Sebastian

1. "Ach Gott, vom Himmel sieh' Darein," BWV 2, mm. 1–4

Chopin, Frédéric

1. Nocturne in B-flat minor, op. 9 no. 1, mm. 12–18
2. Nocturne in f minor, op. 55 no. 1, mm. 1–8
3. Valse brilliante, op. 34 no. 2, mm. 69–84
4. Prelude in b minor, op. 28 no. 6 (other position)
5. Prelude in c minor, op. 28 no. 20, mm. 1–8 (other position)
6. Mazurka in C-sharp minor, op. 30 no. 4, mm. 13–28
7. Etude in E-flat minor, op. 10 no. 6, mm. 1–8

Brahms, Johannes

1. "Wie Melodien zieht es Mir" from *Five Songs*, op. 105 no. 1, mm. 1–13

Beethoven, Ludwig van

1. String Quartet in B-flat major, op. 130, II, mm. 13–16
2. Piano Sonata no. 14 in C-sharp minor, op. 27 no. 2 (*Moonlight*), I, mm. 1–5
3. Piano Sonata no. 17 in d minor, op. 31 no. 2, III, mm. 1–15 (root position)
4. Piano Sonata no. 21 in C major, op. 53 (*Waldstein*), I, mm. 134–36; mm. 237–39

Mendelssohn, Felix

1. "Help, Lord!" from *Elijah*, mm. 54–58

Mozart. Wolfgang Amadeus

1. Sonata in F major, K. 280, II, mm. 45–60
2. Fantasia in c minor, K. 475, mm. 170–73

Donizetti, Gaetano

1. *Lu trademiento*, mm. 1–13

Haydn, Franz Joseph

1. Piano Sonata in D major, Hob. XVI:37, I, mm. 25–35; mm. 51–58

Wolf, Hugo

1. "Wer Sich der Einsamkeit Ergiebt" from *Goethe Songs*, no. 1, mm. 1–6 (also secondary function of German sixth)

Rachmaninoff, Sergei

1. Prelude in G-sharp minor, op. 32 no. 12, mm. 1–8

Lennon, John and Paul McCartney

1. *Do You Want to Know a Secret*
2. *It Won't Be Long*

Common Chord Modulation (Chapter 23)

Beethoven, Ludwig van

1. Piano Sonata no. 9 in E major, op. 14 no. 1, III, mm. 8–21
2. Piano Sonata no. 10 in G major, op. 14 no. 2, II, mm. 1–8
3. Piano Sonata no. 14 in C-sharp minor, op. 27 no. 2 (*Moonlight*), I, mm. 5–9
4. Piano Sonata no. 4 in E-flat major, op. 7, III, mm. 1–24

Bach, Johann Sebastian

1. "Aria" from *Goldberg Variations*, BWV 988, mm. 1–16
2. "Gavotte" from French Suite no. 5 in G major, BWV 816
3. Invention no. 4 in d minor, BWV 775, mm. 1–18

Corelli, Arcangelo

1. Sonata da Camera a Tre, op. 4 no. 8, Preludio, mm. 1–14

Mozart, Wolfgang Amadeus

1. Piano Sonata in D major, K. 284, III, mm. 5–8
2. Piano Sonata in B-flat major, K. 333, I, mm. 11–14
3. *Die Entführung aus dem Serail*, Act 1, no. 5, mm. 36–58; no. 8, mm. 13–24

Haydn, Franz Joseph

1. Piano Sonata in e minor, Hob. XVI:34, III, mm. 1–18
2. Piano Sonata in D major, Hob. XVI:37, III, mm. 1–8

Clementi, Muzio

1. Sonatina in F major, op. 36 no. 4, I, mm. 1–30

Schubert, Franz

1. Impromptu in E-flat major, op. 90 no. 2, mm. 83–102
2. Impromptu in C minor, op. 90 no. 1, mm. 32–41

Schumann, Robert

1. "Aufschwung" from *Phantasiestücke*, op. 12 no. 2, mm. 1–8

Abrupt and Enharmonic Modulation (Chapter 24)

Mozart, Wolfgang Amadeus

1. Piano Sonata in D major, K. 284, III, Var. VII, mm. 1–8
2. Piano Sonata in B-flat major, K. 570, I, mm. 1–40

Haydn, Franz Joseph

1. Piano Sonata in E-flat major, Hob. XVI:52, I, mm. 44–45; mm. 66–68

Beethoven, Ludwig van

1. Piano Sonata no. 8 in c minor, op. 13 (*Pathétique*), I, mm. 132–36; II, mm. 37–44; III, mm. 193–210
2. Piano Concerto no. 4 in G major, op. 58, I, mm. 134–46
3. Piano Sonata no. 17 in d minor, op. 31 no. 2, III, mm. 216–43
4. Piano Sonata no. 23 in f minor, op. 57 (*Appassionata*), I, mm. 1–8
5. Piano Sonata no. 12 in A-flat major, op. 26, III, mm. 7–13

Chopin, Frédéric

1. Mazurka in B major, op. 56 no. 1, mm. 1–26
2. Mazurka in A-flat major, op. 59 no. 2, mm. 1–20
3. Nocturne in C-sharp minor, op. 27 no. 1, mm. 41–52
4. Etude in E-flat minor, op. 10 no. 6 (several examples)

Liszt, Franz

1. *Zweites Sonett von Petrarca*, mm. 10–21

Vivaldi, Antonio

1. "Et in Terra Pax Hominibus" from *Gloria*, RV 589, II, mm. 64–71

Schubert, Franz

1. Piano Sonata in A major, D. 959, III, mm. 38–54
2. Originaltänze, op. 9 no. 14, D. 365
3. Impromptu in A-flat major, op. 90 no. 4, mm. 1–30
4. Waltz in A major, *Wiener-Damen Ländler*, no. 6, D. 734
5. Moment Musical no. 6 in A-flat major, op. 94, D. 780, mm. 25–33
6. Impromptu in E-flat major, op. 90 no. 2, mm. 70–83

Bach, Carl Philipp Emanuel

1. Sonata no. 3 in f minor, I, mm. 1–34

Wolf, Hugo

1. "Er ist's" from *Gedichte von Eduard Mörike*
2. "Der Mond hat eine schwere Klag' erhoben" from *Italienisches Liederbuch*, mm. 1–18

Schumann, Robert

1. "Am leuchtenden Sommermorgen" from *Dichterliebe*, op. 48 no. 12
2. "Wenn ich in deine Augen'seh'" from *Dichterliebe*, op. 48 no. 4, mm. 1–8
3. "Widmung" from *Myrthen*, op. 25 no. 1 (includes borrowed, secondary dominants, and secondary diminished sevenths)

Brahms, Johannes

1. Romance in F major, op. 118 no. 5, mm. 44–48

Weber, Carl Maria von

1. *Polacca brillante*, op. 72, mm. 1–12 (borrowed m. 6)

Appendix C

MUSICAL CALLIGRAPHY

Musical calligraphy is musical handwriting. Just as legible and fluid handwriting is desirable in the communication of the written word, so it is in the communication of written music. Since students will notate a great deal of music in the course of their studies, it will be well worth their while to pay attention to basic calligraphic procedures and to allow their calligraphy to develop until their notation is both legible and mature.

Possibly the most effective way of improving one's calligraphy is by copying printed music and taking note of the construction of the various musical characters. The following example is written for viola and piano. Examine both the format and the formation of the musical symbols. The notes following the example point out some of the basic elements of the notation of music.

Chanson Triste

Note:

a. The title is centered; the composer's name and dates are printed on the right of the page; the tempo mark is printed on the left.

b. Following the clef symbol, the key signature is written *before* the meter signature.

c. The bar lines are perpendicular to the staff and are arranged so that the entire line is embraced.

d. The note heads are lined up vertically according to the metrical organization of the music. Since the meter here is $\frac{4}{4}$, the quarter note beat occupies approximately one-quarter of the space taken up to notate the whole measure.

e. The note head is *oval* and occupies a space equivalent to the distance between two adjacent staff lines.

f. The stems ascend from the right or descend from the left of the note heads, depending upon the position of the note heads on the staff. Common sense largely dictates in which direction the stems go.

g. The dynamic marks are placed below the solo instrument's part, and between the staves in the piano part.

h. The braces, clef symbols, accidentals, and rests are always formed in the same manner. Thus, the student should practice writing them until they can be committed to paper accurately and automatically.

The student is advised to use a medium-density (No. 2 or HB) pencil initially. An automatic 0.5 mm pencil is most useful because it requires no sharpening. A good eraser and transparent ruler should always be at hand.

When the student feels sufficiently confident, work in ink may be attempted. Because such a wide variety of materials is available it is advised that, before making a purchase, he or she consult a book on musical calligraphy with a view to selecting the most suitable equipment.

Since the last part of the twentieth century, the use of computer software for music notation has become commonplace. Programs range from very simple to very complex, from limited in editing tools to more tools than one would ever need. While there is no substitute for knowing the correct notation procedures, today's musician is encouraged to use a good, comprehensive notation program.

INSTRUMENTS

Following is a list of instruments, their common abbreviations, their ranges, and their notation relative to concert pitch.

With respect to the last item, instruments fall into two categories: (a) nontransposing (or concert pitch) instruments, which sound as written; and (b) transposing instruments, which do not sound as written. The B♭ clarinet, for example, sounds a major second lower than written. To compensate, the part for this instrument must be written a major second higher than that for a concert pitch instrument.

This legend is used in the following list to indicate in which part of the instrument's range the performer may have difficulty in producing accurate tones.

(U)—upper extreme

(L)—lower extreme

(UL)—both the upper and lower extremes

The student is advised either to avoid the use of problematic extremes of range or to consult an orchestration text to discover the nature of the problems.

INSTRUMENT	ABBREVIATION	WRITTEN RANGE	ACTUAL SOUND
Piccolo (UL)	Picc.	d^1–c^4	P8 higher
Flute (UL)	Fl.	c^1–d^4	as written
Oboe (UL)	Ob.	b♭–a^3	as written
English horn (U)	Eng. Hrn., E.H.	b–g^3	P5 lower
Clarinet in B♭ (U)	Cl. in B♭	e–c^4	M2 lower
Clarinet in A (U)	Cl. in A	e–c^4	m3 lower
Bassoon (U)	Fag., Bsn.	BB♭–e♭^{2}	as written
Contrabassoon (U)	C. Fag., C. Bsn.	BB♭–b♭^{1}	as written
Alto saxophone in E♭ (L)	Alt. Sax., A. Sax	b♭–f^3	M6 lower
Tenor saxophone in B♭ (L)	Ten. Sax., T. Sax.	b♭–f^3	M9 lower
Baritone saxophone in E♭	Bar. Sax., B. Sax.	b♭–e^3	M13 lower
Horn in F, French horn (UL)	Cor. in F, Hn. in F	F♯–c^3	P5 lower
Trumpet in B♭ (UL)	Tpt. in B♭	F♯–d^3	M2 lower
Trumpet in C (UL)	Tpt. in C	F♯–d^3	as written
Tenor trombone (UL)	Trb.	E–f^2	as written
Bass trombone (U)	B. Trb.	C–b^1	as written
Tuba (UL)	Tba.	DD–f^1	as written
Violin (U)	Vl.	g–g^4	as written
Viola (U)	Vla.	c–e^3	as written
Cello (violoncello) (U)	Vc.	C–g^2	as written
Double bass (U)	D.B., Bs.	E–d^2	P8 lower

TEMPO AND EXPRESSION MARKS

Following is a list of basic terms associated with tempo and expression. As a general rule, tempo marks are placed above the staff. Expression marks are found both above and below the staff.

accelerando	becoming faster	*andante*	moderately slow
agitato	excited	*animato*	animated
allargando	becoming broader	*appassionato*	impassioned
allegretto	moderately fast	*a tempo*	at normal tempo
allegro	fast	*brilliante*	brilliant

cantabile	singing
crescendo (cresc.)	increasing in volume
decrescendo (decresc.)	decreasing in volume
diminuendo (dim.)	decreasing in volume
dolce	sweet, soft
energico	energetic
espressivo (espr.)	expressive
forte (f)	loud
fortissimo (ff)	very loud
furioso	furious
giocoso	humorous
grazioso	graceful
langsam	slow
larghetto	slow
largo	very slow
lento	slow
maestoso	majestic
marcato (marc.)	marked
mezzo forte (mf)	moderately loud
mezzo piano (mp)	moderately soft
moderato	at moderate tempo
pianissimo (pp)	very soft
piano (p)	soft
presto	very fast
rallentando (rall.)	becoming slower
risoluto	determined
ritardando (rit.)	becoming slower
schnell	fast
sostenuto	sustained
spiritoso	spirited
staccato (stacc.)	detached
stringendo (string.)	quickening
tempo primo	at the original tempo
tenuto (ten.)	held, sustained
tranquillo	quiet, calm
vif	lively
vivace	quick
vivo	lively
zart	tender, delicate

Index